Energy Law in Cyprus

Energy Law in Cyprus

Natalia Charalampidou

This book was originally published as a monograph in the International Encyclopaedia of Laws/Energy Law.

Founding Editor: Roger Blanpain
General Editor: Frank Hendrickx
Volume Editors: Kurt Deketelaere & Bram Delvaux

Wolters Kluwer

Published by:
Kluwer Law International B.V.
PO Box 316
2400 AH Alphen aan den Rijn
The Netherlands
E-mail: lrs-sales@wolterskluwer.com
Website: www.wolterskluwer.com/en/solutions/kluwerlawinternational

Sold and distributed by:
Wolters Kluwer Legal & Regulatory U.S.
920 Links Avenue
Landisville, PA 17538
United States of America
E-mail: customer.service@wolterskluwer.com

ISBN 978-94-035-3917-1

e-Book: ISBN 978-94-035-3927-0
web-PDF: ISBN 978-94-035-3937-9

The Author

Natalia Charalampidou, a native of Thessaloniki (Greece), is teaching International Environmental and Energy Law at the Faculty of Law of the Democritus University of Thrace in Greece.

Natalia's areas of expertise include the Energy Charter Treaty, contaminated site investigation and remediation, environmental liability, solid and hazardous waste, environmental due diligence, energy compliance, prospection, research and exploitation of hydrocarbons, renewable electricity, unconventional energy sources and smart grids and cities. She is an author of the International Encyclopaedia of Laws contributing to the Chapters on Energy, Environment and Contract Law in Cyprus.

Prior to focusing on academic research and teaching in 2012, Natalia had joined the corporate and dispute resolution teams of high-profile law firms in Cyprus and overseas and acquired treasured experience in stock-exchange regulations, the European company (Societas Europaea), due diligence, fraud, anti-money laundering and investment arbitration in the energy sector. For these compelling and captivating times, she is much grateful to the heads of the departments and all her colleagues. She has a Diploma in Turkish Language, Institute for Balkan Studies (Greece), 2002; LLB, Democritus University of Thrace (Greece), 2003; LLM, University of Heidelberg, 2004. She is currently doing PhD at the University of Heidelberg. She was admitted to the bars of Cyprus, in 2006, and Thessaloniki (Greece), in 2014. Her indicative list of publications include the monograph 'Environmental Law: The Implementation of Directives of the European Union in Cyprus' (in Greek) (Sakkoulas Publications, Athens, 2013); the following contributions in collective volumes, 'The Energy Charter Treaty' (in Greek) 23–48 in: K. Antonopoulos & H. Aroni (eds) 'Introduction to International Energy Law' (Nomiki Bibliothiki 2020); 'Renewable Energy' (in Greek) 173–188 in: K. Antonopoulos & H. Aroni (eds) 'Introduction to International Energy Law' (Nomiki Bibliothiki 2020); (co-author) 'Cyprus', in: C. Esplugues (ed.) 'Civil and Commercial Mediation in Europe' (Intersentia, Cambridge 2014) 103–124; the following journal publications, 'Pressing Measures in Perilous Times: The Investment Perspective' 18(2) TDM No. 2 (2021); 'Energy Corporations and Their Information Duties Towards State Authorities' 30(2) EEELR 62–71 (2021); 'The Islamic Revolution of 1979 in

The Author

Iran and Oil Disputes' Mobil Oil and Government of Iran (in Greek), 23(4) Periballon & Dikaio (Greek legal journal) 673–678 (2019); 'Smart Buildings: From Flat-Rates to Smart Metering' (in Greek), 23(4) Periballon & Dikaio 540–559 (2019); 'Supply of Fuels and Diesel Generators' *Lighthouse v. Timor-Leste (in Greek)*, 2 (3) Periballon & Dikaio 511–520 (2019); 'International Energy Disputes That Arose from the Financial Crisis in Argentina (1999–2002)' *Pan American & BP v. Argentina* and *Total v. Argentina (in Greek)*, 23(2) Periballon & Dikaio 350–360 (2019); 'International Energy Disputes That Arose from the Financial Crisis in Argentina (1999–2002)' *CMS v. Argentina* and *El Paso v. Argentina (in Greek)*, 23(1) Periballon & Dikaio 142–168 (2019); 'Investment on Oil Refinery and Electricity Production Unit' *Plama v. Bulgaria (in Greek)*, 22(4) Periballon & Dikaio 673–678 (2018); 'The Applicability of the Energy Charter Treaty' *Yukos Universal v. Russia (in Greek)*, 22(3) Periballon & Dikaio 544–552 (2018); 'Issues of Environmental Damage from Oil Activities' *Chevron and Texaco v. Ecuador (in Greek)*, 22(3) Periballon & Dikaio 536–544 (2018); 'Range of Disputes under the Energy Charter Treaty', 15(7) TDM (OGEL/TDM Special Issue with Arbitral Women 'Strategic Considerations in Energy Disputes') No. 10 (2018); 'The Notion of Waste: An Overview of the Legislation on Waste' (in Greek), 22(2) Periballon & Dikaio 246–258 (2018); 'Greek Soil Law', 2 International Yearbook of Soil Law and Policy 245–276 (2017); 'Annulment of Adoption Orders due to Fraud and Perjury Before the Supreme Court of Cyprus' (in Greek), Epitheorisi Politikis Dikonomias (Greek legal journal) 177–186 (2013); 'European Protection of the Soil: The Struggle for Uniform Regulation' (in German), 8(4) Europarecht 593–611 (2011); 'The Protection of Land in Greece', 19(4) EEELR 160–174 (2010).

Table of Contents

List of Abbreviations

Abs.	Paragraph (of Legislation of the Federal Republic of Germany)
ACER	Agency for the Cooperation of Energy Regulators
Am. J. Intl. L. & Policy	American Journal of International Law and Policy
Ambiente cons.	Ambiente, consulenza e pratica per l'impresa
Ann. fr. dr. intern.	Annuaire Français de Droit International
Art.	Article (of Legislation of the European Union or the Constitution of Cyprus)
Austrl. Y.B. Intl. L.	Australian Yearbook of International Law
BauGB	Baugesetzbuch of the Federal Republic of Germany
BB	Betriebs-Berater
Can. Y.B. Intl. L	Canadian Yearbook of International Law
Cap. 6	Civil Procedure relating to Powers of the Courts in Civil Actions and to the Execution of Judgments in such actions
Cap. 44	A Law to enable the Governor to appoint Commissions of Enquiry with Special Powers
Cap. 148	A Law to Define and Amend the Law of Civil Wrongs
Cap. 149	To Amend and Consolidate the Law relating to Contract
Cap. 154	The Cyprus Criminal Code Order in Council
Cap. 155	A Law to Amend and Consolidate the Law Relating to Procedure in Criminal Proceedings
Cap. 170	A Law to Regulate the Supply of Electricity for Lighting and Other Purposes
Cap. 171	A law to provide for the establishment of a Corporate Body to be called the EAC
Cap. 272	Petroleum Law
Cap. 273	Petroleum (Pipelines) Law
CG	The Cyprus Gazette (Issued from 1873–1960)

List of Abbreviations

Ch. Y.B. Int'l L.	Chinese Yearbook of International Law
CLR	Cyprus Law Reports
CO_2	Carbon dioxide
Com. Mkt. L. Rev.	Common Market Law Review
Current Leg. Problems	Current Legal Problems
Dir. pubbl. comp. eur.	Diritto pubblico comparato ed europeo
DVBl.	Deutsches Verwaltungsblatt
Directive 94/22/EC	Directive on the Conditions for Granting and Using Authorizations for the Prospection, Exploration and Production of Hydrocarbons
Directive 2003/96/EC	Directive on Community Framework for the Taxation of Energy Products and Electricity
Directive 2008/98/EC	Directive on Waste
Directive 2009/73/EC	Directive on Common Rules for the Internal Market in Natural Gas
Directive 2011/92/EU	Directive on the Assessment of the Effects of Certain Public and Private Projects on the Environment
Directive 2012/27/EU	Directive on Energy Efficiency
Directive 2013/30/EU	Directive on Safety of Offshore Oil and Gas Operations
Directive (EU) 2018/2001	Directive on the Promotion of Use of Energy from Renewable Resources
Directive (EU) 2019/944	Directive on Common Rules for the Internal Market for Electricity
EAC	Electricity Authority of Cyprus
EU	European Union
EuZW	Europäische Zeitschrift für Wirtschaftsrecht
EwiR	Entscheidungen zum Wirtschaftsrecht
EWS	Europäisches Wirtschafts- & Steuerrecht
GDP	Gross Domestic Product
J	Journal du droit international
J. Design History	Journal of Design History
J. Royal Socy. Arts	Journal of the Royal Society of Arts
KDP 51/2007	Regulations on Hydrocarbons (Prospection, Research and Exploitation)

KDP 359/2021	Announcement of Regulatory Practice and Methodology on Price Assessment of Electricity
KDP 424/2015	Regulations on Safety and Health (Safety of Offshore Oil and Gas Operations)
KDP 429/2006	Road and Building (Energy Performance of Buildings) Regulations
KDP 538/2004	Regulating the Electricity Market (Issuance of Authorizations) Regulations
Law No. 4(I)/2007	Law on Hydrocarbons (Prospection, Research and Exploitation)
Law No. 13(I)/2022	The Protection of Competition Law
Law No. 17(I)/2011	Law on Ecodesign
Law No. 44(I)/2021	Law on Labelling of Energy Efficiency
Law No. 83(I)/2014	The Control of Concentrations Between Undertakings Law
Law No. 91(I)/2004	Law on Consumption Taxes
Law No. 106(I)/2002	Law on Regulating the Pollution of Waters and Soil
Law No. 107(I)/2022	Law on Promoting and Encouraging the Use of Energy from Renewable Sources
Law No. 110(I)/2011	Law Establishing a Scheme for Greenhouse Gas Emission Allowance Trading
Law No. 127(I)/2018	Law on Environmental Impact Assessment
Law No. 130(I)/2021	Law on Regulating the Electricity Market
Law No. 142(I)/2006	Law on Regulating Energy Performance of Buildings
Law No. 152(I)/2003	Law on Protection and Management of Wild Birds and Games
Law No. 153(I)/2003	Law on Protection and Management of Nature and Wild Life
Law No. 158(I)/1999	Law on General Principles of Administrative Law

List of Abbreviations

Law No. 174(I)/ 2006	Law on the Promotion of Cogeneration of Electrical and Thermal Energy
Law No. 183(I)/ 2004	Law on Regulating the Natural Gas Market
Law No. 185(I)/ 2011	Law on Waste
Law No. 187(I)/ 2002	Law on Regulating the Pollution of Air
Law No. 189(I)/ 2007	Law on Environmental Liability
Law No. 215(I)/ 2002	Law on Solid and Dangerous Waste
LNG	Liquefied Natural Gas
NTER	Nederlands Tijdschrift voor Europees Recht
OG	Official Gazette (of Cyprus Issued from 1960 Onwards)
OJ	Official Journal (of the European Union)
Order 2/2006	Order on Urban and Land Planning regarding Localization of Renewable Energy Plants
p.	Page
Pol ètr	Politique ètrangère
R.M.C.U.E.	Revue du marché commun et de l'Union européenne
Reg.	Regulation (of National Secondary Legislation)
Regulation (EU) 1227/2011	Regulation on Wholesale Energy Market Integrity and Transparency
Regulation (EU) 2018/1999	Regulation on the Governance of the Energy Union and Climate Action
Regulation (EU) 2019/942	Regulation Establishing a European Union Agency for the Cooperation of Energy Regulators
Regulation (EU) 2019/943	Regulation on the Internal Market for Electricity
Riv. It. Dir. Pubbl. Com.	Rivista italiana di diritto pubblico comunitario
Riv. Trim. Dir. Proc. Civ.	Rivista trimestrale di diritto e procedura civile
RTD com.	Revue trimestrielle de droit commercial et de droit économique
RW	Rechtskundig weekblad
SEW	Sociaal-economische wetgeving
SMEs	Small and Medium-Sized Enterprises
TEU	Treaty on European Union

TFEU	Treaty on the Functioning of the European Union
Tex. Intl. L.J.	Texas International Law Journal
ZHR	Zeitschrift für das gesamte Handelsrecht und Wirtschaftsrecht

List of Abbreviations

Preface

This monograph outlines the Energy Law in Cyprus. Due to the fact that this legislation is decisively shaped by Brussels, as Cyprus joined the European Union (EU) in 2004, it seemed inevitable to correspond the national provisions with the provisions of the Directives that were implemented. The underlying reasons are twofold. On the one hand, this is essential for anyone wishing to discover and understand the source, for he may then seek the appropriate *travaux préparatoires* of the European legislation, as national preparatory reports are unusually brief and simple. On the other hand, this is vital for finding the relevant case law of the Court of Justice of the EU, as the national courts have not issued to this date any judgment on the energy laws examined herein.

The Cyprus problem[1] has been most excessively discussed and analysed.[2] Hence, it was considered superfluous to enquire about it further here, as nothing new could be added to said discussions and analysis.

I would like to thank Professor Dr Kurt Deketelaere and Professor Dr Bram Delvaux for their kind invitation as well as Professor Achilles Emilianides, PhD (Thessaloniki). My warmest thanks are expressed to Assistant Professor Konstantinos Antonopoulos, LLM (Cantab), PhD (Nottingham) for his valuable critic of a part of the present monograph but most importantly for his most inspiring lectures on Public International Law at Democritus University of Thrace that fascinated me as a student. Lastly, I cordially thank my *Doktormutter*, Professor Dr iur. Ute Mager,

1. *See* to this respect Resolution 3212 (XXIX) on Question of Cyprus of the General Assembly of the United Nations and relevant Resolutions of the Security Council of the United Nations: Resolution 193 (1964) of 9 Aug. 1964, Resolution 353 (1974) of 20 Jun. 1974, Resolution 358 (1974) of 15 Aug. 1974, Resolution 360 (1974) of 16 Aug. 1974, Resolution 361 of 30 Aug. 1974, Resolution 364 (1974) of 13 Dec. 1974, Resolution 367 (1975) of 12 Mar. 1975, Resolution 365 (1974) of 13 Dec. 1974, Resolution 383 (1975) of 13 Dec. 1975 and Resolution 410 (1977) of 15 Jun. 1977, http://www.securitycouncilreport.org/un-documents/cyprus/.
2. Some of the available literature is: Blay, Samuel Kwaw Nyameke, *Self-Determination in Cyprus: The New Dimensions of an Old Conflict*, 10 Austrl. Y.B. Intl. L. 67 (1987); Calogeropoulos-Stratis, Spyros, *Le Problème de Chypre*, 31 Pol ètr 344 (1966); Evriviades, Marios, *The Legal Dimensions of the Cyprus Conflict*, 10 Tex. Intl. L.J. 227 (1975); Flory, Maurice, *La Partition de Chypre*, 30 Ann. fr. dr. intern. 177 (1985); Hargrove, John L., *Cyprus: International Law and the Prospects for Settlement*, 78 Am. Socy. Intl. L. Procs. 107 (1984); Jacovides, Andreas J., *Cyprus: The International Law Dimension*, 10 Am. J. Intl. L. & Policy 1221 (1995); McDonald, Ronald SJ., *International Law and the Conflict in Cyprus*, 19 Can. Y.B. Intl. L. 3 (1981); Talmon, Stefan, *The EU-Turkey Controversy over Cyprus or a Tale of Two Declarations*, 5 Chinese J. Intl. L. 579 (2006); Wippman, David, *International Law and Ethnic Conflict on Cyprus*, 31 Tex. Intl. L.J. 141 (1996); Yilmaz, Altug, *Conflit Chypriote*, 27 Annales de la Faculté de Droit d' Istanbul 375 (1980).

Preface

Professor of Public Law at the University of Heidelberg, and Professor Dr Dres. h.c Burkhard Hess, Founding and Executive Director of Max Planck Institute Luxembourg for International, European and Regulatory Procedural Law, for urging me to strive for excellence.

This book is dedicated to my parents for all the reasons that one is grateful to his parents, but most importantly for being a light for me in dark places when all other lights go out.

Nicosia
November 2014

Disclaimer: The opinions expressed and arguments employed herein do not reflect the official views of the Democritus University of Thrace.

General Introduction

Chapter 1. General Background

§1. Geography and Population

1. Cyprus has a population of approximately 1,172,458, which contains Greek (77%), Turkish (18%) and other (5%) ethnic groups. It is the third-largest island in the Mediterranean Sea after Sicily and Sardinia, in the south of Turkey and west of Syria, whereas it is located in the Middle East, covering a total area of 9,251 square kilometres. Its natural resources include copper, pyrites, asbestos, gypsum, timber, salt, marble and clay earth pigment.[3]

§2. Legal and Political Structure

2. Cyprus is a common law country. Laws are interpreted in accordance with the principles of legal interpretation in England, and expressions used in those are presumed, so far as they are consistent with their context, and except as may be otherwise expressly provided, to be used with the meaning attached to them in English law and are construed in accordance therewith.[4] Certain areas of law, however, have little to do with common law. In particular, legislation on family law has been based on the Greek Civil Code, and therefore Greek case law can be invoked before Cyprus courts.[5] With reference to Administrative Law, it has been held that its basic provision, that being Article 146 of the Constitution, corresponds to the Greek one.

3. Central Intelligence Agency, *The World Factbook, Cyprus – Geography*, https://www.cia.gov/the-world-factbook/countries/cyprus/#geography (24 Jul. 2023). *See also* Cullis, C. Gilbert, *A Sketch of the Geology and Mineral Resources of Cyprus*, 72 (3741) J. Royal Socy. Arts 624 (1924).
4. Section 2(1) a Law to Define and Amend the Law of Civil Wrongs ('Cap. 148') No. 35 of 1932 (CG No. 2223, 10 Jun. 1932, p. 385); s. 2(1) To Amend and Consolidate the Law relating to Contract ('Cap. 149') No. 24 of 1930 (CG No. 2059, 28 May 1930, p. 773); s. 3 The Cyprus Criminal Code Order in Council, 1928 ('Cap. 154') (CG No. 1947, 17 Oct. 1928, p. 695); s. 3 Criminal Procedure – a Law to Amend and Consolidate the Law Relating to Procedure in Criminal Proceedings ('Cap. 155') No. 40 of 1948 (CG No. 3406, 30 Nov. 1948, p. 503).
5. *Menelaou v. Menelaou* (1993) 1 CLR 381. For a comprehensive overview of Cyprus law *see* Neocleous, Andreas, *Neocleous's Introduction to Cyprus Law* (C. Melides et al. eds, 3rd ed., Andreas Neocleous & Co LLC 2011); Andreas Neocleous & Co LLC, *Handbook of Cypriot Laws* (in Greek) (2nd ed., Nomiki Bibliothiki 2013).

Hence, the Supreme Court has been applying Greek case law in order to elaborate on relevant points of law.[6] It has been further ruled that:

> as it appears that under Art. 146, the process of judicial review of administrative acts existing in continental countries such as Greece, France or Germany, has been introduced in Cyprus, it is reasonable to hold that principles of administrative law can be adopted and applied by this Court as Cyprus law laid down by the Courts of Cyprus.[7]

Lastly, Cyprus joined the European Union (EU) in 2004 and, therefore, it bears the obligation to take any appropriate measure, general or particular, to ensure fulfilment of the obligations arising out of the Treaties or resulting from the acts of the institutions of the Union (Article 4(3) TEU).

§3. Economic Characteristics

3. Under British Rule (1878–1960), the economy of Cyprus gradually shifted from agriculture and a small number of handicrafts towards financial institutions, construction, tourism and mining.[8] Today it is dominated by the service sector, that being, tourism, financial services, shipping and real estate.[9] Since independence and until 1994, the average growth of real Gross Domestic Product (GDP) was 6%.[10] During the first five years of the EU Membership, it had an average rate of about 4% GDP, that in current prices, amounts to EUR 17,720 million[11] or USD 21,780 million. In May 2011, Cyprus lost access to international capital markets, and in July 2012, it requested an economic bailout programme from the European Commission, European Central Bank and the International Monetary Fund. The bailout requested triggered a two-week bank closure in March 2013 and, among others, bank deposits were converted into shares.[12] Cyprus implemented an economic

6. *Chrysostomides Kyriakos v. The Greek Communal Chamber through the Disciplinary Council of Elementary School teachers* (1964) 1 CLR 397.
7. *Stelios Morsis v. The Republic of Cyprus* (1965) 1 JSC 12 (16).
8. Angelides, Simoni, *The Cyprus Economy under British Rule (1878–1960)*, in *The Development of the Cypriot Economy* 209 et seq. (V. Karageorghis & D. Michaelides eds, University of Cyprus and Bank of Cyprus 1996); Sinclair, George, *Cyprus Since Independence*, 110 J. Royal Socy. Arts 511 at 516, 517 (1962).
9. Central Intelligence Agency, *The World Factbook*, 26 Sep. 2018, https://www.cia.gov/library/publications/the-world-factbook/.
10. Andreou, Elena, *Cyprus Economy in the Last Three Decades (1960–1994)*, in *The Development of the Cypriot Economy* 232 (V. Karageorghis & D. Michaelides eds, University of Cyprus and Bank of Cyprus 1996).
11. European Commission, *Economic and Financial Affairs, Cyprus – Economic situation*, http://ec.europa.eu/economy_finance/eu/countries/cyprus_en.htm.
12. *See* relevant international investment arbitration cases: *Marfin Investment Group Holdings S.A., Alexandros Bakatselos and others v. Republic of Cyprus* (ICSID Case No. ARB/13/27) award of 26 Jul. 2018; *Cyprus Popular Bank Public Co. Ltd. v. Hellenic Republic* (ICSID Case No. ARB/14/16) award of 15 Apr. 2021.

adjustment programme from April 2013 to March 2016. The fourth Post-Programme Surveillance Report underscored that reducing the high stock of non-performance loans should remain a high priority while affirming that the macroeconomic situation and outlook remain very positive and that fiscal performance has also been remarkably strong.[13]

§4. Social and Cultural Characteristics

4. Greek and Turkish are the official languages of Cyprus pursuant to Article 3(1) of the Constitution. However, cases have been argued in English before the Courts, and relevant judgments have been issued in the same language until the mid-1980s. Today legislation and case laws are written in Greek.

5. Nicosia (Λευκωσία/Lefkoşa), the capital of Cyprus, is a walled city and unique in having successive cultural layers of Byzantine, Frankish, Venetian, Ottoman, British and post-British periods, one on top of another.[14] Modifications had been made in order to suit the climate of the Levant.[15] The House of Dragoman Hadjigeorgakis Kornessios is a fine example of urban architecture of the nineteenth century of Ottoman Rule.[16] Following independence, modern architecture gained importance as a symbol of both decolonization and modernization.[17] The most influential architect was Neoptolemos Michaelides, whose work has been described as explicitly modernist with particular vernacular references.[18] Village houses had until the 1930s a very recognizable structure. Generally, they were built in stone below and mud brick above and had a flat roof. An enclosed courtyard was entered from the street, and a variety of rooms around it was used for living, storage and keeping animals.[19] The sense of community was given by a central church or mosque, around which villages usually clustered, as well as coffee houses, fountains and annual fairs.[20] Picturesque traditions, customs and beliefs are not unusual in Cyprus in both rural and urban areas.[21]

---

13. European Commission, *Post-Programme Surveillance Report, Cyprus Spring 2018, Institutional Paper 083,* Luxembourg, July 2018, https://ec.europa.eu/info/publications/economic-and-financial-affairs-publications_en.
14. Pulhan, Hifsiye & Ibrahim, Numan, *The Traditional Urban House in Cyprus as Material Expression of Cultural Transformation,* 19 J. Design History 105 (2006).
15. Enlart, Camile, *Gothic Art and the Renaissance in Cyprus* 378 (David Hunt ed., 1st ed., Trigraph 1987).
16. Rizopoulou-Egoumenidou, Euphrosyne, *The House of the Dragoman of Cyprus Hadjigeorgakis Kornessions* 11 (Bank Cyprus Cultural Foundation 1991).
17. Pyla, Panayiota & Phokaides, Petros, *Architecture and Modernity in Cyprus*, 2 EAHN Newsltr. 36 at 37 (2009).
18. *Ibid.*, pp. 44, 47.
19. Given, Michael, *Mining Landscapes and Colonial Rule in Early-Twentieth-Century Cyprus,* 39 Hist. Archaeology 49, 56 (2005).
20. *Ibid.*, p. 58.
21. *See* in this respect Argyrou, Vassos, *Under a Spell: The Strategic Use of Magic in Greek Cypriot Society*, 20 AAA/AE 256 (1993).

6. A number of memorable castles are also situated in Cyprus[22] along wit important religious monuments. For example, in the area of South-East Cyprus, th church of St Lazarus, which was built in the tenth century, and the Hala Sulta Tekke (or the Mosque of Umm Haram) are located.[23] Other memorable religiou monuments are the church of Peristeronas of the eleventh century, the church o Christos Antiphonitis of the twelfth century, the church of Apostolos Varnavas o the tenth century[24] and the church of Timios Stavros, Pelendri, which has bee inscribed on the United Nations Educational, Scientific and Cultural Organizatio (UNESCO) World Heritage List along with the church of Timios Stavros tou Agi asmati, Platanistasa, the church of Agios Nikolaos tis Stegis, Kakopetria, the churc of the Transfiguration of the Saviour, Palaichori, the church of Panagia tis Asinou Nikitari, the church of Panagia tou Moutoulla, the church of Panagia tou Arakos Lagoudera, the church of Panagia tis Podithou, Galata, the church of Archangelo Michail, Pedoulas, the monastery of Agios Ioannis Lampadistis, Kalopanagiotis, th site of Choirokoitia, which was founded and inhabited during the fifth millenniun BC, the ancient town of Palaipafos, which is linked to an ancient cult associate with the 'Great Goddess', the goddess of fertility, who was worshipped in Cypru since the Neolithic period and Nea Pafos, a town founded at the end of the fourt century.[25]

§5. Energy Strategy

7. The energy strategy of Cyprus is fully aligned with and in compliance wit the EU strategy 'clean energy for all Europeans'.[26] In order to demonstrate how i plans to meet the EU energy and climate targets for 2030, it has fully drafted an issued a ten-year national energy and climate plan, the 'Integrated National Energ and Climate Plan' (*see* in this respect paragraph 14 below). In practice, electricit produced from fossil fuels in Cyprus is estimated to be 86.8% in 2020, wherea none is produced from nuclear fuels, hydroelectric plants, tide and wave and geo- thermal. The remaining 12% is generated from solar and wind and 1.3% from bio- mass and waste. Estimated carbon dioxide (CO_2) emissions from the consumptio of petroleum and other liquids amounted to 8.024 million metric tonnes in 2019.[27]

22. *See* Rosser, John, *Crusader Castles of Cyprus*, 39 Archaeology 40 (1986); Rosser, John, *Excava- tions at Saranda Kolones, Paphos, Cyprus 1981–1983*, 39 Dumbarton Oaks Papers 81 (1985); Bid- dulph, Robert, *Cyprus,* 13 For. & Cmmw. Off. Collection (1889).
23. Department of Antiquities, *Monuments*, http://www.mcw.gov.cy/mcw/da/da.nsf/DMLmonum_en/ DMLmonum_en?OpenDocument.
24. Hadjidemetriou, Katia, *History of Cyprus* (in Greek) 380 (Nicosia 2010).
25. Minister of Communications and Works, Department of Antiquities, *UNESCO monuments*, av- ailable: http://www.mcw.gov.cy/mcw/DA/DA.nsf/DMLunesco_en/DMLunesco_en?OpenDocument (24 Jul. 2023).
26. Directorate-General for Energy (European Commission), *Clean Energy for All Europeans*, Luxem- bourg: Publications Office of the European Union, 2019, available: https://op.europa.eu/en/ publication-detail/-/publication/b4e46873-7528-11e9-9f05-01aa75ed71a1/language- en?WT.mc_id=Searchresult&WT.ria_c=null&WT.ria_f=3608&WT.ria_ev=search (24 Jul. 2023).
27. Central Intelligence Agency, *The World Factbook, Cyprus – Energy,* available: https://www.cia.gov/ the-world-factbook/countries/cyprus/#energy (24 Jul. 2023).

Chapter 2. Basic Principles of Energy Law

8. No basic principles may be extracted by the national legislation regulating the energy market. However, as this is purely administrative law, the general principles thereof, as codified in Law No. 158(I)/1999,[28] are freely applicable. Hence, actions of the state are bound by the following axioms.

9. First, the principle of legality (*'αρχή της νομιμότητας'*) demands that activities of the state organs are defined and restricted by the then applicable law.[29] It is further clarified that the legislation marking the limits and the extent of the power of public administration is contained in the Constitution, the legislation and the administrative regulations issued by the Council of Ministers or other administrative organs in accordance with the relevant legislation[30] along with the judgments of Supreme Court of Cyprus and case law.[31] The crucial point of time for determining the applicable law is the one of issuing the relevant administrative act and not the one of submitting the same,[32] as long as the administrative act is being issued within a reasonable time ('εύλογος χρόνος') from filing the relevant application. Reasonableness of time is determined by the facts surrounding each case.[33] Time limits set out in law are of indicative nature unless it is explicitly stated that they are mandatory.[34] However, especially the time limits set for the citizens to file applications are mandatory unless it is stated otherwise in the law.[35] Lastly, the authority needs to be legally composed[36] as well as both locally and materially competent.[37]

10. Parallel to the above, the principle of equality ('αρχή της ισότητας') requires that the administration, while performing its discretionary power, handles

28. Law on General Principles of Administrative Law ('περί των Γενικών Αρχών του Διοικητικού Δικαίου Νόμος') No. 158 of 1999 (OG I(I) No. 3378, 31 Dec. 1999, p. 478), as amended.
29. Section 8(1) Law No. 158(I)/1989. *See* relevant case law mostly in relation to due reasoning of administrative acts: *President of the Republic v. Yiannakis Louca and Others* (1984) 3 CLR 241; *Myrtiotis Panayiotis Ioannou* v. The Republic of Cyprus through the Educational Service Common (1975) 3 CLR 58; *Pancyprian Federation of Labour (PEO) v. Board of Cinematograph Films Censors and another* (1965) 3 CLR 27; *Adamides Panos v. The Republic of Cyprus through the Council of Ministers* (1982) 3 CLR 343; *Symboulio Eggrafis Arhitektonon kai Politikon Mihanikon v. Constantinou and Others* (1990) 3 CLR 3303. The principle of legality is also a principle recognized by the Court of Justice of the EU law. *See* in this respect Joined Cases 42/59 and 49/59 *SNUPAT v. High Authority* [1961] ECR 53, 87; Joined Cases 205/82–215/82 *Deutsche Milchkontor and Others* [1983] ECR 2633; Case 134/84 *Williams v. Court of Auditors* [1985] ECR 2225, para. 14; Case 188/83 *Witte v. Parliament* [1984] ECR 3465; Case T-22/96 *Langdon v. Commission* [1996] ECR II-1009; Case C-413/08 *P Lafarge v. Commission* [2010] ECR I-5361; Case C-51/10 P *Agencja Wydawnicza Technopol v. OHIM* [2011] ECR I-0000. Importantly, according to Art. 1A of the Constitution of Cyprus EU law is superior to national law.
30. Section 8(2) Law No. 158(I)/1999.
31. Section 59 *ibid.*
32. Section 9 *ibid.*
33. Section 10 *ibid.*
34. Section 11(1) *ibid.*
35. Section 11(2) *ibid.*
36. Section 15 *ibid.*
37. Section 17 *ibid.*

equally all citizens being under the same or similar circumstances.[38] Should the administration perform its discretionary power illegally, it may not continue such illegality in similar cases in the future, as no equality in illegality is recognized.[39] This law also foresees the equality of genders.[40]

11. The principle of natural justice ('αρχές φυσικής δικαιοσύνης') comprises impartiality ('αμεροληψία'), which requires ensuring the impartial view of every authority[41] and prohibits the issuance of an administrative act by an authority having a special relationship, family ties or major hostility with the citizen.[42] Natural justice further includes the right of every person to be heard ('δικαίωμα ακρόασης') prior to taking any individual measure which would affect him adversely.[43]

12. The last principle that must be taken into consideration by the administration is the one of due administration ('αρχή χρηστής διοίκησης'). According to this, authorities during the performance of their discretionary powers, must act in accordance with the sense of justice and avoid unjust decisions.[44] A special expression of due administration is the principle of good faith ('αρχή καλής πίστης'), which prohibits the administration from acting in an inconsistent and conflicting manner or in bad faith so that citizens are defrauded or suffer undue inconvenience.[45] Under the principle of due administration, equally falls the principle of proportionality ('αρχή της αναλογικότητας'), which demands that all interests involved in each case must be considered by the authorities,[46] whereas the means used must be proportional to the intended purpose. Lastly, any intervention with the

38. Section 38(1) *ibid. Charalambos Papadopoullos v. The Republic of Cyprus* (1965) 3 CLR 401; *Dinos Constantinou as administrator of the estate of the deceased Ekaterini Emmanuel v. The Republic of Cyprus* (1966) 3 CLR 572.
39. Section 39 Law No. 158(I)/1999.
40. Section 40 *ibid. Voyiazianos Praxitelis v. The Republic of Cyprus through the Board for the Reinstatement of Dismissed Public Officers* (1967) 3 CLR 239.
41. Section 42(1) Law No. 158(I)/1999.
42. Section 42(2) *ibid. Kallouris Georghios Michael v. The Republic of Cyprus through the Public Service Commission* (1964) 1 CLR 313; *Maratheftis Mikis v. The Republic of Cyprus through The Public Service Commission* (1965) 3 CLR 576; *Sygahriotis Kyriacos and others v. The Republic of Cyprus through the Dental Council* (1965) 3 CLR 317; *Kontemeniotis Antonios v. The Cyprus Broadcasting Corporation* (1982) 3 CLR 1027; *Cyprus Sulphar and Copper Co Ltd v. The Republic of Cyprus* (2003) 4 CLR 471.
43. Section 43(1) *ibid. Andreas A. Marcoullides and The Republic (Public Service Commission)* 3 RSCC 30; *Nicolaos D. Haros and The Republic (Minister of The Interior)* 4 RSCC 39; *Maro N. Panteilidou and The Republic (Public Service Commission)* 4 RSCC 100; *Christodoulos Fisentzides v. Republic (Public Service Commission)* (1971) 3 CLR 80; *Republic (Public Service Commission) v. Lefkos Georghiades* (1972) 3 CLR 594; *Kypros Kyprianou v. Public Service Commission* (1973) 3 CLR 206; *Iordanis lordanous v. Republic (Public Service Commission)* (1974) 3 CLR 194; *Orphanou v. Registrar Co-operative Societies* (1985) 3 CLR 1022.
44. Section 50 Law No. 158(I)/1999.
45. Section 51(1) *ibid. Tamassos Tobacco Suppliers and Co v. The Republic of Cyprus* (1992) 3 CLR 60.
46. Section 52(1) Law No. 158(I)/1999. *Chrysochou Bros v. The Cyprus Telecommunications Authority a. a.* (1966) 3 CLR 482.

rights of the citizens is allowed only to the extent that this is necessary for the protection of public interest.[47]

47. Section 52(2) Law No. 158(I)/1999.

Chapter 3. Historical Background and Development of Energy Law

13. In Cyprus, the electricity market was first regulated during British Rule with the law on supply of electricity,[48] commonly referred to as Cap. 170, and the law on generation and supply of electricity,[49] commonly referred to as Cap. 171. This legislation, which as amended is still in force, has lost its principal meaning due to the enactment of a series of laws on electricity[50] in view of bringing national legislation in line with the then *acquis communautaire,* and now *Union acquis.*

48. A Law to Regulate the Supply of Electricity for Lighting and Other Purposes ('Cap. 170') No. 26 of 1940, CG No. 2882, 23 Oct. 1940, p. 414, as amended.
49. A law to provide for the establishment of a Corporate Body to be called the EAC and for the exercise and performance by such body of functions relating to generation and supply of electricity and certain other matters; to authorize the acquisition by the said body of electricity undertakings and to regulate the payment of compensation thereof; to provide for the regulation of the supply of electricity; and for purposes connected with the matters aforesaid ('Cap. 171') No. 23 of 1952, CG No. 3650, 29 Oct. 1952, p. 141, as amended.
50. *See* in this respect para. 15 below.

Chapter 4. Role of Government Institutions in the Shaping and Administration of Energy Law and Policy

14. Shaping the energy law of Cyprus takes place at three levels: drafting energy policy; issuing the legislation on energy; and specifying or clarifying any issues through Decrees or Decisions, where the law provides the corresponding competence and discretion. With regard to energy policy, under Article 9(1) of the Regulation on the Governance of the Energy Union,[51] Cyprus has issued the *Integrated National Energy and Climate Plan* ('Εθνικό Σχέδιο της Κύπρου για την Ενέργεια και το Κλίμα')[52] for the period 2021 to 2030. It has set the national objectives and targets with regard to decarbonization, energy efficiency, energy security, the internal energy market as well as research, innovation and competitiveness, along with the corresponding policies and measures and their impact assessment. According to said plan, Cyprus shall reach the new renewable energy sources targets of 23% by 2030, as the market parity has already been achieved and since 2013, electricity from renewable sources is no longer promoted through subsidies. Renewable heating and cooling is promoted by support schemes offering grants to households and through obligatory measures to new buildings; however, renewable energy sources in transport are the most challenging sector. With reference to energy efficiency, policies and measures shall enable Cyprus to meet the national target of energy savings by 2030. Cyprus has strengthened its focus on energy efficiency in the transport sector. In relation to energy security, the energy isolation of Cyprus shall come to an end through the introduction of natural gas via Liquified Natural Gas imports and the development of the necessary infrastructure to import natural gas in Cyprus via the project of common interest named 'CyprusGas2EU'. These measures shall also diversify the national energy mix and contribute to energy security.[53] With reference to the internal energy market, a number of key projects are expected to contribute to electricity being traded on competitive terms. These are the Meter Data Management System and the Market Management System, along with rolling out the Advanced Metering Infrastructure with 400,000 smart meters and better controlling the distribution system.[54]

15. The national legislation on energy (*see* in this respect paragraph 18 below) which consists mainly of national statutes transposing EU legislation is issued by

51. Regulation (EU) 2018/1999 of the European Parliament and of the Council of 11 Dec. 2018 on the Governance of the Energy Union and Climate Action, amending Regulations (EC) No. 663/2009 and (EC) No. 715/2009 of the European Parliament and of the Council, Directives 94/22/EC, 98/70/EC, 2009/31/EC, 2009/73/EC, 2010/31/EU, 2012/27/EU and 2013/30/EU of the European Parliament and of the Council, Council Directives 2009/119/EC and (EU) 2015/652 and repealing Regulation (EU) No. 525/2013 of the European Parliament and of the Council, OJ L 328, 21 Dec. 2018, p. 1.
52. Th. Mesimeris et al., Cyprus' Integrated National Energy and Climate Plan under the Regulation (EU) 2018/1999 of the European Parliament and of the Council of 11 Dec. 2018 on the Governance of the Energy Union and Climate Action, Nicosia: Republic of Cyprus, January 2020, available (in Greek): https://meci.gov.cy/assets/modules/wnp/articles/202101/103/docs/necpgr.pdf & available (in English): https://meci.gov.cy/assets/modules/wnp/articles/202101/103/docs/cynecp.pdf (4 Jul. 2023).
53. *Ibid.* pp. 18–19.
54. *Ibid.* pp. 19–20.

the House of Representatives, is shaped in essence by Brussels and, in essence, i harmonized throughout the Union. Nonetheless, the EU has allowed for derogation from the EU statutory provisions specifically for Cyprus. These provisions relate tc ownership unbundling of transmission systems and transmission system operators independence of system operators; unbundling of transmission system owners assets, equipment, staff and identity of independent transmission operators; independence of the transmission system operator; independence of the staff and the management of the transmission system operator; supervisory body; compliance programme and compliance officer and designation and certification of transmission system operators; and at least until 1 January 2025, market-based supply prices.[55] Furthermore, until the transmission system of Cyprus is connected to other Member States' transmission systems via interconnections, the following EU provisions on the internal market for electricity do not apply: principles regarding the operation of electricity markets; balance responsibility; balancing market; certain aspects of day-ahead and intraday markets; trade on day-ahead and intraday markets; forward markets; technical bidding limits; value of lost load; dispatching of generation and demand response; dispatching; capacity allocation; certain aspects of network charges and congestion income; certain aspects of resource adequacy; certain aspects of regional cooperation of transmission system operators; establishment, mission, geographical scope and tasks of regional coordination centres cooperation within and between regional coordination centres; working arrangements, consultation procedure and transparency of regional coordination centres adoption and review of coordinated actions and recommendations; management board of regional coordination centres; organizational structure, equipment and staff of regional coordination centres; monitoring and reporting performed by regional coordination centres and their liability; certain aspects of the ten-year network development plan; the inter-transmission system operator compensation mechanism; and certification of transmission system operators.[56]

16. Finally, Decrees and Decisions are issued by the Minister, occasionally following consultation with other governmental bodies, interested parties or the public, in order to elaborate, clarify or explain a statutory provision, as long as such a power is derogated by the law.

17. The administration of energy law is entrusted to the Minister and, mainly, to Cyprus Energy Regulatory Authority. They ensure, promote and control its application under each particular chapter of energy law, those being electricity, natural gas and renewable energy. No further elaborations may be made at this point, as general legislation applicable to all aforementioned aspects of energy law, from which general powers and duties of those bodies derive, is absent.

55. Articles 43 to 50, 52 and 5 Directive (EU) 2019/944. *See* Art. 66(3) Directive (EU) 2019/944.
56. Articles 3, 5–6, 7(1) & (2) (c) & (g), 8–17, 18(5) & (6), 19, 20, 21(1), (2) & (4) to (8), 22(1)(c), (2)(b) & (c) and the last subparagraph, 23–27, 34(1), (2) & (3), 35–47, 48(2), 49 and 51 Regulation 2019/943. *See* Art. 64(2) Regulation 2019/943.

Chapter 5. Sources of Energy Law

18. Energy law is regulated by a series of laws, which were issued for the purpose of implementing directives of the EU and facilitating the application of regulations of the EU. These are the new Law on Electricity Market Regulation[57] (hereinafter 'Law No. 130(I)/2021') that repealed and replaced the previous Law on Regulating the Electricity Market of 2003.[58] Pursuant to its preamble, Law No. 130(I)/2021 implements fully the directive on the internal market for electricity[59] and partially the directives on renewable electricity[60] and energy efficiency.[61] It equally facilitates the application of the regulation of the wholesale energy market,[62] the trans-European energy infrastructure,[63] the internal market for electricity[64] and the electricity transmission system.[65] The natural gas market is regulated

57. Law on Electricity Market Regulation ('ο περί Ρύθμισης της Αγοράς Ηλεκτρισμού Νόμος') No. 130 of 2021, OG I(I) No. 4850 of 7 Oct. 2021, p. 1010, as last amended by Amending Law No. 224 of 2022, OG I(I) No. 4931 of 22 Dec. 2022, p. 1665.
58. Law on Regulating the Electricity Market ('περί Ρύθμισης της Αγοράς Ηλεκτρισμού Νόμος') No. 122 of 2003, OG I(I) No. 3742, 25 Jul. 2003, p. 737, as last amended by Amending Law No. 145 of 2018, OG I(I) No. 4678 of 18 Dec. 2018, p. 1024.
59. Directive (EU) 2019/944 of the European Parliament and of the Council of 5 Jun. 2019 on common rules for the internal market for electricity and amending Directive 2012/27/EU, OJ L 158, 14 Jun. 2019, p. 125, as last amended by Regulation (EU) 2022/869 of the European Parliament and of the Council of 30 May 2022 on guidelines for trans-European energy infrastructure, amending Regulations (EC) No 715/2009, (EU) 2019/942 and (EU) 2019/943 and Directives 2009/73/EC and (EU) 2019/944, and repealing Regulation (EU) No 347/2013, OJ L 152, 3 Jun. 2022, p. 45.
60. Directive (EU) 2018/2001 of the European Parliament and of the Council of 11 Dec. 2018 on the promotion of the use of energy from renewable sources, OJ L 328, 21 Dec. 2018, p. 82, as last amended by Commission Delegated Regulation (EU) 2022/759 of 14 Dec. 2021 amending Annex VII to Directive (EU) 2018/2001 of the European Parliament and of the Council as regards a methodology for calculating the amount of renewable energy used for cooling and district cooling, OJ L 139, 18 May 2022, p. 1.
61. Directive 2012/27/EU of the European Parliament and of the Council of 25 Oct. 2012 on energy efficiency, amending Directives 2009/125/EC and 2010/30/EU and repealing Directives 2004/8/EC and 2006/32/EC Text with EEA relevance, OJ L 315, 14 Nov. 2012, p. 1, as last amended by Directive (EU) 2019/944 of the European Parliament and of the Council of 5 Jun. 2019 on common rules for the internal market for electricity and amending Directive 2012/27/EU, OJ L 158, 14 Jun. 2019, p. 125.
62. Regulation (EU) No. 1227/2011 of the European Parliament and of the Council of 25 Oct. 2011 on wholesale energy market integrity and transparency, OJ L 326, 8 Dec. 2011, p. 1. Amendment has been proposed by European Commission, Proposal for a Regulation of the European Parliament and of the Council amending Regulations (EU) No. 1227/2011 and (EU) 2019/942 to improve the Union's protection against market manipulation in the wholesale energy market, COM/2023/147 final of 14 Mar. 2023, available: https://eur-lex.europa.eu.
63. Regulation (EU) No. 347/2013 of the European Parliament and of the Council of 17 Apr. 2013 on guidelines for trans-European energy infrastructure and repealing Decision No. 1364/2006/EC and amending Regulations (EC) No. 713/2009, (EC) No. 714/2009 and (EC) No. 715/2009 Text with EEA relevance, OJ L 115, 25 Apr. 2013, p. 39, as last amended by Commission Delegated Regulation (EU) 2022/564 of 19 Nov. 2021 amending Regulation (EU) No. 347/2013 of the European Parliament and of the Council as regards the Union list of projects of common interest, OJ L 109, 8 Apr. 2022, p. 14.
64. Regulation (EU) 2019/943 of the European Parliament and of the Council of 5 Jun. 2019 on the internal market for electricity, OJ L 158, 14 Jun. 2019, p. 54, as last amended by Regulation (EU)

by Law on Regulating the Natural Gas Market[66] (hereinafter 'Law No. 183(I)/2004'), which was laid down for the purpose of implementing Directive 2003/55/EC[67] pursuant to its preamble. However, amending laws have been issued, and accordingly, the latest natural gas directives have been implemented.[68] In particular, prospection, research and exploitation of hydrocarbons, those being oil and gas, is regulated by the Law on Hydrocarbons[69] (hereinafter 'Law No. 4(I)/2007'), as well as its secondary legislation.[70] Finally, renewable energy is regulated by the Law on

---

2022/869 of the European Parliament and of the Council of 30 May 2022 on guidelines for trans-European energy infrastructure, amending Regulations (EC) No. 715/2009, (EU) 2019/942 and (EU) 2019/943 and Directives 2009/73/EC and (EU) 2019/944, and repealing Regulation (EU) No. 347/2013, OJ L 152, 3 Jun. 2022, p. 45.

65. Commission Regulation (EU) 2017/1485 of 2 Aug. 2017 establishing a guideline on electricity transmission system operation, OJ L 220, 25 Aug. 2017, p. 1, as last amended by Commission Implementing Regulation (EU) 2021/280 of 22 Feb. 2021 amending Regulations (EU) 2015/1222, (EU) 2016/1719, (EU) 2017/2195 and (EU) 2017/1485 in order to align them with Regulation (EU) 2019/943, OJ L 62, 23 Feb. 2021, p. 24.

66. Law on Regulating the Natural Gas Market No. 183 of 2004, OG I(I) No. 3852, 30 Apr. 2004, p. 3289, as last amended by Law on Regulating the Natural Gas Market (Amendment) ('περί Ρύθμισης της Αγοράς Φυσικού Αερίου (Τροποποιητικός) Νόμος') No. 190 of 2022, OG I(I) No. 4927, 9 Dec. 2022, p. 1537.

67. Directive 2003/55/EC of the European Parliament and of the Council of 26 Jun. 2003 concerning common rules for the internal market in natural gas and repealing Directive 98/30/EC, OJ L 176, 15 Jul. 2003, p. 57.

68. Law on Regulating the Natural Gas Market (Amendment) ('περί της Ρύθμισης της Αγοράς Φυσικού Αερίου (Τροποποιητικός) Νόμος') No. 219 of 2012, OG I(I) No. 4374, 28 Dec. 2012, p. 2413, which implements Directive 2009/73/EC of the European Parliament and of the Council of 13 Jul. 2009 concerning common rules for the internal market in natural gas and repealing Directive 2003/55/EC, OJ L 211, 14 Aug. 2009, p. 94; Law on Regulating the Natural Gas Market (Amendment) ('περί της Ρύθμισης της Αγοράς Φυσικού Αερίου (Τροποποιητικός) Νόμος') No. 148 of 2018, OG I(I) 4678, 18 Dec. 2018, p. 1032, which implemented Arts 3(5), 27(1), 31(3), 31(4) and Annex I(1)(a) Directive 2009/73/EC as well as Arts 2, 9(1) and (2), 10(2), 11(1) and 15(2) Directive 2012/27/EU; Law on Regulating the Natural Gas Market (Amendment) ('περί Ρύθμισης της Αγοράς Φυσικού Αερίου (Τροποποιητικός) Νόμος') No. 103 of 2022, OG (I) 4772, 14 Aug. 2020, p. 444, which implemented amending Directive (EU) 2019/692 and Art. 70 Directive (EU) 2019/944.

69. Law on Hydrocarbons (Prospection, Research and Exploitation) ('περί Υδρογονανθράκων (Αναζήτηση, Έρευνα και Εκμετάλλευση) Νόμος') No. 4 of 2007, OG I(I) No. 4109, 26 Jan. 2007, p. 81. This legislation was enacted for the purposes of implementing Directive 94/22/EC of the European Parliament and of the Council of 30 May 1994 on the conditions for granting and using authorizations for the prospection, exploration and production of hydrocarbons, OJ L 164, 30 Jun. 1994, p. 3. Law No. 4(I)/2007 has been amended by Law on Hydrocarbons (Prospection, Research and Exploitation) (Amendment) ('περί Υδρογονανθράκων (Αναζήτηση, Έρευνα και Εκμετάλλευση) (Τροποποιητικός) Νόμος') No. 126 of 2013, OG I(I) No. 4410, 25 Oct. 2013, p. 1108, and by Law on Hydrocarbons (Prospection, Research and Exploitation) (Amendment) ('περί Υδρογονανθράκων (Αναζήτηση, Έρευνα και Εκμετάλλευση) (Τροποποιητικός) Νόμος') No. 29 of 2014, OG I(I) No. 4433, 7 Mar. 2014, p. 157.

70. Regulations on Hydrocarbons (Prospection, Research and Exploitation) ('οι περί Υδρογονανθράκων (Αναζήτηση, Έρευνα και Εκμετάλλευση) Κανονισμοί') No. 51 of 2007, OG I(III) No. 4170, 26 Jan. 2007, p. 345, which have been amended by Regulations on Hydrocarbons (Prospection, Research and Exploitation) (Amendment) ('οι περί Υδρογονανθράκων (Αναζήτηση, Έρευνα και Εκμετάλλευση) (Τροποποιητικοί) Κανονισμοί') No. 113 of 2009, OG I(III) No. 4342, 13 Mar. 2009, p. 627 (hereinafter 'KDP 51/2007').

Promoting and Encouraging the Use of Energy from Renewable Sources[71] (hereinafter 'Law No. 107(I)/2022'), which partially implements Directive 2018/2001/[72] pursuant to its preamble.

71. Law on Promotion and Encouragement of Use of Renewable Energy Sources ('περί Προώθησης και Ενθάρρυνσης της Χρήσης Ανανεώσιμων Πηγών Ενέργειας Νόμος') No. 107 of 2022, OG I(I) No. 4902, 15 Jul. 2022, p. 1039.
72. *See* n 57 above.

Part I. Regulatory Framework Concerning Electricity

Chapter 1. Introduction

§1. Objective of Law No. 130(I)/2021

19. Following the spirit of the implemented EU provisions, Law No. 130(I)/2021 aims to regulate the electricity market as well as to set out common rules concerning generation ('παραγωγή'),[73] transmission ('μεταφορά'),[74] distribution ('διανομή')[75] and supply ('προμήθεια')[76] of electricity, as well as protection of consumers, with a view to creating truly integrated competitive, consumer-centred, flexible, fair and transparent electricity markets in the Union. Moreover, using the advantages of an integrated market, this Directive aims to ensure affordable, transparent energy prices and costs for consumers, a high degree of security of supply and a smooth transition towards a sustainable low-carbon energy system. It lays down key rules relating to the organization and functioning of the Union electricity sector, in particular, rules on consumer empowerment and protection, open access to the integrated market, third-party access to transmission and distribution infrastructure. It further ensures that electricity undertakings ('επιχειρήσεις ηλεκτρικής ενέργειας')[77] function with the aim of achieving a competitive, safe

73. *Generation* ('production' in French, 'Erzeugung' in German, 'productie' in Dutch) in relation to electrical energy means production of electricity (s. 2 Law No. 130(I)/2021, which corresponds to Art. 2(37) Directive (EU) 2019/944).
74. *Transmission* ('transport' in French, 'Übertragung' in German, 'transmissie' in Dutch) in relation to electricity stands for transmission of electricity through a transmission system, that being, a system comprised fully or mainly of lines and electrical installations of high-voltage and used for the transmission of electricity from a power plant to a substation or from a power plant to another or from a substation to another or to and from any interconnection or to final customers or to distributors, but does not include supply (s. 2 Law No. 130(I)/2021, which corresponds to Art. 2(34) Directive (EU) 2019/944).
75. *Distribution* ('distribution' in French, 'Verteilung' in German, 'distributie' in Dutch) in relation to electricity means the the transport of electricity on high-voltage, medium-voltage and low-voltage distribution systems with a view to its delivery to customers,, but does not include supply (s. 2 Law No. 130(I)/2021, which corresponds to Art. 2(34) Directive (EU) 2019/944).
76. *Supply* ('fourniture' in French, 'Versorgung' in German, 'levering' in Dutch) is the sale, including resale, of electricity to customers (s. 2 Law No. 130(I)/2021, which corresponds to Art. 2(12) Directive (EU) 2019/944).
77. *Electricity undertaking* ('entreprise d'électricité' in French, 'Elektrizitätsunternehmen' in German, 'elektriciteitsbedrijf' in Dutch) means a natural or legal person who carries out at least one of the

and environmentally sustainable market of electricity energy and are not subject to discrimination with regard to their rights or duties.[78]

20. Furthermore, Law No. 130(I)/2021 establishes a new regime for issuing authorizations regarding generation, transmission, distribution, supply and storage of electricity ('αποθήκευση ενέργιας'),[79] including function of the market and linking electricity systems. It has created the Transmission System Operator ('Διαχειριστή Συστήματος Μεταφοράς Κύπρου') and has set up dispute resolution mechanisms for disputes between the Transmission System Owner and the Transmission System Operator, between the Transmission System Operator and the Distribution System Operator and between the Interconnector Owner, the Transmission System Operator, the Interconnector Operator and the neighbouring transmission system operators. At the same time, Law No. 130(I)/2021 regulates access to the transmission and distribution system while introducing public service obligations and consumer protection, including vulnerable customers and energy poverty.[80]

21. Especially with reference to environmental protection, it must be stressed that Law No. 130(I)/2021, unlike its repealed predecessor, does set out that the main players take environmental protection into account while exercising their rights and complying with their duties. This applies to the Transmission System Owner, the Distribution System Owner, the Transmission System Operator, the Distribution System Operator, the Interconnector Owner and the Interconnector Operator.[81] Environmental protection is also a condition to be considered for the authorization of electricity production.[82] Parallel to those, the environment is protected in Cyprus through a complex of laws issued for the purposes of implementing directives of the EU.[83] These are relevant to energy law to the extent that environmental permissions are essential for the lawful operation of electricity undertakings.

§2. Regulatory Mechanism

22. The regulatory mechanism of Law No. 130(I)/2021 is run by the Cyprus Energy Regulatory Authority ('Ρυθμιστική Αρχή Ενέργειας Κύπρου'), while the

---

following functions: generation, transmission, distribution, aggregation, demand response, energy storage, supply or purchase of electricity, and who is responsible for the commercial, technical or maintenance tasks related to those functions, but does not include final customers (s. 2 Law No. 130(I)/2021, which corresponds to Art. 2(57) Directive (EU) 2019/944).

78. Section 3(1) Law No. 130(I)/2021, which in part corresponds to Art. 1 Directive (EU) 2019/944.
79. *Energy storage* ('stockage d'énergie' in French, 'Energiespeicherung' in German, 'energieopslag' in Dutch) means in the electricity system, deferring the final use of electricity to a moment later than when it was generated, or the conversion of electrical energy into a form of energy which can be stored, the storing of such energy, and the subsequent reconversion of such energy into electrical energy or use as another energy carrier (s. 2 Law No. 130(I)/2021, which corresponds to Art. 2(59) Directive (EU) 2019/944).
80. Section 3(2) Law No. 130(I)/2021.
81. *See* ss 41, 42(b), 48(1), 70(1)(a), 103, 105 & 111(1)(d) *ibid.*
82. *See* s. 25(2)(b) *ibid.*
83. On protection of the environment *see* paras 415 et seq. below.

Council of Ministers and the Minister of Energy, Commerce and Industry (hereinafter 'the Minister') are entrusted with policy drafting and supervision. Equally important is the role of the EU Agency for the Cooperation of Energy Regulators (hereinafter 'ACER'), as explained below. Furthermore, an essential principle that does affect the regulatory mechanism is that of unbundling of transmission systems and electricity production and supply, which has been introduced already in the First Energy Package.[84] This principle, now evolved into 'effective unbundling'[85] applies throughout the Union and is deemed in fact necessary to ensure the functioning of the internal energy market (Article 194(1) TFEU) and the security of supply, in the sense of allowing for non-discriminatory network access.[86] It has also resulted in the creation of four persons, the Transmission System Owner, the Transmission System Operator, the Distribution System Owner and the Distribution System Operator. All and each of them are an indispensable part of the regulatory system; albeit they, their duties and responsibilities are portrayed in the relevant subchapters (*see* in this regard paragraphs 144 et seq., 147 et seq., 166 et seq. and 168 et seq. below).

I. Cyprus Energy Regulatory Authority

23. Cyprus Energy Regulatory Authority has general objectives, general duties and powers, duties and competence with regard to regional coordination centres, the authority to issue regulatory decisions and other decisions, and when competition issues arise, it has the authority to cooperate with the Cyprus Commission for the Protection of Competition.

24. Cyprus Energy Regulatory Authority, in carrying out the regulatory tasks specified in this law, takes all reasonable measures in pursuit of the following objectives within the framework of its duties and powers as laid down in section 5 of this law (*see* in this regard paragraphs 23 et seq. below), in close consultation with other relevant national authorities, including competition authorities, as well as authorities, including regulatory authorities, from neighbouring Member States and neighbouring third countries, as appropriate, and without prejudice to their competence:

– promoting, in close cooperation with regulatory authorities of other Member States, the Commission and ACER, a competitive, flexible, secure and environmentally sustainable internal market for electricity within the Union, and effective market opening for all customers and suppliers in the Union, and ensuring

84. *See* Arts 13 to 15 Directive 96/92/EC of the European Parliament and of the Council of 19 Dec. 1996 concerning common rules for the internal market in electricity, OJ L 27, 30 Jan. 1997, p. 20, Arts 10, 15, 18 & 19 Directive 2003/54/EC of the European Parliament and of the Council of 26 Jun. 2003 concerning common rules for the internal market in electricity and repealing Directive 96/92/EC, OJ L 176, 15 Jul. 2003, p. 37, Arts 9, 14, 26, 30 & 31 Directive 2009/72/EC of the European Parliament and of the Council of 13 Jul. 2009 concerning common rules for the internal market in electricity and repealing Directive 2003/54/EC, OJ L 211, 14 Aug. 2009, p. 55.
85. *See* the provisions now in force: Arts 35, 43, 55 & 56 Directive (EU) 2019/944.
86. *See* CJEU Case C-718/18, *European Commission v. Federal Republic of Germany,* Judgment of 2 Sep. 2021, digital ECJ paras 35, 36, 54, 55; C-347/16, *Balgarska energiyna borsa*, Judgment of 26 Oct. 2017, para. 34.

appropriate conditions for the effective and reliable operation of electricity networks, taking into account long-term objectives;
- facilitating the development of competitive and properly functioning regional cross-border markets within the Union with a view to achieving the objectives referred to in the aforementioned point;
- facilitating the elimination of restrictions on trade in electricity between Member States, including developing appropriate cross-border transmission capacities to meet demand and enhancing the integration of national markets which may facilitate electricity flows across the Union;
- helping to achieve, in the most cost-effective way, the development of secure, reliable and efficient non-discriminatory systems that are consumer-oriented, and promoting system adequacy and, in accordance with general energy policy objectives, energy efficiency, as well as the integration of large and small-scale production of electricity from renewable sources and distributed generation in both transmission and distribution networks, and facilitating their operation in relation to other energy networks of gas or heat;
- facilitating access to the network for new generation capacity and energy storage facilities, in particular removing barriers that could prevent access for new market entrants and of electricity from renewable sources;
- ensuring that system operators and system users are granted appropriate incentives, in both the short and the long term, to increase efficiencies, especially energy efficiency, in system performance and to foster market integration;
- ensuring that customers benefit through the efficient functioning of their national market, promoting effective competition and helping to ensure a high level of consumer protection, in close cooperation with relevant consumer protection authorities; and
- helping to achieve high standards of universal service and of public service in electricity supply, contributing to the protection of vulnerable customers and contributing to the compatibility of necessary data exchange processes for customer switching.[87]

25. At the same time, Cyprus Energy Regulatory Authority in carrying out the regulatory tasks set out in this law, takes all reasonable measures in order to ensure the protection of customers and especially vulnerable customers, high levels of customer protection, especially with regard to transparency of contractual terms and conditions and dispute resolution, the satisfaction of all reasonable demands and needs with regard to electricity, as well as safety, continuity, quality and reliability of providing electricity. It also ensures that electricity undertakings comply with this law, in order to achieve a competitive, safe and environmentally sustainable electricity market and do not discriminate between said undertakings regarding their rights or duties. Further, it monitors security of supply, save for Regulations (EU) 2019/941 and 2019/943, while promoting optimisation of electricity use among electricity undertakings and ensuring that administrative procedures do not discriminate against suppliers of undertakings already registered in another Member State.

87. Section 4(a) to (h) Law No. 130(I)/2021, which corresponds to Art. 58(a) to (h) Directive (EU) 2019/944.

It finally takes appropriate measures for the protection of customers and especially ensures that sufficient safeguards for the protection of vulnerable customers and customers at remote areas are in place.[88]

26. The general duties and powers of Cyprus Energy Regulatory Authority are the following:

- fixing or approving, in accordance with transparent criteria, transmission or distribution tariffs or their methodologies, or both;
- ensuring the compliance of transmission system operators and distribution system operators and, where relevant, system owners, as well as the compliance of any electricity undertakings and other market participants, with their obligations under this Directive, Regulation (EU) 2019/943, the network codes and the guidelines adopted pursuant to Articles 59, 60 and 61 of Regulation (EU) 2019/943, and other relevant Union law, including as regards cross-border issues, as well as with ACER's decisions;
- in close coordination with the other regulatory authorities, ensuring the compliance of the ENTSO for Electricity and the EU DSO entity with their obligations under this law, Regulation (EU) 2019/943, the network codes and guidelines adopted pursuant to Articles 59, 60 and 61 of Regulation (EU) 2019/943, and other relevant Union law, including as regards cross-border issues, as well as with ACER's decisions, and jointly identifying non-compliance of the ENTSO for Electricity and the EU DSO entity with their respective obligations; where the regulatory authorities have not been able to reach an agreement within a period of four months after the start of consultations for the purpose of jointly identifying non-compliance, the matter shall be referred to the ACER for a decision, pursuant to Article 6(10) of Regulation (EU) 2019/942;
- approving products and procurement process for non-frequency ancillary services;
- implementing the network codes and guidelines adopted pursuant to Articles 59, 60 and 61 of Regulation (EU) 2019/943 through national measures or, where so required, coordinated regional or Union-wide measures;
- cooperating in regard to cross-border issues with the regulatory authority or authorities of the Member States concerned and with ACER, in particular through participation in the work of ACER's Board of Regulators pursuant to Article 21 of Regulation (EU) 2019/942;
- complying with, and implementing, any relevant legally binding decisions of the Commission and of ACER;
- ensuring that transmission system operators make available interconnector capacities to the utmost extent pursuant to Article 16 of Regulation (EU) 2019/943;
- reporting annually on its activity and the fulfilment of its duties to the Minister, the Commission and ACER, including on the steps taken and the results obtained as regards each of the tasks listed herein;

88. Section 4(2)(a) to (i) Law No. 130(I)/2021.

- ensuring that there is no cross-subsidization between transmission, distribution and supply activities or other electricity or non-electricity activities;
- monitoring investment plans of the transmission system operators and providing in its annual report an assessment of the investment plans of the transmission system operators as regards their consistency with the Union-wide network development plan, which may include recommendations to amend those investment plans;
- monitoring and assessing the performance of transmission system operators and distribution system operators in relation to the development of a smart grid that promotes energy efficiency and the integration of energy from renewable sources, based on a limited set of indicators, and publish a national report every two years, including recommendations;
- setting or approving standards and requirements for quality of service and quality of supply or contributing thereto together with other competent authorities and monitoring compliance with and reviewing the past performance of network security and reliability rules;
- monitoring and ensuring the level of transparency, including of wholesale prices according to Regulation 1227/2011, and ensuring compliance of electricity undertakings with transparency and integrity obligations;
- monitoring the level and effectiveness of market opening and competition at wholesale and retail levels, including on electricity exchanges, prices for household customers including prepayment systems, the impact of dynamic electricity price contracts and of the use of smart metering systems, switching rates, disconnection rates, charges for maintenance services, the execution of maintenance services, the relationship between household and wholesale prices, the evolution of grid tariffs and levies, and complaints by household customers, as well as any distortion or restriction of competition, including by providing any relevant information, and bringing any relevant cases to the Cyprus Commission for the Protection of Competition;
- monitoring the occurrence of restrictive contractual practices, including exclusivity clauses which may prevent customers from contracting simultaneously with more than one supplier or restrict their choice to do so, and, where appropriate, informing the Cyprus Commission for the Protection of Competition of such practices;
- monitoring the time taken by transmission system operators and distribution system operators to make connections and repairs;
- helping to ensure, together with other relevant authorities, that the consumer protection measures are effective and enforced;
- publishing recommendations, at least annually, in relation to compliance of supply prices with Article 5 of Directive 2019/944, and providing those recommendations to the Cyprus Commission for the Protection of Competition, where appropriate;
- ensuring non-discriminatory access to customer consumption data, the provision, for optional use, of an easily understandable harmonized format at national level for consumption data, and prompt access for all customers to such data pursuant to section 127;

- monitoring the implementation of rules relating to the roles and responsibilities of transmission system operators, distribution system operators, suppliers, customers and other market participants pursuant to Regulation (EU) 2019/943;
- monitoring investment in generation and storage capacities in relation to security of supply;
- monitoring technical cooperation between Union and third-country transmission system operators;
- contributing to the compatibility of data exchange processes for the most important market processes at regional level;
- monitoring the availability of comparison tools that meet the requirements set out in section 121 and in the Annex;
- monitoring the removal of unjustified obstacles to and restrictions on the development of consumption of self-generated electricity and citizen energy communities;
- advise the Minister on all matters related to electricity;
- save for Regulations (EU) 2019/941 and 2019/943, ensure electricity sufficiency to satisfy all reasonable electricity needs and demands;
- act in accordance with the directions of the Council of Ministers in the event of defence or national security;
- act as the competent authority for out-of-court settlement of disputes; and
- ensure that customers are provided with all necessary information regarding their rights, the laws in force and the manner of applying to the dispute resolution mechanisms.[89]

27. Cyprus Energy Regulatory Authority further has the authority to cooperate closely with the Transmission System Operator and other national authorities while exercising said duties.[90] In order to ensure that the Transmission System Operator fulfils its duties, the Cyprus Energy Regulatory Authority may do the following:

- monitor the Transmission System Owner's and the Transmission System Operator's compliance with their obligations under section 5 of this law and issue penalties for non-compliance;
- monitor the relations and communications between the Transmission System Operator and the Transmission System Owner so as to ensure compliance of the first with its obligations, and in particular approve contracts and act as a dispute settlement authority between the two with respect to any complaint submitted by either party;
- regarding the first ten-year network development plan, approve the investments planning and the multi-annual network development plan submitted at least every two years by the Transmission System Operator;
- ensure that network access tariffs collected by the Transmission System Operator include remuneration for the Transmission System Owner, which provides for adequate remuneration of the network assets and of any new investments made therein, provided they are economically and efficiently incurred;

89. Section 5(1) *ibid.*, which partially corresponds to Art. 59(1) Directive (EU) 2019/944.
90. Section 5(2) Law No. 130(I)/2021.

- have the powers to carry out inspections, including unannounced inspections, a the premises of Transmission System Owner and Transmission System Operator and
- monitor the use of congestion charges collected by the Transmission System Operator in accordance with Article 19(2) of Regulation (EU) 2019/943.[91]

28. Furthermore, in order to ensure the independence of the Transmission System Operator, Cyprus Energy Regulatory Authority has been granted the following duties and powers:

- to impose penalties for discriminatory behaviour in favour of the vertically integrated undertaking;
- to monitor communications between the Transmission System Operator and the vertically integrated undertaking so as to ensure compliance of the Transmission System Operator with its obligations;
- to act as dispute settlement authority between the vertically integrated undertaking and the transmission system operator with respect to any submitted complaint;
- to monitor commercial and financial relations including loans between the vertically integrated undertaking and the Transmission System Operator;
- to approve all commercial and financial agreements between the vertically integrated undertaking and the Transmission System Operator on the condition that they comply with market conditions; and
- to carry out inspections, including unannounced ones, on the premises of the vertically integrated undertaking and the Transmission System Operator.[92]

29. In addition, Cyprus Energy Regulatory Authority has the power to fix and/or approve national methodologies that are made public, for the calculation and establishment of the terms and conditions of the following, save for ACER competence under Regulations (EU) 2019/943 and 2019/942:

- connection and access to national networks, including transmission and distribution tariffs or their methodologies, those tariffs or methodologies shall allow the necessary investments in the networks to be carried out in a manner allowing those investments to ensure the viability of the networks;
- the provision of ancillary services which shall be performed in the most economic manner possible and provide appropriate incentives for network users to balance their input and off-takes, such ancillary services shall be provided in a fair and non-discriminatory manner and be based on objective criteria; and

91. Section 5(5)(a) to (f) Law No. 130(I)/2021, which corresponds to Art. 59(5)(a) to (f) Directive (EU) 2019/944.
92. Section 5(6)(a) to (f) Law No. 130(I)/2021, which corresponds to Art. 59(6)(a) to (e) & (g) Directive (EU) 2019/944.

– access to cross-border infrastructures, including the procedures for the allocation of capacity and congestion management.[93]

30. With reference to congestion, Cyprus Energy Regulatory Authority has the authority to monitor congestion management of the national electricity system including, interconnectors and the implementation of congestion management rules that are part of the Transmission Rules, the Distribution Rules or the Electricity Market Rules. These rules, including capacity allocation, are submitted by the Transmission System Operator or the Distribution System Operator, as the case may be, to Cyprus Energy Regulatory Authority that may request amendments thereto.[94]

31. In connection to electricity undertakings, Cyprus Energy Regulatory Authority has the authority to issue, amend and revoke authorizations issued under this law[95] (*see* in this regard paragraphs 41 et seq below) as well as make binding decisions for electricity undertakings,[96] including whether an authorized electricity undertaking violates the law, regulatory decisions, terms and conditions of their authorizations.[97] It also carries out investigations into the functioning of the electricity markets, including investigations relating to competition law in cooperation with the Cyprus Commission for the Protection of Competition, and decides upon and imposes any necessary and proportionate measures to promote effective competition and ensure the proper functioning of the market.[98] In the same spirit, it ensures a level playing field compatible with the TFEU, and especially Article 36 thereof, and with Union law. In doing so, it takes measures proportionate, non-discriminatory and transparent that may be implemented only following the notification to and approval by the Commission, unless the latter does not act within two months.[99] It may also require any information from electricity undertakings relevant for the fulfilment of its tasks,[100] and upon infringement of this law, Regulation (EU) 2019/943 or any relevant legally binding decisions of Cyprus Energy Regulatory Authority or of ACER, it has the authority to impose effective, proportionate and dissuasive penalties of up to 10% of the annual turnover, as well as when

93. Section 5(7)(a) to (c) & (8) Law No. 130(I)/2021, which corresponds to Art. 59(7)(a) to (c) & (8) Directive (EU) 2019/944.
94. Section 5(10) Law No. 130(I)/2021, which corresponds to Art. 59(10) Directive (EU) 2019/944.
95. Section 5(3) Law No. 130(I)/2021, which partially corresponds to Art. 59(2) Directive (EU) 2019/944.
96. Section 5(4)(a) Law No. 130(I)/2021, which partially corresponds to Art. 59(3)(a) Directive (EU) 2019/944.
97. Section 12(a), (b) & (c) Law No. 130(I)/2021.
98. Section 5(4)(b) *ibid.*, which corresponds to Art. 59(3)(b) Directive (EU) 2019/944. *See also* s. 18 Law No. 130(I)/2021. Competition law includes The Protection of Competition Law ('περί της Προστασίας του Ανταγωνισμού Νόμος') No. 13 of 2022, OG I(I) No. 4875 of 23 Feb. 2022, p. 87, as amended, and The Control of Concentrations between Undertakings for the purpose of Safeguarding Fair Competition Law ('περί Ελέγχου των Συγκεντρώσεων Επιχειρήσεων Νόμος') No. 83 of 2014, OG I(I) No. 4448, 20 Jun. 2014, p. 583. In this regard *see* paras 359 et seq. below.
99. Section 11(1), (2) & (3) Law No. 130(I)/2021, which corresponds to Art. 65(1), (2) & (3) Directive (EU) 2019/944.
100. Section 5(4)(c) Law No. 130(I)/2021, which corresponds to Art. 59(3)(c) Directive (EU) 2019/944.

suppliers follow unfair or misleading selling methods.[101] Finally, it has appropriate rights of investigation and relevant powers of instruction for dispute settlement.[102]

32. Cyprus Energy Regulatory Authority further has certain duties at the regional level. More specifically, it closely consults and cooperates with other regulatory authorities, in particular, within ACER, and provides them with any information necessary for the fulfilment of their tasks under this law, while ensuring the same level of confidentiality of the exchanged information among the different authorities. It also cooperates at least at a regional level to:

- foster the creation of operational arrangements in order to enable an optimal management of the network, promote joint electricity exchanges and the allocation of cross-border capacity, and to enable an adequate level of interconnection capacity, including through new interconnection, within the region and between regions to allow for development of effective competition and improvement of security of supply, without discriminating between suppliers in different Member States;
- coordinate the joint oversight of entities performing functions at regional level;
- coordinate, in cooperation with other involved authorities, the joint oversight of national, regional and European resource adequacy assessments;
- coordinate the development of all network codes and guidelines for the relevant transmission system operators and other market actors; and
- coordinate the development of the rules governing the management of congestion.[103]

33. In addition, it cooperates closely with the regulatory authorities of the regional coordination centre, where it is established, in order to perform the following functions:

- approve the proposal for the establishment of regional coordination centres in accordance with Article 35(1) of Regulation (EU) 2019/943;
- approve the costs related to the activities of the regional coordination centres, which are to be borne by the transmission system operators and to be taken into account in the calculation of tariffs, provided that they are reasonable and appropriate;
- approve the cooperative decision-making process;
- ensure that the regional coordination centres are equipped with all the necessary human, technical, physical and financial resources for fulfilling their obligations under this Directive and carrying out their tasks independently and impartially;
- propose jointly with other regulatory authorities of a system operation region possible additional tasks and additional powers to be assigned to the regional coordination centres by the Member States of the system operation region;

---

101. Section 5(4)(d) & (f) Law No. 130(I)/2021, which partially corresponds to Art. 59(3)(d) Directive (EU) 2019/944.
102. Section 5(4)(e) Law No. 130(I)/2021, which corresponds to Art. 59(3)(e) Directive (EU) 2019/944.
103. Section 6(1) & (2) Law No. 130(I)/2021, which corresponds to Art. 61(1) & (2) Directive (EU) 2019/944.

– ensure compliance with the obligations under this Directive and other relevant Union law, in particular as regards cross-border issues, and jointly identify non-compliance of the regional coordination centres with their respective obligations; where the regulatory authorities have not been able to reach an agreement within a period of four months after the start of consultations for the purpose of jointly identifying non-compliance, the matter shall be referred to ACER for a decision, pursuant to Article 6(10) of Regulation (EU) 2019/942; and
– monitor the performance of system coordination and report annually to ACER in this respect in accordance with Article 46 of Regulation (EU) 2019/943.[104]

34. In order to do so, it has the power to request information from the regional coordination centre and together with other regulatory authorities, it may issue joint binding decisions on the regional coordination centre. When said centre is located in Cyprus, the Cyprus Energy Regulatory Authority may carry out inspections at its premises and impose effective, proportionate and dissuasive penalties on it where it does not comply with its obligations under this law, Regulation (EU) 2019/943 or any relevant legally binding decisions of the regulatory authorities or of ACER.[105]

35. With regard to network codes and guidelines, that consist of network and reliability rules, capacity allocation and congestion management rules, rules relating to non-discriminatory, transparent provision of non-frequency ancillary services as well as in relation to demand response, energy storage and demand curtailment rules,[106] Cyprus Energy Regulatory Authority has the power to request the opinion of ACER on compliance of its decisions with said codes and guidelines set out in this law and Regulation (EU) 2019/943.[107] It also has the power to inform the Commission where it considers that a decision relevant for cross-border trade taken by another regulatory authority does not comply with said legislation and submit observations, where the Commission decides to examine the case further.[108]

II. The Minister of Energy, Commerce and Industry

36. Turning to the powers of the Minister, provisions for his competence are widespread within the legislation. At the outset, he has the authority to suggest the introduction of simplified and streamlined authorization procedures for small decentralized and/ or distributed generation. He may also set guidelines for that specific authorization procedure.[109] He further issues government energy decisions that

104. Section 7(1)(a) to (g) Law No. 130(I)/2021, which corresponds to Art. 62(1)(a) to (g) Directive (EU) 2019/944.
105. Section 7(2) & (3) Law No. 130(I)/2021, which corresponds to Art. 62(2) & (3) Directive (EU) 2019/944.
106. *See* Art. 59 Regulation (EU) 2019/943.
107. Networks and guidelines are regulated in Arts 58, 59, 60, 61 & 62 *ibid*.
108. Section 8(1), (3) & (4) Law No. 130(I)/2021, which corresponds to Art. 63(1), (4) & (5) Directive (EU) 2019/944.
109. Section 25(3)(a) & (b) Law No. 130(I)/2021. *See also* Art. 8(3) Directive (EU) 2019/944.

entail guidelines also on the matter of tariffs and prices.[110] Especially with regard to recourse adequacy assessment, the Minister, following him being informed of an assessment denoting that the already installed electricity capacity does not suffice for ensuring electricity provision in a satisfactory manner, has the power to issue a decree on the necessary electricity production and initiate a public tender in this regard.[111] In extraordinary cases, he has the authority to allow the use of the distribution system for purposes unrelated to electricity as long as doing so is not in conflict or does not constrain the fulfilment of the Distribution System Owner's duties as set out in the relevant authorization.[112] The same may be granted to the Distribution System Operator,[113] including recharging points for electric vehicles,[114] and the Transmission System Operator.[115] The Minister may further authorize the operation and management of energy storage units by the Distribution System Operator.[116] Finally, he receives an annual report on the activity of Cyprus Energy Regulatory Authority, including measures taken and results achieved for each of its statutory duties, and an annual report on the activities of the Transmission System Operator that includes the financial statements.[117] These financial statements are also received by the Minister of Finance.[118]

III. The Council of Ministers

37. The Council of Ministers generally approves plans, issues regulations and oversees simplified authorization procedures for electricity generation of limited size. However, in cases of war or other public danger, it has the power to declare an electricity crisis. In such an event, Cyprus Energy Regulatory Authority is obliged to proceed with notifying interested parties and disclosing information, as set out in Regulation (EU) 2019/941.[119]

38. The Council of Ministers is entrusted with approving the network development plan for distribution of electricity (*see* in this regard paragraph 172 below) as well as the network development plan for electricity transmission[120] (*see* in this regard paragraphs 159 et seq below), although ensuring that said plans are in line with the objectives, targets, contributions and measures of the Integrated National Energy and Climate Plan prepared according to Regulation (EU) 2018/1999 is the task of Cyprus Energy Regulatory Authority. The Council of Ministers further appoints and, under certain conditions, removes the Director of the Transmission

110. Section 22(2) Law No. 130(I)/2021.
111. Section 34(2) & (3) *ibid. See also* Arts 20 to 22 Regulation (EU) 2019/943.
112. Section 44 Law No. 130(I)/2021.
113. Section 48(10)(a) & (b) *ibid.*
114. Section 51(3) & (5) *ibid.*
115. Section 70(7) *ibid.*
116. Section 53(2) *ibid.*
117. Sections 5(1)(i), 68(2) and 69(1) & (2) *ibid.*
118. Section 68(2) *ibid.*
119. Section 5(13) *ibid.* & Art. 14(2) Regulation (EU) 2019/941.
120. Sections 50(3)(c) and 73(7) Law No. 130(I)/2021.

System Operator and is also involved in the appointment of this operator's staff and their employment conditions.[121] With regard to certification of a transmission system owner or a transmission system operator that is controlled by persons from third countries, the Council of Ministers has the right, and the power, to refuse certification on the grounds of endangering the national security of supply or the security of supply of another Member State.[122] Additionally, it has the authority to ensure that simplified and streamlined authorization procedures for small decentralized and/ or distributed generation that have considered their limited size and potential impact and have been already suggested by the Minister, are being followed.[123] The Council of Ministers may also approve Regulations prepared by Cyprus Energy Regulatory Authority with regard to setting out objective and non-discriminatory criteria for approving authorizations for the construction of direct lines.[124]

IV. The EU Agency of the Cooperation of Energy Regulators

39. ACER is established by Regulation (EU) 2019/942.[125] Its purpose is to assist the regulatory authorities in exercising at the Union level the regulatory tasks performed in the Member States and, where necessary, to coordinate their action and to mediate and settle disagreements between them. ACER also contributes to the establishment of high-quality common regulatory and supervisory practices, thus contributing to the consistent, efficient and effective application of Union law in order to achieve the Union's climate and energy goals.[126] The general tasks appointed to ACER is providing, upon request of the European Parliament, the Council or the European Commission or on its own initiative, an opinion or a recommendation to the same on any of the issues relating to the purpose for which it has been established.[127] At ACER's request, the regulatory authorities, the ENTSO for Electricity, the ENTSO for Gas, the regional coordination centres, the EU DSO (Distribution System Operator) entity, the transmission system operators and the nominated electricity market operators bear the obligation to provide to ACER the information necessary for the purpose of carrying out ACER's tasks under this Regulation unless ACER has already requested and received such information. For the purpose of said information requests, ACER has the power to issue decisions specifying the purpose of its request, making a reference to the legal basis under which the information is requested, and stating a time limit within which the information is to be provided. That time limit has to be proportionate to the request.

---

121. Sections 57, 58, 60, 61, 66 & 69 *ibid.*
122. Section 81(7) *ibid. See also* Art. 53(8) Directive (EU) 2019/944.
123. Section 25(3)(a) Law No. 130(I)/2021. *See also* Art. 8(3) Directive (EU) 2019/944.
124. Section 100(4) & 138 Law No. 130(I)/2021. *See also* Art. 7(2) Directive (EU) 2019/944.
125. Regulation (EU) 2019/942 of the European Parliament and of the Council of 5 Jun. 2019 establishing a European Union Agency for the Cooperation of Energy Regulators, OJ L 158, 14 Jun. 2019, p. 22. This has repealed Regulation (EC) No. 713/2009 of the European Parliament and of the Council of 13 Jul. 2009 establishing an Agency for the Cooperation of Energy Regulators, OJ L 211, 14 Aug. 2009, p. 1.
126. Article 1(2) Regulation (EC) 2019/942.
127. Article 3(1) *ibid.*

ACER has the power to use confidential information received pursuant to this Regu lation only for the purpose of carrying out its tasks while ensuring the appropriat data protection of the information.[128] Its tasks as regards the cooperation of trans mission system operators and distribution system operators, the development an implementation of network codes and guidelines, the national regulatory authori ties, regional coordination centres, nominated electricity market operators, genera tion adequacy and risk preparedness, exemptions, infrastructure, wholesale marke integrity and transparency, monitoring and reporting on the electricity and natura gas sectors and combating fraud are set out in detail in the regulation.[129]

128. Article 3(2) *ibid.*
129. Articles 4, 5, 6, 7, 8, 9, 10, 11, 12, 15 and 37 *ibid.*

Chapter 2. Production & Generation

40. Generation ('παραγωγή') in relation to electrical energy means production of electricity.[130] In this chapter, the issues of authorization, regulated tariffs, charges and fees are explained, along with the electricity market rules, resource adequacy and new capacity, the protection of fair competition, confidentiality and publicly available information and compliance.

§1. Authorization for Electricity-Related Activities

41. As a general rule, construction and operation of power plants and energy storage facilities ('εγκατάσταση αποθήκευσης ηλεκτρικής ενέργειας'),[131] is prohibited unless the proper authorization has been obtained both under this law and under any other legislation.[132] This prohibition extends to supplying electricity to final customers[133] or wholesale customers[134] as well as performing any of the activities of the Transmission System Operator,[135] of the Distribution System Operator or a Closed Distribution System Operator,[136] of the Transmission System Owner,[137] of the Distribution System Owner,[138] of the Market Official, of the Balance Responsible Party, of the Independent Aggregator or the Aggregator, of the Interconnector Operator or Owner[139] and, finally, constructing a direct line.[140] Self-evidently, this authorization does not acquit the holder from acquiring any further permits or authorizations foreseen in the law.[141] Such may be environmental permits, obligations set out in competition laws and regulations, as well as supplementary supervision pursuant to the regulations on financial conglomerates[142] that could freely be applicable.

130. 'Production' in French, 'Erzeugung' in German, 'productie' in Dutch. Section 2(1) Law No. 130(I)/2021, which corresponds to Art. 2(37) Directive (EU) 2019/944.
131. Energy storage facility ('installation de stockage d'énergie' in French, 'Energiespeicheranlage' in German, 'energieopslagfaciliteit' in Dutch) means, in the electricity system, a facility where energy storage occurs. Energy storage ('stockage d'énergie' in French, 'Energiespeicherung' in German, 'energieopslag' in Dutch) is, in the electricity system, deferring the final use of electricity to a moment later than when it was generated, or the conversion of electrical energy into a form of energy which can be stored, the storing of such energy, and the subsequent reconversion of such energy into electrical energy or use as another energy carrier. Section 2(1) Law No. 130(I)/2021, which corresponds to Art. 2(60) & (59) Directive (EU) 2019/944 respectively.
132. Sections 25(1) and 26(1)(a) & (m) Law No. 130(I)/2021.
133. Section 26(1)(b) *ibid.*
134. Section 26(1)(c) *ibid.*
135. Sections 26(1)(d) and 60 *ibid.*
136. Sections 26(1)(e), 47 and 56 *ibid.*
137. Sections 26(1)(f) and 36 *ibid.*
138. Sections 26(1)(g), 41 and 42 *ibid.*
139. Section 26(1)(h), (i), (j), (k) & (l) *ibid.*
140. Sections 26(1)(m) and 100 *ibid.*
141. Section 27(5) *ibid.*
142. Directive OD 144-2007-16 of 2015 of Cyprus Securities and Exchange Commission on supplementary supervision of investment firms that belong to financial conglomerates (Financial Conglomerates Directive) ('Οδηγία σχετικά με τη συμπληρωματική εποπτεία των επιχειρήσεων παροχής επενδυτικών υπηρεσιών, εταιρειών διαχείρισης περιουσιακών στοιχείων ή

42. Electricity activities could be excluded from authorization, should Cyprus Energy Regulatory Authority reach such a decision, under the terms and conditions specified therein.[143] Such exclusion may be granted for generation of electricity greater than 30 kilowatts and less than up to 1 megawatt for self-consumption,[144] for generation of electricity from renewable energy sources greater than 50 kilowatts and less than 8 megawatts. Any such decision may not create or allow discrimination among the persons having been granted said exemption.[145] A relevant application in the form specified by the authority needs to be filed with the same by the interested party, along with the requested information and fees.[146] Granted exceptions entail terms and conditions according to which they may be amended for the purpose of compliance with any amendment of the applicable legislation. Further, their holder is obliged to pay the relevant fees and to keep separate accounts for each exempted activity.[147] Any exemption granted under the repealed legislation on electricity is still valid under the law now in force for as long as specified in its terms and conditions.[148]

I. Application for Authorization

43. Application for authorization may be submitted by any natural person who is an EU national and lives in a Member State,[149] as well as by any legal person that is registered in a Member State. Especially in the case of a company, it needs to have been incorporated in accordance with the legislation of a Member State and have its statutory seat, central management or place of business within the EU.[150] The application is submitted to the Cyprus Energy Regulatory Authority in the provided form,[151] along with necessary information and fees.[152] Such information includes:

διαχειριστών οργανισμών εναλλακτικών επενδύσεων οι οποίες ανήκουν σε χρηματοπιστωτικό όμιλο ετερογενών δραστηριοτήτων') (OG III(I) No. 4895, 25 Sep. 2015, p. 1955), that implements Directive 2002/87/EC of the European Parliament and of the Council of 16 Dec. 2002 on the supplementary supervision of credit institutions, insurance undertakings and investment firms in a financial conglomerate and amending Council Directives 73/239/EEC, 79/267/EEC, 92/49/EEC, 92/96/EEC, 93/6/EEC and 93/22/EEC, and Directives 98/78/EC and 2000/12/EC of the European Parliament and of the Council, OJ L 035, 11 Feb. 2003, p. 1, as amended.

143. Section 27(4)(a) Law No. 130(I)/2021.
144. Section 27(4)(a)(i) *ibid.*
145. Section 27(4)(a)(ii) *ibid.*
146. Section 27(4)(b) *ibid.*
147. Section 27(4)(c)(i), (ii) & (iii) *ibid.*
148. Section 27(4)(d) *ibid.*
149. Section 29(2)(a) *ibid.*
150. Section 29(2)(b) *ibid.*
151. The form has been set out in Reg. 3(1)(a), Annex I Regulating the Electricity Market (Issuance of Authorizations) Regulations ('περί Ρυθμίσεως της Αγοράς Ηλεκτρισμού (Έκδοση Αδειών) Κανονισμοί') No. 538 of 2004, OG III(I) No. 3850, 30 Apr. 2004, p. 5235 (hereinafter 'KDP 538/2004').
152. Section 37(1) Law No. 122(I)/2003.

- approved financial statements of the past three years;[153]
- a general declaration of business proposal for the next five years;[154]
- a schedule of construction and activation of the plant;[155]
- details of the applicant or any business partner or subcontractor that evidence their necessary know-how to perform the activity of the application;[156]
- details on the efficiency of energy expected to be achieved by the proposed plant;[157]
- a summary of the financial plan of the activities in the application indicating the annual estimation for cash inflow for the next five years or of the technical life of the plan, should it be longer;[158] and
- a statement on the possible provider of finance.[159]

44. The authority may request additional information on the application within two months of the submission[160] as well as one month after the submission of the additional information.[161] Should the applicant fail to submit the requested information timely, the authority may reject the application.[162] Upon provision of the additional information as well as in the event that the authority does not ask for such,[163] the application is considered to be full. Within five days, the applicant is obliged to publish a copy of the submitted application and an announcement that the submitted information, along with a map, when applicable, may be inspected by the public at the offices of authority,[164] but for confidential information, which is qualified as such by the applicant.[165] It also announces that any person may submit information in writing within a time limit that may not be shorter than fifteen days from the date that the application was full.[166] The authority receives such information under no obligation to reply. However, such is forwarded to the applicant, who may express his views at the same.[167]

45. The application will be examined by the Cyprus Energy Regulatory Authority with objective, transparent and non-discriminatory criteria.[168] During evaluation, it will take into account the following criteria: security of the electricity system, power plants and electricity lines; energy efficiency; the nature of the primary sources; the characteristics of the applicant, such as technical, economic and

153. Annex I Part II(1) KDP 538/2004.
154. Annex I Part II(2) *ibid.*
155. Annex I Part II(3)(a) *ibid.*
156. Annex I Part II(3)(b) *ibid.*
157. Annex I Part II(3)(c) *ibid.*
158. Annex I Part II(4) *ibid.*
159. Annex I Part II(5) *ibid.*
160. Regulation 4(1) *ibid.*
161. Regulation 4(4) *ibid.*
162. Regulation 4(3) *ibid.*
163. Regulation 4(2) *ibid.*
164. Regulation 5(1) *ibid.*
165. Regulation 5(4) *ibid.*
166. Regulation 5(2) *ibid.*
167. Regulations 6(1), (3)(a) *ibid.*
168. Section 30(1) Law No. 130(I)/2021.

financial capabilities; compliance with other statutory measures; and the contribution of generating capacity to meeting the overall Union target of at least a 32% share of energy from renewable sources in the Union's gross final consumption of energy in 2030; and the alternatives to the construction of new generating capacity, such as demand response solutions and energy storage.[169] It shall equally consider the outcome of the comprehensive assessment under section 14C Law No. 174(I)/2006[170] and the outcome of cost-benefit analysis under section 14A Law No. 174(I)/2006, save for exceptions on considering said outcomes granted by the authority on imperative reasons of law, ownership or finance. In such event, the Minister shall be duly informed, along with the European Commission.[171] The authority reached a decision taking into consideration all information available within three months after the application was full.[172] This time limit may be extended for a further three-month period. The applicant is then informed accordingly in writing by the authority.[173]

II. Granting of Authorization

46. The decision of the authority to grant authorization is valid upon its publication in the Official Gazette (OG).[174] Within forty-five days of this decision, the authorization is issued by the Cyprus Energy Regulatory Authority.[175] Such authorization may include any terms and conditions the authority deems necessary, which in any event, may not create or allow for any discrimination among the holders of authorizations.[176] Various drafts of terms and conditions are foreseen in Annexes 2–6 of KDP 538/2004, which may at any time undergo a change pursuant to a decision of the authority.[177] Within fifteen days of the aforementioned publication, the authority enters the details of the authorization in the relevant register.[178] The holder pays an annual fee and keeps separate accounts for every activity, for which authorization is required pursuant to this law.[179]

47. Authorizations may be amended, revoked, transferred or extended.[180] The authority may announce a suggestion of amendment of any authorization through

169. Section 30(2)(a), (b), (c), (d), (e), (f) & (g) and 111 *ibid.*, which correspond to Art. (2)(a), (f), (g), (h), (i), (j), (l) and 9 Directive (EU) 2019/944. On the overall Union target *see* Art. 3(1) Directive (EU) 2018/2001.
170. Section 30(2)(h) Law No. 130(I)/2021. On the comprehensive analysis *see* Art. 14 Directive 2012/27/EU.
171. Section 30(2)(i) 2nd sentence Law No. 130(I)/2021.
172. Regulation 7(3) KDP 538/2004.
173. Regulation 7(4) *ibid.*
174. Regulation 9(5) *ibid.*
175. Regulation 10(1) *ibid.*
176. Section 28(1) Law No. 130(I)/2021.
177. Regulation 14 KDP 538/2004.
178. Regulation 10(3) *ibid.*
179. Section 28(2)(b) and (c) Law No. 130(I)/2021.
180. Section 32 *ibid.*, Reg. 11 KDP 538/2004.

publication in the OG and additionally in a daily newspaper if considered appropriate,[181] whereas a copy thereof is forwarded to the authorization holder.[182] This suggestion includes the grounds that trigger it, the expected result of the suggested amendment and a time period, which cannot be less than thirty days from the date that the announcement was made, and during which any representations or objections by any affected person may be brought forward.[183] Following due consideration of representations and objections received regarding the suggested amendment, it may decide or not, the alteration or revocation thereof. The holder will be then informed accordingly, and the resolved amendment will be published in the above-mentioned means within forty-five days.[184]

48. The authorization may also be amended following prior consent of the holder. In such a case, the amendment may be decided solely on the grounds of facing particular circumstances as long as the holder or a holder of authorization of the same type is not disadvantaged with regard to competition.[185] The decided amendment is published as described above.[186]

49. Turning to revocation of the authorization, specific grounds for this are set out in the law. These include a relevant application of the holder in agreement with the authority's views,[187] granting of the authorization under false or deceptive representations,[188] a change in the ownership control of the holder, which the authority does not approve,[189] no payment of duty,[190] non-compliance with the terms and conditions of the authorization[191] or with a decision of the authority or the Minister on permitted activities,[192] permanent termination of approved activities according to the authority's views[193] and declaration of bankruptcy by the holder.[194] Should the authority believe that one of the above takes place, it gives notice to the holder stating that the authorization will be revoked unless the infringement is upheld within due time. In the event that the holder fails to comply, the authority decides the time of revocation and informs the holder accordingly.[195]

50. Lastly, authorization may be transferred following a specific procedure. The holder submits an application to Cyprus Energy Regulatory Authority indicating the person to which it is intended to transfer the authorization at least three months

181. Regulation 12(1), (3)(a) *ibid.*
182. Regulation 12(3)(b) *ibid.*
183. Regulation 12(2)(a), (b), (c) *ibid.*
184. Regulation 12(4) *ibid.*
185. Regulation 13(1)(a) and (b)(i) and (ii) *ibid.*
186. Regulation 13(2) and (3) *ibid.*
187. Regulation 15(a) *ibid.*
188. Regulation 15(b) *ibid.*
189. Regulation 15(c) *ibid.*
190. Regulation 15(d) *ibid.*
191. Regulation 15(e) *ibid.*
192. Regulation 15(f) *ibid.*
193. Regulation 15(g) *ibid.*
194. Regulation 15(h) *ibid.*
195. Regulation 16(1) and (2) *ibid.*

before the planned action.[196] At the same time, the person wishing to acquire th authorization submits an application for granting authorization, as describe above.[197] Both applications are published in the above-mentioned way, and accord ingly, all documentation is available for inspection.[198]

III. Denial of Authorization

51. In the event that the application for authorization is rejected, the authorit informs the applicant of the reasons for it, which must be objective, non discriminatory, well-founded and duly substantiated.[199] Further, it must communi cate in writing the reasons for such rejection to the European Commission withi twenty-eight days.[200] Pursuant to general administrative law and, more precisely Article 146 of the Constitution and the Administrative Court Law,[201] the addresse may further lodge an appeal against this administrative action with the Administra tive Court of Cyprus, requesting its annulment and hence the re-evaluation of hi application by the authority. The procedure is regulated by Articles 146 as well a 135 and 163 of the Constitution, the Law on Administration of Justice,[202] the pro cedural regulations issued by the Supreme Court[203] and jurisprudence.

IV. Special Authorization Procedures for Small, Decentralized and Distributed Generation

52. The Council of Ministers, following the suggestion of the Minister, ensure that specific authorization procedures exist for small decentralized and/or distrib uted generations, which take into account their limited size and potential impact.[20 The Minister may specify guidelines for this special procedure that are examine

196. Regulation 18(1)(a) *ibid.*
197. Regulation 18(1)(b) *ibid.*
198. Regulation 18(1)(c) and (d) *ibid.*
199. Section 31(1) Law No. 130(I)/2021.
200. Section 39(b) *ibid.*
201. Section 3 Law on Establishment and Operation of the Administrative Court ('Νόμος πoυ Προβλέπει για την Ίδρυση και Λειτουργία Διοικητικού Δικαστηρίου') No. 131 of 2015, OG I(I) No. 4526 of 21 Jul. 2015, p. 1108, as last amended by Law on Establishment and Operation o the Administrative Court – Amendment ('Νόμος που Προβλέπει για την Ίδρυση κα Λειτουργία Διοικητικού Δικαστηρίου (Τροποποιητικός)') No. 3 of 2021, OGI(I) No. 4803 o 4 Feb. 2021, p. 7.
202. Law on Administration of Justice (Miscellaneous Provisions) ('Ο περί Απονομής της Δικαιο- σύνης (Ποικίλες Διατάξεις) Νόμος') No. 33 of 1964, OG I(I) 331 of 9 Jul. 1964, p. 398, as las amended by Law on Administration of Justice (Miscellaneous Provisions) – Amendment No. 3 ('Ο περί Απονομής της Δικαιοσύνης (Ποικίλες Διατάξεις) Νόμος (Τροποποιητικός) (Αρ. 3)') No. 223 of 2022, OG I(I) No. 4930 of 16 Dec. 2022, p. 1662.
203. Procedural Regulations on the Operation of the Administrative Court (No. 1) ('Οι περί της Λειτουργίας του Διοικητικού Δικαστηρίου (Αρ. 1) Διαδικαστικοί Κανονισμοί') No. 6 of 2015, OG II(I) 4102 of 31 Dec. 2015, p. 23, as last amended by Procedural Regulations on the Operation of the Administrative Court – Amendment (No. 3) ('Ο περί της Λειτουργίας του Διο- ικητικού Δικαστηρίου (Τροποποιητικός) (Αρ. 3) Διαδικαστικός Κανονισμός') No. 27 of 2022, OG II(I) 4147 of 27 May 2022, p. 39.
204. Section 25(3)(a) Law No. 130(I)/2021 that corresponds to Art. 8(3) Directive (EU) 2019/944.

by the Cyprus Energy Regulatory Authority as well as other competent authorities. These may propose amendments to it.[205] Where under the Law on Urban and Land Planning (*see* in this regard paragraph 352 below), particular land-use permit procedures apply to major new infrastructure projects in generation capacity, the construction of new generation capacity shall be included within the scope of those procedures, as the case may be. These shall be implemented in a non-discriminatory manner and within an appropriate time frame.[206]

V. Existing Authorizations

53. Authorizations issued on the basis of the repealed electricity legislation are still valid under Law No. 130(I)/2021, and their holders need to comply with the legislation now in force.[207]

§2. Regulated Tariffs, Charges and Fees of Electricity

54. The regulatory frame on electricity sets out three sets of rules with regard to tariffs, charges and fees of electricity. The first set consists of general principles, the second of customers' rights and the third of obligations of electricity undertakings. With regard to the general principles, all regulated tariffs and charges for services regulated by this law reflect the relevant costs and do not discriminate among the receivers of said services.[208] Still, Cyprus Energy Regulatory Authority may require an authorization holder to deviate from this rule, as long as this person shall be able to recover its costs and said tariffs shall not lead to exploitation of customers.[209] Further, Cyprus Energy Regulatory Authority ensures the removal of those incentives in transmission and distribution of tariffs that are detrimental to the overall efficiency (including energy efficiency) of the generation, transmission, distribution and supply of electricity or those that might hamper the participation of demand response, in balancing markets and ancillary services procurement.[210] It also ensures that network operators are incentivized to improve efficiency in infrastructure design and operation, and that tariffs allow suppliers to improve consumer participation in system efficiency, including demand response.[211]

55. Cyprus Energy Regulatory Authority has the power to issue regulatory decisions during the performance of its duties, competences and powers (*see* in this regard paragraph 31 above). Said regulatory decisions set out the manner in which

205. Section 25(3)(b) and (c) Law No. 130(I)/2021 that corresponds to Art. 8(3) Directive (EU) 2019/944.
206. Section 25(3)(d) Law No. 130(I)/2021 that corresponds to Art. 8(3) Directive (EU) 2019/944.
207. Section 142(3) Law No. 130(I)/2021.
208. Section 22(1) *ibid.*
209. Section 22(2) *ibid.*
210. Section 22(3) *ibid.*, which corresponds to (repealed) Art. 15(4) Directive 2012/27/EU.
211. Section 22(4) and (5) Law No. 130(I)/2021, which corresponds to (repealed) Art. 15(4) Directive 2012/27/EU.

the electricity market shall be regulated, as well as name the holders of authorizations that are to be bound by them.[212] The authority may further reach decisions pursuant to the provisions of Law No. 130(I)/2021 and the regulations issued according to the same.[213] Such regulations shall also provide for charges and tariffs methodology.[214]

56. The authority made use of this broad power and has issued a number of regulatory decisions, among which stands the Announcement of Regulatory Practice and Methodology on Price Assessment of Electricity[215] of 2021. The general scope of these regulatory decisions is to maximize the long-term advantage of competitiveness of the economy of Cyprus, protect the interests of consumers in the short and long term against prices established on a monopoly basis, meet public service obligations, safeguard the security of electricity supply and promote energy efficiency and quality of the services provided by the authorization holders.[216] The specific aims are to:

– reflect the cost of service so as to enhance economic efficiency;[217]
– allow the reasonable prospect of recovery of efficient costs;[218]
– be fair and non-discriminatory unless justified on the grounds of other tariff objectives such as enhancing economic efficiency;[219]
– avoid cross-subsidies between different electricity sector activities (i.e., generation, transmission system ownership, transmission system operation, distribution system ownership, distribution system operation and supply or other non-regulated activities);[220]
– be simple, transparent and predictable;[221]
– encourage efficient consumption decisions by consumers;[222]
– be compatible with the clear environmental objectives set by the Republic of Cyprus;[223]

212. Section 9(1)(a) Law No. 130(I)/2021.
213. Section 9(1)(b) *ibid.*
214. Section 23 *ibid.*
215. Regulatory Decision No. 1/2021 pursuant to s. 26 Law No. 122(I)/2003, Announcement of Regulatory Practice and Methodology on Price Assessment of Electricity ('Δήλωση Ρυθμιστικής Πρακτικής και Μεθοδολογία Διατιμήσεων Ηλεκτρισμού') No. 359 of 2021, OG III(I) No. 5581, 13 Aug. 2021, p. 2658 (hereinafter 'KDP 359/2021'), as amended by Regulatory Decision No. 05/2022 Announcement of Regulatory Practice and Methodology on Price Assessment (Amendment) ('Δήλωση Ρυθμιστικής Πρακτικής Και Μεθοδολογία Διατιμήσεων Ηλεκτρισμού (Τροποποίηση)') No. 183 of 2022, OG III(I) No. 5697, 13 May 2022, p. 1321.
216. Paragraph 3.1 KDP 359/2021.
217. Paragraph 3.2(a) *ibid.*
218. Paragraph 3.2(b) *ibid.*
219. Paragraph 3.2(c) *ibid.*
220. Paragraph 3.2(d) *ibid.*
221. Paragraph 3.2(e) *ibid.*
222. Paragraph 3.2(f) *ibid.*
223. Paragraph 3.2(g) *ibid.*

– allow the recovery of efficiently incurred costs related to public service obligations and the promotion of generation of electricity from renewable energy sources and high-efficiency cogeneration;[224]
– encourage security of electricity supply;[225]
– provide incentives to regulated undertakings to operate efficiently;[226] and
– promote efficiency and quality of the service provided by authorization holders.[227]

57. Lastly, electricity tariffs are regulated in accordance with said general scope and the principle that tariffs to end consumers may differentiate between customer classes according to characteristics that reflect costs but may not differentiate according to the geographical location of the consumer.[228] Said principles form the base of tariffs for goods and services provided via a regulated activity.[229] At a more specific level, tariff methodologies have been set out for wholesale electricity,[230] for use of transmission system,[231] for use of distribution system at medium voltage,[232] for use of distribution system at low voltage,[233] for the provision of ancillary services,[234] for public benefit services fees,[235] for expenses of the Transmission System Operator,[236] for metering expenses,[237] for supply and sale of electricity[238] and for use of the interconnector.[239]

58. Turning to customers' rights with regard to tariffs, charges and fees, the following has been decided for household customers, small enterprises, final customers, active customers, citizen energy communities, renewables self-consumers and renewable energy communities, respectively. Household customers ('οικιακοί πελάτες')[240] and small enterprises ('μικρές επιχειρήσεις')[241] are not charged any switch-related fees as a general rule. However, they may be charged contract termination fees, when said customers voluntarily terminate fixed-term, fixed-price

224. Paragraph 3.2(h) *ibid.*
225. Paragraph 3.2(i) *ibid.*
226. Paragraph 3.2(j) *ibid.*
227. Paragraph 3.2(k) *ibid.*
228. Paragraph 6.13 *ibid.*
229. Paragraph 6.1 *ibid.*
230. Paragraphs 6.8 and 7.6 to 7.15 *ibid.*
231. Paragraphs 6.8 and 7.16 to 7.28 *ibid.*
232. Here, medium voltage stands for greater than 1 kV and less than 36 kV. This tariff includes a charge component related to the Distribution System Operator. Paragraphs 6.8 and 7.29 to 7.37 *ibid.*
233. Here, low voltage stands for at or below 1 kV. This tariff includes a charge component related to the Distribution System Operator. Paragraphs 6.8 and 7.38 to 7.44 *ibid.*
234. Paragraphs 6.8 and 7.45 to 7.47 *ibid.*
235. Paragraphs 6.8 and 7.59 to 7.64 *ibid.*
236. Paragraphs 6.8 and 7.65 to 7.67 *ibid.*
237. This is a tariff for the recovery of expenses of metering incurred by the Distribution System Operator (for users connected to the distribution network). Paragraphs 6.8 and 7.68 to 7.73 *ibid.*
238. Paragraphs 6.8 and 7.74 to 7.77 *ibid.*
239. Paragraphs 6.8 and 7.78 and 7.79 *ibid.*
240. *Household customer* ('client résidentiel' in French, 'Haushaltskunde' in German, 'huishoudelijke afnemer' in Dutch) is a customer who purchases electricity for the customer's own household consumption, excluding commercial or professional activities. Section 2(1) Law No. 130(I)/2021, which corresponds to Art. 2(4) Directive (EU) 2019/944.

electricity supply contracts before their maturity, provided that such fees are part of a contract that the customer has voluntarily entered into and that such fees are clearly communicated to the customer before the contract is entered into. Such fees shall be proportionate and shall not exceed the direct economic loss to the supplier or the market participant engaged in aggregation resulting from the customer's termination of the contract, including the costs of any bundled investments or services that have already been provided to the customer as part of the contract. The burden of proving the direct economic loss is on the supplier or market participant engaged in aggregation, and the permissibility of contract termination fees is monitored by Cyprus Energy Regulatory Authority.[242]

59. Final customers ('τελικοί πελάτες'), as ensured by Cyprus Energy Regulatory Authority, are not subjected to discriminatory charges by their supplier on the basis of having a contract with market participants engaged in aggregation. It is here noted that aggregation ('σωρευτική εκπροσώπηση') is a function performed by a natural or legal person who combines multiple customer loads or generated electricity for sale, purchase or auction in any electricity market.[243] Final customers are also not subjected to discrimination as regards cost for their right to conclude an aggregation contract or to receive all relevant demand response data or data on supplied and sold electricity.[244] At least once every billing period, final customers receive free of charge all relevant demand response data or data on supplied and sold electricity if requested by them.[245] Also free of charge, they receive all their bills and billing information.[246] With regard to payment methods or prepayment systems, final customers are not subjected to unduly discrimination, when a difference in charges occurs. Any such difference shall be objective, non-discriminatory and proportionate and shall not exceed the direct costs borne by the payee for the use of a specific payment method or prepayment system in line with Directive 2015/2366.[247,248] Final customers also have the right to switch supplier or market participants engaged in aggregation and they can exercise it in a non-discriminatory manner as regards cost, effort and time.[249] Similarly, they are not charged additional

241. *Small enterprise* ('petite entreprise' in French, 'Kleinunternehmen' in German, 'kleine onderneming' in Dutch) means an enterprise which employs fewer than 50 persons and whose annual turnover and/or annual balance sheet total does not exceed EUR 10 million. Section 2(1) Law No. 130(I)/2021, which corresponds to Art. 2(7) Directive (EU) 2019/944.
242. Section 22(6)(a) & (b) Law No. 130(I)/2021, which corresponds to Art. 12(2) & (3) Directive (EU) 2019/944.
243. 'Agrégation' in French, 'Aggregierung' in German, 'aggregatie' in Dutch. Section 2(1) Law No. 130(I)/2021, which corresponds to Art. 2(18) Directive (EU) 2019/944.
244. Section 22(7)(b) Law No. 130(I)/2021, which corresponds to Art. 13(2), (3) & (4) Directive (EU) 2019/944.
245. Section 22(7)(c) Law No. 130(I)/2021, which corresponds to Art. 13(3) Directive (EU) 2019/944.
246. Section 22(7)(d) Law No. 130(I)/2021, which corresponds to Art. 18(2) Directive (EU) 2019/944.
247. Directive (EU) 2015/2366 of the European Parliament and of the Council of 25 Nov. 2015 on payment services in the internal market, amending Directives 2002/65/EC, 2009/110/EC and 2013/36/EU and Regulation (EU) No. 1093/2010, and repealing Directive 2007/64/EC, OJ L 337, 23 Dec. 2015, p. 35.
248. Section 22(7)(e) Law No. 130(I)/2021 and Art. 62 Directive 2015/2366, which corresponds to Art. 10(6) Directive (EU) 2019/944.
249. Section 22(7)(f) Law No. 130(I)/2021, which corresponds to Art. 12(4) Directive (EU) 2019/944.

costs for access to their data or for requesting to make their data available.[250] In particular, final customers that offer demand response through aggregation are not subjected to payments by their suppliers due to having a contract with independent aggregators.[251] Such customers or the electricity undertakings that represent them, pay financial compensation to other market participants or to the market participants' balance responsible parties that are directly affected by demand response activation, when the benefits for all suppliers, customers and balance responsible parties do not exceed the direct costs. Such financial compensation is strictly limited to covering the resulting costs incurred by the suppliers of participating customers or the suppliers' balance responsible parties during the activation of demand response. The method for calculating compensation takes account of the benefits brought about by the independent aggregators to other market participants and creates neither a barrier to market entry for market participants engaged in aggregation nor a barrier to flexibility. It is applied only following the apposite approval by Cyprus Energy Regulatory Authority.[252]

60. In particular, active customers (‘ενεργοί πελάτες’)[253] that own an energy storage facility are not subject to any double charges, including network charges, for stored electricity remaining within their premises or when providing flexibility services to system operators. They are also not subject to disproportionate licensing requirements or fees.[254] Final customers acting as active customers are not subject to network charges that are not cost-effective. However, they are subject to cost-reflective, transparent and non-discriminatory network charges. Such charges account separately for the electricity fed into the grid and the electricity consumed from the grid, in accordance with Article 59(9) of this Directive and Article 18 of Regulation (EU) 2019/943, ensuring that they contribute in an adequate and balanced way to the overall cost sharing of the system.[255] Lastly, customers subject to existing schemes have the possibility at any time to opt for a new scheme that accounts separately for the electricity fed into the grid and the electricity consumed from the grid as the basis for calculating network charges.[256]

---

250. Section 22(7)(g) Law No. 130(I)/2021, which corresponds to Art. 23(5) Directive (EU) 2019/944.
251. Section 22(11)(a) Law No. 130(I)/2021, which corresponds to Art. 17(3)(e) Directive (EU) 2019/944. The European provision refers to *undue payments, penalties or other undue contractual restrictions* and not merely to *payments*.
252. Section 22(11)(b) & (c) Law No. 130(I)/2021, which partially corresponds to Art. 17(4) Directive (EU) 2019/944.
253. Active customer (‘client actif’ in French, ‘aktiver Kunde’ in German, ‘actieve afnemer’ in Dutch) is a final customer, or a group of jointly acting final customers, who consumes or stores electricity generated within its premises located within confined boundaries or, where permitted by a Member State, within other premises, or who sells self-generated electricity or participates in flexibility or energy efficiency schemes, provided that those activities do not constitute its primary commercial or professional activity. Section 2(1) Law No. 130(I)/2021, which corresponds to Art. 2(8) Directive (EU) 2019/944.
254. Section 22(9)(a) & (b) Law No. 130(I)/2021, which corresponds to Art. 15(5)(b) & (c) Directive (EU) 2019/944.
255. Sections 22(8)((a) & (b) and 5(9) Law No. 130(I)/2021, which correspond to Art. 15(1) & (2)(e) Directive (EU) 2019/944.
256. Section 22(8)(c) Law No. 130(I)/2021, which corresponds to Art. 15(4) Directive (EU) 2019/944.

61. Specific provisions have been set out on pricing of citizen energy communities ('ενεργειακές κοινότητες πολιτών'), that being a legal entity that: (a) is based on open and voluntary participation and is effectively controlled by shareholders or members that are natural persons, local authorities, including municipalities or small enterprises; (b) has for its primary purpose to provide environmental, economic or social community benefits to its members or shareholders or to the local areas where it operates rather than to generate financial profits; and (c) may engage in generation, including from renewable sources, distribution, supply, consumption, aggregation, energy storage, energy efficiency services or charging services for electric vehicles or provide other energy services to its members or shareholders.[257] In this regard, Cyprus Energy Regulatory Authority assesses the payment of fair compensation to the Transmission System Operator or the Distribution System Operator for facilitating electricity transmission within energy communities in order to ensure that said payment is fair. It also ensures that said communities are subject to transparent network charges and reflect cost, according to Article 18 Regulation (EU) 2019/943, ensuring that they contribute to the overall system cost sharing in an adequate and balanced manner. In case electricity is shared, such sharing is effective save for applicable network charges, tariffs and levies according to transparent cost-benefit analysis of the allocated energy resources that Cyprus Energy Regulatory Authority has developed. Lastly, with regard to consumption of self-generated electricity, Cyprus Energy Regulatory Authority ensures that network charges are transparent, non-discriminatory and cost-reflective and such network charges account separately for the electricity fed into the distribution network and the electricity consumed from the distribution network outside the citizen energy community is in accordance with Article 18 Regulation (EU) 2019/943, ensuring that they contribute to the overall system cost sharing in an adequate and balanced manner.[258]

62. Cyprus Energy Regulatory Authority is further entrusted with ensuring that renewables self-consumers ('αυτοκαταναλωτές ενέργειας από ανανεώσιμες πηγές'), individually or through aggregators are not subject to discriminatory or disproportionate fees and network charges that do not reflect cost with regard to the electricity that they consume from the grid or they feed into same.[259] It further ensures that same consumers are not subject to any charge or fee in relation to their self-generated renewable electricity remaining within their premises in one or more of the following cases: (a) if the self-generated renewable electricity is effectively supported via support schemes, only to the extent that the economic viability of the project and the incentive effect of such support are not undermined; (b) from 1 December 2026, if the overall share of self-consumption installations exceeds 8% of the total installed electricity capacity and if it is demonstrated, by means of a

257. In French 'communauté énergétique citoyenne', in German 'Bürgerenergiegemeinschaft', in Dutch 'energiegemeenschap van burgers'. Section 2(1) Law No. 130(I)/2021, which corresponds to Art. 2(11) Directive (EU) 2019/944.

258. Section 22(11)(a), (b) & (c) Law No. 130(I)/2021, which corresponds to Art. 16(1)(d), (3) & (4)(b) Directive (EU) 2019/944.

259. Section 22(12)(a) Law No. 130(I)/2021, which corresponds partially to Art. 21(2)(a)(i) Directive (EU) 2018/2001.

cost-benefit analysis performed by Cyprus Energy Regulatory Authority, which is conducted by way of an open, transparent and participatory process, that the here described lack of charges and fees either results in a significant disproportionate burden on the long-term financial sustainability of the electric system, or creates an incentive exceeding what is objectively needed to achieve cost-effective deployment of renewable energy, and that such burden or incentive cannot be minimized by taking other reasonable actions; or (c) if the self-generated renewable electricity is produced in installations with a total installed electrical capacity of more than 30 kW. The aforementioned charges and fees are imposed non-discriminatory and proportionate.[260] Finally, the renewables self-consumers have the right to instal and operate electricity storage systems combined with installations generating renewable electricity for self-consumption without liability for any double charge, including network charges, for stored electricity remaining within their premises.[261]

63. The last cost regulation relates to renewable energy communities ('ενεργειακές κοινότητες πολιτών'), which are a legal entity: (a) that is based on open and voluntary participation, is autonomous, and is effectively controlled by shareholders or members that are located in the proximity of the renewable energy projects that are owned and developed by that legal entity; (b) the shareholders or members of which are natural persons, SMEs or local authorities, including municipalities; and (c) the primary purpose of which is to provide environmental, economic or social community benefits for its shareholders or members or for the local areas where it operates, rather than financial profits.[262] These are subject to cost-reflective network charges as well as charges, levies and taxes, so that these communities contribute, in an adequate, fair and balanced way, to the overall cost sharing of the system. To this end, Cyprus Energy Regulatory Authority has developed a transparent cost-benefit analysis of distributed energy sources.[263]

64. Turning to the obligations of electricity undertakings, it is provided that bills and billing information are accurate, easy to understand, clear, concise, user-friendly and presented in a manner that facilitates comparison by final customers. Further, electricity undertakings provide final customers a clear and understandable explanation of how their bill was derived, especially where bills are not based on actual consumption, upon request by said customers. They also offer the option of electronic bills and billing information as well as flexible arrangements for the actual payment of the bills.[264] Finally, the electricity undertakings are obliged to provide minimum information on the bill and in the billing information, such as

---

260. Section 22(12)(b) Law No. 130(I)/2021, which corresponds to Art. 21(3)(a), (b) & (c) Directive (EU) 2018/2001.
261. Section 22(12)(c) Law No. 130(I)/2021, which corresponds to Art. 21(2)(b) Directive (EU) 2018/2001.
262. In French 'frais de résiliation du contrat', in German 'Kündigungsgebühren', in Dutch 'opzegvergoeding'. Section 2(1) Law No. 130(I)/2021, which corresponds to Art. 2(16) Directive 2018/2021.
263. Section 22(13)(a) & (b) Law No. 130(I)/2021, which corresponds to Art. 22(4)(d) Directive (EU) 2018/2001.
264. Section 24(2), (3) & (4) Law No. 130(I)/2021, which corresponds to Art. 18(1) & (3) Directive (EU) 2019/944.

electricity consumption for the billing period, frequency of billing and the provision of billing information, breakdown of the final customer's price, access to complementary information on historical consumption and disclosure of energy sources.[265]

§3. ELECTRICITY MARKET RULES

65. Electricity Market Rules that have the form of a regulatory decision regulate mechanisms, price and other terms and regulations applicable to authorization holders selling or buying electricity based on arrangements of the Transmission System Operator.[266] They ensure that authorization holders asked to participate in such transactions of electricity are not discriminated[267] against while promoting efficiency and economy and facilitating fair competition.[268] Electricity Market Rules also set out charges for non-compliance that the Transmission System Operator imposes on any participant in the electricity market that fails to comply with any obligation set out therein. Finally, they are in full compliance with Regulation (EU) 2019/943, where the area of application overlaps.[269] They are being drafted by the Transmission System Operator following the relevant request of the Cyprus Energy Regulatory Authority.[270] The latter consults the informal advisory committee[271] on the draft,[272] which must be approved by the same and the Minister.[273] Upon approval, the rules are published by the Transmission System Operator.[274] All holders of authorizations or exclusions as well as final customers are bound by those to the extent that this is required by the specific authorizations or exclusions.[275]

66. The Energy Market Rules may be revised as well as amended from time to time, including for the purpose of complying with Regulation (EU) 2019/943. In all cases, the Cyprus Energy Regulatory Authority after consultations with the authorization holders and other persons, as it deems appropriate, gives appropriate instructions to the Transmission System Operator,[276] indicating the matters to be

265. Section 132 Law No. 130(I)/2021, which corresponds to Art. 18(6) & Annex I Directive (EU) 2019/944.
266. Section 94(1)(a) Law No. 130(I)/2021.
267. Section 94(1)(b) *ibid.*
268. Section 94(1)(c) *ibid.*
269. Section 94(1)(d) & (e) *ibid.*
270. Section 93(1) *ibid.*
271. The Advisory Committee on Energy Market Rules ('Συμβουλευτική Επιτροπή Κανόνων Αγοράς Ηλεκτρισμού') that had been established via the repealed Law on Regulating the Electricity Market No. 122 of 2003 is absent in Law No. 130(I)/2021. To the contrary the now valid legislation provides for an informal advisory committee that consists of representatives of the authorization holders and other interested parties directly affected by the purpose of such change – not by the Electricity Market Rules. The specific participants of said committee are the subject of decision of Cyprus Energy Regulatory Authority (s. 94(2) Law No. 130(I)/2021).
272. Section 93(2)(a) *ibid.*
273. Section 93(2)(b) *ibid.*
274. Section 93(2) *ibid.*
275. Section 94(2) *ibid.*
276. Section 93(3)(a) *ibid.*

determined in the rules.[277] Cyprus Energy Regulatory Authority has the power to issue a regulatory decision on transitional regulation of the electricity market, as long as the Minister approves it. A revision can be further requested by the Minister,[278] the Transmission System Operator itself, under the condition that such was proposed by the authorization holders or other interested parties[279] or the Distribution System Operator.[280] During the procedure of revision, consultation with authorization holders and other interested parties takes place whereas the suggested amendments are then put into public consultation.[281] Amendments to these rules are suggested by the Transmission System Operator following a revision of the same. These are drafted by the said operator and forwarded to the authority for approval taking into account the policy directives on the operation of the electricity market as they have been decided by the Minister.[282] The amendments only come into force following publication in the OG.[283]

§4. Resource Adequacy and New Capacity

67. Cyprus Energy Regulatory Authority assesses on a regular basis the national resource adequacy with regard to electricity. In addition, it timely takes measures to ensure adequacy via self-generation, energy storage, demand response and energy efficiency elimination of any identified regulatory distortions and a cost-efficient and market-based procurement of balancing and ancillary services,[284] After Cyprus' transmission system is connected to other Member States' transmission systems via interconnections, said authority shall also have to consider removing regulatory distortions, removing price caps, introducing a shortage pricing function for balancing energy, increasing interconnection and internal grid capacity and removing regulated prices.[285] Should an adequacy assessment demonstrate that the already installed electricity capacity does not suffice to ensure a satisfactory electricity supply and this makes capacity mechanism measures necessary, Cyprus Energy Regulatory Authority informs the Minister accordingly.[286] *Capacity mechanism* is here understood as 'a temporary measure to ensure the achievement of the necessary level of resource adequacy by remunerating resources for their availability, excluding measures relating to ancillary services or congestion management'.[287] The Minister shall initiate a public tender published in the official gazette of Cyprus with the terms, conditions and criteria with which the applicants must comply in order to participate. Furthermore, the tenders shall have to comply with the design principles

277. Section 93(3)(b) *ibid.*
278. Section 94(3)(a) *ibid.*
279. Section 94(3)(b) *ibid.*
280. Section 94(3)(c) *ibid.*
281. Section 94(4) *ibid.*
282. Section 94(5) & (6) *ibid.*
283. Section 94(7) *ibid.* These are available at: http://www.dsm.org.cy/.
284. Section 34(1)(a) to (e) Law No. 130(I)/2021. *See* Art. 20(3)(e) & (f) Regulation (EU) 2019/943.
285. Articles 64(2), 20(3)(a), (b), (c), (d) & (f) and 10 *ibid.*, Art. 44(3) Regulation (EU) 2017/2195 and Art. 4(d)(1) Regulation (EU) 2018/1999.
286. Section 34(2) Law No. 130(I)/2021.
287. Article 2(22) Regulation (EU) (EU) 2019/944.

set by the EU.[288] In other words, the suggested capacity mechanism shall have to be temporary and neither create undue market distortions nor limit cross-zonal trade.[289] It shall not go beyond what is necessary to address the adequacy concerns. The process shall be transparent, non-discriminatory and competitive and through this competitive process, the remuneration shall be determined.[290] Further, incentives shall be given for capacity providers to be available in times of expected system stress.[291] Finally, the suggested capacity mechanism shall set out the technical conditions for the participation of capacity providers in advance of the selection process and shall be open to participation of all resources that are capable of providing the required technical performance, including energy storage and demand side management.[292]

§5. Protection of Fair Competition

68. The measures that the Cyprus Energy Regulatory Authority takes on the basis of its statutory powers for the purpose of ensuring fair competition in compliance with both domestic and Union law, especially Article 36 of the TFEU and Union law, are proportionary, transparent and non-discriminatory.[293] Cyprus Energy Regulatory Authority ensures that appropriate and effective mechanisms of regulation, control and transparency are in place so that abuse of dominant position, especially towards consumers, and any aggressive behaviour are avoided.[294] However, they may only be implemented following their communication to the Commission and approval by the same. This is assumed when the Commission does not object within two months since the relevant notification.[295]

69. In addition, Cyprus Energy Regulatory Authority cooperates closely with the Commission for the Protection of Competition with regard to violations of the Law of Competition that fall within the competence of the latter. Both authorities share the mutual duty of information regarding the exercise of their duties.[296] Cooperation takes place in the following fashion. Should Cyprus Energy Regulatory Authority while conducting inquiries on competition issues, as per its statutory authority, notice a possible violation of the legislation on competition, it notifies accordingly the Commission for the Protection of Competition that shall conduct an investigation.[297]

288. Section 34(3), (4) & (5) Law No. 130(I)/2021 and Art. 22 Regulation (EU) 2019/943.
289. Article 20(1)(a) & (b) *ibid.*
290. Article 20(1)(c), (d) & (f) *ibid.*
291. Article 20(1)(e) *ibid.*
292. Article 20(1)(g) &(h) *ibid.*
293. Sections 11(1) & (2) and 4(1) Law No. 130(I)/2021.
294. Section 19(4) *ibid.*
295. Section 11(2) & (3) *ibid.*
296. Sections 18(1) & (3) *ibid.*
297. Section 18(3) *ibid.*

§6. CONFIDENTIALITY AND AUTHORITY TO PUBLISH INFORMATION

70. Pivotal to the duty of confidentiality is the notion of commercially sensitive information ('εμπορικά ευαίσθητη πληροφορία') that means any information, the disclosure of which may substantially damage the financial interest of any person.[298] With this in mind, it is noted that Cyprus Energy Regulatory Authority, the Distribution System Owner, the Distribution System Operator, the Transmission System Owner, the Transmission System Operator or any other person exercising its duties under this law, has the duty to preserve the confidentiality of commercially sensitive information obtained in the course of carrying out their activities. It is prohibited to disclose or communicate in any way confidential data or information that has been communicated to them during the exercise of their activities, to third parties. They further have the duty to prevent disclosure in a discriminatory manner of information related to their activities and may be commercially advantageous, as well as to protect any intellectual property rights related to such data or information.[299] In particular, the Transmission System Owner does not disclose any commercially sensitive information to the remaining parts of Cyprus Energy Authority ('Αρχή Ηλεκτρισμού Κύπρου') unless such disclosure is necessary for carrying out a business transaction. In order to ensure the full respect of the rules on information unbundling, the transmission system owner and the remaining part of Cyprus Energy Authority do not use joint services, such as joint legal services, apart from purely administrative or IT functions.[300] Similarly, the Transmission System Operator does not, in the context of sales or purchases of electricity-related undertakings, misuse commercially sensitive information obtained from third parties in the context of providing or negotiating access to the system.[301] Nonetheless, information necessary for effective competition and the efficient functioning of the market shall be made public. That obligation shall be without prejudice to preserving the confidentiality of commercially sensitive information.[302]

71. Cyprus Energy Regulatory Authority has the power to publish information for the purpose of informing the public on electricity issues as well as facilitating their understanding. However, it shall not reveal any confidential information with regard to any specific person or enterprise without their consent, unless it is given an apposite statutory authority by this law or relevant regulations. Such would be the case when releasing confidential information serves the purpose of facilitating duties' fulfilment or power exercising, including commercial sensitive information contained in accounts of electricity enterprises, as long as this is necessary and,

298. Section 2(1) *ibid.*
299. Section 19(5)(a)(i) *ibid*, which corresponds to Art. 41(1) Directive (EU) 2019/944.
300. Section 19(5)(a)(ii) & (iii) Law No. 130(I)/2021, which partially corresponds to Art. 41(1) Directive (EU) 2019/944.
301. Section 19(5)(a)(iv) Law No. 130(I)/2021, which corresponds to Art. 41(2) Directive (EU) 2019/944.
302. Section 19(5)(a)(v) Law No. 130(I)/2021, which corresponds to Art. 41(3) Directive (EU) 2019/944.

where appropriate, Cyprus Energy Regulatory Authority takes measures for safe guarding the confidential information from the persons to which this is exposed.[30 Confidential information may also be released within the frame of criminal inves tigations or civil proceedings.[304]

72. Similarly, Cyprus Energy Regulatory Authority cooperates closely both wit national authorities of Cyprus, such as the Commission for the Protection of Com petition, and with national authorities of other Member States, for example withi ACER. During such cooperation that inevitably includes exchange of informatior the authority receiving information is bound to ensure the same level of protectio as the authority that dispatched it.[305]

73. Any violation of the provisions on confidentiality is treated as a crimina offence. Conviction may lead to imprisonment of up to two years and/ or a mon etary fine of up to EUR 100,000.[306]

§7. Monitoring Compliance

74. Breaching authorizations and provisions of Law No. 130(I)/2021 may resul in a penal conviction and administrative fines. With reference to penal offences, i is set out that any person, who in breach of section 26 Law No. 130(I)/2021, per forms any of the electricity-related activities that require authorization, commits a crime. Should this person be held guilty, he can be convicted to imprisonment of up to three years and/or to a fine not exceeding EUR 200,000.[307] Imprisonment of up to three years and/ or a fine not exceeding EUR 90.000 may be imposed in case of conviction of a person, who in person or via his employee or via his representative

- violates or fails to adhere to any term of an authorization, exemption or decree;[308]
- reveals commercial sensitive information, in the sense of any information the revealing of which may cause harm to the financial interests of any person, that he receives during the performance of his duties unless such exposure is foreseen in this law;[309]
- violates or fails to adhere to a regulatory decision or a decision of Cyprus Energy Regulatory Authority issued in accordance with said legislation;[310]
- discriminates between persons or categories of persons or between users of the transmission or the distribution system;[311]

303. Sections 20(1), (2) & (3)(a) and 137(2) Law No. 130(I)/2021.
304. Section 20(3)(b) & (c) *ibid.*
305. Sections 6(1) and 18(4) *ibid*, which correspond to Arts 41(3) and 61(1) Directive (EU) 2019/944.
306. Section 19(5)(b) Law No. 130(I)/2021.
307. Section 134 *ibid.*
308. Section 133(a) *ibid.*
309. Sections 133(b) and 2 *ibid.*
310. Section 133(c) *ibid.*
311. Section 133(d) *ibid.*

- fails to provide Cyprus Energy Regulatory Authority or the Minister with any information, document or other material requested for the purpose of exercising its powers pursuant to said legislation;[312]
- deters or hinders an authorized officer, who acts pursuant to section 14 Law No. 130(I)/2021, from performing his duties, such as entering any building that belongs or is held by an authorization holder, demanding any documentation to be presented to him and inspecting any books, documents and registers;[313]
- fails to adhere to any demand imposed by an authorized officer within the powers set out in section 14 of this law;[314]
- makes untruthful or misleading statements to an authorized officer, either intentional or unintentional;[315]
- fails to adhere to or violates his obligations relating to accounts;[316]
- fails to present himself before Cyprus Energy Regulatory Authority or to furnish or present any documentation in violation of section 13 of this law, which includes investigations on its own initiative or following a complaint about the activities and acts of any electricity undertaking;[317]
- denies answering any reasonable question submitted by Cyprus Energy Regulatory Authority or the Minister within the above-mentioned investigations. However, a person is not obliged to answer any question that could incriminate him;[318]
- intentionally hinders or disrupts an investigation, as the ones mentioned above;[319] and
- violates or fails to adhere to any prohibitive or mandatory proviso of any regulations or decrees that may be issued in accordance with the said legislation.[320]

75. Within the frame of wholesale energy market, the obligation to refrain from insider trading is ensured by special sanctions. It is here briefly noted that under the relevant EU legislation persons who possess inside information in relation to a wholesale energy product are prohibited from using that information for their own account or for the account of a third party. Also, they may nether disclose that information to any other person nor recommend or induce another person, on the basis of inside information.[321] Inside information ('εμπιστευτικές πληροφορίες')[322] means 'information of a precise nature which has not been made public, which relates, directly or indirectly, to one or more wholesale energy products and which, if it were made public, would be likely to significantly affect the prices of those

312. Section 133(e) *ibid.*
313. Sections 133(f) and 14 *ibid.*
314. Sections 133(g) and 14 *ibid.*
315. Section 133(h) *ibid.*
316. Sections 133(i) and 10 *ibid.*
317. Sections 133(j) and 13 *ibid.*
318. Sections 133(k) and 13 *ibid.*
319. Sections 133(l) and 13 *ibid.*
320. Section 133(m) *ibid.*
321. Article 3(1)(a), (b) & (c) Regulation (EU) 1227/2011 of the European Parliament and of the Council of 25 Oct. 2011 on wholesale energy market integrity and transparency, OJ L 326, 8 Dec. 2011, p. 1.
322. In French 'information privilégiée', in German 'Insider-Information', in Dutch 'voorwetenschap'.

wholesale energy products'. For the purpose of this definition, information ('πληροφορίες')[323] stands for '(a) information which is required to be made public in accordance with Regulations (EC) No 714/2009 and (EC) No 715/2009, including guidelines and network codes adopted pursuant to those Regulations; (b) information relating to the capacity and use of facilities for production, storage, consumption or transmission of electricity or natural gas or related to the capacity and use of LNG facilities, including planned or unplanned unavailability of these facilities; (c) information which is required to be disclosed in accordance with legal or regulatory provisions at Union or national level, market rules, and contracts or customs on the relevant wholesale energy market, in so far as this information is likely to have a significant effect on the prices of wholesale energy products; and (d) other information that a reasonable market participant would be likely to use as part of the basis of its decision to enter into a transaction relating to, or to issue an order to trade in, a wholesale energy product'. Finally, information is deemed to be of a precise nature 'if it indicates a set of circumstances which exists or may reasonably be expected to come into existence, or an event which has occurred or may reasonably be expected to do so, and if it is specific enough to enable a conclusion to be drawn as to the possible effect of that set of circumstances or event on the prices of wholesale energy products'.[324] Anyone violating these statutory obligations, both in person, via an employee or a representative, has committed a criminal offence and may face imprisonment of up to five years and/ or a monetary fine of up to EUR 350,000.[325] These penalties also apply to anyone violating regulatory decisions.[326] In addition, any person convicted of such a criminal offence is automatically deprived of the right to enter into transactions in wholesale energy products both directly and indirectly. Equally, any such person may not enter into transactions, including the placing of orders to trade, in one or more wholesale energy markets for a period of five years.[327] Performing such transactions notwithstanding said prohibition constitutes independently a crime leading to imprisonment of up to one year and/ or a monetary fine of up to EUR 50,000.[328] Conviction of this latter crime automatically causes further transaction prohibition in wholesale energy, as already depicted, for a period of five more years.[329]

76. In the event that a criminal offence foreseen in Law No. 130(I)/2021 is committed by a legal person, and it is proven that the said crime has been committed with the consent or in collaboration of or is attributed to a person being director, secretary or another officer thereof, this natural person along with the legal person is liable to criminal prosecution.[330]

---

323. In French 'information', in German 'Information', in Dutch 'informatie'.
324. Article 2(1) Regulation (EU) 1227/2011.
325. Section 133(2)(a) Law No. 130(I)/2021.
326. Sections 133(2)(a) and 9(1)(b)(i) *ibid.*
327. Section 133(2)(b) *ibid.*
328. Section 133(2)(c) *ibid.*
329. Section 133(2)(d) *ibid.*
330. Section 140(1) *ibid.*

77. Apart from the above, violation of regulatory decrees issued by Cyprus Energy Regulatory Authority necessary for the purpose of ensuring compliance with this law, constitutes a penal offence. In case of conviction, it may lead to conviction of up to six months and/or a monetary fine of up to EUR 50,000.[331]

78. Turning to administrative fines, a detailed procedure for investigating violations of statutory obligations or obligations stemming from issued authorizations is foreseen in this law. At the outset, it is noted that Cyprus Energy Regulatory Authority may, on its own initiative or following a complaint, examine whether a holder of the authorization or a person to whom exemption has been granted violates or fails to comply with the terms and conditions of its authorization, any regulatory decision or decision of Cyprus Energy Regulatory Authority or any provision of this law, including regulations of the same authority.[332] To this end, said authority may investigate the activities and actions of any electricity entity and is entrusted with the following powers: have access to any relevant archive or document in any form, and to receive a copy of it or the original; demand information from any relevant person, including those who are successively involved in the transmission of orders or conduct of the operations concerned, as well as their principals, and, if necessary, the right to summon and hear any such person or principal; carry out on-site inspections;[333] enter the establishment of natural and legal persons in order to confiscate archives, documents and data in any form, as long as it is suspected that such objects are related to the investigation and it is possible that they are crucial for the suspected violations (entering a home is performed only following a court order); summoning witnesses and interested parties as well as forcing them to appear, and instructing them to bring or present documents, books, plans and registers; and examine both the authority itself and via lawyers witnesses and interested parties.[334] Specifically with regard to investigations into the wholesale energy market, Cyprus Energy Regulatory Authority has the following powers, further to and in addition to the aforementioned: require existing telephone and existing data traffic records; require the cessation of any practice that is contrary to Regulation (EU) 1227/2011 or delegated acts or implementing acts adopted on the basis thereof; request a court to freeze and/ or sequester assets; request a court, the Cyprus Securities and Exchange Commission or other competent authority to impose a temporary prohibition of professional activity; and take all necessary measures for properly informing the public, including the correction of false or misleading information that had been made public, requesting from any person that spread such false and misleading information to publish a corrected declaration.[335] Interested parties may be represented before the Cyprus Energy Electricity Authority by an advocate

331. Section 135(1) & (4) *ibid.*
332. Section 12(a), (b) & (c) *ibid.*
333. Section 13(1) & (2) (a), (b) & (c) *ibid*, which is similar to Art. 13(2)(a), (b) & (c) Regulation (EU) 1227/2011.
334. Section 13(2)(d), (e) & (f) Law No. 130(I)/2021.
335. Section 13(3)(a), (b), (c), (d), (e) & (f) *ibid*, which is similar to Art. 13(2)(d), (e), (f) & (g) Regulation (EU) 1227/2011.

and may summon witnesses pursuant to the Civil Procedure Rules[336] and the Law on Courts, which are applied *mutatis mutandis*.[337]

79. Should the investigation lead to a prima facie violation, the authority serves notification to persons who are believed to have violated the terms of the authorization, exemption, regulatory decision or decision, as the case may be. Therein, the allegedly violated term(s) is specified[338] along with the actions or omissions that result or may result in such a violation.[339] It is further mentioned that the addressee of the notification may submit written objections within a certain time limit that may not be longer than thirty days after serving the notification.[340] Following examination of such objections by the authority as well as after having taken into consideration any opinion, information or documents put before it, but regardless of any criminal procedures being pending or having been concluded, the authority may impose an administrative fine to the holder of the authorization or the receiver of the exemption. It may also decide the imposition of an administrative fine depending on the nature, the seriousness and the duration of the act or omission for every day that the relevant act or omission continues to exist. Similarly, it may suspend the issued authorization or exemption for as long as it considers necessary under the circumstances or even revoke it.[341]

80. Should the violation of terms and conditions of an authorization or of technical rules result in direct danger to human lives, property or the environment, Cyprus Energy Regulatory Authority may decide the immediate suspension of the relevant authorization or exemption for as long as it deems necessary under those specific conditions.[342]

81. Specifically with regard to investigations into the wholesale energy market, Cyprus Energy Regulatory Authority, may take the following decisions and impose administrative sanctions and other measures, regardless of any criminal investigations: order the termination of unlawful behaviour and abstain from repeating it; berefting the acquired profits or the avoided damage due to the violation, to the extent that these can be calculated; public warning stating the person responsible and the nature of the violation; revocation or suspension of the operation licence of the undertaking; temporary prohibition of performing managing duties within an undertaking for the person performing such duties or any other natural person responsible for the violation;[343] in case of multiple violations of the prohibition of insider trading and market manipulation, permanent prohibition of exercising said

336. Civil Procedure relating to Powers of the Courts in Civil Actions and to the Execution of Judgments in such actions ('Cap. 6') X of 1885, The Statute Laws of Cyprus, p. 183, as amended.
337. Section 13(4)(a) & (b) Law No. 130(I)/2021.
338. Section 15(1)(a) *ibid.*
339. Section 15(1)(b) *ibid.*
340. Section 15(1)(c) *ibid.*
341. Section 15(2)(a), (b), (c) & (d) *ibid.*
342. Section 15(3) *ibid.*
343. Section 15(4)(a), (b), (c), (d) & (e) *ibid.*

managing duties;[344] temporary prohibition of conducting transactions for the same account to anyone performing managing duties within an undertaking or any other natural person liable for violation; maximum administrative fines up to three times the profit acquired or damage avoided due to the violation, if such amount may be determined;[345] administrative fines of up to EUR 5 million for violation of prohibition of insider trading and market manipulation, up to EUR 1 million for violation of the obligation to publish inside information, up to EUR 500,000 for violation of regulatory decisions, when the violator is a natural person;[346] and administrative fines of up to EUR 15 million for violation of prohibition of insider trading and market manipulation, up to EUR 2.5 million for violation of the obligation to publish inside information, up to EUR 1 million for violation of regulatory decisions, when the violator is a legal person.[347] Finally, if Regulation (EU) 1227/2011 is violated in any manner not foreseen in this law, Cyprus Energy Regulatory Authority may impose an administrative fine of up to EUR 350,000 on the violator. Such a fine may also be imposed on anyone failing to comply with any order or prohibition that the same authority issued. Repeating the same violations leads to an administrative fine of up to EUR 700,000.[348] However, should the violator have obtained profit from that violation that is greater than the described amount of monetary fines, the authority has the power to impose a fine up to double the amount of the acquired profit.[349]

82. Each and every administrative decision must be in writing and have due reasoning.[350] The specific conditions that the authority is obliged to consider, while exercising its discretion, are the following, in addition to all case-specific relevant circumstances: the seriousness and the duration of the violation; the level of responsibility of the violator; the monetary robustness of the violator, as indicated by the total turnover of a legal person or the annual income of a natural person; the importance of the acquired profit or the avoided loss, to the extent that this is determinable; the level of cooperation of the violator with the authority; any previous violations; and the measures taken by the violator in order to avoid repeating the violation.[351]

83. During this examination, the authority may impose on the addressee the obligation to reach measures necessary for making good of the violation or prohibiting any future breach.[352] Should the addressee fail to comply with such an obligation within one month of serving of the relevant administrative act or within a reasonable time, as the case may be, the authority may impose on him an administrative fine in accordance with the nature, the seriousness and the duration of the breach.[353]

---

344. Section 15(4)(f) *ibid.*, Art. 3 and 5 Regulation (EU) 1227/2011.
345. Section 15(4)(g) & (h) Law No. 130(I)/2021.
346. Section 15(4)(i) *ibid.* and Arts 3,5 & 4 Regulation (EU) 1227/2011.
347. Section 15(4)(j) Law No. 130(I)/2021 and Arts 3, 5 & 4 Regulation (EU) 1227/2011.
348. Section 15(6) Law No. 130(I)/2021.
349. Section 15(7) *ibid.*
350. Section 15(8) *ibid.*
351. Section 15(9)(a) to (g) *ibid.*
352. Section 27(4) Law No. 122(I)/2003.
353. Section 27(5)(a) *ibid.*

Further, administrative fine for every day of continuing the breach may b imposed.[354] Lastly, revocation of the authorization, exclusion or decree may b ordered.[355] Administrative acts imposing such fines need to be in writing and du reasoned.[356] This proviso is not particularly necessary, as under general administra tive law, acts issued following the exercise of discretion need to be fully and du reasoned, especially when they are negative for the citizen, when they are contrar to the content of the previous opinion, suggestion, proposal or report of a compe tent authority or to the specifics of a file, when they are contrary to establishe policy or tactic, when they introduce extraordinary measures and when they are t be reasoned by the law.[357] The reasoning is due when it is clear so that no doubt exist as to the actual grounds that lead the administration to reach such a deci sion.[358] General characterizations that are applicable to any case or a simple refer ence to general terms of law equally applicable to any case are no due reasoning.[35 The said administrative acts imposing fines are served to the addressee,[360] who ma within thirty days of the service submit written suggestions ('προτάσεις') to th Cyprus Energy Regulatory Authority.[361] As stated above, the addressee may withi seventy-five days lodge an appeal with the Supreme Court of Cyprus requesting it annulment. Only after the lapse of the said limitation or the giving of judgment when an appeal is filed, is the fine collectable by the authority.[362] In case th addressee does not opt to pay it, the authority can collect it as a civil debt owed t the Treasury of Cyprus Energy Regulatory Authority by filing a civil action.[363]

354. Section 27(5)(b) *ibid.*
355. Section 27(5)(c) *ibid.*
356. Section 27(6) *ibid.*
357. Section 26(1)(a)–(e) Law No. 158(I)/1999. *See* relevant case law: *Pancyprian Federation o Labour (Peo) v. 1. The Board of Cinematograph Films Censors 2. The Minister of Interior* (1965 3 CLR 27; *The Cyprus Palestine Plantations Co. Ltd. v. the Republic* (1965) 3 CLR 271; *Kasapi v. the Council for Registration of Architects and Civil Engineers* (1967) 3 CLR 270; *Georgiades a o. v. the Republic* (1967) 3 CLR 653; *K.M.C. Motors Limited v. the Republic* (1985) 3 CLR 1235 *A. Trikomitis Limited v. the Republic* (1986) 3 CLR 262.
358. Section 28(1) Law No. 158(I)/1999. Due reasoning was considered in the following case law: *Con stantinides v. the Republic* (1967) 3 CLR 7; *Tourpeki v. Demokratias* (1973) 3 CLR 592; *Savva Nisiotis v. the Republic* (1977) 3 CLR 388; *Savva v. the Republic* (1980) 3 CLR 675; *Markides v the Republic* (1985) CLR 1393; *Tsountas a.o. v. EEY* (1985) 3 CLR 784; *Pericleous v. Kypriako Organismou Tourismou* (1989) 3C CLR 1116; *Frangou v. Demokratias* (1998) 3 CLR 270.
359. Section 28(2) Law No. 158(I)/1999. *See* relevant case law: *Petrondas v. the Attorney-General o the Republic* (1969) 3 CLR 214; *Zavros v. the Council for Registration of Architects and Civil Engi neers* (1969) 3 CLR 310; *Papageorgiou v. the Republic* (1984) 3 CLR 1348.
360. Section 28(1) Law No. 122(I)/2003.
361. Section 28(2) *ibid.*
362. Section 28(3) *ibid.*
363. Section 28(4) *ibid.*

Chapter 3. Prospection, Research and Exploitation of Hydrocarbons

84. Prospection, research and exploitation of hydrocarbons are regulated by Law No. 4(I)/2007,[364] as well as its secondary legislation.[365] Hydrocarbons, which stand in the foreground of this legislation, are any type of mineral oils in solid, liquid or gas form and include mineral oil, benzene, natural hydrocarbon gases and any relevant fossils or substances excavated with those.[366]

§1. Objective

85. Besides implementing Directive 94/22/EC into national law, Law No. 4(I)/2007 is silent on its objective. Therefore, it can be safely assumed that the scope of the said directive is at the same time the scope of the national law. As it can be extracted from the preamble of this directive, its scope includes encouraging the best possible prospection, exploration and production of the resources located in the Union, ensuring non-discriminatory access to and pursuit of activities relating to prospection, exploration and production of hydrocarbons under conditions which encourage greater competition in this sector and thereby favour the best prospection, exploration and production of resources in the Member States. It is further aimed to reinforce the integration of the internal energy market and hence to set up common rules for ensuring that the procedures for granting authorizations for the prospection, exploration and production of hydrocarbons must be open to all entities possessing the necessary capabilities. Equally important, it is intended that the

364. Law on Hydrocarbons (Prospection, Research and Exploitation) ('περί Υδρογονανθράκων (Αναζήτηση, Έρευνα και Εκμετάλλευση) Νόμος') No. 4 of 2007, OG I(I) No. 4109, 26 Jan. 2007, p. 81. This legislation was enacted for the purposes of implementing Directive 94/22/EC of the European Parliament and of the Council of 30 May 1994 on the conditions for granting and using authorizations for the prospection, exploration and production of hydrocarbons, OJ L 164, 30 Jun. 1994, p. 3. Law No. 4(I)/2007 has been amended by Law on Hydrocarbons (Prospection, Research and Exploitation) (Amendment) ('περί Υδρογονανθράκων (Αναζήτηση, Έρευνα και Εκμετάλλευση) (Τροποποιητικός) Νόμος') No. 126 of 2013, OG I(I) No. 4410, 25 Oct. 2013, p. 1108, by Law on Hydrocarbons (Prospection, Research and Exploitation) (Amendment) ('περί Υδρογονανθράκων (Αναζήτηση, Έρευνα και Εκμετάλλευση) (Τροποποιητικός) Νόμος') No. 29 of 2014, OG I(I) No. 4433, 7 Mar. 2014, p. 157 and by Law on Hydrocarbons (Prospection, Research and Exploitation) (Amendment) ('περί Υδρογονανθράκων (Αναζήτηση, Έρευνα και Εκμετάλλευση) (Τροποποιητικός) Νόμος') No. 186 of 2015, OG I(I) No. 4544, 16 Dec. 2015, p. 1380.

365. Regulations on Hydrocarbons (Prospection, Research and Exploitation) ('περί Υδρογονανθράκων (Αναζήτηση, Έρευνα και Εκμετάλλευση) Κανονισμοί') No. 51 of 2007, OG I(III) No. 4170, 26 Jan. 2007, p. 345, which have been amended by Regulations on Hydrocarbons (Prospection, Research and Exploitation) (Amendment) ('περί Υδρογονανθράκων (Αναζήτηση, Έρευνα και Εκμετάλλευση) (Τροποποιητικοί) Κανονισμοί') No. 113 of 2009 OG I(III) No. 4342, 13 Mar. 2009, p. 627, and Regulations on Hydrocarbons (Prospection, Research and Exploitation) (Amendment) ('περί Υδρογονανθράκων (Αναζήτηση, Έρευνα και Εκμετάλλευση) (Τροποποιητικοί) Κανονισμοί') No. 574 of 2014 OG I(III) No. 4840, 23 Dec. 2014, p. 3210 (hereinafter 'KDP 51/2007').

366. Section 2 Law No. 4(I)/2007.

Member States' entities enjoy in third countries a treatment comparable to that enjoyed by third countries' entities in the EU by virtue of the laid provisions.[367]

§2. Regulatory Mechanism

I. The Council of Ministers

86. The Council of Ministers holds a key position regarding the implementation of the present legislation, as it defines the areas, where activities relevant to hydrocarbons may take place,[368] issues relevant authorizations, renews them as well as revokes, annuls and suspends the same.[369] For the optimal application of this law, the Council of Ministers may issue regulations.[370] These may refer to the form of any documentation used,[371] to defining the manner in which the applications for issuing, renewing or transferring an authorization or assigning rights deriving from the same are to be submitted, as well as the eligible applicants,[372] to renewal and/or extension of authorizations,[373] to regulating authorizations for hydrocarbons research and exploitation as well as to protection of hydrocarbon deposits.[374] These may further determine the way of providing information or updates to the Minister by the authorization holders[375] and regulate non-intervention to other activities in or near the area, for which an authorization has been issued[376] as well as any matters regarding duties and powers of the authorized public servants.[377] Lastly, the regulations may regulate matters relevant to the conclusion of contracts ('*Συμβόλαια*') between the state and authorization holders.[378] Interestingly, in said regulation, criminal offences may be established. However, the relevant penalties may not exceed imprisonment for four years and a monetary fine of EUR 8,500,000.[379]

II. The Minister

87. The Minister of Energy, Commerce, Industry and Tourism (hereinafter 'the Minister') plays a rather executive role, as he publishes calls for applications and

367. Recitals to the preamble of Directive 94/22/EC. This is an expression of the well-established principle of reciprocity of public international law (*see* Shaw, Malcom N., *International Law* 7 (4th ed., Cambridge University Press 1997)).
368. Section 4 Law No. 4(I)/2007.
369. Sections 5, 15 and 23 *ibid.*
370. Section 30(1) *ibid.*
371. Section 30(2)(a) *ibid.*
372. Section 30(2)(b) *ibid.*
373. Section 30(2)(g) *ibid.*
374. Section 30(2)(c) *ibid.*
375. Section 30(2)(d) *ibid.*
376. Section 30(2)(e)(i) *ibid.*
377. Section 30(2)(e)(ii) *ibid.*
378. Section 30(2)(f) *ibid.*
379. Section 30(3) *ibid.*

announcements in the OG or the Official Journal (OJ) of the EU,[380] receives applications for authorizations,[381] asks for information from the authorization holders[382] and convenes a meeting of the Advisory Committee for the initiation of the examination process of the applications.[383] Apart from the above-mentioned competence of the Council of Ministers, the Minister may issue decrees for the optimal application of this law.[384] Such decrees may set out provisions relevant to keeping a registry of hydrocarbons by the Minister,[385] the construction of joint establishments[386] and the fixing of fees for any application.[387]

88. Interestingly, the Minister may delegate in writing to any public servant any duty appointed to him by this law or regulations.[388] The relevant public servant has an obligation to perform the duties delegated to him according to any relevant instructions of the Minister,[389] who reserves the right to amend and revoke this delegation via written notification.[390]

III. The Advisory Committee

89. The Advisory Committee ('Συμβουλευτική Επιτροπή'), which is established in this law,[391] plays a vital role mainly in examining the applications submitted. It is comprised of the Permanent Secretary of the Ministry of Energy, Commerce, Industry and Tourism or its representative, who is the President of the Advisory Committee,[392] the Attorney General of the Republic or its representative,[393] the Permanent Secretary of the Ministry of Foreign Affairs or its representative,[394] the Permanent Secretary of the Ministry of Finance or its representative,[395] the Permanent Secretary of the Ministry of Agriculture, Rural Development and Environment or its representative,[396] the Director of the Department of Geological Survey or its representative[397] and the Director of the Department of Energy or its representative.[398]

---

380. Sections 5(1)(b), 5(5) and 18 *ibid.*
381. Section 6(2) *ibid.*
382. Section 17 *ibid.*
383. Section 6(2) *ibid.*
384. Section 30(1) *ibid.*
385. Section 30(4)(a) *ibid.*
386. Section 30(4)(b) *ibid.*
387. Section 30(4)(c) *ibid.*
388. Section 33(1) *ibid.*
389. Section 33(2) *ibid.*
390. Section 33(3) *ibid.*
391. Section 6(1) *ibid.*
392. Section 6(1)(a) *ibid.*
393. Section 6(1)(b) *ibid.*
394. Section 6(1)(c) *ibid.*
395. Section 6(1)(d) *ibid.*
396. Section 6(1)(e) *ibid.*
397. Section 6(1)(f) *ibid.*
398. Section 6(1)(g) *ibid.*

90. The main duty of the Advisory Committee is to study the content of applications for prospection, research and exploitation of hydrocarbons as well as to evaluate any matter that arises in relation to the applications or that is tabled before it. It further advises the Minister on any matter that comes up during the application of this law.[399] In particular, the committee may examine and submit its views to the Minister on any matter occurring before the initiation of the submission of applications,[400] on whether a submitted application should be granted or not,[401] on the transfer of authorization or the concession of rights deriving from the same to another body,[402] on defining any terms in the event of accepting an application, as well as any revision of the same,[403] on environmental threat rating due to granting the authorization and the contingent protection measures,[404] on the safety measures that need to be imposed and the measures reassuring that the persons performing activities related to hydrocarbons have the appropriate scientific qualifications,[405] on navigation of safety measures[406] and anything else related to the applications that the committee deems proper to examine.[407]

91. The Advisory Committee has the power to invite to a meeting any special expert on prospection, research and exploitation of hydrocarbons and may be advised by him. This expert may be any public servant or private employee as well as any person, whose views or specialized knowledge on a specific matter may be regarded as useful or necessary for its duties.[408] The Committee may also appoint special technical committees for the study of specialized matters arising during the examination of any application or other matters, as well as define the terms of their mandate and function. It shall have regard for the results of their research.[409]

IV. Authorized Public Servants

92. The Minister may appoint proper person(s) as authorized public servants ('εξουσιοδοτημένοι λειτουργοί') for the purpose of monitoring the application of and adherence to this law, the regulations issued in accordance with same and the terms of authorizations.[410] In this respect, authorized public servants may enter at any reasonable time without prior notice into any building, premises or other areas, in which they reasonably think that a violation takes place. It is self-evident that for entering residential premises, a relevant court order is needed.[411] They may

399. Section 8(1) *ibid.*
400. Section 8(2)(a) *ibid.*
401. Section 8(2)(b) *ibid.*
402. Section 8(2)(c) *ibid.*
403. Section 8(2)(d) *ibid.*
404. Section 8(2)(e) *ibid.*
405. Section 8(2)(f) *ibid.*
406. Section 8(2)(g) *ibid.*
407. Section 8(2)(h) *ibid.*
408. Section 9(1) *ibid.*
409. Section 9(2) *ibid.*
410. Section 19(1) *ibid.*
411. Section 19(2)(a) *ibid.*

conduct investigations, examinations, tests, controls and inquiries deemed necessary in order to establish, whether a violation takes place, and inspect, and take parts of documentation related to hydrocarbon activities or copies thereof.[412] They may further keep copies of any data or records, when they may reasonably think that such may be needed in a criminal or civil procedure relating to an offence foreseen in this law, and copies of any information provided to the Minister, under the condition that the Law on the Protection of Natural Persons from Processing of Personal Data and Free Movement of those Data[413] is applied.[414] They may do anything considered proper and reasonable for ensuring the application of this law and issued regulations,[415] such as entering at a reasonable time and without prior notice into any building, premises, area, vehicle, ship or aircraft and examining any machine or equipment, which has been used, is being used or will be used and is related to hydrocarbon activities.[416] Lastly, an authorized public servant may take samples of hydrocarbons, water or other liquids, gaseous or solid substances, and perform investigations, analysis, tests, research and inquiries for the purpose of establishing any violation of the terms of the authorization or of this law.[417] For the effective exercise of these duties, every authorization holder and any owner, occupier or person in control of buildings, premises, areas, vehicles, ships or aircraft is obliged to provide every reasonable help, including necessary means of transportation.[418]

§3. Authorization for Prospection, Research and Exploitation of Hydrocarbons

93. Ownership of hydrocarbons anywhere in Cyprus, including the territorial sea, continental shelf and exclusive economic zone belongs and has always belonged to the state.[419] Prospection ('αναζήτηση υδρογονανθράκων'),[420]

412. Section 19(2)(b) *ibid.*
413. Law on the Protection of Natural Persons from Processing of Personal Data and Free Movement of those Data ('περί της Προστασίας των Φυσικών Προσώπων Έναντι της Επεξεργασίας των Δεδομένων Προσωπικού Χαρακτήρα και της Ελεύθερης Κυκλοφορίας των Δεδομένων Αυτών Νόμος') No. 125 of 2018, OG I(I) No. 4670, 31 Jul. 2018, p. 827. This law aims to fostering the implementation of Regulation (EU) 2016/679 of the European Parliament and of the Council of 27 Apr. 2016 on the protection of natural persons with regard to the processing of personal data and on the free movement of such data, and repealing Directive 95/46/EC (General Data Protection Regulation), OJ L 119, 4 May 2016, p. 1. Hence, the relevant case law of the Court of Justice of the EU is of profound importance for its proper interpretation and application. Related cases are the following: Case C-673/17 *Bundesverband der Verbraucherzentralen und Verbraucherverbände – Verbraucherzentrale Bundesverband e.V. v. Planet49 GmbH*, digital ECJ; Case C-520/18 *Ordre des barreaux francophones et germanophone, Académie Fiscale ASBL, UA, Liga voor Mensenrechten ASBL, Ligue des Droits de l'Homme ASBL, VZ, WY, XX v. Conseil des ministres* (pending – the opinion of Advocate General was delivered on 15 Jan. 2020.); Case C-272/19 *VQ v. Land Hesse* (digital ECR); Case C-439/19 *B v. Latvijas Republikas Saeima*, digital ECJ.
414. Section 19(2)(c) Law No. 4(I)/2007.
415. Section 19(2)(d) *ibid.*
416. Section 19(2)(e) *ibid.*
417. Section 19(2)(f) *ibid.*
418. Section 19(3) *ibid.*
419. Section 3(1) *ibid.*

research ('έρευνα υδρογονανθράκων')[421] or exploitation of hydrocarbon ('εκμετάλλευση υδρογονανθράκων')[422] prerequisite the issuance of appropriat authorizations. In the event this does not take place, a criminal offence is being com mitted. This is punished with the conviction of no more than two years and/or monetary fine of not more than EUR 1,710,000 unless authorization is granted. I case of a second or further conviction, imprisonment of no more than four year and/or a monetary fine of no more than EUR 8,550,000 is imposed.[423] Hence, th necessary authorizations for the lawful performance of these activities are authori zation for the prospection of hydrocarbons ('άδεια αναζήτησης υδρογονανθ ράκων'), authorization for research of hydrocarbons ('άδεια έρευνα υδρογονανθράκων') and authorization for the exploitation of hydrocarbon ('άδεια εκμετάλλευσης υδρογονανθράκων').

94. The Council of Ministers specifies the areas eligible to perform said activi ties.[424] Once the area is defined, the Council of Ministers ensures non discriminatory access to and performance of such activities.[425] However, on th grounds of national security ('εθνική ασφάλεια'), the Council of Ministers ma deny such access to any person being substantially controlled by a third country o by citizens thereof.[426]

95. Lastly, it should be noted that certain decisions of the Council of Minister related to hydrocarbons are not to be deemed as authorizations. These involve th issuance of an authorization solely due to a change of name, ownership or corporat structure of the holder to transfer the authorization or assignment of rights derivin from the same.[427] No authorization in the meaning of this law constitutes furthe authorization to a person holding another authorization when the latter implies issu ance of the first,[428] and decision of the Council of Ministers reached within a authorization and related to initiation, interruption, extension or pause of the activi ties of the granted authorization.[429] Lastly, a decision of the Council of Ministers t proceed with research on evaluating oil reserves ('πετρελαϊκό δυναμικό') by pub lic bodies and due support from special counsels and experts is no authorization.[430]

---

420. *Prospection of hydrocarbons* stands for efforts of localizing hydrocarbons in any appropriat approach, but for drilling (s. 2 *ibid.*).
421. *Research of hydrocarbons* means research for discovery of hydrocarbon fields in any appropriat approach, including drilling (s. 2 *ibid.*).
422. *Exploitation of hydrocarbons* is understood as development and generation of hydrocarbons or any processing, so that they become marketable, including storage and transport of those and thei by-products to the cargo facilities for further disposal, excluding refining (s. 2 *ibid.*).
423. Section 22 *ibid.*
424. Section 4(1) *ibid.*, Reg. 3(4) KDP 51/2007.
425. Section 4(2) Law No. 4(I)/2007.
426. Section 4(3) *ibid.*
427. Section 5(7)(a)(i) *ibid.*, which corresponds to Art. 3(5)(a) Directive 94/22/EC. In such a case, the Minister must be informed immediately of the changes. Should this not be done, the authorization may be annulled according to s. 5(7)(b) Law No. 4(I)/2007.
428. Section 5(7)(a)(ii) *ibid.*, which corresponds to Art. 3(5)(b) Directive 94/22/EC.
429. Section 5(7)(a)(iii) Law No. 4(I)/2007, which corresponds to Art. 3(5)(c) Directive 94/22/EC.
430. Section 5(7)(a)(iv) Law No. 4(I)/2007.

I. Applications for Authorizations

96. The relevant call for applications can be initiated either on the initiative of the Council of Ministers, which triggers the Minister to call for submission of applications published in the OG and the OJ of the EU at least ninety days prior to the end of the relevant time limit[431] or following a submission of application by a body, which causes announcement of a call for applications in the OG and the OJ of the EU by the Minister in consensus with the Council of Ministers. In the latter case, any interested party may submit an application at least ninety days after the announcement.[432] Said call for applications must define the type of authorization, all geographical areas that are or may be in whole or in part subject of the application, projected date or time limit of authorization issuance, any terms or conditions that the Council of Ministers deems proper to be announced at this stage of proceedings, whether preference is made towards independent and uncontrolled applicants, as well as anything else deemed proper to be included in the announcement.[433]

97. Applications for prospection of hydrocarbons need to include the name, address and citizenship ('υπηκοότητα') of the applicant,[434] the place of registration or incorporation as well as the principal place of business, the members of its board of directors and the main directors, their citizenship and place of residence, the capital structure and full details on any control performed by other natural or legal person on the applicant.[435] Financial arrangement of the prospection, in the event that the application is accepted, must also be submitted along with security regarding fulfilment of the obligations of the applicant.[436] Lastly, the former experience of the applicant on hydrocarbon prospection must be stated.[437]

98. Applications for research on hydrocarbons must submit in addition to the above details,[438] the type of the legal form of the applicant, including information on the connection with the parent company, if applicable, and on any associated persons,[439] as well as the financial structure of the applicant and the parent company, if applicable, including approved financial statements and annual returns for the last three years and any other statements that they have submitted to an authority competent for supervising the capital market and transferable securities ('συναλλαγών κινητών αξιών').[440] In addition, the special information that follows below is equally to be included. The area(s) for which the application is filed as well as the

431. Section 5(1)(a) *ibid.*
432. Section 5(1)(b) *ibid.*
433. Section 5(2) *ibid.*
434. Regulation 6(1)(a) KDP 51/2007.
435. Regulation 6(1)(b) *ibid.*
436. Regulation 6(1)(c) *ibid.*
437. Regulation 6(1)(d) *ibid.*
438. Regulation 6(2)(a), (b), (e) and (f) *ibid.*
439. Regulation 6(2)(c) *ibid.*
440. Regulation 6(2)(d) *ibid.*

priority order, if applicable, must be elaborated,[441] the exploitation programme suggested for the area(s) along with the geographical distribution is to be described in detail[442] and the minimum obligations undertaken regarding the works and expenses during the research period must be stated.[443] Also, a short notice on environmental effects of the research activities and the intended response measures is to be submitted[444] as well as proposals on training and employment of Cypriot nationals, including the minimum expenses to this aim.[445] Further proposals on the financial terms and conditions demanded as criteria for the evaluation of the application, such as the financial consideration and/or the allocation of production between the applicant and the state, need to be submitted.[446] Lastly, any agreement on financing the activities[447] or any other information that the Minister asks for or that the applicant wishes to submit needs to be included.[448]

99. Holders of authorization of exploitation of hydrocarbons need to file an Environmental Impact Assessment according to the relevant provisions of Law on the Assessment of the Effects of Certain Projects on the Environment.[449,450] This assessment requires a series of information, that being a description of the project, including, in particular, a description of the location of the project, the physical characteristics of the whole project and the land-use requirements during the construction and operational phases, a description of the main characteristics of the operational phase of the project, for instance, energy demanded and energy used, nature and quantity of the materials and natural resources used, and an estimate, by type and quantity, of expected residues and emissions (such as water, air and soil pollution, noise, vibration, light, heat, radiation) and quantities and types of waste produced during the construction and operation phases,[451] alongside a digital archive of the geographical data of the location of the project.[452] Further, an outline of the reasonable alternatives studied by the developer and an indication of the main

441. Regulation 6(6)(a) *ibid.*
442. Regulation 6(6)(b) *ibid.*
443. Regulation 6(6)(c) *ibid.*
444. Regulation 6(6)(d) *ibid.*
445. Regulation 6(6)(e) *ibid.* Restricting the training to Cypriot nationals constitutes clearly a violation of Art. 21(1) Charter of Fundamental Rights of the EU, OJ C 83, 30 Mar. 2010, p. 389 (396), which prohibits discrimination based on any ground such as sex, race, colour, ethnic or social origin, genetic features, language, religion or belief, political or any other opinion, membership of a national minority, property, birth, disability, age or sexual orientation.
446. Regulation 6(6)(f) KDP 51/2007.
447. Regulation 6(6)(g) *ibid.*
448. Regulation 6(6)(h) *ibid.*
449. Law on the Assessment of the Effects of Certain Projects on the Environment ('ο Περί Εκτίμησης των Επιπτώσεων στο Περιβάλλον από Ορισμένα Έργα Νόμος') No. 127 of 2018, OG I(I) No. 4055, 2 Dec. 2005, p. 851 (hereinafter 'Law No. 127(I)/2018'), which has been enacted for the purpose of implementing Directive 2011/92/EU of the European Parliament and of the Council of 13 Dec. 2011 on the assessment of the effects of certain public and private projects on the environment (OJ L 26, 28 Jan. 2012, p. 1), as amended by Directive 2014/52/EU, according to national law's preamble.
450. Section 11(2)(a) and (b) Law No. 4(I)/2007.
451. Annex V(1)(a), (b), (c) and (d) Law No. 127(I)/2018, which corresponds to Annex IV(1)(a), (b), (c) and (d) Directive 2011/92/EU.
452. Annex V(1)(e) Law No. 127(I)/2018.

reasons for selecting the chosen option, including a comparison of the environmental effects must be submitted.[453] The relevant aspects of the current state of the environment (baseline scenario) and an outline of the likely evolution thereof without implementation of the project as far as natural changes from the baseline scenario can be assessed with reasonable effort on the basis of the availability of environmental information and scientific knowledge also need to be described,[454] as well as factors likely to be significantly affected by the project: population, human health, biodiversity, land, soil, water, air, climate, material assets, cultural heritage, including architectural and archaeological aspects, and landscape.[455] Equally, a description of the likely significant effects of the project on the environment must be set out.[456] Also, the forecasting methods or evidence used to identify and assess the significant effects on the environment, including details of difficulties encountered, compiling the required information, and the main uncertainties involved need to be explained.[457] Measures envisaged to prevent, reduce and where possible offset any significant adverse effects on the environment are also to be set out,[458] alongside a description of the expected significant adverse effects of the project on the environment deriving from the vulnerability of the project to risks of major accidents and/or disasters which are relevant to the project concerned.[459] All the above should be included in a non-technical summary.[460] Lastly, a reference list detailing the sources used for the descriptions and assessments included in the report,[461] and data for the Study Group ('Ομάδα Μελέτης' in original),[462] a rather vague requirement not further explained in the law must be included.

100. Should the applications for prospection and research be submitted by two or more persons, the aforementioned are to be submitted for each one of them. In addition, one person needs to be specified as their representative.[463] Also, in the event that any change of the submitted information takes place, the Minister must immediately be informed accordingly.[464] Upon payment of the respective fee, the Minister files the application to the relevant register, including the date of submission, the relevant area, the paid amount and the status of the application.[465]

II. Derogation from the Process of Application for Authorization

101. The above-described application procedure for authorization can be disregarded, and authorizations are granted by the Council of Ministers in the following

453. Annex V(2) *ibid.*, which corresponds to Annex IV(2) Directive 2011/92/EU.
454. Annex V(3) Law No. 127(I)/2018, which corresponds to Annex IV(3) Directive 2011/92/EU.
455. Annex V(4) Law No. 127(I)/2018, which corresponds to Annex IV(4) Directive 2011/92/EU.
456. Annex V(5) Law No. 127(I)/2018, which corresponds to Annex IV(5) Directive 2011/92/EU.
457. Annex V(6) Law No. 127(I)/2018, which corresponds to Annex IV(6) Directive 2011/92/EU.
458. Annex V(7) Law No. 127(I)/2018, which corresponds to Annex IV(7) Directive 2011/92/EU.
459. Annex V(8) Law No. 127(I)/2018, which corresponds to Annex IV(8) Directive 2011/92/EU.
460. Annex V(9) Law No. 127(I)/2018, which corresponds to Annex IV(9) Directive 2011/92/EU.
461. Annex V(10) Law No. 127(I)/2018, which corresponds to Annex IV(10) Directive 2011/92/EU.
462. Annex V(10) Law No. 127(I)/2018.
463. Regulation 6(3) KDP 51/2007.
464. Regulation 6(4) *ibid.*
465. Regulation 6(5) *ibid.*

cases. First, this applies, when the area for which authorization is requested is available on a permanent basis.[466] Deviation may further occur when the same area has been the subject of a previous procedure, which has not resulted in the granting of authorization.[467] Lastly, the same takes place when the said area has been relinquished by an entity and does not fall automatically under the first described case.[468] To this respect, the Minister arranges for the publication in the OG of Cyprus and the OJ of the EU of a notice indicating the areas which are available according to the above and where detailed information in this regard can be obtained. Any significant change in this information is subject to additional notice.[469]

102. Said provisions on the application are not applied when geological or production considerations justify the granting of the authorization for an area to the holder of an authorization for a contiguous area. In such a case, the Council of Ministers ensures that the holders of authorizations for any other contiguous areas are eligible to submit applications in such a case and are given sufficient time to do so.[470]

III. Evaluation of Applications

103. After the submission of the application to the Minister and the summoning of a meeting of the Advisory Committee, the President of the latter sends without any delay a copy of the application to the members of the Committee and calls a meeting within thirty days for its evaluation.[471] During this meeting, the Advisory Committee examines whether the application has been filed in accordance with the provisions of this law and whether the data provided are sufficient for its evaluation and the issuance of the authorization.[472] Should it establish that the information before it is not sufficient or full, it may ask from the applicant or any third party any additional information or data considered necessary, as well as the performance of controls or ensuring opinions and reports from experts or other specialized professionals.[473] As soon as the Advisory Committee establishes that the information before is sufficient, it examines the application, in a procedure set out by the same, and submits a reasoned proposal on whether the authorization should be granted and in the affirmative its terms. This reasoned proposal is submitted in the form of an explanatory report ('εισηγητική έκθεση') to the Minister. He forwards this along with his proposal to the Council of Ministers that reaches the final decision on these matters.[474]

---

466. Section 5(4)(a) Law No. 4(I)/2007, which corresponds to Art. 3(3)(a) Directive 94/22/EC.
467. Section 5(4)(b) Law No. 4(I)/2007, which corresponds to Art. 3(3)(b) Directive 94/22/EC.
468. Section 5(4)(c) Law No. 4(I)/2007, which corresponds to Art. 3(3)(c) Directive 94/22/EC.
469. Section 5(5) Law No. 4(I)/2007, which corresponds to Art. 3(3) Directive 94/22/EC.
470. Section 5(6) Law No. 4(I)/2007, which corresponds to Art. 3(4) Directive 94/22/EC.
471. Section 10(1) Law No. 4(I)/2007.
472. Section 10(2) *ibid.*
473. Section 10(3) *ibid.*
474. Section 10(4) *ibid.*

104. The Council of Ministers evaluates the applications on the basis of ensuring that a decision on granting authorization to carry out offshore oil and gas operations takes into account the capability of an applicant for such an authorization to meet the requirements for operations within the framework of the authorization as required by the Directive on safety of offshore oil and gas operations.[475,476] In particular, when assessing the technical and financial capability of the applicant for authorization, due account is taken of the following:

- the risk, the hazards and any other relevant information relating to the licensed area concerned, including, where appropriate, the cost of degradation of the marine environment referred to in section 9(1)(c) Law on Marine Strategy;
- the particular stage of offshore oil and gas operations;
- the applicant's financial capabilities, including any financial security, to cover liabilities potentially deriving from the offshore oil and gas operations in question including liability for potential economic damages where such liability is provided for by national law; and
- the available information relating to the safety and environmental performance of the applicant, including in relation to major accidents, as may be appropriate to the operations for which the licence was requested.[477] The Council of Ministers requires applicants to provide, in an appropriate manner, evidence of technical and financial capacity and any other relevant information relating to the area covered by the authorization and the particular stage of offshore oil and gas operations,[478] while facilitating the deployment of sustainable financial instruments and other arrangements to assist applicants in demonstrating their financial capacity.[479] When assessing the technical and financial capabilities of an applicant, special attention is paid to any environmentally sensitive marine and coastal environments, in particular, ecosystems which play an important role in mitigation and adaptation to climate change, such as salt marshes and seagrass beds, and marine protected areas, such as special areas of conservation pursuant to Law on Protection and Management of Nature and Wild Life,[480] special protection areas pursuant to Law on Protection and Management of Wild Birds,[481] and marine

475. Directive 2013/30/EU of the European Parliament and of the Council of 12 Jun. 2013 on safety of offshore oil and gas operations and amending Directive 2004/35/EC, OJ L 178, 28 Jun. 2013, p. 66.
476. Section 12A(1) Law No. 4(I)/2007, which corresponds to Art. 4(1) Directive 2013/30/EU.
477. Section 4(2) Law No. 4(I)/2007, which corresponds to Art. 4(2) Directive 2013/30/EU.
478. Section 12A(3) Law No. 4(I)/2007, which corresponds to Art. 4(3) Directive 2013/30/EU.
479. Section 12A(4) Law No. 4(I)/2007, which corresponds to Art. 4(3) Directive 2013/30/EU.
480. Law on Protection and Management of Nature and Wild Life ('Νόμος περί Προστασίας και Διαχείρισης της Φύσης και της Αγριας Ζωής') No. 153 of 2003, OG I(I) No. 3758, 3 Oct. 2003, p. 1149, as amended, that implements Council Directive 92/43/EEC of 21 May 1992 on the conservation of natural habitats and of wild fauna and flora, OJ L 206, 22 Jul. 1992, p. 7.
481. Law on Protection and Management of Wild Birds and Games ('Νόμος περί Προστασίας και Διαχείρισης Αγριων Πτηνών και Θηραμάτων') No. 152 of 2003, OG I(I) No. 3758, 3 Oct. 2003, p. 1030, as amended, that implements Directive 2009/147/EC of the European Parliament and of the Council of 30 Nov. 2009 on the conservation of wild birds, OJ L 20, 26 Jan. 2010, p. 7.

protected areas as agreed by the Union or Cyprus concerned within the framework of any international or regional agreements to which they are a party.[482]

105. It may take into account further criteria, which are published in the OG of the Republic and the OJ of the EU. In the event that those have been published in the Gazette, the publication in the journal may simply make a reference to the first publication. Any change in criteria is to be published in full in both the OG and the OJ of the EU.[483] These criteria may refer to national security or public interest,[484] the technical and financial capability of the applicant,[485] the way in which they propose to prospect, explore and/or bring into production the geographical area in question,[486] the price which the entity is prepared to pay in order to obtain the authorizations if the authorization is put up for sale[487] and any lack of efficiency and responsibility that the applicant has demonstrated during previous authorization.[488] If two or more applications have equal merit, the Council of Ministers may adopt other criteria in order to make a final choice among those. These criteria need to be published in the OG of the Republic and the OJ of the EU.[489]

IV. Granting of Authorizations

A. *Content of Authorizations*

106. An application for prospection authorization is granted only when the competent authority is satisfied with evidence from the applicant that the applicant has made or will make adequate provision, on the basis of arrangements to be decided by the Council of Ministers, to cover liabilities potentially deriving from the applicant's offshore oil and gas operations. This is valid and effective from the start of offshore oil and gas operations. The Council of Ministers, while assessing the application submitted, may ask for the opinion of the Department of Labour Inspection if it deems it fit, whereas it examines whether the applicant has sufficient financial resources for the immediate launch and uninterrupted continuation of all measures necessary for effective emergency response and subsequent remediation.[490] Should an application for prospection authorization be granted, it gives the holder prospection rights in the specific area under specific terms and conditions.[491] A research authorization provides exclusive research rights in the given area under certain terms and conditions. In addition, the right to be granted an exploitation authorization is given, in the event of discovering financially exploitable hydrocarbon

482. Section 12A(2) Law No. 4(I)/2007, which corresponds to Art. 4(6) Directive 2013/30/EU.
483. Section 12(1) Law No. 4(I)/2007, which corresponds to Art. 5(1) Directive 94/22/EC.
484. Section 12(1)(a) Law No. 4(I)/2007.
485. Section 12(1)(b) *ibid.*, which corresponds to Art. 5(1)(a) Directive 94/22/EC.
486. Section 12(1)(c) Law No. 4(I)/2007, which corresponds to Art. 5(1)(b) Directive 94/22/EC.
487. Section 12(1)(d) Law No. 4(I)/2007, which corresponds to Art. 5(1)(c) Directive 94/22/EC.
488. Section 12(1)(e) Law No. 4(I)/2007, which corresponds to Art. 5(1) Directive 94/22/EC.
489. Section 12(2) Law No. 4(I)/2007.
490. Section 12A(3) *ibid.*, which corresponds to Art. 4(3) Directive 2013/30/EU.
491. Section 14(1) Law No. 4(I)/2007.

reserves.[492] An exploitation authorization provides exclusive exploitation rights in the given area under the terms and conditions of the authorization.[493] Said terms and conditions ensure the proper performance of authorized activities,[494] contribution in money or in hydrocarbons,[495] national security,[496] public security,[497] public health,[498] transport safety,[499] environmental protection,[500] protection of biological and mineral resources, as well as state treasures that are of artistic, historical or archaeological value,[501] safety of facilities and employees,[502] programmed administration of hydrocarbon reserves,[503] the need to ensure proceedings for the state,[504] and that the authorization holders have sufficient abilities to meet their financial obligations, which result from the hydrocarbons activities.[505] Terms and conditions are not to discriminate between authorization holders.[506] Terms and conditions relating to performance and suspension of activities that are applied to any authorization due to statutory provisions as well as any change are communicated to the holders.[507]

107. The duration of the authorization does not exceed the time demanded for the completion of the activities authorized.[508] In particular, prospection authorizations are issued for one year,[509] research authorizations for an initial period of no more than three years and may be renewed for additional two periods of no more than two years each,[510] whereas exploitation authorizations for no more than twenty-five years.[511] Renewal of research authorizations depends on fulfilling the obligations deriving from the granted authorization and submitting a relevant application at least two months prior to the expiration thereof.[512] However, the Council of Ministers may decide on the renewal despite not fulfilling said obligations, if it deems it proper.[513] In every renewal of research authorization, the holder releases at

492. Section 14(2) *ibid.*
493. Section 14(3) *ibid.*
494. Section 13(1)(a) *ibid.*
495. Section 13(1)(b) *ibid.*
496. Section 13(1)(c) *ibid.*
497. Section 13(1)(d) *ibid.*
498. Section 13(1)(e) *ibid.*
499. Section 13(1)(f) *ibid.*
500. Section 13(1)(g) *ibid.*
501. Section 13(1)(h) *ibid.*
502. Section 13(1)(i) *ibid.*
503. Section 13(1)(j) *ibid.*
504. Section 13(1)(k) *ibid.*
505. Section 13(1)(l) *ibid.*
506. Section 13(2) *ibid.*
507. Section 13(3) *ibid.*
508. Section 15 *ibid.*
509. Regulation 8 KDP 51/2007.
510. Regulation 9(1) *ibid.*
511. Regulation 11(1) *ibid.*
512. Regulation 11(2) *ibid.*
513. Regulation 11(4) *ibid.*

least 25% of the initial area authorized,[514] whereas, upon the termination of the second renewal, the holder releases all areas authorized. Still, areas included in exploitation authorization are not to be released.[515] In the terms and conditions of the authorization, it may also be foreseen that in case the research activities relating to discovery are in progress and are not completed until the expiration of the authorization, the holder may apply for an extension of no more than six months with the Council of Ministers.[516] Lastly, exploitation authorizations may be renewed for an additional period of ten years.[517]

108. The specific terms and conditions are negotiated between the Minister and the authorization holder. In the event of successful negotiations, the text of the contract is submitted to the Council of Ministers for approval. As soon as this is approved and signed by the two parties, the relevant authorization is granted.[518]

The authorization holder is not necessarily the person who shall conduct the authorized activities. In fact, the authorization holder or the Council of Ministers appoints an operator ('φορέας εκμετάλλευσης')[519] that being the entity appointed by the authorization holder or the authorizing authority to conduct offshore oil and gas operations, including planning and executing a well operation or managing and controlling the functions of a production installation.[520] The operator bears a series of duties and responsibilities, apart and distinct from the authorization holder. Most importantly, he has the duty to ensure that he takes all suitable and sufficient measures to prevent major accidents caused by offshore oil and natural gas operations.[521] In the event of a major accident, operators have to take all proper measures to limit its effects on human health and the environment.[522] At all times, operators have to ensure that offshore oil and gas operations are carried out on the basis of systematic risk management so that the residual risks of major accidents to persons, the environment and offshore installations are acceptable.[523] If the authorization holder intends to appoint an operator, he needs to inform in advance the Council of Ministers, which does have the right to object to such an appointment. While deliberating on expressing an objection, the Council of Ministers may, if it deems it necessary, consult the Director of the Department of Labour Inspection on grounds related to the Regulations on Safety and Health (Safety of Offshore Oil and Gas

514. Regulation 10(1) *ibid.*
515. Regulation 10(2) *ibid.*
516. Regulation 11(3) *ibid.*
517. Regulation 11(1) *ibid.*
518. Regulation 7 *ibid.*
519. Section 15A(1) Law No. 4(I)/2007.
520. Section 2 *ibid.* and Reg. 2 Regulations on Safety and Health (Safety of Offshore Oil and Gas Operations) of 2015 ('Οι περί Ασφάλειας και Υγείας στην Εργασία (Ασφάλεια των Υπεράκτιων Εργασιών Πετρελαίου και Φυσικού Αερίου) Κανονισμοί') No. 424 of 2015, OG I(III) No. 4911, 11 Dec. 2015, p. 2513 (hereinafter 'KDP 424/2015'), which corresponds to Art. 2(5) Directive 2013/30/EU of the European Parliament and of the Council of 12 Jun. 2013 on safety of offshore oil and gas operations, OJ L 178, 28 Jun. 2013, p. 66.
521. Regulation 7(1) KDP 424/2015, which corresponds to Art. 3(1) Directive 2013/30/EU.
522. Regulation 7(3) KDP 424/2015, which corresponds to Art. 3(3) Directive 2013/30/EU.
523. Regulation 7(4) KDP 424/2015, which corresponds to Art. 3(4) Directive 2013/30/EU.

Operations) of 2015.[524] In such an event, the Council of Ministers asks the authorization holder to appoint another appropriate operator or to take over the duties of the operator set out in said safety and health regulations of 2015.[525] Lastly, the ability of the operator to fulfil the duties set in the same regulations is periodically reviewed ex officio by the Director of the Department of Labour Inspection.[526] The Minister is informed in this regard and, if he deems it proper, instructs the authorization holder to take the necessary measures for compliance with the same regulations.[527] Then the authorization holder bears the responsibility for fulfilling the relevant duties and without any delay suggests a deputy operator, who is then appointed under the condition that he is previously approved by the Council of Ministers.[528]

B. Obligations of Authorization Holders

109. Authorization holders bear statutory obligations. The first set of obligations relates to the way the authorized activities are performed. In particular, hydrocarbon activities are to be performed in a due and safe manner and in accordance with the prevailing working practices and the good practice of hydrocarbons. The authorization holder has to comply with labour legislation, as well as legislation on safety and health at work.[529] He must further ensure that material, equipment, construction and facilities used by him or by sub-contractors comply with generally accepted standards in the international oil industry are duly constructed and are kept in good condition.[530] He is obliged to use natural resources as productively as possible[531] and prevent damages in the discovered reserve while ensuring that hydrocarbons, sludge or other liquids or substances do not escape and are not being dumped.[532] The authorization holder must further prevent damage to nearby hydrocarbon reserves and water-bearing strata. Equally, he has to prevent water from entering into any hydrocarbon reserves but for any such method for secondary extraction or in accordance with international standards of the oil industry.[533] He is also obliged to store hydrocarbons in vessels designed for this purpose. Crude oil is not to be stored in soil tanks, except for cases of emergency in a temporary manner.[534] Lastly, the provisions of Law on Solid and Dangerous Waste[535] need to be taken into consideration by the authorization holder.[536]

524. Section 15A(2) Law No. 4(I)/2007.
525. Section 15A(3) *ibid.*
526. Section 15A(5) *ibid.*
527. Section 15A(6) *ibid.*
528. Section 15A(7) *ibid.*
529. Regulation 13(1) KDP 51/2007.
530. Regulation 13(2)(a) *ibid.*
531. Regulation 13(2)(b) *ibid.*
532. Regulation 13(2)(c) *ibid.*
533. Regulation 13(2)(d) *ibid.*
534. Regulation 13(2)(e) *ibid.*
535. Law on Solid and Dangerous Waste ('περί Στερεών και Επικίνδυνων Αποβλήτων Νόμος') No. 215 of 2002, OG I(I) No. 3666, 27 Dec. 2002, p. 3375, has been repealed by Law on Waste ('περί Αποβλήτων Νόμος') No. 185 of 2011, OG I(I) No. 4313, 23 Dec. 2011, p. 1531, which according

110. The second set of obligations relates to environmental protection. Generally, it must be ensured that hydrocarbon activities are performed in an environmentally acceptable and safe manner that is compatible with environmental legislation in force and good practices of the oil industry. In this regard, effective control must be exercised.[537] More specifically, prior to initiating any offshore works, they must acquire the licence set out in Article 4 of the Protocol for the Protection of the Mediterranean Sea against pollution resulting from exploration and exploitation of the continental shelf and the seabed and its subsoil.[538] In addition, all necessary measures need to be taken in order to restrict to a minimum all environmental pollution or damage to water, soil and air in relation to hydrocarbon activities.[539] These measures and methods, which adhere to relevant international standards, are agreed in advance with the Minister at the beginning of hydrocarbon activities or at any significant change in the performance of said activities.[540] Obligations deriving from the International Convention on Civil Liability for Oil Pollution Damage of 1969[541] must also be met.[542] In the event that the holder fails to comply with these obligations and pollution is caused to water, soil or air, he has to take all reasonable and necessary measures to restrict or eliminate such pollution.[543] Should any works or activities performed by authorization holders or any facilities built by the same endangered persons or property or pollute the environment, flora, fauna or marine organisms at a non-acceptable level, the Minister may ask the authorization holder to take corrective measures and rehabilitate the environmental damage. The possibility of said danger and pollution may equally lead to such an order. Said corrective measures have to be taken within a reasonable time period, as this will be considered proper by the Minister. Under the circumstances and at the discretion of the Minister, suspension of the authorization may be decided by the

---

to its preamble implements the following directives: Council Directive 96/59/EC of 16 Sep. 1996 on the disposal of polychlorinated biphenyls and polychlorinated terphenyls (PCB/PCT), OJ L 243, 24 Sep. 1996, p. 31; Council Directive 1999/31/EC of 26 Apr. 1999 on the landfill of waste, OJ L 182, 16 Jul. 1999, p. 1; Directive 2002/96/EC of the European Parliament and of the Council of 27 Jan. 2003 on waste electrical and electronic equipment (WEEE), OJ L 037, 13 Feb. 2003, p. 24; Directive 2006/66/EC of the European Parliament and of the Council of 6 Sep. 2006 on batteries and accumulators and waste batteries and accumulators, OJ L 266, 26 Sep. 2006, p. 1; Directive 2008/98/EC of the European Parliament and of the Council of 19 Nov. 2008 on waste, OJ L 312, 22 Nov. 2008, p. 3; and Directive 2011/65/EU of the European Parliament and of the Council of 8 Jun. 2011 on the restriction of the use of certain hazardous substances in electrical and electronic equipment (recast), OJ L 174, 1 Jul. 2011, p. 88.

536. Regulation 13(2)(f) KDP 51/2007.
537. Regulation 15(1) *ibid.*
538. Section 11A Law No. 4(I)/2007, which corresponds to recital No. 51 to the preamble of Directive 2013/30/EU.
539. Regulation 15(2)(a) KDP 51/2007.
540. Regulation 15(5) *ibid.*
541. It should be noted that this has been replaced by the International Convention of 27 Nov. 1992 on Civil Liability for Oil Pollution Damage. The latter has been signed and ratified by Cyprus (OG I(III) No. 3150, 19 May 1997, p. 825).
542. Regulation 15(2)(b) KDP 51/2007.
543. Regulation 15(3) *ibid.*

Council of Ministers following a proposal of the Minister until all corrective measures and rehabilitation of environmental damage have been taken.[544]

111. A further set of obligations relate to facilities, pipes and relevant equipment. The authorization holder must maintain and repair all construction, equipment and other facilities used for hydrocarbon activities, which are situated within the area for which authorization was granted.[545] During offshore works, the authorization holder ensures that according to the practice of the international oil industry and relevant legislation and regulations, constructions and facilities that shall be erected are constructed, situated, marked, equipped and maintained in order to provide safe and proper routes of sea navigation.[546] Provisions of relevant international conventions must be applied.[547] They must also be maintained in a good functional condition,[548] so they may not obstruct navigation and fishery or pollute the sea or rivers.[549] No authorization holder may construct, convert or operate pipelines, pumping stations, storage areas or any other facility for hydrocarbon transport or storage from the authorized area without a written application to the Minister and approval thereof.[550] This application must contain information on proposed planning and construction of pipelines, pumping station, storage room or other facilities,[551] on the suggested work programme, budget, available technical and financial resources for construction, conversion or operation of the pipeline, pumping station, storage area or other relevant facilities[552] and on proposed laying of pipelines and placing of the said constructions.[553] The Minister may order the construction of common facilities, including pipelines, storage, communication and other transport facilities, for separate areas of different authorizations on the grounds of public interest.[554] In such an event, authorization holders take all necessary measures for reaching an agreement on the construction of joint facilities and inform the Minister every fifteen days of the progress of negotiations. If no agreement is reached within three months, the Minister may bring this matter to mediation.[555]

112. A certain set of obligations arises upon expiration of the authorization or the termination thereof. In such a case the authorization holder must remove equipment, facilities, constructions, laboratories, appliances, mechanisms and pipelines

544. Regulation 15(4) *ibid.*
545. Regulation 19(1) *ibid.*
546. Regulation 19(2)(a) *ibid.*
547. These are International Convention for the Prevention of Pollution from Ships (MARPOL) of 1973 (Convention), 1978 (1978 Protocol) and resolutions MEPC 14(20) of 1984, MEPC 16(22) and MEPC 21(22) of 1985, http://www.imo.org/ (ratified in Cyprus by the relevant law published in: OG I(III) No. 3489, 12 Apr. 2001, p. 869).
548. Regulation 19(2)(c) KDP 51/2007.
549. Regulation 19(2)(d) *ibid.*
550. Regulation 19(3) *ibid.*
551. Regulation 19(4)(a) *ibid.*
552. Regulation 19(4)(b) *ibid.*
553. Regulation 19(4)(c) *ibid.*
554. Regulation 19(5)(a) *ibid.*
555. Regulation 19(5)(b) *ibid.*

from the area, according to the Abandonment Plan in the Contract.[556] He must fur ther perform all necessary rehabilitation actions according to the good practice c the international oil industry and take all necessary measures to avert endangermen of human lives, properties or the environment.[557] To this respect, the Minister ma instruct authorization holders to deposit a guarantee or to establish a fund for th purpose of covering expenses in case of abandonment and rehabilitation of areas.[55

113. Following a set of obligations relates to information. Every authorizatio holder must acquire, operate and maintain equipment to measure the quantity an quality of hydrocarbons produced and stored.[559] Prior to the operation of this equip ment, it must be approved by the Minister.[560] Said measurements are performed i the method(s) usually used in the international oil industry, whereas the Ministe must approve the necessary frequency and methods.[561] Further, two days prior t measurement, the authorization holder informs the Minister, and an authorized civi servant may be present during performance thereof.[562] Measurement equipment an machines are available for inspection and tests by authorized public servants at an reasonable time, without obstructing the proper operation of related facilities.[56 Should during such an inspection be established that the measurement procedur performed was inaccurate, this inaccuracy is deemed to have been effective for al the period since the last inspection or test, unless proved otherwise. Authorizatio holders perform necessary adjustments within thirty days of the establishment o such inaccuracy.[564]

114. In addition, every authorization holder is obliged to keep precise records or the areas, where geological or geophysical activities took place,[565] on exact geo logical maps and plans, geophysical archives and relevant interpretations,[566] or drilling, including operation, deepening, sealing and abandonment,[567] on layers o peat and subsoil drilled,[568] on shield of the drilling,[569] on any discovered hydrocar bons, water and other minerals or dangerous substances[570] and on any other matte specified in the contract or deemed proper by the Minister.[571] Exact records o hydrocarbon production must also be kept by the authorization holder. These state

556. Regulation 16(1)(a) *ibid.*
557. Regulation 16(1)(b) *ibid.*
558. Regulation 16(2) *ibid.*
559. Regulation 20(1)(a) *ibid.*
560. Regulation 20(1)(b) *ibid.*
561. Regulation 20(2) *ibid.*
562. Regulation 20(3) *ibid.*
563. Regulation 20(4) *ibid.*
564. Regulation 20(5) *ibid.*
565. Regulation 22(1)(a) *ibid.*
566. Regulation 22(1)(b) *ibid.*
567. Regulation 22(1)(c) *ibid.*
568. Regulation 22(1)(d) *ibid.*
569. Regulation 22(1)(e) *ibid.*
570. Regulation 22(1)(f) *ibid.*
571. Regulation 22(1)(g) *ibid.*

the total amount of crude oil and natural gas produced and stored,[572] the quality, specific weight and composition of crude oil and the composition of natural gas produced,[573] the amount of oil, natural gas and sulphur of any kind being disposed, the consideration received and the details of the person who purchased it,[574] the amount of crude oil, natural gas and other liquids or gases passed in geological formation,[575] the amount of crude oil and natural gas consumed during production,[576] the amount of crude oil being refined[577] and of natural gas being processed[578] or burned[579] and any other information foreseen in the contract or reasonably demanded in writing by the Minister.[580]

115. Generally, the Minister may ask the authorization holders to provide information on existing or foreseen supply sources, on obligations deriving from the granted authorizations or any other matter considered necessary by the Minister. This can be done only if it is justified on grounds of public morality ('δημόσια ηθική'),[581] public order ('δημόσια τάξη'),[582] public security,[583] protection of human health and life, as well as of flora and fauna,[584] protection of state treasures of artistic, historical or archaeological value,[585] protection of industrial and commercial property[586] and national and international laws.[587] In particular, authorization holders communicate to the Minister all important developments regarding the course of hydrocarbon activities.[588] They submit copies of geological, geophysical and other technical reports, registrations of drillings, maps, diagrams, magnetic strips, electronically or otherwise stored data, reports and interpretations prepared

572. Regulation 24(1)(a) *ibid.*
573. Regulation 24(1)(b) *ibid.*
574. Regulation 24(1)(c) *ibid.*
575. Regulation 24(1)(d) *ibid.*
576. Regulation 24(1)(e) *ibid.*
577. Regulation 24(1)(f) *ibid.*
578. Regulation 24(1)(g) *ibid.*
579. Regulation 24(1)(h) *ibid.*
580. Regulation 24(1)(i) *ibid.*
581. Section 17(a) Law No. 4(I)/2007. The term 'public morality' (in French 'moralité publique', in German 'öffentliche Sittlichkeit' and in Dutch 'openbare zedelijkheid') has its origins in EU law. It has been held that Member States are free to establish their own standards of public morality in accordance with its own scale of values and in the form selected by it the requirements of public morality in its territory. However, this may not justify restrictions on the free movement of goods (Case 121/85, *Conegate Limited v. HM Customs & Excise* [1986] ECR 1007, paras 14, 15).
582. Section 17(b) Law No. 4(I)/2007. The term 'public order' (in French 'l'ordre public', in German 'öffentliche Ordnung' and in Dutch 'openbare orde') equally has its origins in EU law. It has been settled that this requires a genuine and sufficiently serious threat affecting one of the fundamental interests of society (*see* Case 30/77, *R v. Bouchereau* [1977] ECR I-1999, para. 36; Case C-114/97, *Commission v. Spain* [1998] ECR I-6717, para. 47; Case C-348/96, *Calfa* [1999] ECR I-11, para. 21; Case C-476/98, *Commission of the European Communities v. Federal Republic of Germany* [2002] ECR I-09855, para. 158).
583. Section 17(c) Law No. 4(I)/2007.
584. Section 17(d) *ibid.*
585. Section 17(e) *ibid.*
586. Section 17(f) *ibid.*
587. Section 17(g) *ibid.*
588. Regulation 23(1) KDP 51/2007.

by or on behalf of the authorization holder, as soon as these are done.[589] The same applies to representative geological samples, including duly marked rock cores and fragments from all performed drillings.[590] Every six months, the Minister is informed of a summary of all geological and geophysical activities and their results,[591] a summary of all drilling activities and relevant results[592] and a catalogue of maps, reports and other geological and geophysical information prepared by or on behalf of the authorization holder regarding this period.[593] Every year, the Minister receives a report on the results of hydrocarbon activities performed by the authorization holder within this period[594] and on estimations of the amount of financial marketable crude oil and natural gas.[595] Within six months, the authorization holder submits a summary of research drilling performed. Should this not be possible in this period, it can be done after the lapse thereof, however, as soon as possible.[596] Lastly, any other available information, data, reports, evaluations and interpretations on hydrocarbon activities that the Minister may reasonably demand is communicated to the same.[597]

116. Certain restrictions apply to the information described above. Original registers, magnetic strips and electronically or otherwise stored files may not be transported abroad unless this is authorized by the Minister,[598] whereas the ownership of all information and data belongs to the state.[599] In addition, the Minister has access to original files, magnetic strips and electronically or otherwise stored files and he may request two copies of those from the authorization holder without any charge.[600] The authorization holder may keep the originals after the expiration of the contract, only if a relevant proviso is foreseen therein.[601]

117. Joint exploitation of hydrocarbons introduces certain obligations. This is the case of activities of extracting hydrocarbons, being performed at present or future time in a certain authorized area where hydrocarbon reserves exist as long as these reserves extend into another. The latter area must be further included in the authorization of a different person, who currently performs or shall perform hydrocarbon extraction activities. The authorization of the latter area may have been granted by a different state.[602] When these prerequisites are fulfilled, the authorization holders involved may enter into an agreement regarding joint exploitation only

589. Regulation 23(2)(a)(i) *ibid.*
590. Regulation 23(2)(a)(ii) *ibid.*
591. Regulation 23(2)(b)(i) *ibid.*
592. Regulation 23(2)(b)(ii) *ibid.*
593. Regulation 23(2)(b)(iii) *ibid.*
594. Regulation 23(2)(c)(i) *ibid.*
595. Regulation 23(2)(c)(ii) *ibid.*
596. Regulation 23(2)(d) *ibid.*
597. Regulation 23(2)(e) *ibid.*
598. Regulation 23(3) *ibid.*
599. Regulation 23(4) *ibid.*
600. Regulation 23(5) *ibid.*
601. Regulation 23(6) *ibid.*
602. Regulation 21(1) *ibid.*

if the said agreement has been submitted and approved by the Minister.[603] Negotiations for reaching such an agreement within a certain period of time can be initiated on the parties' own initiative or by an invitation of the Minister.[604] In the event that no agreement has been reached within this time period or that an agreement was reached but not communicated to the Minister, he may give notice to the authorization holder to submit an action plan on joint exploitation of hydrocarbons within a specific time period.[605] Should hydrocarbon reserves extend beyond the exclusive economic zone of Cyprus, relevant international agreements[606] are applied.[607]

C. *Obligations of the Minister*

118. The Minister is obliged to communicate to the European Commission information on hydrocarbon activities on a yearly basis. This includes information on the geographical areas which have been opened for prospecting, exploration and production, authorizations granted, entities holding authorizations and the composition thereof and the estimated reserves contained in Cyprus.[608] The same information is published in the OG.

119. The Minister also informs the European Commission of any general difficulty encountered, de jure or de facto, by entities in access to or exercise of the activities of prospecting, exploring for and producing hydrocarbons in third countries, which have been brought to their attention.[609] Persons engaged in hydrocarbon activities may provide to the Minister or any authorized public officer relevant information.[610]

V. Especially Drilling

120. Specific and much detailed provisions are foreseen for drilling activities. Every authorization holder ensures that drilling planning and performance of such activities correlate to the generally accepted practice of the international oil industry.[611] Every drilling is recognized by name, number and geographical coordinates presented in maps, plans and relevant records that authorization holders are obliged to keep. They are further obliged to inform the Minister of any change thereof.[612]

603. Regulation 21(2) *ibid.*
604. Regulation 21(3) *ibid.*
605. Regulation 21(4) *ibid.*
606. All treaties that Cyprus has entered into are listed in, http://www.olc.gov.cy/olc/olc.nsf/inttreatiesarch_el/inttreatiesarch_el?openDocument.
607. Regulation 21(5) KDP 51/2007.
608. Section 18 Law No. 4(I)/2007, which corresponds to Art. 9 Directive 94/22/EC. The directive in addition clarifies that no information of a commercially confidential nature need to be published.
609. Section 29(2) Law No. 4(I)/2007, which corresponds to Art. 8(1) Directive 94/22/EC.
610. Section 29(1) Law No. 4(I)/2007.
611. Regulation 17(1) KDP 51/2007.
612. Regulation 17(2) *ibid.*

121. At least seven days prior to initiation of any drilling or other activity in drilling or restart of drilling or other activity that has been suspended for more than six months, authorization holders forward to the Minister a written communication.[613] This includes the name and number of the drilling,[614] a description of the precise location with reference to the geographical coordinates,[615] a detailed report on the drilling method, estimated time and depth, material and safety measures to be used[616] and a report on the location of the drilling, the geological and geophysical data and interpretations due to which the specific location was chosen.[617] In addition to this communication, an emergency plan for hydrocarbon leaks and fire is prepared and submitted to the Minister for approval. This plan is to be implemented should such an event arise.[618] Should any other emergency event or accident that affects the environment occur, the authorization holder takes reasonable and necessary measures in accordance with the generally accepted practice of the international oil industry.[619] If the authorization holder fails to take such measures, the Minister may order their implementation and retrieve the costs from the authorization holder.[620]

122. The Minister is equally informed in writing when any drilling or other activity is disrupted for a period of more than thirty days.[621] Should the disruption or other related activity last for more than thirty days but less than six months, authorization holders need to inform the Minister at least two days prior to restarting those.[622] In particular, intended drillings at a location of less than 200 metres from the limits of the authorized area require prior written approval by the Minister under the terms and conditions specified therein.[623]

123. Abandonment of drillings gives rise to further obligations. Prior to any such abandonment, authorization holders must inform in writing the Minister of their intention. The relevant time period is thirty days in case of production drilling and two days in case of any other drilling. This information includes a full programme and time-schedule for abandonment and sealing of the drill.[624] The authorization holder may initiate abandonment upon the lapse of the relevant time period or upon receiving the approval of the Minister, whichever takes place sooner.[625] In particular, the authorization holder must seal the drilling in order to avoid pollution and probable damage to the reservoir and to remove any relevant equipment, material and facilities unless a different proviso is included in the contract or the Minister

613. Regulation 17(3) *ibid.*
614. Regulation 17(3)(a) *ibid.*
615. Regulation 17(3)(b) *ibid.*
616. Regulation 17(3)(c) *ibid.*
617. Regulation 17(3)(d) *ibid.*
618. Regulation 17(6)(a) *ibid.*
619. Regulation 17(6)(b) *ibid.*
620. Regulation 17(7) *ibid.*
621. Regulation 17(4) *ibid.*
622. Regulation 17(5) *ibid.*
623. Regulation 17(6) *ibid.*
624. Regulation 18(1) *ibid.*
625. Regulation 18(2) *ibid.*

reaches a relevant decision.[626] He must also ensure that cemented cables or other forms of the shield are to be removed only under prior written approval of the Minister.[627] Any authorized public servant may inspect abandonment works.[628]

VI. Transfer of Authorization and Assignment of Rights

124. Authorization can be transferred, and relevant rights can be assigned, under the condition that approval of the Council of Ministers has been given.[629] In particular, a relevant written application is submitted to the Minister.[630] This application includes the name and citizenship of the intended transferee as well as the place of incorporation and the principal place of business if the transferee is a legal person.[631] Documentation proving its technical and financial ability to cover contractual obligations and other commitments also needs to be provided,[632] along with any agreement related to financing hydrocarbon activities.[633] The intended transferee must lastly declare in writing its unconditional consent to assume the obligations of the authorization holder,[634] as well as any further information the Minister may reasonably demand.[635] Should the authorization holder not submit the additional information within the specified time, the application is deemed to be withdrawn.[636]

125. The Minister evaluates this application and forwards a proposal to the Council of Ministers.[637] While discussing whether such approval may be given, the Council of Ministers considers national security[638] and qualities of the person to whom the authorization is intended to be transferred or the rights to be assigned. These include technical knowledge, experience and financial resources for ensuring proper performance of prospection, research and exploitation of hydrocarbons.[639] The willingness of the same person to comply with any terms and conditions which the Council of Ministers may wish to impose is also regarded.[640]

126. With reference to the legal effect of a transfer of authorization and assignment of rights, it must be noted that the previous authorization holder is not freed from any liability that was due before the transfer or assignment. In addition, he is also liable for the due performance of the contractual obligations by the transferee

626. Regulation 18(3)(a) *ibid.*
627. Regulation 18(3)(b) *ibid.*
628. Regulation 18(3)(c) *ibid.*
629. Section 27(1) Law No. 4(I)/2007.
630. Regulation 12(1) KDP 51/2007.
631. Regulation 12(2)(a) *ibid.*
632. Regulation 12(2)(b) *ibid.*
633. Regulation 12(2)(c) *ibid.*
634. Regulation 12(2)(d) *ibid.*
635. Regulation 12(2)(e) *ibid.*
636. Regulation 12(3) *ibid.*
637. Regulation 12(1) *ibid.*
638. Section 27(1)(a) Law No. 4(I)/2007.
639. Section 27(1)(b) *ibid.*
640. Section 27(1)(c) *ibid.*

unless otherwise foreseen in the contract.[641] Hence, any court proceedings agains the previous authorization holder may be continued or initiated regardless of an transfer or assignment.[642]

VII. Refusal of Authorization

127. The Council of Ministers may refuse to grant authorization under the condition that it does not discriminate.[643] Such a refusal must be reasoned.[644] A refusa ground can constitute the fact that the applicant is effectively controlled by thir countries or third-country nationals under the condition that this third country is nc granting entities of Cyprus or of the EU, as regards access to or exercise of prospecting, exploring for and producing hydrocarbons, treatment comparable to tha which Cyprus or the EU grants entities from that third country with reference to th same activities. For this ground to be effective, it must be approved by the European Council.[645]

128. Against such refusal, the addressee may lodge an appeal with the Suprem Court of Cyprus requesting its annulment pursuant to Article 146 of the Constitution, in view of the fact that said refusal constitutes an administrative act that negatively affects the addressee.

§4. State Participation in Activities of Hydrocarbons' Prospection, Research and Exploitation

129. Contribution of authorization holders may be in money or in hydrocarbons This is specified by the Council of Ministers that must, in any case, ensure management independence of the authorization holders.[646] Management of the state participation in activities of hydrocarbons' prospection, research and exploitation is rur either by the state or by a legal person appointed by the Council of Ministers.[647] Ir the event that issuance of authorization depends on state participation and at th same time a legal person has been incorporated solely for the purpose of managing such participation, the state underlies certain obligations. It may not be informed or

641. Regulation 12(4) KDP 51/2007.
642. Regulation 12(5) *ibid.*
643. Section 12(4) Law No. 4(I)/2007.
644. Section 12(5) *ibid.*
645. Section 29(3) *ibid.*, which corresponds to Art. 8(3) and (4) Directive 94/22/EC. This European provision, which originates from Art. 9 of the proposed directive of 11 May 1992, aims to establishing a procedure for evaluation and initiating negotiations with third countries and not blocking third countries from obtaining authorizations (Commission of the European Communities, Proposal for a Council Directive on the conditions for granting and using authorizations for the prospection exploration and extraction of hydrocarbons, dd. 11 May 1992, COM(92) 110 final, para. 27, http:/ eur-lex.europa.eu/).
646. Sections 16(2) and 13(1)(b) Law No. 4(I)/2007.
647. Section 16(1) *ibid.*

anything relating to supply commissions of the authorization holder and have voting rights related to such commissions[648] or majority voting rights in combination with any public bodies.[649] Its vote must be based only on transparent, non-discriminatory and objective principles. In addition, it may not hinder that relevant administrative decisions are based on usual commercial principles.[650] Should the state not adhere to these obligations, it may be prohibited from enjoying the rights and carrying the obligations associated with said participation.[651] However, the state or the legal person managing state participation may in any case object to any decision of the authorization holder in violation of the terms and conditions of the authorization regarding exhaustion of reserves and protection of state financial interests. Such an objection must still respect non-discrimination unless national legislation and international legitimacy are violated.[652]

130. Should the management of state participation be performed by a legal person who also holds the relevant authorizations, two specific obligations are foreseen in the law. First, the legal person has to keep separate accounts for its commercial capacity and its capacity for managing state participation.[653] Further, no flow of information may take place between the part of this person managing state participation and the one holding the authorization.[654] In the case, however, that the first part is being advised by the latter, it may provide information that is necessary for the performance of its duties as an advisor. Any authorization holders related to the said information are previously informed of its content. Should they have any objections to such communication, these may be filed with the Minister, who after hearing the views of both sides reaches a decision.[655]

§5. Confidentiality

131. Any information data compiled and used by an authorized public servant is deemed to be confidential in the meaning of the Law on Statistics.[656,657] All accounts, reports, plans, data and other information submitted to the Minister fall under the meaning of information. These are not to be revealed to third parties prior to abandonment of the area, to which they are related or alternatively expiration of

648. Section 16(3)(a) *ibid.*
649. Section 16(3)(b) *ibid.*
650. Section 16(3)(c) *ibid.*
651. Section 16(3) *ibid.*
652. Section 16(4) *ibid.*
653. Section 16(5)(a) *ibid.*
654. Section 16(5)(b) *ibid.*
655. Section 16(6) *ibid.*
656. Law on Statistics ('περί Στατιστικής Νόμος') No. 15 of 2000, OG I(I) No. 3386, 4 Feb. 2000, p. 59.
657. Section 20(1) *ibid.*

the research period unless the contract contains a different proviso.[658] Also, authorization holders may not publish or communicate any information kept or submitted to authorities in accordance with this legislation without the prior written consent of the Minister.[659]

132. It should be noted that confidentiality is not effective, when the person responsible for management, function, maintenance or keeping of the building or facilities, where research, examinations, tests, controls, inspections and investigations are given, consents in writing.[660] Equally, no confidentiality may be invoked before a court,[661] a Commission of Inquiry ('Ερευνητική Επιτροπή') appointed and functioning in accordance with Law on Commissions of Inquiry,[662,663] an examining magistrate ('ποινικός ανακριτής'),[664,665] the Unit for Combating Money Laundering ('Μονάδα Καταπολέμησης Αδικημάτων Συγκάλυψης'),[666] and the Commission for the Protection of Competition ('Επιτροπή Προστασίας Ανταγωνισμού').[667] In addition, any geological charts and interpretations may be used at any time by the competent authorities of Cyprus for the creation of official maps[668] and yearly statistical data may be published at any time by the state, as long as the activities of certain authorization holders are not made public.[669] The state

658. Regulation 26(1) KDP 51/2007.
659. Regulation 26(3) *ibid.*
660. Section 20(2)(a) Law No. 4(I)/2007.
661. Section 20(2)(b) *ibid.*
662. A Law to enable the Governor to appoint Commissions of Enquiry with Special Powers ('Cap. 44') No. 8 of 1942, CG No. 2993, 14 May 1942, p. 109, as amended.
663. Section 20(2)(c) Law No. 4(I)/2007.
664. He is appointed in accordance with the relevant provisions of Cap. 155.
665. Section 20(2)(d) Law No. 4(I)/2007.
666. Section 20(2)(e) *ibid.* This Unit is established for the purpose of seeing to the application of Law on the Prevention and Suppression of Money Laundering and Terrorist Financing ('περί της Παρεμπόδισης και Καταπολέμησης της Νομιμοποίησης Εσόδων από Παράνομες Δραστηριότητες Νόμος') No. 188 of 2007, OG I(I) No. 4154, 31 Dec. 2007, p. 1715, as last amended by Law on the Prevention and Suppression of Money Laundering and Terrorist Financing (Amendment) ('περί της Παρεμπόδισης και Καταπολέμησης Εσόδων από Παράνομες Δραστηριότητες (Τροποποιητικός) Νόμος'), No. 81 of 2019, OG I(I) No. 4708, 31 May 2019, p. 499, which implements Directive 2005/60/EC of the European Parliament and of the Council of 26 Oct. 2005 on the prevention of the use of the financial system for the purpose of money laundering and terrorist financing, OJ L 309, 25 Nov. 2005, p. 15, as amended. Hence relevant case law of the Court of Justice of the EU is of importance for its interpretation, that being Case C-212/11, *Jyske Bank Gibraltar Ltd v. Administración del Estado*, digital ECR (*see* Steck, Kai-Uwe, *Rechtsunsicherheit in Kollisionsfällen kann Rückzug von Banken aus bestimmten Zielstaaten zur Folge haben*, 68 BB 1684 (2013); Lecocq, Arnaud, *Arrêt 'Jyske Bank Gibraltar': le contrôle exercé sur la libre prestation de services financiers au titre de la lutte contre le terrorisme et le blanchiment de capitaux*, 14 J.D.E. 231 (2013); Incalza, Thomas, *De meldingsplicht wegens witwassen ten aanzien van de ontvangstlidstaat in het licht van de vrijheid van dienstverrichting: een Spaanse armada tussen droom en daad?*, 78 RW 1362 (2014)); Case C-235/14, *Safe Interenvíos, S.A. v. Liberbank, S.A. and Others*, digital ECR; Case C-668/15, *Jyske Finans A/S v. Ligebehandlingsnævnet, acting on behalf of Ismar Huskic*, digital ECR.
667. Section 20(2)(f) Law No. 4(I)/2007.
668. Regulation 26(2)(a) KDP 51/2007.
669. Regulation 26(2)(b) *ibid.*

may further communicate at any time accounts, reports, plans, data and other information to counsels, lawyers, legal advisors, accountants, creditors, state authorities and organizations and legal persons governed by public law if this is deemed necessary.[670] Authorization holders may on their part communicate any information to the same persons, as long as the latter has the right to be informed thereof.[671] Any such communication or publication is performed under the condition that this is to be treated and used in confidentiality by the receiver of this information.[672]

133. Breach of confidentiality constitutes a penal offence. In particular, any authorized public servant participating in investigations or controls, who publishes or communicates to a non-authorized person any information that was provided to him with the exercise of his duties without the prior approval of the Minister, commits a criminal offence. In case of conviction, he faces imprisonment of no more than twelve months and/or a fine of no more than EUR 34,200.[673]

§6. MONITORING COMPLIANCE

134. Compliance with the legislation in force and terms and conditions of authorizations is monitored by authorized public servants, whose duties and powers have been set out above. In the event of a breach either by action or by omission, penal and administrative penalties are imposed.

135. More specifically, when a person acts in violation of the law by hindering any authorized public servant from entering into any premises,[674] performing investigations, tests and inspections,[675] keeping copies of any information,[676] doing anything deemed necessary with the aim of enforcing this law[677] or entering and inspecting as foreseen in secondary legislation issued,[678] he commits a crime. Should he be found guilty, he is imprisoned for a period of no more than six months and/or a monetary fine of no more than EUR 17,100 is imposed.[679] In the event of a second or subsequent conviction, he faces imprisonment of no more than twelve months and/or a monetary fine of no more than EUR 34,200.[680] In addition, the Council of Ministers may revoke, suspend or annul the authorization issued.[681]

136. Should any person perform prospection, research or exploitation of hydrocarbons without authorization or in violation of the terms of authorization, he also

670. Regulation 26(2)(c) *ibid.*
671. Regulation 26(4) *ibid.*
672. Regulation 26(5) *ibid.*
673. Section 20(2) Law No. 4(I)/2007.
674. Sections 21(1)(a) and 19(2)(a) *ibid.*
675. Sections 21(1)(b) and 19(2)(b) *ibid.*
676. Sections 21(1)(c) and 19(2)(c) *ibid.*
677. Sections 21(1)(d) and 19(2)(d) *ibid.*
678. Section 21(1)(e) *ibid.*
679. Section 21(2)(a) *ibid.*
680. Section 21(2)(b) *ibid.*
681. Section 23(1) *ibid.*

commits a crime. Should he be convicted, imprisonment of no more than two years and/or a monetary fine of no more than EUR 1,710,000 may be imposed. In the event of second or subsequent conviction imprisonment of no more than four years and/or a fine of no more than EUR 8,550,000 may be ordered.[682] However, no person, releasing hydrocarbons, while legally drilling for freshwater or performing other law-abiding activities, is to be found guilty.[683]

137. Crime is also committed when an authorization holder transfers an authorization or assigns rights without the prior approval of the Council of Ministers. He may be then imprisoned for a period of no more than twelve months and/or requested to pay a monetary fine of no more than EUR 855,000.[684] The same penalties may be imposed on any authorization holder changing his name or the name of the company, as the case may be, or the structure of the same without the prior approval of the Council of Ministers.[685] In particular, no authorization holder may come under the direct or indirect control of a third country or a third-country citizen without the prior approval of the Council of Ministers.[686] In the event that this is done and the accused is convicted, he faces the above-mentioned penalties, those being imprisonment of no more than twelve months and/or a monetary fine of no more than EUR 855,000.[687]

138. In the event that the above-mentioned crimes are committed by legal persons, it is enquired whether this has been performed with the consent or tolerance of its chief executive officer, director, secretary or other officer or if it is due to their negligence. In the affirmative, the relevant natural person(s) is (are) guilty of the crime along with the legal one.[688]

139. Turning to some procedural matters, the competent court is generally established by the rules set out in section 23 Law on Courts.[689] However, the above-mentioned crimes are to be heard exclusively by the President of the Nicosia District Court. He shall also determine the penalties to be imposed in each case.[690] Further, he may order any amount of hydrocarbons acquired as a result of illegal activity, as well as any equipment, machine, vehicle, ship or aeroplane and any construction used, to be confiscated. If it is not possible to confiscate hydrocarbons, he may then order a monetary fine of no less than their value to the convicted person.[691]

---

682. Section 22 *ibid.*
683. Section 24 *ibid.*
684. Section 27(2) *ibid.*
685. Section 5(7)(c) and (d) *ibid.*
686. Section 28(1) *ibid.*
687. Section 28(2) *ibid.*
688. Section 25 *ibid.*
689. Law on Courts ('περί Δικαστηρίων Νόμος') No. 14 of 1969 (OG No. 24, 17 Dec. 1960, p. 83), as amended.
690. Section 32 Law No. 4(I)/2007.
691. Section 26 *ibid.*

140. Administrative fines are imposed by the Minister when any provision of Law No. 4(I)/2007 or secondary legislation issued in accordance with the same is violated. This may amount to less than EUR 427,000, whereas the exact figure depends on the nature, gravity and duration of the violation. In the case of a second or subsequent violation, an administrative fine of no more than EUR 1,710,000 may be imposed.[692] The relevant decision of the Minister is to be duly reasoned and may only be reached if the offender has been heard by the administration or if he has been given the opportunity to communicate his views.[693]

141. Against this decision, an administrative appeal ('ιεραρχική προσφυγή')[694] may be filed in writing within thirty days with the Council of Ministers.[695] This examines the appeal, while it gives the opportunity to the parties to express their views.[696] It may then confirm, annul or amend the appealed decision or issue a new one replacing the same.[697] It is self-evident that the addressee may file an appeal against the decision with the Supreme Court in accordance with Article 146 of the Constitution.

142. Lastly, if the addressee does not pay the imposed fines, the Minister may initiate court proceedings to collect the same as a civil debt owed to the state.[698]

---

692. Section 31(1) *ibid.*
693. Section 31(2) *ibid.*
694. The institution of administrative appeal is common in continental countries. In Greece *ιεραρχική προσφυγή* is regulated in s. 24 Code of Administrative Procedure ('Κώδικας Διοικητικής Διαδικασίας') (Law No. 2690/1999 FEK A 45), whereas the equivalent institution in Germany is the *Widerspruch* (§70 Abs. 1 Satz 1 VwGO).
695. Section 31(3) Law No. 4(I)/2007.
696. Section 31(4) *ibid.*
697. Section 31(5)(a), (b), (c) and (d) *ibid.*
698. Section 31(6) *ibid.*

Chapter 4. Transmission

143. Transmission ('μεταφορά') in relation to electricity stands for transmission of electricity through a transmission system, that being, a system comprise fully or mainly of lines and electrical installations of high-voltage and used for th transmission of electricity from a power plant to a substation or from a power plar to another or from a substation to another or to and from any interconnection or t final customers or to distributors, but does not include supply.[699] In this chapter, th items discussed are concentrated on the issue of transmission and relate to the owne and operator of the transmission system, their duties and obligations, the transmission rules, independence, certification and investment.

§1. Transmission System Owner

144. Transmission System Owner ('Ιδιοκτήτης Συστήματος Μεταφοράς') i the Electricity Authority of Cyprus (EAC) under its capacity as owner of the transmission system.[700] It is obliged to construct and maintain an efficient, coordinated safe, non-hazardous, reliable and economical transmission system according to th ten-year development plan for the transmission system (*see* in this respect paragraphs 159 et seq. below) and the transmission control protocol (*see* in this regar paragraphs 157 et seq. below)[701] demonstrating due care for environmental protection.[702] More specifically, it has the authority to perform works of maintenance an construction pursuant to the ten-year development programme and the terms in th Transmission Control Protocol, as well as of planning and developing assigned to i by the same protocol.[703] In addition, it implements anything further required pursuant to the same ten-year programme and complies with any other relevant reques in accordance with the present legislation with due attention and care for environmental protection.[704] Before implementing measures of said ten-year programm according to the Transmission Control Protocol, it notifies the Transmission Systen Operator and Cyprus Energy Regulatory Authority accordingly within the time limi set by the latter.[705]

699. 'Transport' in French, 'Übertragung' in German, 'transmissie' in Dutch. Section 2(1) Law No 130(I)/2021, which corresponds to Art. 2(34) Directive (EU) 2019/944.
700. Section 2(1) Law No. 130(I)/2021.
701. Transmission Control Protocol ('Πρωτόκολλο Συστήματος Μεταφοράς') is a protocol agreed between the Transmission System Owner and the Transmission System Operator. It includes standard requirements for establishing which assets of the Transmission System Owner shall form the transmission system, provisions for maintenance and development of same system, as well as construction, connection and use of it by third parties. It further provides for information flow betweer owner and operator regarding the development plan, its application and expenses and for rights and obligations relating deactivation and disconnection. It lastly foresees details on insurance coverage of the parties and evaluation of the application of this protocol as well as duration, expiration and renewal thereof (ss 2 and 69(a)–(h) *ibid.*).
702. Section 35 *ibid.*
703. Section 36(a) *ibid.*
704. Section 36(b) *ibid.*
705. Section 36(c) *ibid.*

145. The Transmission System Owner is also bound by two statutory obligations. Firstly, it may neither sell nor take out of service any asset that is part of the transmission system nor mortgage the same without the prior written approval of Cyprus Energy Regulatory Authority.[706] Secondly, it may not function in any way that causes negative discrimination between persons or categories of persons or between users of the system or categories thereof. Especially it may not negatively discriminate to the benefit of its subsidiaries or related undertakings or joint ventures, in which it participates.[707]

146. Finally, the Transmission System Owner has the option to use the transmission system for purposes other than electricity, as long as Cyprus Energy Regulatory Authority and any other competent authority have authorized it in writing. Cyprus Energy Regulatory Authority while exercising its discretion before reaching a decision, must be satisfied that the activity in question neither restricts nor collides with the fulfilment of its obligations as Transmission System Owner set out in the relevant authorization and the fulfilment of the obligations of the Transmission System Operator.[708]

§2. Transmission System Operator

147. The Transmission System Operator ('Διαχειριστής Συστήματος Μεταφοράς Κύπρου') means a legal person who is responsible for operating, ensuring the maintenance of and, if necessary, developing the transmission system and its interconnections with other systems, and for ensuring the long-term ability of the system to meet reasonable demands for the transmission of electricity.[709] It is a legal person governed by public law.[710] The Executive Director of the Transmission System Operator is appointed for a six-year period by the Council of Ministers.[711] During his appointment, an Executive Director may not perform, or in some instances have performed, any of the following: (i) during the last two years prior to its appointment, he has not held any position with a legal person that was authorized to produce or supply electricity; (ii) having a position with a legal person governed by public law the benefits of which are under the control of the state; (iii) being employed by a legal person authorized to perform electricity-related activities, with the exception of retirement benefits, other payments, acquiring any – direct or indirect – interest, shares, bonds or other securities; (iv) holding any office with a political party; (v) accepting an employment offer or maintaining employment with any undertaking in the private sector regardless of payment or its form, as long as payment is reasonably expected.[712] During the same period, he may also neither act in any way that raises doubts regarding the independence of his office,

706. Section 37 *ibid.*
707. Section 38 *ibid.*
708. Section 39(1) & (2) *ibid.*
709. Sections 2(1) and 57 *ibid,* which corresponds to Art. 2(35) Directive (EU) 2019/944.
710. Section 57(1) Law No. 130(I)/2021.
711. Section 57(2) *ibid.*
712. Sections 57(6)(a) to (e) & 60(7)(b) *ibid.*

nor use nor reveal confidential information, unless this is demanded by a public authority or a Court according to the applicable legislation.[713] Further, the Executive Director is entrusted with preparing the budget of the Transmission System Operator that is submitted by the Minister to the Minister of Finance and the Council of Ministers for their approval and ensuing voting by the House of Representatives.[714]

148. The Transmission System Operator has the following specific, statutory foreseen, duties:

- ensuring the long-term ability of the system to meet reasonable demands for the transmission of electricity, operating, maintaining and developing under economic conditions secure, reliable and efficient transmission system with due regard to the environment, in close cooperation with neighbouring transmission system operators and the Distribution System Operator;
- research and promotion of interconnection of the transmission system with other systems following relevant instructions of the Minister and relevant information of Cyprus Energy Regulatory Authority by the Transmission System Operator;
- enquire and promote the implementation of projects of common interest under Regulation (EU) 347/2013 that relate to the transmission system and are located within Cyprus;
- where this is technically and economically feasible with the mode of operation of the high-efficiency cogeneration installation, it is ensured that high-efficiency cogeneration operators offer balancing services and other operational services as well as that such services are part of a services bidding process which is transparent, non-discriminatory and open to scrutiny;
- sign protocols with the Distribution System Operator, with the view to encourage security of operation of the transmission and distribution systems;
- during dispatching, give priority to generating installations that use renewable energy sources and high-efficiency cogeneration and ensure that the energy it uses to cover energy losses and reserve capacity in the system is procured according to transparent, non-discriminatory and market-based procedures pursuant to the terms included in the authorization provided, the Transmission and Distribution Rules and the Electricity Market Rules;
- developing and publicizing procedures for using interconnectors with other transmission and distribution systems, where necessary;
- fees for connection to and use of the transmission system;
- propose terms and conclude protocols or contracts for connection to the transmission system and its use by the persons using or seeking to use said system;
- ensuring adequate means to meet its obligations;
- contributing to security of supply through adequate transmission capacity and system reliability;
- managing electricity flows on the system, taking into account exchanges with other interconnected systems. To that end, the Transmission System Operator

713. Section 60(7)(a) & (c) *ibid.*
714. Section 61(a) *ibid.*

shall be responsible for ensuring a secure, reliable and efficient electricity system and, in that context, for ensuring the availability of all necessary ancillary services, including those provided by demand response and energy storage facilities, insofar as such availability is independent from any other transmission systems with which its system is interconnected;
- providing to the operator of other systems with which its system is interconnected sufficient information to ensure the secure and efficient operation, coordinated development and interoperability of the interconnected system;
- ensuring non-discrimination as between system users or classes of system users, particularly in favour of its related undertakings;
- providing system users with the information they need for efficient access to the system;
- collecting congestion rents and payments under the inter-transmission system operator compensation mechanism, in accordance with Article 49 Regulation (EU) 2019/943, granting and managing third-party access and giving reasoned explanations when it denies such access, which shall be monitored by the regulatory authorities; in carrying out these tasks the Transmission System Operators primarily facilitates market integration;
- procuring ancillary services to ensure operational security;
- adopting a framework for cooperation and coordination between the regional coordination centres;
- participating in the establishment of the European and national resource adequacy assessments pursuant to Chapter IV of Regulation (EU) 2019/943;
- the digitalisation of transmission systems;
- data management, including the development of data management systems, cybersecurity and data protection, subject to the applicable rules, and without prejudice to the competence of other authorities; and
- drafting proper communication and cooperation protocols in cooperation with the Transmission System Operators.[715]

149. Specifically with regard to procuring ancillary services, the Transmission System Operator does so subject to transparent, non-discriminatory and market-based procedures, as well as the participation of all qualified electricity undertakings and market participants, including market participants offering energy from renewable sources, market participants engaged in demand response, operators of energy storage facilities and market participants engaged in aggregation.[716] However, if certain ancillary services are not provided frequently, Cyprus Energy Regulatory Authority may grant a deviation from the aforementioned rule provided it assesses that the market-based provision of non-frequency ancillary services is economically not efficient.[717] Still, this obligation does not apply to fully integrated network components.[718] Specifications for the non-frequency ancillary services

715. Section 70(1) Law No. 130(I)/2021, which partially corresponds to Art. 15(6) Directive 2012/27 and Art. 40(1) Directive 2019/944.
716. Section 62(3) *ibid.*, which corresponds to Art. 40(3) Directive (EU) 2019/944.
717. Section 62(4)(a) Law No. 130(I)/2021, which corresponds to Art. 40(5) Directive (EU) 2019/944.
718. Section 62(6) Law No. 130(I)/2021, which corresponds to Art. 40(7) Directive (EU) 2019/944.

procured and, where appropriate, standardised market products for such services at national level are established in a transparent and participatory process that includes all relevant system users and the Distribution System Operator by the latter subject to approval by Cyprus Energy Regulatory Authority. These specifications shall ensure the effective and non-discriminatory participation of all market participants, including market participants offering energy from renewable sources, market participants engaged in demand response, operators of energy storage facilities and market participants engaged in aggregation.[719]

150. The Transmission System Operator is obliged to not discriminate between persons or classes of persons both with regard to system use and to suggesting terms for system connection works.[720]

151. At the same time, the Transmission System Operator is independent. This independence is safeguarded via statutory rights that are entrusted upon it, as well as via obligations imposed both on it, on the Transmission System Owner and on other persons. At the outset, it is prohibited for the Transmission System Owner to manage or give instructions to the Transmission System Operator with regard to any of its statutory duties.[721] Similarly, it is prohibited for anyone supplying or producing electricity to control, exercise any right or provide consultation to the Transmission System Operator.[722] In the same vein, the Transmission System Operator may not control, exercise any right or provide consultation to anyone producing or supplying electricity.[723] The Transmission System Owner is further obliged to comply with any demands that the Transmission System Operator deems necessary that are essential for performing its duties. This statutory obligation is interpreted in a way so that the terms and conditions set out in the respective authorizations, as well as any protocols and agreements with regard to connection to the transmission system and its use, are not affected.[724] At the same time, the Transmission System Owner is obliged to: exercise its ownership rights in a manner that does not interfere with the performance of the operator's duties; provide any relevant cooperation and support the operator for the performance of the latter's duties, including all relevant information; fund the investment set out in the ten-year development programme of the transmission system or agrees to their funding by a third party, including the system operator; provide for the coverage of liability relating to the network assets, excluding the liability relating to the tasks of the independent system operator; and provide guarantees to facilitate financing any network expansions with the exception of those investments where it has given its agreement to financing by any interested party including the system operator.[725] Furthermore, the Transmission System

719. Section 64(5)(a) & (c) Law No. 130(I)/2021, which corresponds to Art. 40(6) Directive (EU) 2019/944.
720. Section 96 Law No. 130(I)/2021.
721. Section 78(2) *ibid.*
722. Section 78(6) *ibid.*
723. Section 78(7) *ibid.*
724. Section 78(3) & (8) *ibid.*
725. Section 78(5)(a) to (e) *ibid.*, which partially corresponds to Art. 44(5)(a) to (c) Directive (EU) 2019/944.

Operator bears the following obligations: it must not participate in company structures of the integrated electricity undertaking responsible, directly or indirectly, of the day-to-day operation of the generation, transmission or supply of electricity; the professional interests of the persons responsible for the management of the distribution system operator are taken into account in a manner that ensures that they are capable of acting independently; it must have effective decision-making rights, independent from the integrated electricity undertaking, with respect to assets necessary to operate, maintain or develop the network; and it must establish and implement a compliance programme which sets out the measures taken in order to ensure that discriminatory conduct is excluded, and ensure that the compliance with that programme is adequately monitored, while elaborating an annual report, setting out the measures taken and the extent to which the programme has been implemented.[726] Finally, the personnel and the assets of the Transmission System Operator are housed at a property that is separated in a natural manner from the establishment of any person active in electricity generation or supply.[727]

152. In particular, third parties do have access to the transmission system on the basis of published tariffs applicable to all customers that are applied objectively and without discrimination between system users. The relevant methodologies for calculating the tariffs are both approved and published prior to their entry into force. Still, third parties may be denied access for lack of the necessary capacity. Such refusal is accompanied by duly substantiated reasons and is based on objective and technically and economically justified criteria. In such cases, the Transmission System Operator provides relevant information on measures that would be necessary to reinforce the network and the party requesting such information may be charged a reasonable fee reflecting the cost of providing such information.[728]

153. The Transmission System Operator may perform activities other than those described here and set out in this law and Regulation (EU) 2019/943, where such other activities are necessary for it to fulfil its statutory obligations, provided that Cyprus Energy Regulatory Authority has assessed a derogation necessary.[729]

154. In carrying out his tasks, the Transmission System Operator primarily facilitates market integration[730] and targets minimizing total expenses of generation, transmission, distribution and supply of electricity to consumers.[731] Its Director prepares an annual report on its activities which is submitted to Cyprus Energy Regulatory Authority and forms part of the annual report of the latter.[732]

726. Section 78(9)(a) to (d) Law No. 130(I)/2021, which partially corresponds to Art. 50 Directive (EU) 2019/944. The obligations of the Transmission System Operator set out in the national law remind the obligations of a transmission system owner under the EU law and specifically set out in Art. 35(2)(a) to (d) *ibid.*
727. Section 78(10) Law No. 130(I)/2021.
728. Section 97(1), (2), (3) & (4) *ibid.*, which corresponds to Art. 6 (1) & (2) Directive (EU) 2019/944.
729. Section 62(7) Law No. 130(I)/2021, which corresponds to Art. 40(7) Directive (EU) 2019/944.
730. Section 62(1)(q) Law No. 122(I)/2003, which corresponds to Art. 12(h) Directive 2009/72/EC.
731. Section 62(2) Law No. 122(I)/2003.
732. Sections 62(3) and 18 *ibid.*

§3. Transmission Rules and the Transmission System Protocol

155. The Transmission System Operator, following instructions from Cypru Energy Regulatory Authority, drafts technical rules on the operation of the trans mission system. These are part of the Transmission Rules ('Κανόνε Μεταφοράς') that are formally issued following consultation and approval by th same authority, via a regulatory decision.[733] The Transmission Rules have the fol lowing content. They set out the technical requirements and restrictions to b applied by the authorization holders, when they connect with the transmission c distribution system or when they use these to transmit electricity.[734] These rules als ensure that the technical terms applied to authorization holders during the abov activities do not create unjustified discrimination towards them,[735] whereas effi ciency, reliability and economy in using and developing the transmission system ar promoted.[736] At the same time, Transmission Rules are fully harmonized with th provisions of Regulation (EU) 2019/943.[737] Same rules are addressed to all fina customers to the extent that the authorization terms require, to all holders of autho rization or to the persons that have been granted exclusion, to the extent required b the relevant authorization or exclusion.[738] Cyprus Energy Regulatory Authority ha the authority to issue from time to time instructions on matters that may be deter mined in the Transmission Rules.[739]

156. Transmission Rules may be reviewed and amended from time to time. A revision may take place upon request by Cyprus Energy Regulatory Authority, th Transmission System Operator, the Distribution System Operator or for the purpos of harmonizing with Regulation (EU) 2019/943, when the Transmission Systen Operator deems this necessary.[740] Any review is made by the Transmission Systen Operator in consultation with an atypical consultation committee formed by repre sentatives of the authorization holders and other interested parties that are directl affected by the purpose of this review. The exact participants of said atypical com mittee are determined by Cyprus Energy Regulatory authority. The Transmission System Operator after taking dully into account the written or oral views of saic atypical committee, decides on suggested amendments and offers them for public consultation. Should it then deem an amendment ('τροποποίηση') of the Trans mission Rules necessary, it publishes the suggested amendments on its website anc forwards them to the Cyprus Energy Regulatory Authority for approval, along witl any other information the latter deems necessary.[741] Cyprus Energy Regulatory Authority has the power to approve, reject or amend the suggested amendments.[742]

733. Section 85(1) & (3) *ibid.*
734. Section 86(1)(a) *ibid.*
735. Section 86(1)(b) *ibid.*
736. Section 86(1)(c) *ibid.*
737. Section 86(1)(d) *ibid.*
738. Section 86(2) *ibid.*
739. Section 85(2) *ibid.*
740. Section 87(1)(b) *ibid.*
741. Section 87(3) *ibid.*
742. Section 87(2)(a) & (b) and (3)(a) & (b) *ibid.*

The amended rules enter into force upon their approval and publication by Cyprus Energy Regulatory Authority.[743] Cyprus Energy Regulatory Authority has the authority to issue from time to time instructions on the review and reconsideration of the Transmission Rules.[744]

157. The Transmission System Protocol ('Πρωτόκολλο Συστήματος Μεταφοράς') regulates the relationship between the owner and the operator of the transmission system.[745] This set of rules provides: the standards according to which the assets of the Transmission System Owner constitute the transmission system, including the technical operation limits of those elements and the manner in which such standards may be altered in the future; maintenance and development of the transmission system; construction, connection and use of the transmission system by third parties;[746] arrangements for information sharing among the owner and the operator of the transmission system with regard to the development programme as well as its application and costs; rights and responsibilities for disabling and disconnection; insurance coverage for the owner and operator of the transmission system; duration, expiration and renewal of this protocol; and assessment of the implementation of this same protocol by the owner and the operator of the transmission system.[747]

§4. Transmission System and Investment

158. The Transmission System Operator has the following statutory rights with regard to acquiring, disposing and investing assets: acquire movable or immovable property for its accommodation and operation; accept donations from the state of Cyprus, the EU or other international organization; dispose any movable or immovable property as well as mortgage or pledge such property for fulfilling its statutory duties and obligations, as long as the Council of Ministers has approved it; take loans necessary for implementing the above following authorization by the Minister of Finance, who decides the manner and the terms of such a loan and who has the

743. Section 88 *ibid.*
744. Section 85(2) *ibid.*
745. Section 78(4) *ibid.*
746. On open access of third parties to electricity transmission and distribution systems *see* Case C-439/06, *Energy management proceedings citiworks AG* [2008] ECR I-03913 (*see* Scholtka, Boris & Helmes, Sebastian, *Das Objektnetz ist tot. Es lebe das Industrienetz*, 21 NVwZ 1310 (2008); Pront-van Bommel, S., *Particuliere elektriciteitsnetten onder communautair vuur?*, 50 SEW 244 (2009); Petruzzo, Chiara, *Accesso dei terzi alla rete elettrica: un diritto 'biunivoco' e direttamente applicabile*, 18 Riv. it. dir. pubbl. com. 1558 (2008); Becker, Sebastian, *Kurzbesprechung der Schlussanträge des Generalanwalts Jan Mazak vom 12.12.2007 in der Rechtssache C-439/06 (citiworks AG/Sächsiches Staatsministerium für Wirtschaft und Arbeit)*, 11 EuZW 101 (2008); Geldhof, Wouter & Tormans, Stefan, *Case C-439/06 – ECJ Leaves Limited Scope for Exemptions from Third Party Access Obligations for So-Called Operational Networks*, 17 Eur. Energy & Envtl. L. Rev. 256 (2008)); Case C-239/07, *Julius Sabatauskas and Others* [2008] ECR I-07523 (*see* Pirstner-Ebner, Renate, *Kein Recht zum Anschluss an das Übertragungsnetz*, 12 EuZW 15 (2009); Pront-van Bommel, S., *Particuliere elektriciteitsnetten onder communautair vuur?*, 50 SEW 310 (2009)).
747. Section 75(a) to (h) Law No. 130(I)/2021.

authority to provide guarantee for such loans; and make contracts as well as anything else necessary for implementing the above.[748]

159. Furthermore, the Transmission System Operator is obliged to prepare annually the ten-year network development plan ('δεκαετές πρόγραμμα ανάπτυξης του συστήματος μεταφοράς') and submit it to Cyprus Energy Regulatory Authority for approval. On the basis of existing and forecasted supply and demand and consultation with all the relevant stakeholders, this plan contains efficient measures in order to guarantee the adequacy of the system and the security of supply. At the same time, it indicates to market participants the main transmission infrastructure that needs to be built or upgraded over the next ten years. Also, this plan contains all the investments already decided and identifies new investments which have to be executed in the next three years, while setting a time frame for all investment projects.[749] While drafting the same plan, the Transmission System Operator takes fully into account the potential for the use of demand response, energy storage facilities or other resources as alternatives to system expansion, as well as expected consumption, trade with other countries and investment plans for Union-wide and regional networks as well as projects of common interest under Regulation (EU) 347/2013.[750] It shall also consult all actual or potential system users on the ten-year network development plan in an open and transparent manner while having the option to ask potential system users to substantiate their claims. The result of the consultation process and especially possible needs for investments shall be made public.[751]

160. Cyprus Energy Regulatory Authority examines, whether the ten-year development programme of the transmission system covers all development needs identified during the consultation process and whether it is consistent with the Union-wide network development plan ('διενωσιακό πρόγραμμα ανάπτυξης δικτύων').[752] If any doubt arises as to the consistency with the Union-wide network development plan, Cyprus Energy Regulatory Authority consults ACER. It also has the authority to require the Transmission System Operator to amend its ten-year development plan of the transmission system, while ensuring that said ten-year plan is consistent with the national energy and climate plan.[753] Furthermore, Cyprus Energy Regulatory Authority monitors and evaluates the implementation of said ten-year development plan.[754] More specifically, when the Transmission System Owner does not execute an investment in accordance with the ten-year development plan, Cyprus Energy Regulatory Authority is obliged by law to take one of the

748. Sections 66(a) to (e) and 67 *ibid.*
749. Section 73(1)(a) to (c) *ibid.*, which corresponds to Art. 51(1) & (2) Directive (EU) 2019/944.
750. Section 73(4) Law No. 130(I)/2021, which corresponds to Art. 51(3) Directive (EU) 2019/944.
751. Section 73(5) Law No. 130(I)/2021, which corresponds to Art. 51(4) Directive (EU) 2019/944.
752. In French 'plan de développement du réseau dans l'ensemble de l'Union', in German 'unionsweiter Netzentwicklungsplan', in Dutch 'Uniebreed netontwikkelingsplan'. *See* in this regard Art. 30(1)(b) Regulation (EU) 2019/943.
753. Section 73(6)(a), (b) & (c) & (7) Law No. 130(I)/2021, which corresponds to Art. 51(5) Directive (EU) 2019/944.
754. Section 73(8) Law No. 130(I)/2021, which corresponds to Art. 51(6) Directive (EU) 2019/944.

following measures, under the condition that such investment is still relevant on the basis of the most recent ten-year development plan of the transmission system. Firstly, it has the power to require the Transmission System Owner to execute the investments in question. At the same time, it may organize a tender procedure open to any investors for the investment in question. Finally, it has the authority to oblige the Transmission System Owner to accept a capital increase to submit a supplementary budget in order to finance the necessary investments.[755] The costs of the investments in question are covered by the relevant tariff regulations.[756] When it decides to organize a tender procedure, it may oblige to Transmission System Owner to agree to one or more of the following: (a) construction by any third party; (b) building the new assets concerned itself; and (c) operating the new assets concerned itself.[757] Cyprus Energy Regulatory Authority is deprived of said powers, when the investment in question was not performed for overriding reasons beyond the control of the Transmission System Owner.[758] The Transmission System Operator provides the investors with all information needed to realize the investment, connects new assets to the transmission network and generally makes its best efforts to facilitate the implementation of the investment project. The relevant financial arrangements are subject to approval by Cyprus Energy Regulatory Authority.[759]

161. Energy storage facilities ('εγκαταστάσεις αποθήκευσης ενέργειας') are specifically regulated. *Energy storage* means, in the electricity system, deferring the final use of electricity to a moment later than when it was generated, or the conversion of electrical energy into a form of energy which can be stored, the storing of such energy, and the subsequent reconversion of such energy into electrical energy or use as another energy carrier.[760] As a general rule, the Transmission System Operator is prohibited from owning, developing, managing and operating energy storage facilities.[761] By way of derogation, it may be allowed for the Transmission System Operator to perform such activities, where energy storage facilities are fully integrated network components and Cyprus Energy Regulatory Authority. It may also be allowed to do so, when all of the following conditions are fulfilled. Firstly, other parties, following an open, transparent and non-discriminatory tendering procedure that is subject to review and approval by Cyprus Energy Regulatory Authority, must have not been awarded a right to own, develop, manage or operate such facilities, or could not deliver those services at a reasonable cost and in a timely manner. At the same time, such facilities or non-frequency ancillary services are necessary for the Transmission System Operators to fulfil their obligations under

755. Section 73(9)(a), (b) & (c) Law No. 130(I)/2021, which partially corresponds to Art. 51(7)(a), (b) & (c) Directive (EU) 2019/944.
756. Section 73(11) Law No. 130(I)/2021, which corresponds to Art. 51(9) Directive (EU) 2019/944.
757. Section 73(10)(a) Law No. 130(I)/2021, which partially corresponds to Art. 51(8) Directive (EU) 2019/944.
758. Section 73(9) Law No. 130(I)/2021, which partially corresponds to Art. 51(7) Directive (EU) 2019/944.
759. Section 73(10)(b) & (c) Law No. 130(I)/2021, which partially corresponds to Art. 51(8) Directive (EU) 2019/944.
760. In French 'stockage d'énergie', in German 'Energiespeicherung', in Dutch 'energieopslag'. Section 2(1) Law No. 130(I)/2021, which partially corresponds to Art. 2(59) Directive (EU) 2019/944.
761. Section 82(1) Law No. 130(I)/2021, which corresponds to Art. 54(1) Directive (EU) 2019/944.

this law for the efficient, reliable and secure operation of the transmission system and they are not used to buy or sell electricity in the electricity markets. Finally, Cyprus Energy Regulatory Authority must have assessed the necessity of such a derogation, has carried out an *ex ante* review of the applicability of a tendering procedure, including the conditions of the tendering procedure, and has granted its approval.[762] A fair tendering procedure is ensured by guidelines or procurement clauses set up by Cyprus Energy Regulatory Authority.[763] Should Cyprus Energy Regulatory Authority decide to grant a derogation under said conditions, it has the obligation to notify the Commission and ACER together with relevant information about the request and the reasons for granting the derogation.[764]

162. At regular intervals or at least every five years, Cyprus Energy Regulatory Authority performs a public consultation on the existing energy storage facilities in order to assess the potential availability and interest of other parties in investing in such facilities. Where the public consultation, as assessed by Cyprus Energy Regulatory Authority, indicates that other parties are able to own, develop, operate or manage such facilities in a cost-effective manner, it ensures that the Transmission System Operators' activities in this regard are phased out within eighteen months. As part of the conditions of that procedure, Cyprus Energy Regulatory Authority may allow the Transmission System Operator to receive reasonable compensation, in particular, to recover the residual value of their investment in the energy storage facilities.[765] Said public consultation does not apply to fully integrated network components or for the usual depreciation period of new battery storage facilities with a final investment decision until 2024, provided that such battery storage facilities are: (a) connected to the grid at the latest two years thereafter; (b) integrated into the transmission system; (c) used only for the reactive instantaneous restoration of network security in the case of network contingencies where such restoration measure starts immediately and ends when regular re-dispatch can solve the issue; and (d) not used to buy or sell electricity in the electricity markets, including balancing.[766]

§5. Confidentiality

163. Both the Transmission System Operator and the Transmission System Owner are statutory obligated to treat commercially sensitive information in a confidential manner. The aforementioned (*see* in this regard paragraphs 131 et seq above) apply *mutatis mutandis*.

762. Section 82(2) Law No. 130(I)/2021, which corresponds to Art. 54(2) Directive (EU) 2019/944.
763. Section 82(3) Law No. 130(I)/2021, which corresponds to Art. 54(2) Directive (EU) 2019/944.
764. Section 82(4) Law No. 130(I)/2021, which corresponds to Art. 54(3) Directive (EU) 2019/944.
765. Section 82(5) Law No. 130(I)/2021, which corresponds to Art. 54(4) Directive (EU) 2019/944.
766. Section 82(6) Law No. 130(I)/2021, which corresponds to Art. 54(5) Directive (EU) 2019/944.

§6. Disputes Between the Transmission System Operator and the Transmission System Owner

164. Cyprus Energy Regulatory Authority is the dispute settlement authority for any dispute between the Transmission System Operator and the Transmission System Owner. It shall issue a decision, with which the Transmission System Operator and the Transmission System Owner bear via law the obligation to comply therewith.[767]

767. Section 77(1) & (2) Law No. 130(I)/2021.

Chapter 5. Distribution

165. Distribution ('διανομή') in relation to electricity means the transport c electricity on high-voltage, medium-voltage and low-voltage distribution system with a view to its delivery to customers, but does not include supply.[768] The issue discussed in this chapter rotate around this notion; more specifically, they include the duties and powers of the owner and the operator of the distribution system, elec tromobility, electricity storage as well as rules and development programme.

§1. Distribution System Owner

166. Distribution System Owner ('Ιδιοκτήτης Συστήματος Διανομής') i EAC in its capacity as a distribution system owner.[769] It is operational after obtain ing authorization for distribution activities of the system owner under this law.[77 Its general obligation is to construct and maintain an efficient, coordinated, secure non-hazardous, reliable and financially sustainable electricity distribution system i its area according to the ten-year development plan of the distribution system (*se* in this regard paragraphs 159 et seq. below), with due regard for the environmen and energy efficiency.[771] Furthermore, it performs maintenance and constructio works according to said development program, as well as planning and develop ment works. It also makes any other works necessary under the same developmen programme and complies with any other demand related thereto under this law wit due regard for the environment and energy efficiency. Before performing works i accordance with the same programme, it shall inform the Distribution Systen Operator and Cyprus Energy Regulatory Authority. Also, on the basis of existing needs and available options, it signs cooperation protocols ('πρωτόκολλο συνεργασίας') with telecommunications network providers regarding the distribu tion system and the telecommunications network, in the form, the manner and wit the content approved by Cyprus Energy Regulatory Authority.[772] At all times, the Distribution System Owner may not function in a manner that creates discrimina tion between persons, categories of persons, or system users and specifically, it may not discriminate in favour of its subsidiaries, affiliated companies or joint ventures in which it participates.[773]

167. The Distribution System Owner may use the distribution system for pur poses other than electricity, under the condition that written approvals of the Min ister[774] and the Cyprus Energy Regulatory Authority are provided.[775] The authority

768. In French 'distribution', in German 'Verteilung', in Dutch 'distributie'. Section 2(1) *ibid.*, which corresponds to Art. 2(28) Directive (EU) 2019/944.
769. Section 2(1) Law No. 130(I)/2021.
770. Sections 26(1)(g), 41 & 32 *ibid.*
771. Section 41 *ibid.*
772. Section 42(a), (b) & (c) *ibid.*
773. Section 46 *ibid.*
774. The approval is regulated in s. 12 Cap. 171.
775. Section 51(2) Law No. 122(I)/2003.

grants such usage if it is satisfied that such other activity neither collides with nor limits the fulfilment of the obligations of the Distribution System Owner set out in its authorization.[776] Lastly, it is obliged not to sell or take out of service any asset that is part of the transmission system nor mortgage the same without the prior written approval of Cyprus Energy Regulatory Authority,[777] similar to the relevant obligation of the Transmission System Owner.

§2. Distribution System Operator

168. Distribution System Operator ('Διαχειριστής Συστήματος Διανομής') is EAC under its capacity as operator of the distribution system that has the statutory duties and powers and, as the case may be, its interconnections with other systems and for ensuring the long-term ability of the system to meet reasonable demands for the distribution of electricity.[778] The Distribution System Operator has both duties and powers that are set out in detail in this law. Its duties entail:

- ensuring the long-term ability of the system to meet reasonable demands for the distribution of electricity, operating, maintaining and developing under economic conditions a secure, reliable and efficient electricity distribution system in its area with due regard for the environment and energy efficiency;[779]
- avoiding any discrimination between system users or classes of system users, particularly in favour of its related undertakings;[780]
- providing system users with the information they need for efficient access to, including use of, the system;[781]
- when dispatching generating installations, giving priority to generating installations using renewable energy sources or using high-efficiency cogeneration;[782]
- acting as a neutral market facilitator in procuring the energy it uses to cover energy losses in its system in accordance with transparent, non-discriminatory and market-based procedures, where it has such a function;[783]
- where it is responsible for the procurement of products and services necessary for the efficient, reliable and secure operation of the distribution system, the rules adopted for that purpose are objective, transparent and non-discriminatory, and are developed in coordination with the Transmission System Operator and other relevant market participants. The terms and conditions for the provision of such products and services to the Distribution System Operator are established in a

---

776. Section 44 *ibid.*
777. Section 51(1) *ibid.*
778. Section 2(1) *ibid.*, which partially corresponds to Art. 2(29) Directive (EU) 2019/944.
779. Section 48(1) Law No. 130(I)/2021, which corresponds to Art. 31(1) Directive (EU) 2019/944.
780. Section 48(2) Law No. 130(I)/2021, which corresponds to Art. 31(2) Directive (EU) 2019/944.
781. Section 48(3) Law No. 130(I)/2021, which corresponds to Art. 31(3) Directive (EU) 2019/944.
782. Section 48(4) Law No. 130(I)/2021, which corresponds to Art. 31(4) Directive (EU) 2019/944. With regard to high-efficiency cogeneration *see* s. 102 Law No. 130(I)/2021 and Art. 12 Regulation (EU) 2019/943.
783. Section 48(5) Law No. 130(I)/2021, which corresponds to Art. 31(5) Directive (EU) 2019/944.

non-discriminatory and cost-reflective way and are published; is responsible for balancing the distribution system;[784] and

- cooperating with the Transmission System Operator for the effective participation of market participants connected to their grid in retail, wholesale and balancing markets and agreeing with the Transmission System Operator on providing balancing services from resources within the distribution system.[785]

169. At the same time, the Transmission System Operator may be allowed to perform activities other than those provided for in this law and Regulation (EU) 2019/943, where such activities are necessary for fulfilling its obligations under said legislations provided that the Minister has authorized it and Cyprus Energy Regulatory Authority has assessed the necessity for such a derogation.[786]

170. In addition to the above-mentioned duties, the Distribution System Operator establishes protocols together with the Transmission System Operator to improve the function of a coordinated transmission and distribution system.[787] It provides terms and comes into agreements or protocols with electricity undertakings that intend to use or connect to the distribution system[788] and prepares a distribution development programme that aims to safeguard the supply of electricity.[789] It also charges for usage of and connection to the distribution system.[790]

171. With regard to third-party access to the distribution system and non-discrimination, the aforementioned with regard to the Transmission System Operator (*see* in this regard paragraph 148 above) apply *mutatis mutandis*.[791] In addition, it is here noted that said rules on third-party access also apply to citizen energy communities that manage distribution networks.[792] Lastly, the Distribution System Operator has a specific non-discrimination duty on two occasions. Firstly, with regard to electromobility, it is obliged to cooperate on a non-discriminatory basis with any undertaking that owns, develops, operates or manages recharging points for electric vehicles, including with regard to connection to the grid. Cyprus Energy Regulatory Authority is entrusted with providing the necessary regulatory framework to facilitate the connection of publicly accessible and private recharging points to the distribution networks.[793] Further, with regard to data management performed

784. Sections 48(6) and 5(7) Law No. 130(I)/2021, which correspond to Arts 31(6) and 59(7) Directive (EU) 2019/944. On procuring non-frequency ancillary services needed for the distribution system *see* s. 48(7) & (8) Law No. 130(I)/2021, which correspond to Art. 31(7) & (8) Directive (EU) 2019/944.
785. Section 48(9) Law No. 130(I)/2021, which corresponds to Art. 31(9) Directive 2019/944. *See also* Art. 57 Regulation (EU) 2019/943 and Art. 182 Regulation (EU) 2017/1485.
786. Section 48(10) Law No. 130(I)/2021, which corresponds to Art. 31(10) Directive (EU) 2019/944.
787. Section 53(a) Law No. 130(I)/2021.
788. Section 53(c) *ibid.*
789. Section 53(d) *ibid.*
790. Section 53(b) *ibid.*
791. Section 97(1), (2), (3) & (4) *ibid.*, which corresponds to Art. 6 (1) & (2) Directive (EU) 2019/944.
792. Section 97(5) Law No. 130(I)/2021, which corresponds to Art. 6(3) Directive (EU) 2019/944.
793. Section 51(1) Law No. 130(I)/2021, which corresponds to Art. 33(1) Directive (EU) 2019/944.

by the Distribution System Operator, eligible parties must have access to data in a non-discriminatory manner under clear and equal terms and in accordance with the national legislation on personal data.[794] Cyprus Energy Regulatory Authority is the authority ensuring that this is done. Specifically within the frame of smart meters, Cyprus Energy Regulatory Authority ensures that vertically integrated undertakings do not have privileged access to data for the conduct of their supply activities.[795]

§3. Distribution Rules

172. The Distribution System Operator following instructions by Cyprus Energy Regulatory Authority drafts distribution rules that come into force upon their approval by said authority and the ensuing publication.[796] The aforementioned on Transmission Rules (*see* in this respect paragraphs 155 et seq. above) apply *mutatis mutandis.*

§4. Distribution System and Investment

173. The Distribution System Owner faces restrictions on disposal of its assets.[797] The aforementioned on the transmission system (*see* in this respect paragraph 158 above) apply *mutatis mutandis.*

174. The Distribution System Operator may not own energy storage units, in principle, although derogations are possible.[798] The aforementioned under the transmission system (*see* in this respect paragraphs 161 & 162 above) apply *mutatis mutandis.*

§5. Confidentiality

175. Both the Distribution System Operator and the Distribution System Owner are statutorily obligated to treat commercially sensitive information in a confidential manner. The aforementioned (*see* in this regard paragraph 163 above) apply *mutatis mutandis.*

---

794. Law on the Protection of Natural Persons with Regard to the Processing of Personal Data and on the Free Movement of Such Data ('περί της Προστασίας των Φυσικών Προσώπων Έναντι της Επεξεργασίας των Δεδομένων Προσωπικού Χαρακτήρα και της Ελεύθερης Κυκλοφορίας των Δεδομένων αυτών Νόμο') No. 125 of 2018, OG I(I) No. 4670 of 31 Jul. 2018, p. 827.
795. Section 52(1) & (2) Law No. 130(I)/2021, which corresponds to Art. 34 Directive (EU) 2019/944.
796. Sections 89 to 92 Law No. 130(I)/2021.
797. Section 43 *ibid.*
798. Section 53 *ibid.*

§6. Disputes between the Distribution System Owner and the Distribution System Operator

176. Disputes between the owner and the operator of the distribution system are solved by Cyprus Energy Regulatory Authority.[799] The aforementioned on transmission (*see* in this respect paragraph 164 above) apply *mutatis mutandis*.

799. Section 54 *ibid.*

Chapter 6. Interconnector

177. Interconnector ('γραμμή διασύνδεσης') means a transmission line, including equipment and stations used to link electricity systems, which crosses or spans a border between Member States and which connects the national transmission systems of the Member States and which connects the transmission system or network of Cyprus with the national transmission system or network of another Member State and/ or with the transmission system network or system of a third state.[800] In this chapter, the themes discussed are the interconnector owner, the interconnector operator and the interconnector system protocols.

§1. Interconnector Owner

178. The Interconnector Owner has the same general obligations and competences as the Transmission System Owner,[801] but for the competence to perform works necessary under a ten-year development program. Thus, the aforementioned (*see* in this regard paragraphs 159 et seq. above) apply *mutatis mutandis*.

§2. Interconnector Operator

179. The Interconnector Operator is devoid of general obligations; nonetheless, it has been given the following specific competences:

- operating an efficient, coordinated, secure, non-hazardous, reliable and financially sustainable electricity interconnector and ensuring the interconnector's long-term capacity to respond to reasonable demand for transmission and transboundary supply of electricity under financially acceptable conditions with due regard to the environment;
- ensuring the development and maintenance of an efficient, coordinated, secure, non-hazardous, reliable and financially sustainable electricity interconnector and ensuring the interconnector's long-term capacity to respond to reasonable demand for transmission and transboundary supply of electricity under financially acceptable conditions with due regard to the environment;
- making Interconnector Protocols with the Interconnector Owner, the Transmission System Operator and the neighbouring transmission system operators while promoting and ensuring, among others, the interoperability of the interconnected systems and the good, safe and seamless function of the electricity lines and the interconnector;

800. 'Interconnexion' in French, 'Verbindungsleitung' in German, 'interconnector' in Dutch. Section 2(1) *ibid*, which corresponds to Art. 2(39) Directive (EU) 2019/944 & Art. 2(1) Regulation (EU) 2019/943.
801. Sections 105 & 106 Law No. 130(I)/2021.

– managing the transboundary flows of electricity of the interconnected systen and
– preparing a development program of the interconnector.[802]

§3. Interconnected System Protocols

180. Interconnected system protocols ('πρωτόκολλα διασυνδεδεμένου συσ τήματος') are made between the Interconnector Owner and the Transmission Sys tem Operator, the Interconnector Owner and the Interconnector Operator, th Interconnector Operator and the Transmission System Operator, the Interconnecto Operator and neighbouring transmission system operators as well as the Transmis sion System Operator and neighbouring transmission system operators. Such pro tocols serve the aim of enabling the Interconnector Operator to perform it duties.[803] At the outset, the Interconnected System Protocols provide that the Inter connector Owner maintains the interconnector and performs construction work according to the development programme of the interconnector as prepared by th Interconnector Operator.[804] Generally, such protocols provide the following:

– making the Interconnector Operator capable of fully and effectively performin its duties;
– making the Transmission System Operator capable of fully and effectively per forming its duties;
– ensuring that the Transmission System Operator helps the Interconnector Opera tor with performing its duties;
– ensuring that the Interconnector Owner helps the Interconnector Operator wit performing its duties;
– ensuring that the Interconnector Owner performs its duties and responsibilities;
– setting out common operational demands and safety principles;
– setting out common operational principles for design of the interconnected sys tem;
– setting out common procedures for control of load/ frequency and control struc tures;
– ensuring the conditions for maintaining operational safety throughout the Union;
– ensuring the conditions for maintaining high-quality frequency of all the syn chronized areas throughout Europe;
– promoting the coordination of system operation and the operational planning;
– ensuring and promoting the transparency and reliability of information regarding the operation of the transmission system; and
– promoting the effective function and development of the electricity transmission system and the electricity sector in the Union.[805]

---

802. Section 103(a) to (e) *ibid.*
803. Section 108(1)(a) *ibid.*
804. Section 108(6) *ibid.*
805. Section 108(5) *ibid.*

181. More specifically, Interconnected System Protocols have a form or type approved by Cyprus Energy Regulatory Authority and include specifics on the following:

- standards according to which the assets of the Interconnector Owner constitute the interconnector of the interconnected system, including the technical operation limits of these assets and the manner in which these standards may be amended in the future;
- maintaining and developing the interconnector of the interconnected system;
- construction, connection and use of the interconnector of the interconnected system by third parties, where applicable;
- arrangements for communication and information exchange between the Interconnector Owner and the Transmission System Operator as well as between the Interconnector Owner and the Interconnector Operator as well as between the Interconnector Operator and the Transmission System Operator with regard to the development program, its application and its expenses;
- arrangements, in order to ensure good, safe and seamless function of the electricity lines and the interconnector for which responsible is the Transmission System Operator and the Interconnector Operators, long-term ability, reliability and effectiveness of the interconnected system, respond to reasonable demand for transmission and cross-border electricity supply, operation, maintenance, development of safe, reliable and effective transmission system, performing their duties and providing sufficient information for safe and efficient operation, as well as coordinated development and interoperability of the interconnected system;
- the rights and responsibilities for deactivation and disconnection;
- the insurance coverage that the Interconnector Owner, the Interconnector Operator and the Transmission System Operator shall have;
- duration, termination and renewal of the Interconnector Protocols; and
- assessing the application of the Interconnector Protocols by the Transmission System Operator, the Interconnector Owner and the Interconnector Operator.[806]

182. Interconnected System Protocols must be approved by Cyprus Energy Regulatory Authority that consults the Commission for the Protection of Competition, as the case may be. Cyprus Energy Regulatory Authority also has the authority to instruct the Transmission System Operator, the Interconnector Owner and the Interconnector Operator to include in such protocols terms and development programme of the Interconnector, as it may seem necessary.[807]

183. The Interconnected System Protocols are reviewed when the Transmission System Operator, the Interconnector Operator, the Interconnector Owner or Cyprus Energy Regulatory Authority deem it necessary. Specifically where the latter thinks that an amendment is necessary, it may demand from the Transmission System

806. Section 109 *ibid.*
807. Section 108(1)(b), (4) & (2) *ibid.*

Operator, the Interconnector Operator and the Interconnector Owner to amend the protocols according to the amendments suggested by the same.[808]

184. Cyprus Energy Regulatory Authority has the authority to monitor the application of the Interconnector Protocols. Should it deem that the Interconnector Owner, the Interconnector Operator or the Transmission System Operator systematically fail to comply with the terms of such protocol, statutory provisions or terms of its authorization in a manner that may substantially affect public interest, it may take a decision following consultations with the Minister. Such a decision may demand the relevant operator or owner to comply with specific terms or provisions and to specify the manner in which the relevant operator or owner must comply with this decision.[809] Specifically for violation of obligations of the Interconnector Owner under the Interconnected System Protocol, the Interconnector Operator may take immediate steps for works to be performed by a contractor as long as Cyprus Energy Regulatory Authority authorizes it. The relevant expenses are borne by the Interconnector Owner.[810]

808. Section 108(1)(c) & (3) *ibid.*
809. Section 110(1) & (2)(a) & (b) *ibid.*
810. Section 110(3) *ibid.*

Chapter 7. Consumption

§1. Consumers

185. Law on electricity differentiates between different types of customers. Generally, a customer ('πελάτης') is a wholesale or final customer of electricity.[811] A particular form of customer is household customer ('οικιακός πελάτης'), which means a customer purchasing electricity for his own household consumption, excluding commercial or professional activities.[812] Non-household customer ('μη οικιακός πελάτης') is a natural or legal person purchasing electricity which is not for their own household use and includes producers, industrial customers, Small and Medium-sized Enterprises (SMEs), businesses and wholesale customers.[813] Wholesale customer ('πελάτης χονδρικής') stands for a natural or legal person purchasing electricity for the purpose of resale inside or outside the system where he is established.[814] Lastly, the final customer ('τελικός πελάτης') is a customer purchasing electricity for his own use.[815]

§2. Public Service and Universal Service Obligations

186. Customers are benefitted from the obligation of public service and the obligation of universal service that electricity undertakings have under this law. Starting with public service ('δημόσια υπηρεσία'),[816] the Minister after consultations with Cyprus Energy Regulatory Authority, having full regard to the relevant provisions of the TFEU, in particular, Article 106 thereof, may impose on undertakings operating in the electricity sector, in the general economic interest, public service obligations which may relate to security, including the security of supply, regularity, quality and price of supplies and environmental protection, including energy efficiency, energy from renewable sources and climate protection.[817] Such obligations are clearly defined, transparent, non-discriminatory and verifiable, and guarantee equality of access for electricity undertakings of the Union to national

811. Section 2(1) Law No. 130(I)/2021, which corresponds to Art. 2(1) Directive (EU) 2019/944. The French term is 'client', the German 'Kunden' and the Dutch 'afnemer'.
812. Section 2(1) Law No. 130(I)/2021, which corresponds to Art. 2(4) Directive 2019/944. The French term is 'client résidentiel', the German 'Haushalts-Kunde' and the Dutch 'huishoudelijke afnemer'.
813. Section 2(1) Law No. 130(I)/2021, which corresponds to Art. 2(5) Directive (EU) 2019/944. The French term is 'client non résidentiel', the German 'Nichthaushaltskunde' and the Dutch 'niet-huishoudelijke afnemer'.
814. Section 2(1) Law No. 130(I)/2021, which corresponds to Art. 2(2) Directive (EU) 2019/944. The French term is 'client grossiste', the German 'Großhändler' and the Dutch 'grootafnemer'.
815. Section 2(1) *ibid.*, which corresponds to Art. 2(3) Directive (EU) 2019/944. The French term is 'client final', the German 'Endkunden' and the Dutch 'eindafnemer'.
816. In French 'service public', in German 'Gemeinwirtschaftliche Verpflichtungen', in Dutch 'Openbaredienstverplichtingen'.
817. Section 111(1)(a) to (d) Law No. 130(I)/2021, which corresponds to Art. 9(2) Directive (EU) 2019/944.

consumers.[818] Where the State grants financial compensation, other forms of compensation and exclusive rights for the fulfilment of the aforementioned obligations, this is done in a non-discriminatory and transparent way.[819] For the purpose of implementing said measures, Cyprus Energy Regulatory Authority issues regulatory decisions that must be approved by the Council of Ministers and provide, among others, provisions on recovery of additional expenses of the electricity undertakings in the form of charges on the consumers for the electricity provided.[820]

187. Universal service ('καθολική υπηρεσία') is the right to be supplied with electricity of a specified quality within their territory at competitive, easily and clearly comparable, transparent and non-discriminatory prices.[821] It is stated explicitly in the law that all household customers have the right to enjoy universal service, which shall be implemented in a transparent and non-discriminatory way, and shall not impede the free choice of supplier. *Small enterprises*, that being an enterprise which employs fewer than fifty persons and whose annual turnover and/or annual balance sheet total does not exceed EUR 10 million, might be eligible for enjoying universal service, when the Minister deems this necessary and issues a relevant decree.[822] To ensure the provision of universal service, Cyprus has appointed a supplier of last resort, whereas the Distribution System Operator has an obligation to connect customers to their network under certain terms, conditions and tariffs (*see* in this regard paragraphs 168 et seq. above).[823]

188. The Minister informs the Commission on all measures adopted for fulfilling universal service and public service obligations, including protection of consumers and of the environment and their possible effect on national and international competition.[824]

§3. Customers' Rights and Protection

189. Customers' rights and protection measures consist of general rights, basic rights and a series of special rights, as described below.

---

818. Section 111(2) Law No. 130(I)/2021, which corresponds to Art. 9(2) Directive (EU) 2019/944.
819. Section 111(3) Law No. 130(I)/2021, which corresponds to Art. 9(3) Directive (EU) 2019/944.
820. Section 112(1) Law No. 130(I)/2021.
821. In French 'service universel', in German 'Grundversorgung', in Dutch 'universele dienstverlening'. Section 113(1) *ibid.*, which corresponds to Art. 27(1) Directive (EU) 2019/944.
822. Section 113(1), (6) & (2) Law No. 130(I)/2021, which corresponds to Arts 2(7) and 27(1) Directive (EU) 2019/944.
823. Sections 113(4) & (5) and 5(7)(a) Law No. 130(I)/2021, which corresponds to Arts 27(1) and 59(7) Directive (EU) 2019/944.
824. Sections 111(4) and 113(9) Law No. 130(I)/2021, which corresponds to Art. 9(4) Directive (EU) 2019/944.

I. General Rights

190. Consumers in their capacity as customers have two general rights. At the outset, they have the right to purchase electricity from a supplier of their choice. They also have the right to make more than one electricity supply contract simultaneously, under the condition that the necessary connection and measurement points have been specified.[825]

II. Basic Rights

191. Without prejudice to Union rules on consumer protection and the relevant national legislation, Cyprus Energy Regulatory Authority ensures that all final customers have the following basic rights:

(1) the right to have their electricity provided by a supplier, subject to the supplier's agreement, regardless of the Member State in which the supplier is registered, provided that the supplier follows the applicable trading and balancing rules;
(2) the right to a contract with their supplier that specifies:
   (a) the identity and address of the supplier;
   (b) the services provided, the service quality levels offered, as well as the time for the initial connection;
   (c) the types of maintenance service offered;
   (d) the means by which up-to-date information on all applicable tariffs, maintenance charges and bundled products or services may be obtained;
   (e) the duration of the contract, the conditions for renewal and termination of the contract and services, including products or services that are bundled with those services, and whether terminating the contract without charge is permitted;
   (f) any compensation and the refund arrangements which apply if contracted service quality levels are not met, including inaccurate or delayed billing;
   (g) the method of initiating an out-of-court dispute settlement procedure in accordance with section 128;
   (h) information relating to consumer rights, including information on complaint handling and all of the information referred to therein, that is clearly communicated on the bill or the electricity undertaking's web site.
(3) the right to know in advance the terms and conditions of a contract with a supplier that must be fair and provided prior to the conclusion or confirmation of the contract, along with any information relating to the matters set out above, where contracts are concluded through intermediaries;
(4) the right to be provided with a summary of the key contractual conditions in a prominent manner and in concise and simple language;
(5) the right to be given adequate notice of any intention to modify contractual conditions and to be informed about their right to terminate the contract when

825. Section 116(a) & (b) Law No. 130(I)/2021.

the notice is given. Suppliers notify their final customers, in a transparent an comprehensible manner, directly of any adjustment in the supply price and c the reasons and preconditions for the adjustment and its scope, at an appro priate time no later than two weeks, or no later than one month in the case c household customers, before the adjustment comes into effect. Also, Cypru Energy Regulatory Authority ensures that final customers are free to terminat contracts if they do not accept the new contractual conditions or adjustment in the supply price notified to them by their supplier;

(6) the right to be provided with transparent information on applicable prices an tariffs and on standard terms and conditions, in respect of access to and use c electricity services;

(7) the right to be offered a wide choice of payment methods;

(8) the right of household customers that have access to prepayment methods no be placed at a disadvantage by the prepayment systems;

(9) the right to be offered fair and transparent general terms and conditions tha are provided in plain and unambiguous language and do not include non contractual barriers to the exercise of customers' rights, such as excessive con tractual documentation and protection against unfair or misleading selling methods;

(10) the right to a good standard of service and complaint handling by their sup pliers. Suppliers shall handle complaints in a simple, fair and prompt manner

(11) the right to be informed about their rights regarding universal service unde section 113;

(12) the right to receive a final closure account after any switch of supplier no late than six weeks after such a switch has taken place;

(13) the right of household customers to be provided with adequate information or alternative measures to disconnection sufficiently in advance of any plannec disconnection and not pay extra costs in case they face disconnection; and

(14) the right of taking alternative measures towards disconnection of householc customers and being informed on such measures sufficiently in advance of any planned disconnection and avoiding additional charges by the customers fac ing disconnection. Such alternative measures may refer to sources of suppor to avoid disconnection, prepayment systems, energy audits, energy consul tancy services, alternative payment plans, debt management advice or discon nection moratoria.[826]

III. Specific Rights

192. The specific rights that final customers have related to dynamic electricity price contracts, switching suppliers, aggregation, comparison tools, active customers and out-of-court dispute settlement.

---

826. Section 117(a) to (n) Law No. 130(I)/2021, which corresponds to Art. 10(1) to (12) Directive 2019/ 944.

193. Dynamic electricity price contract ('σύμβαση δυναμικής τιμολόγησης ηλεκτρικής ενέργειας') is an electricity supply contract between a supplier and a final customer that reflects the price variation in the spot markets, including in the day-ahead and intraday markets, at intervals at least equal to the market settlement frequency.[827] Final customers who have a smart meter (*see* in this regard paragraphs 205 et seq. below) can request to conclude a dynamic electricity price contract with the supplier that has the biggest number of final customers in the electricity sector and with every supplier that has more than 200 000 final customers. This opportunity is optional for suppliers that do not meet said criteria. All suppliers have the statutory duty to fully inform final customers of the opportunities, costs and risks of such dynamic electricity price contracts, and the need to have an electricity smart meter installed.[828] Before a final customer is switched to a dynamic electricity price contract, the supplier must have given his consent.[829] Cyprus Energy Regulatory Authority is entrusted with monitoring market developments and assessing the risks that the new products and services may entail and dealing with abusive practices.[830]

194. With regard to switching suppliers or market participants engaged in aggregation, it is ensured that a customer wishing to do so, shall be entitled to such a change within three weeks, and from January 2026, this procedure shall last no longer than twenty-four hours and shall be possible on any working day.[831] This right is granted to customers in a non-discriminatory manner as regards cost, effort and time.[832] Specifically, household customers are entitled to participate in collective switching schemes. Cyprus Energy Regulatory Authority in a regulatory decision sets the frame under which customers may do so while removing all regulatory or administrative barriers for collective switching and providing a framework that ensures the utmost consumer protection to avoid any abusive practices.[833]

195. Turing to aggregation contracts, all customers are free to purchase and sell electricity services, including aggregation, other than supply, independently from their electricity supply contract and from an electricity undertaking of their choice.[834] A final customer wishing to conclude an aggregation contract shall be entitled to do so without the consent of his electricity undertaking. Market participants engaged in aggregation have the duty to fully inform customers of the terms

827. In French 'contrat d'électricité à tarification dynamique', in German 'Vertrag mit dynamischen Stromtarifen', in Dutch 'contract op basis van een dynamische elektriciteitsprijs'. Section 2(1) Law No. 130(I)/2021, which corresponds to Art. 2(15) Directive (EU) 2019/944. Section 2(1) Law No. 130(I)/2021, which corresponds to Art. 2(15) Directive (EU) 2019/944.
828. Section 118(1) & (2) Law No. 130(I)/2021, which corresponds to Art. 11(1) & (2) Directive (EU) 2019/944.
829. Section 118(3) Law No. 130(I)/2021, which corresponds to Art. 11(3) Directive (EU) 2019/944.
830. Section 118(4)(b) Law No. 130(I)/2021, which corresponds to Art. 11(4) Directive (EU) 2019/944.
831. Section 119(1)(a) & (b) Law No. 130(I)/2021, which corresponds to Art. 11(1) Directive (EU) 2019/944.
832. Section 119(2) Law No. 130(I)/2021, which corresponds to Art. 12(4) Directive (EU) 2019/944.
833. Section 119(3)(a) & (b) Law No. 130(I)/2021, which corresponds to Art. 12(5) Directive (EU) 2019/944.
834. Section 120(1) Law No. 130(I)/2021, which corresponds to Art. 13(1) Directive (EU) 2019/944.

and conditions of the contracts that they offer to them.[835] Cyprus Energy Regulatory Authority ensures that said right is granted in a non-discriminatory manner as regards cost, effort or time. In particular, customers are not subject to discriminatory technical and administrative requirements, procedures or charges by their supplier on the basis of whether they have a contract with a market participant engaged in aggregation.[836]

196. Household customers and microenterprises with an expected yearly consumption of below 100 000 kWh, have access, free of charge, to a tool comparing the offers of suppliers, that is managed by Cyprus Energy Regulatory Authority or, alternatively by another non-governmental entity.[837] This comparison tool, which covers the entire market and has the trust mark issued by Cyprus Energy Regulatory Authority,[838] satisfies the following requirements:

- it is independent from market participants and ensures that electricity undertakings are given equal treatment in search results;
- it clearly discloses its owners and the natural or legal person operating and controlling the tools, as well as information on how the tools are financed;
- it sets out clear and objective criteria on which the comparison is to be based, including services, and discloses them;
- it uses plain and unambiguous language;
- it provides accurate and up-to-date information and state the time of the last update;
- it is accessible to persons with disabilities, by being perceivable, operable, understandable and robust;
- it provides an effective procedure for reporting incorrect information on published offers;
- it performs comparisons, while limiting the personal data requested to that strictly necessary for the comparison; and
- includes comparative criteria with regard to the nature of the services provided by the suppliers.[839]

197. Customers are informed of the availability of such a tool in their bills or documents accompanying their bills and ensure easy access thereto through their website. Cyprus Energy Regulatory Authority ensures that electricity undertakings provide precise and updated information.[840] Finally, should multiple tools cover the

835. Section 120(2) & (3) Law No. 130(I)/2021, which corresponds to Art. 13(2) Directive (EU) 2019/944.
836. Section 120(4) Law No. 130(I)/2021, which corresponds to Art. 13(4) Directive (EU) 2019/944.
837. Section 121(4) & (1) Law No. 130(I)/2021, which partially corresponds to Art. 14(1) Directive (EU) 2019/944.
838. Section 121(3) Law No. 130(I)/2021, which partially corresponds to Art. 14(1) Directive (EU) 2019/944.
839. Section 121 and Annex (a) to (i) Law No. 130(I)/2021, which partially corresponds to Art. 14(1) Directive 2019/944.
840. Section 121(5) & (6) Law No. 130(I)/2021, which partially corresponds to Art. 14(1) Directive (EU) 2019/944.

market, those tools include, as complete as practicable, a range of electricity offers covering a significant part of the market and, where those tools do not completely cover the market, a clear statement to that effect, before displaying results.[841]

198. Furthermore, final customers have the right to act as active customers and/ or renewables self-consumers without being subject to disproportionate or discriminatory technical requirements, administrative requirements, procedures and charges. To this end, Cyprus Energy Regulatory Authority ensures that active customers: (a) are entitled to operate either directly or through aggregation; (b) are entitled to sell self-generated electricity, including through power purchase agreements; (c) are entitled to participate in flexibility schemes and energy efficiency schemes; (d) are entitled to delegate to a third party the management of the installations required for their activities, including installation, operation, data handling and maintenance, without that third party being considered to be an active customer;[842] (e) pay the network charges;[843] (f) are financially responsible for the imbalances they cause in the electricity system; to that extent they shall balance responsible parties or shall delegate their balancing responsibility; and (g) have systems that account separately for the electricity fed into the grid and the electricity consumed from the grid.[844] Cyprus Energy Regulatory Authority may have different provisions applicable to individual and jointly-acting active customers, provided that all rights and obligations mentioned above apply to all active customers and any difference in the treatment of jointly-acting active customers is proportionate and duly justified.[845] Specifically with regard to active customers that own an energy storage facility, it is ensured that: (a) they have the right to a grid connection within a reasonable time after the request, provided that all necessary conditions, such as balancing responsibility and adequate metering, are fulfilled;[846] (b) they are not subject to any double charges, including network charges, for stored electricity remaining within their premises or when providing flexibility services to system operators;[847] (c) they are not subject to disproportionate licensing requirements or fees; and (d) are allowed to provide several services simultaneously, if technically feasible.[848]

199. Finally, final customers have the right to out-of-court dispute settlement, as explained in detail below (*see* in this respect paragraph 216 below).

---

841. Section 121(9) Law No. 130(I)/2021, which partially corresponds to Art. 14(1) Directive (EU) 2019/944.
842. Section (1) & (2)(a) to (d) Law No. 130(I)/2021, which partially corresponds to Art. 15(1) & (2)(a) to (d) Directive (EU) 2019/944.
843. Sections 122(2)(e) and 22(8)(b) Law No. 130(I)/2021.
844. Section 122(2)(f) & (g) *ibid*, which corresponds partially to Art. 15(2)(f) & (e) Directive (EU) 2019/944.
845. Section 122(3) Law No. 130(I)/2021, which corresponds to Art. 15(3) Directive (EU) 2019/944.
846. Section 122(4)(a) Law No. 130(I)/2021, which corresponds to Art. 15(5)(a) Directive (EU) 2019/ 944.
847. Sections 122(4)(b) and 22(9)(a) Law No. 130(I)/2021, which corresponds to Art. 15(5)(b) Directive (EU) 2019/944.
848. Section 122(4)(c) & (d) Law No. 130(I)/2021, which corresponds to Art. 26(1)(c) & (d) Directive (EU) 2019/944.

IV. Rights with Regard to Access to Information

200. Final customers have specific rights with regard to access to certain information, that being energy sources and billing. At the outset, they have the right to receive clarifications and information on the contribution of each energy source to the electricity purchased separately for every product included in the electricity supply contract. In this spirit, final customers are informed on the contribution of each energy source to the overall energy mix of the supplier both at the national level and at the level of the supplier, if the supplier is active in several Member States, over the preceding year in a comprehensible and clearly comparable manner. They are also informed on the environmental impact, in at least terms of CO2 emissions and the radioactive waste resulting from the electricity produced by the overall energy mix of the supplier over the preceding year. Specifically regarding electricity from high-efficiency cogeneration and from renewable sources, this disclosure duty is fulfilled by using the apposite guarantees of origin.[849] Cyprus Energy Regulatory Authority ensures that suppliers provide the aforementioned information and clarifications.[850]

201. At the same time, final customers have the right to access *billing information* ('πληροφορίες τιμολόγησης'), which is specified as 'the information provided on a final customer's bill, apart from a request for payment'.[851] This information, which has to be prominently displayed in their bills, consists of: (a) the price to be paid and a breakdown of the price together with a clear statement that all energy sources may also benefit from incentives that were not financed through the levies indicated in the breakdown of the price; (b) the date on which payment is due; (c) electricity consumption for the billing period; (d) the name and contact details of the supplier, including a consumer support hotline and email address; (e) the tariff name; (f) the end date of the contract, as the case may be; (g) information on the availability and benefits of switching; (g) information on the final customer's switching code or unique identification code for the final customer's supply point; (h) information on final customers' rights as regards out-of-court dispute settlement, including the contact details of the entity responsible; (i) the single point of contact, in the sense of the contact, where customers can be provided with all necessary information about their rights, the applicable law and available dispute settlement mechanisms that may be part of general consumer information points; and (j) a link or reference to where comparison tools can be found.[852] Depending on bills being based on actual consumption or remote reading by the operator, final customers further have the right to access the following information: (a) comparisons of

849. *See* in this regard Law No. 174(I)/2006 and Law No. 107(I)/2022 that implement Directive 2012/27/EU and Directive (EU) 2018/2001, respectively.

850. Section 131 Law No. 130(I)/2021, which corresponds to Annex I.5 Directive (EU) 2019/944.

851. In French 'informations relatives à la facturation', in German 'Abrechnungsinformationen', in Dutch 'factureringsinformatie'. Section 2(1) Law No. 130(I)/2021, which corresponds to Art. 2(21) Directive (EU) 2019/944.

852. Section 132(1)(a) & (b) and (2)(a) to (i) Law No. 130(I)/2021, which corresponds to Annex I.1.1 & I.1.2 and Art. 25 Directive (EU) 2019/944.

the final customer's current electricity consumption with the final customer's consumption for the same period in the previous year in graphic form; (b) contact information for consumer organizations, energy agencies or similar bodies, including website addresses, from which information may be obtained on available energy efficiency improvement measures for energy-using equipment; and (c) comparisons with an average normalized or benchmarked final customer in the same user category.[853] With regard to the frequency of billing and the provision of billing information the following apply: (a) billing on the basis of actual consumption takes place at least once a year; (b) where final customers do not have a meter that allows remote reading by the Transmission System Operator, or where final customers have actively chosen to disable remote reading, accurate billing information based on actual consumption is made available to them at least every six months, or once every three months, if requested or where final customers have opted to receive electronic billing; (c) where final customers do not have a meter that allows remote reading by the Transmission System Operator, or where final customers have actively chosen to disable remote reading, the obligations in the aforementioned two points may be fulfilled by means of a system of regular self-reading by the final customer, whereby final customers communicate readings from the meter to the supplier; billing or billing information may be based on estimated consumption or a flat rate only where the final customer has not provided a meter reading for a given billing interval; and (d) where the final customer has a meter that allows remote reading by the Transmission System Operator, accurate billing information based on actual consumption is provided at least every month; such information may also be made available via the internet, and shall be updated as frequently as allowed by the measurement devices and systems used.[854] With respect to breakdown of the final customer's price, it is provided that said price is the sum of: (a) the energy and supply component; (b) the network component (transmission and distribution); and (c) the component comprising taxes, levies, fees and charges.[855] Finally, complementary information on historical consumption is made available at the request of the final customer, to the supplier or service provider designated by the final customer. Where final customers have a meter that allows remote reading by the Transmission System Operator, they have easy access to complementary information on historical consumption allowing detailed self-checks. Complementary information on historical consumption include: (a) cumulative data for at least the three previous years or the period since the start of the electricity supply contract, if that period is shorter. The data correspond to the intervals for which frequent billing information has been produced; and (b) detailed data according to the time of use for any day, week, month and year, which is made available to the final customer without

853. Section 132(3)(a) to (c) Law No. 130(I)/2021, which corresponds to Annex I.1.3 Directive (EU) 2019/944.
854. Section 132(4)(a) to (d) Law No. 130(I)/2021, which corresponds to Annex I.2 Directive (EU) 2019/944.
855. Section 132(5)(a) Law No. 130(I)/2021, which corresponds to Annex I.3 Directive (EU) 2019/944.

undue delay via the internet or the meter interface, covering the period of at leas the previous twenty-four months or the period since the start of the electricity sup ply contract, if that period is shorter.[856]

202. All aforementioned information, that being billing information and infor mation on energy sources, constitute 'the minimum requirements for billing an billing information' under EU law.[857]

§4. Citizen Energy Communities

203. Citizen energy communities ('ενεργειακές κοινότητες πολιτών') hav the following characteristics, as ensured by Cyprus Energy Regulatory Authority (a) participation is open and voluntary; (b) its members or shareholders have th right to leave the community; (c) its members or shareholders do not lose thei rights and obligations as household customers or active customers; (d) the Trans mission System Operator cooperates with such communities to facilitate electricity transfers within them; (e) they are subject to non-discriminatory, fair, proportionate and transparent procedures and charges, including with respect to registration and licensing, and to transparent, non-discriminatory and cost-reflective network charges;[858] (f) citizen energy communities are subject to the exceptions set out with regard to closed distribution systems;[859] (g) they are able to access all electricity markets, either directly or through aggregation, in a non-discriminatory manner; (h they are treated in a non-discriminatory and proportionate manner with regard to their activities, rights and obligations as final customers, producers, suppliers, dis tribution system operators or market participants engaged in aggregation; (i) they are responsible for the imbalances they cause in the electricity system and bear the relevant financial responsibility; (j) with regard to consumption of self-generated electricity, citizen energy communities are treated like active customers; and (k they have the right to arrange within the citizen energy community the sharing of electricity that is produced by the production units owned by the community, subject to other requirements, as explained in this paragraph, and subject to the community members retaining their rights and obligations as final customers.[860] It is further ensured that citizen energy communities are open to cross-border participation and are entitled to own, establish, purchase or lease distribution networks and to autonomously manage them subject to conditions applicable to Distribution System Operators.[861]

---

856. Section 132(6)(a) to (c) Law No. 130(I)/2021, which corresponds to Annex I.4 Directive (EU) 2019/944.
857. *See* Annex I *ibid*.
858. Section 123(1)(a) to (e) Law No. 130(I)/2021, which corresponds to Art. 16(1)(a) to (e) Directive (EU) 2019/944.
859. Sections 123(1)(f) and 56(3) Law No. 130(I)/2021.
860. Section 123(1)(g) to (k) *ibid*., which corresponds to Art. 16(3)(a) & (e) Directive (EU) 2019/944.
861. Section 123(2)(a) & (b) Law No. 130(I)/2021, which corresponds to Art. 16(2)(a) & (b) Directive (EU) 2019/944.

§5. Demand Response and Smart Meters

204. Directive 2019/944 aims to foster consumers' direct participation in the market, especially via adjusting their consumption in response to market signals and thus, benefiting from lower prices or other incentive payments.[862] Allowing consumers to change the manner they consume electricity in order to reap benefits, such as consuming electricity at a lower price or from a particular source prerequisites three notions: aggregation; demand response; and smart meters. These have been statutorily defined. *Aggregation*, as already noted (*see* in this regard paragraph 59 above), stands for a function performed by a natural or legal person who combines multiple customer loads or generated electricity for sale, purchase or auction in any electricity market.[863] *Demand response* ('απόκριση ζήτησης') is the change of electricity load by final customers from their normal or current consumption patterns in response to market signals, including in response to time-variable electricity prices or incentive payments, or in response to the acceptance of the final customers bid to sell demand reduction or increase at a price in an organized market.[864] A *smart metering system* ('έξυπνο σύστημα μέτρησης') is an electronic system that is capable of measuring electricity fed into the grid or electricity consumed from the grid, providing more information than a conventional meter, and that is capable of transmitting and receiving data for information, monitoring and control purposes, using a form of electronic communication.[865]

205. Participation in demand response is both allowed and fostered through aggregation, allowing final customers to participate alongside producers in a non-discriminatory manner in all electricity markets.[866] To this end, Cyprus Energy Regulatory Authority ensures: (a) that the Transmission System Operator and the Distribution System Operator when procuring ancillary services, treat market participants engaged in the aggregation of demand response in a non-discriminatory manner alongside producers on the basis of their technical capabilities;[867] (b) the right for each market participant engaged in aggregation, including independent aggregators, to enter electricity markets without the consent of other market participants; (c) non-discriminatory and transparent rules that clearly assign roles and responsibilities to all electricity undertakings and customers; (d) non-discriminatory and transparent rules and procedures for the exchange of data between market participants engaged in aggregation and other electricity undertakings that ensure easy

862. Recital no. 37 to the preamble of Directive (EU) 2019/944.
863. Section 2(1) Law No. 130(I)/2021, which corresponds to Art. 2(18) Directive (EU) 2019/944.
864. In French 'participation active de la demande', in German 'Laststeuerung', in Dutch 'vraagrespons'. Section 2(1) Law No. 130(I)/2021, which corresponds to Art. 2(20) Directive (EU) 2019/944.
865. In French 'système intelligent de mesure', in German 'intelligentes Messsystem', in Dutch 'slimme-metersysteem'. Section 2(1) Law No. 130(I)/2021, which corresponds to Art. 2(23) Directive (EU) 2019/944.
866. Section 124(1) Law No. 130(I)/2021, which corresponds to Art. 17(1) Directive (EU) 2019/944.
867. Section 124(2)(a) Law No. 130(I)/2021, which corresponds to Art. 17(2) Directive (EU) 2019/944.

access to data on equal and non-discriminatory terms while fully protecting commercially sensitive information and customers' personal data;[868] (e) an obligation on market participants engaged in aggregation to be financially responsible for the imbalances that they cause in the electricity system; to that extent they shall balance responsible parties or shall delegate their balancing responsibility;[869] (f) that final customers having made a contract with independent aggregators not to be subject to undue payments, penalties or other undue contractual restrictions by their suppliers;[870] (g) paying financial compensation to other market participants or to the market participants' balance responsible parties, if those market participants or balance responsible parties are directly affected by demand response activation. The financial compensation is strictly limited to covering the resulting costs incurred by the suppliers of participating customers or the suppliers' balance responsible parties during the activation of demand response, whereas the method for calculating it, takes account of the benefits brought about by the independent aggregators to other market participants. It creates a barrier neither to market entry for market participants engaged in aggregation nor to flexibility and is applied only following the approval of the calculation method by Cyprus Energy Regulatory Authority;[871] (h) that the Transmission System Operator and the Distribution System Operator acting in close cooperation with market participants and final customers, establish the technical requirements for participation of demand response in all electricity markets on the basis of the technical characteristics of those markets and the capabilities of demand response.[872]

206. At the same time, Cyprus Energy Regulatory Authority ensures the deployment of smart metering systems throughout Cyprus in order to assist the active participation of customers in the electricity market.[873] In a regulatory decision, it sets out the minimum functional and technical requirements for the smart metering systems to be deployed that must comply with European standards and the following principles:[874] (a) the smart metering systems shall accurately measure actual electricity consumption and shall be capable of providing to final customers information on actual time of use. Validated historical consumption data are made easily and securely available and visualized to final customers on request and at no additional cost. Non-validated near real-time consumption data are made easily and securely available to final customers at no additional cost, through a standardized interface

868. Section 124(2)(b) to (d) Law No. 130(I)/2021, which corresponds to Art. 17(3)(a) to (c) Directive (EU) 2019/944.
869. Section 124(2)(e) Law No. 130(I)/2021, which corresponds to Art. 17(3)(d) Directive (EU) 2019/944 and Art. 5 Regulation (EU) 2019/943.
870. Section 124(2)(f) Law No. 130(I)/2021, which corresponds to Art. 17(3)(e) Directive (EU) 2019/944.
871. Sections 124(2)(g) and 22(11)(b) & (c) Law No. 130(I)/2021, which correspond to Art. 17(4) Directive (EU) 2019/944.
872. Section 124(2)(h) Law No. 130(I)/2021, which corresponds to Art. 17(5) Directive (EU) 2019/944.
873. Section 125(1)(a) Law No. 130(I)/2021, which corresponds to Art. 19(2) Directive (EU) 2019/944.
874. Section 125(1)(b) Law No. 130(I)/2021, which corresponds to Art. 20 Directive (EU) 2019/944.

or through remote access, in order to support automated energy efficiency programmes, demand response and other services; (b) the security of the smart metering systems and data communication shall comply with relevant Union security rules, having due regard of the best available techniques for ensuring the highest level of cybersecurity protection while bearing in mind the costs and the principle of proportionality; (c) the privacy of final customers and the protection of their data shall comply with relevant Union data protection and privacy rules; (d) the Transmission System Operator shall ensure that the meters of active customers who feed electricity into the grid can account for electricity fed into the grid from the active customers' premises; (e) if final customers request it, data on the electricity they fed into the grid and their electricity consumption data shall be made available to them through a standardized communication interface or through remote access, or to a third party acting on their behalf, in an easily understandable format allowing them to compare offers on a like-for-like basis; (f) appropriate advice and information shall be given to final customers prior to or at the time of installation of smart meters, in particular concerning their full potential with regard to the management of meter reading and the monitoring of energy consumption, and concerning the collection and processing of personal data in accordance with the applicable Union data protection rules; (g) smart metering systems shall enable final customers to be metered and settled at the same time resolution as the imbalance settlement period set in the Electricity Market Rules.[875]

207. Deployment of smart metering systems is subject to a cost-benefit assessment performed under the following principles: (a) an economic assessment of all of the long-term costs and benefits to the market and the individual consumer or which form of smart metering is economically reasonable and cost-effective and which time frame is feasible for their distribution; (b) such assessment takes into consideration specific methodology for the cost-benefit analysis and some minimum functionalities for smart metering systems,[876] as well as the best available techniques for ensuring the highest level of cybersecurity and data protection; (c) subject to that assessment, Cyprus Energy Regulatory Authority prepares a timetable with a target of up to ten years for the deployment of smart metering systems. Where the deployment of smart metering systems is assessed positively, at least 80% of final customers shall be equipped with smart meters either within seven years of the date of the positive assessment or by 2024 for those Member States that have initiated the systematic deployment of smart metering systems before 4 July 2019.[877]

208. Where the performed cost-benefit assessment results in a positive outcome, Cyprus Energy Regulatory Authority decides to develop smart metering systems according to said standards and principles and within the explained time frame and

875. Section 125(4)(a) to (g) Law No. 130(I)/2021, which corresponds to Arts 19(3) and 20(a) to (g) Directive (EU) 2019/944.
876. *See* in this regard Commission Recommendation 2012/148/EU of 9 Mar. 2012 on preparations for the roll-out of smart metering systems, OJ L 73, 13 Mar. 2012, p. 9.
877. Section 125(2)(a) to (c) Law No. 130(I)/2021, which corresponds to Art. 19(2) and Annex II (1) and (3) Directive (EU) 2019/944.

instructs the Transmission System Operator to do so. It ensures the interoperability of those metering systems, as well as their ability to provide output for consumer energy management systems, while having due regard to the use of the relevant available standards, including those enabling interoperability, best practices and the importance of the development of smart grids and the development of the internal market for electricity.[878] Final customers contribute to the associated costs of the deployment in a transparent and non-discriminatory manner, while taking into account the long-term benefits to the whole value chain. Cyprus Energy Regulatory Authority regularly monitors such deployment in their territories to track the delivery of benefits to consumers.[879]

209. However, should the cost-benefit assessment lead to a negative result, Cyprus Energy Regulatory Authority ensures that the assessment is repeated at least every three years or sooner, should the market or technology developments demand so. It communicates the results to the Minister as soon as these are made available.[880] At the same time, every final customer is entitled on request to the Distribution System Operator to have installed or, where applicable, to have upgraded, under fair, reasonable and cost-effective conditions, a smart meter. This is equipped with certain functionalities and is interoperable and able to deliver the desired connectivity of the metering infrastructure with consumer energy management systems in near real-time.[881]

210. Already installed smart metering systems as of 4 July 2019, may remain in operation over their lifetime; however, if such systems do not meet the statutory requirements, their operation is limited up to 5 July 2031, at the latest.[882]

211. Where final customers do not have smart meters, they are provided with individual conventional meters that accurately measure their actual consumption. They must be able to easily read their convention meters, either directly or indirectly through an online interface or through another appropriate interface. This is ensured by the Distribution System Operator.[883]

§6. Vulnerable Customers and Energy Poverty

212. Vulnerable customers ('ευάλωτοι καταναλωτές') is a notion created at the EU level, albeit its content is specified at the national level. In Cyprus, persons

878. Section 125(3) & (5) Law No. 130(I)/2021, which corresponds to Art. 19(3) Directive (EU) 2019/944.
879. Section 125(6) Law No. 130(I)/2021, which corresponds to Art. 19(4) Directive (EU) 2019/944.
880. Section 125(7)(a) & (b) Law No. 130(I)/2021.
881. Section 125(7)(c) & (9)(a) *ibid*, which corresponds to Art. 21(1) Directive (EU) 2019/944. With regard to fuctionalities *see* s. 125(4) Law No. 130(I)/2021, which corresponds to Art. 20 Directive (EU) 2019/944.
882. Section 125(8) Law No. 130(I)/2021, which corresponds to Art. 19(6) Directive (EU) 2019/944.
883. Section 126(1) & (2) Law No. 130(I)/2021, which corresponds to Art. 22(1) & (2) Directive (EU) 2019/944.

with the following characteristics are treated as vulnerable customers: (a) the beneficiaries of minimum guaranteed income; (b) the receivers of a public allowance; (c) the receivers of grave mobility disability; (d) the receivers of allowance for retirees with low income of more than 70 years of age, under the condition that they do not cohabitate with a younger person; (e) the receivers of allowance for care of tetraplegic persons; (f) the receivers of allowance for blindness; and (g) large or five-member families that receive child allowance.[884]

213. The measures that Cyprus has set as adequate safeguards for the protection of vulnerable customers[885] are the following: (a) including the aforementioned categories of vulnerable customers, but for the fourth and seventh one, to a special valorization of lower charges; (b) providing monetary incentives to all aforementioned categories of vulnerable customers in order to instal domestic photovoltaic system of up to 3kW with the method of offsetting produced and consumed electricity; (c) providing monetary incentives to all aforementioned categories of vulnerable customers in order to improve the energy efficiency of their homes; (d) not disrupting or reconnecting electricity during crucial periods for all aforementioned categories of vulnerable customers for which continuous supply of electricity is necessary for reasons associated with their health.[886] Such measures must not impede the effective opening of the market or market functioning and need to be notified to the Commission, where relevant. Such notifications may also include measures taken within the general social security system.[887] Cyprus Energy Regulatory Authority controls and monitors, whether suppliers fulfil their obligations that correspond to said rights of vulnerable customers. When they fail to do so, it imposes sanctions.[888]

214. Specifically with regard to *energy poverty* ('ενεργειακή φτώχεια'), the Minister, following consultation with the Minister of Labor and Social Insurance, issues a Decree establishing and publishing the set of criteria for the purpose of defining this notion, which may include low income, high expenditure of disposable income on energy and poor energy efficiency.[889] These criteria shall include guidance provided by the Commission with regard to the notion of 'significant number of households in energy poverty' starting from the premise that any proportion of households in energy poverty can be considered to be significant.[890]

884. Regulation 4(1)(a) to (h) KDP 289/2015.
885. Article 28(1) Directive (EU) 2019/944.
886. Regulation 5(a) to (d) KDP 289/2015.
887. Section 129(3)(b) & (c) Law No. 130(I)/2021, which corresponds to Art. 28(2) Directive (EU) 2019/944.
888. Section 129(5) Law No. 130(I)/2021.
889. Section 130(1) *ibid.*, which corresponds to Art. 29 Directive (EU) 2019/944.
890. Section 130(2) Law No. 130(I)/2021, which corresponds to Art. 29 Directive (EU) 2019/944.

§7. Disputes Between Final Customers and Operators

215. Should a dispute arise, aside from the ordinary option of filing a lawsu with the competent courts, final customers have the option of out-of-court settle ment. More specifically, Cyprus Energy Regulatory Authority has the duty to pro vide simple, fair, transparent, independent, effective and efficient out-of-cou mechanisms for the settlement of disputes, to which final customers have acces concerning rights and obligations established under this law.[891] Where the final cus tomer is a *consumer* within the meaning of 'any natural person who is acting fo purposes which are outside his trade, business, craft or profession',[892] such out-of court dispute settlement mechanisms comply with the quality requirements set ou in the opposite legislation and provide a proper system of reimbursement and com pensation.[893] Cyprus Energy Regulatory Authority cooperates with other alternativ dispute resolution entities in order to provide for simple, fair, transparent, indepen dent, effective and efficient out-of-court dispute settlement mechanisms for any dis pute that arises from products or services that are tied to, or bundled with, an product or service falling under the scope of this law.[894] The participation of elec tricity undertakings in out-of-court dispute settlement mechanisms for househol customers is mandatory, when the relevant dispute arises between household cus tomers and electricity undertakings.[895]

891. Section 128(1) Law No. 130(I)/2021, which corresponds to Art. 26(1) Directive (EU) 2019/944.
892. Section 2(1) Law on Alternatve Dispute Resolution for Consumer Disputes ('ο περί της Εναλ-λακτικής Επίλυσης Καταναλωτικών Διαφορών Νόμος') No. 85 of 2017, OG I(I) No. 4610 of 7 Jul. 2017, p. 718, which corresponds to Art. 4(1)(a) Directive 2013/11/EU of the European Parliament and of the Council of 21 May 2013 on alternative dispute resolution for consumer disputes and amending Regulation (EC) No. 2006/2004 and Directive 2009/22/EC, OJ L 165, 18 Jun. 2013, p. 63.
893. Section 128(2) Law No. 130(I)/2021, which corresponds to Art. 26(1) Directive (EU) 2019/944.
894. Section 128(3) Law No. 130(I)/2021, which corresponds to Art. 26(2) Directive (EU) 2019/944.
895. Section 128(4) Law No. 130(I)/2021, which corresponds to Art. 26(3) Directive (EU) 2019/944.

Part II. Regulatory Framework Concerning Gas

Chapter 1. Introduction

§1. OBJECTIVE

216. Law No. 183(I)/2004 sets out the regulation of the natural gas market and, among others, establishes rules for the transmission ('μεταφορά'),[896] distribution ('διανομή'),[897] supply ('προμήθεια')[898] and storage ('αποθήκευση')[899] of natural gas. It also lays down rules relating to the organization and functioning of the natural gas sector, access to the market, operation of systems, criteria and procedures applicable to the granting of authorizations for transmission, distribution, supply and storage of natural gas.[900] The rules established by this law for natural gas, including Liquefied Natural Gas (LNG), also apply on a non-discriminatory basis to biogas ('βιοαέριο') and gas from biomass or other types of gas insofar as such gases can technically and safely be injected into, and transported through, the natural gas system.[901]

896. Transmission ('transport' in French, 'Fernleitung' in German, 'transmissie' in Dutch) means the transport of natural gas through a network, which mainly contains high-pressure pipelines, other than an upstream pipeline network and other than the part of high-pressure pipelines primarily used in the context of local distribution of natural gas, with a view to its delivery to customers, but not including supply. Section 2(1) Law No. 183(I)/2004, which corresponds to Art. 2(3) Directive 2009/73/EC.
897. Distribution ('distribution' in French, 'Verteilung' in German, 'distributie' in Dutch) means the transport of natural gas through local or regional pipeline networks with a view to its delivery to customers, but not including supply. Section 2(1) Law No. 183(I)/2004, which corresponds to Art. 2(5) Directive 2009/73/EC.
898. Supply ('fourniture' in French, 'Versorgung' or 'Lieferung' in German, 'levering' in Dutch) means the sale, including resale, of natural gas, including LNG, to customers. Section 2(1) Law No. 183(I)/2004, which corresponds to Art. 2(7) Directive 2009/73/EC.
899. Storage facility ('εγκατάσταση αποθήκευσης' in original, 'installation de stockage' in French, 'Speicheranlage' in German, 'opslaginstallatie' in Dutch) means a facility used for the stocking of natural gas and owned and/or operated by a natural gas undertaking, including the part of LNG facilities used for storage but excluding the portion used for production operations, and excluding facilities reserved exclusively for transmission system operators in carrying out their functions. Section 2(1) Law No. 183(I)/2004, which corresponds to Art. 2(9) Directive 2009/73/EC.
900. Section 3(1) Law No. 183(I)/2004, which corresponds to Art. 1(1) Directive 2009/73/EC.
901. Section 3(1) Law No. 183(I)/2004, which corresponds to Art. 1(2) Directive 2009/73/EC.

§2. REGULATORY MECHANISM

217. The natural gas market is regulated by the Cyprus Energy Regulatory Authority, the Minister and the Agency, who bear different duties and authorities, as demonstrated below.

I. Cyprus Energy Regulatory Authority

218. Cyprus Energy Regulatory Authority that has extended duties and rights under Law No. 130(I)/2021, plays a vital role in the natural gas market as well. The duties and powers assigned to the same via this law are set out below:

- issuing, controlling, amending, transferring, suspending or revoking authorizations or exclusions from authorization foreseen in this law;[902]
- approving terms and conditions of connection and access to the network, including transmission and distribution tariffs, and terms, conditions and tariffs for access to LNG and storage facilities;[903]
- defining management rules and interconnection capacity allocation rules in consultation with the competent authority or authorities of the Member States with which an interconnection exists;[904]
- drafting or approving of congestion response mechanism for the gas system;[905]
- consumer protection;[906]
- consulting the Minister on deciding on applications submitted by natural gas undertakings for temporary deviation from certain provisions;[907]
- denying authorization for building and operating distribution pipeline systems;[908]
- regulating tariffs, charges and other terms and conditions imposed by natural gas undertakings for any offered service;[909]
- laying down and publishing regulations on quality standards that natural gas undertakings need to comply with;[910]
- issuing regulations;[911]
- resolving disputes;[912]
- taking appropriate and effective measures for control and transparency in order to avoid any abuse of a dominant position, in particular to the detriment of consumers;[913]

902. Section 7(1)(1) Law No. 183(I)/2004.
903. Section 7(1)(2) *ibid.*, which corresponds to Art. 41(6)(a) Directive 2009/73/EC.
904. Section 7(1)(3) Law No. 183(I)/2004.
905. Section 7(1)(4) *ibid.*
906. Sections 7(1)(5) and 40 *ibid.*
907. Sections 7(1)(6) and 43(2) *ibid.*
908. Sections 7(1)(7) and 14 *ibid.*
909. Section 7(1)(8) *ibid.*
910. Section 7(1)(9) *ibid.*
911. Section 7(1)(10) *ibid.*
912. Sections 7(1)(11), 36, 37 and 40(1) and (11) *ibid.*
913. Section 7(1)(12) *ibid.*, which corresponds to Art. 41(13) Directive 2009/73/EC.

- establishing, keeping and managing a record pursuant to section 7B Law No. 182(I)/2004;[914]
- monitoring compliance of the transmission and distribution system operators with minimum standards for maintenance and development of the transmission and distribution systems, including interconnection capacity, where applicable;[915]
- ensuring compliance of transmission and distribution system operators, and where relevant, system owners, as well as of any natural gas undertakings, with their obligations under this law and other relevant EU legislation, including cross-border issues;[916]
- cooperating in regard to cross-border issues with the regulatory authority or authorities of Member States concerned and with the Agency, including infrastructure to and from a third country;[917]
- complying with, and implementation of, any relevant legally binding decisions of the Agency and the European Commission;[918]
- reporting annually on its activity and the fulfilment of its duties to the President of the Republic, the Agency and the European Commission. Such reports cover steps taken and results obtained as regards each of the tasks listed in this section. The authority deposits a copy of this report to the Council of Ministers and the House of Representatives and takes the necessary steps for easy access to it by the public;[919]
- ensuring that there are no cross-subsidies between transmission, distribution, storage, LNG and supply activities;[920]
- monitoring investment plans of the transmission system operators, and providing in its annual report an assessment of the investment plans of the transmission system operators as regards their consistency with the Union-wide network development plan referred to in Article 8(3)(b) Regulation (EC) No. 715/2009; such assessment may include recommendations to amend those investment plans;[921]
- monitoring compliance with and reviewing the past performance of network security and reliability rules and setting or approving standards and requirements for quality of service and supply or contributing thereto together with other competent authorities;[922]
- monitoring the level of transparency, including wholesale prices, and ensuring compliance of natural gas undertakings with transparency obligations;[923]
- monitoring the level and effectiveness of market opening and competition at wholesale and retail levels, including natural gas exchanges, prices for household customers including prepayment systems, switching rates, disconnection rates,

914. Sections 7(1)(13) and 7B Law No. 183(I)/2004.
915. Section 7(1)(14) *ibid.*, which partially corresponds to Art. 13(4) Directive 2009/73/EC, as the European proviso refers only to transmission.
916. Section 7(1)(15) Law No. 183(I)/2014, which corresponds to Art. 41(1)(b) Directive 2009/73/EC.
917. Section 7(1)(16) Law No. 183(I)/2014, which corresponds to Art. 41(1)(c) Directive 2009/73/EC.
918. Section 7(1)(17) Law No. 183(I)/2014, which corresponds to Art. 41(1)(d) Directive 2009/73/EC.
919. Section 7(1)(18) Law No. 183(I)/2004, which corresponds to Art. 41(1)(e) Directive 2009/73/EC.
920. Section 7(1)(19) Law No. 183(I)/2004, which corresponds to Art. 41(1)(f) Directive 2009/73/EC.
921. Section 7(1)(20) Law No. 183(I)/2004, which corresponds to Art. 41(1)(g) Directive 2009/73/EC.
922. Section 7(1)(21) Law No. 183(I)/2004, which corresponds to Art. 41(1)(h) Directive 2009/73/EC.
923. Section 7(1)(22) Law No. 183(I)/2004, which corresponds to Art. 41(1)(i) Directive 2009/73/EC.

charges for and execution of maintenance services and complaints by household customers, as well as any distortion or restriction of competition, including providing any relevant information. Cyprus Energy Regulatory Authority must bring any relevant cases to the relevant competition authorities;[924]

- monitoring the occurrence of restrictive contractual practices, including exclusivity clauses which may prevent large non-household customers from contracting simultaneously with more than one supplier or restrict their choice to do so, and, where appropriate, informing the National Commission for the Protection of Competition of such practices;[925]
- respecting contractual freedom with regard to interruptible supply contracts as well as with regard to long-term contracts, provided that they are compatible with EU law and consistent with policies of the same;[926]
- monitoring the time taken by transmission and distribution system operators to make connections and repairs;[927]
- monitoring and reviewing the access conditions to storage, line pack and other ancillary services as provided for in sections 30 ff. Law No. 183(I)/2004;[928]
- ensuring the effectiveness and enforcement of consumer protection measures;[929]
- publishing recommendations, at least annually, in relation to supply prices and providing those to the competent authorities, where appropriate;[930]
- ensuring access to customer consumption data, the provision for optional use, of an easily understandable harmonized format at the national level for consumption data and prompt access for all customers to such data;[931]
- monitoring the implementation of rules relating to the roles and responsibilities of transmission system operators, distribution system operators, suppliers and customers and other market parties pursuant to Regulation (EC) No. 715/2009;[932]
- monitoring the correct application of the criteria determining regulation of a storage facility;[933]
- issuing binding decisions for natural gas undertakings;[934]
- carrying out investigations into the functioning of the gas markets, and deciding upon and imposing any necessary and proportionate measures to promote effective competition and ensure the proper functioning of the market. Where appropriate, the authority also has the power to cooperate with the Commission for the

---

924. Section 7(1)(23) Law No. 183(I)/2004, which corresponds to Art. 41(1)(j) Directive 2009/73/EC.
925. Section 7(1)(24) Law No. 183(I)/2004, which corresponds to Art. 41(1)(k) Directive 2009/73/EC.
926. Section 7(1)(25) Law No. 183(I)/2004, which corresponds to Art. 41(1)(l) Directive 2009/73/EC.
927. Section 7(1)(26) Law No. 183(I)/2004, which corresponds to Art. 41(1)(m) Directive 2009/73/EC.
928. Section 7(1)(27) Law No. 183(I)/2004, which corresponds to Art. 41(1)(n) Directive 2009/73/EC.
929. Sections 7(1)(28) and 40 Law No. 183(I)/2004, which correspond to Art. 41(1)(o) Directive 2009/73/EC.
930. Sections 7(1)(29), 6(1)(k), 6(1)(l), 39, 40(2)(a)(ix), 40(6) and 40(7) Law No. 183(I)/2004, which correspond to Art. 41(1)(p) Directive 2009/73/EC.
931. Sections 7(1)(30) and 40(2)(h) Law No. 183(I)/2004, which corresponds to Art. 41(1)(q) Directive 2009/73/EC.
932. Section 7(1)(31) Law No. 183(I)/2004, which corresponds to Art. 41(1)(r) Directive 2009/73/EC.
933. Sections 7(1)(32) and 31(2), (3) and (4) Law No. 183(I)/2004, which correspond to Art. 41(1)(s) Directive 2009/73/EC.
934. Section 7(1)(33) Law No. 183(I)/2004, which corresponds to Art. 41(4)(a) Directive 2009/73/EC.

Protection of Competition and the financial market regulators or the European Commission in conducting an investigation relating to competition law;[935]

- requiring any information from natural gas undertakings relevant to the fulfilment of its tasks, including the justification for any refusal to grant third-party access, and any information on measures necessary to reinforce the network;[936]
- imposing effective, proportionate and dissuasive penalties on natural gas undertakings not complying with their obligations under this law or any relevant legally binding decisions of the authority or of the Agency, or seeking the imposition of such penalties by the competent court. This includes the power to impose or propose the imposition of penalties of up to 10% of the annual turnover of the transmission system operator or of up to 10% of the annual turnover of the vertically integrated undertaking on the transmission system operator or on the vertically integrated undertaking, as the case may be, for non-compliance with their respective obligations pursuant to this law;[937] and
- appropriate rights of investigations and relevant powers of instructions for dispute settlement.[938]

219. Cyprus Energy Regulatory Authority is further competent in certain methodologies. In particular, it is responsible for fixing or approving sufficiently in advance of their entry into force at least the methodologies used to calculate or establish the terms and conditions for:

- connection and access to national networks, including transmission and distribution tariffs, and terms and conditions and tariffs for access to LNG facilities. Those tariffs or methodologies allow the necessary investments in the networks and LNG facilities to be carried out in a manner allowing those investments to ensure the viability of the networks and LNG facilities;[939]
- the provision of balancing services which is performed in the most economical manner and provide appropriate incentives for network users to balance their input and off-takes. Balancing services are provided in a fair and non-discriminatory manner and are based on objective criteria;[940] and
- access to cross-border infrastructures, including the procedures for the allocation of capacity and congestion management.[941]

220. These methodologies and terms and conditions must be published,[942] although the manner of publication is not fixed in the law. Furthermore, in fixing or approving the tariffs or methodologies and the balancing services, the authority ensures that transmission and distribution system operators are granted appropriate

935. Section 7(1)(34) Law No. 183(I)/2004, which corresponds to Art. 41(4)(b) Directive 2009/73/EC.
936. Section 7(1)(35) Law No. 183(I)/2004, which corresponds to Art. 41(4)(c) Directive 2009/73/EC.
937. Section 7(1)(37) Law No. 183(I)/2004, which corresponds to Art. 41(4)(d) Directive 2009/73/EC.
938. Section 7(1)(38) Law No. 183(I)/2004, which corresponds to Art. 41(4)(e) Directive 2009/73/EC.
939. Section 7(2)(a)(i) Law No. 183(I)/2004, which corresponds to Art. 41(6)(a) Directive 2009/73/EC.
940. Section 7(2)(a)(ii) Law No. 183(I)/2004, which corresponds to Art. 41(6)(b) Directive 2009/73/EC.
941. Section 7(2)(a)(iii) Law No. 183(I)/2004, which corresponds to Art. 41(6)(c) Directive 2009/73/EC.
942. Section 7(2)(b) Law No. 183(I)/2004, which corresponds to Art. 41(7) Directive 2009/73/EC.

incentive, over both the short and long term, to increase efficiencies, foster market integration and security of supply and support the related research activities.[943] The authority also monitors congestion management of national gas transmission networks including interconnectors, and the implementation of congestion management rules. To that end, transmission system operators or market operators submit their congestion management rules, including capacity allocation, to the authority. The latter may request amendments to those rules.[944] In particular, it has the authority to require transmission, storage, LNG and distribution system operators, if necessary, to modify the terms and conditions, including tariffs and methodologies referred to in this section, to ensure that they are proportionate and applied in a non-discriminatory manner. In the event of a delay in fixing transmission and distribution tariffs, regulatory authorities have the power to fix or approve provisional transmission and distribution tariffs or methodologies and to decide on the appropriate compensatory measures if the final tariffs or methodologies deviate from those provisional tariffs or methodologies.[945] The decisions reached by the authority are to be fully reasoned and justified to allow for judicial review, along with being available to the public while preserving the confidentiality of commercially sensitive information.[946]

221. The authority is further entrusted to create appropriate and efficient mechanisms for regulation, control and transparency so as to avoid any abuse of a dominant position, in particular, to the detriment of consumers, and any predatory behaviour.[947]

222. Further duty of Cyprus Energy Regulatory Authority is to ensure and publish measures taken in case of an unforeseeable crisis in the energy market or when the safety of persons, works or installations or the safety of the system is threatened.[948] In addition, it cooperates with the competent authorities of other Member States in order to promote regional and bilateral solidarity. Such cooperation covers situations resulting or likely to result in the short term in a severe disruption of supply affecting a Member State and include:

- coordination of national emergency measures referred to in Article 8 Council Directive 2004/67/EC of 26 April 2004 concerning measures to safeguard security of natural gas supply;[949]

943. Section 7(2)(c) Law No. 183(I)/2004, which corresponds to Art. 41(8) Directive 2009/73/EC.
944. Section 7(2)(d) Law No. 183(I)/2004, which corresponds to Art. 41(9) Directive 2009/73/EC.
945. Section 7(2)(e) Law No. 183(I)/2004, which corresponds to Art. 41(10) Directive 2009/73/EC.
946. Section 7(2)(k) Law No. 183(I)/2004, which corresponds to Art. 41(16) Directive 2009/73/EC.
947. Section 7(2)(h) Law No. 183(I)/2004, which corresponds to Art. 41(13) Directive 2009/73/EC. However, the directive imposes this obligation on the state and not solely on the regulatory authority.
948. Section 6(3)(a) Law No. 183(I)/2004.
949. Section 6(3)(c) *ibid.*, which corresponds to Art. 6(2)(a) Directive 2009/73/EC.

– identification and, where necessary, development or upgrading of electricity and natural gas interconnections;[950] and
– conditions and practical modalities for mutual assistance.[951]

223. Cyprus Energy Regulatory Authority is also the competent authority for ensuring the application of measures set out in regulation concerning measures to safeguard security of gas supply.[952,953]

224. In addition, Cyprus Energy Regulatory Authority is entrusted with certain energy efficiency duties, including the deployment of individual meters. Cyprus Energy Regulatory Authority ensures that an assessment is undertaken of the energy efficiency potentials of the gas and electricity infrastructure, in particular, regarding transmission, distribution, load management and interoperability, and connection to energy-generating installations, including access possibilities for micro-energy generators.[954] In addition, it ensures that concrete measures and investments are identified for the introduction of cost-effective energy efficiency improvements in the network infrastructure, with a timetable for their introduction.[955] Further, Cyprus Energy Regulatory Authority ensures that, in so far as it is technically possible, financially reasonable and proportionate in relation to the potential energy savings, final customers for electricity, natural gas, district heating, district cooling and domestic hot water are provided with competitively priced individual meters that accurately reflect the final customer's actual energy consumption and that provide information on actual time of use. In any event, such a competitively priced individual meter is always provided when an existing meter is replaced, unless this is technically impossible or not cost-effective in relation to the estimated potential savings in the long term.[956] Such a meter is equally provided when a new connection is made in a new building or a building undergoes major renovations, as set out in the Law on Energy Efficiency of Buildings.[957,958]

225. The general objectives of the authority are equally set out in the law in a very informative and detailed way. The authority acts in such a way so as to:

---

950. Section 6(3)(c) Law No. 183(I)/2004, which corresponds to Art. 6(2)(b) Directive 2009/73/EC.
951. Section 6(3)(c) Law No. 183(I)/2004, which corresponds to Art. 6(2)(c) Directive 2009/73/EC.
952. Regulation (EU) 2017/1938 of the European Parliament and of the Council of 25 Oct. 2017 concerning measures to safeguard the security of gas supply and repealing Regulation (EU) No. 994/2010, OJ L 280, 28 Oct. 2017, p. 1.
953. Section 6(4) Law No. 183(I)/2004.
954. Section 7(3)(a) *ibid.*, which corresponds to Art. 15(2)(a) Directive 2012/27/EU.
955. Section 7(3)(b) Law No. 183(I)/2004, which corresponds to Art. 15(2)(b) Directive 2012/27/EU.
956. Section 7(4) Law No. 183(I)/2004, which corresponds to Art. 9(1)(a) Directive 2012/27/EU.
957. Law on Regulation of Energy Efficiency of Buildings ('περί Ρύθμισης της Ενεργειακής Απόδοσης των Κτιρίων Νόμος') No. 142 of 2016, OG I(I) No. 4095 of 3 Nov. 2006, as amended, which implements Directive 2012/27/EU of the European Parliament and of the Council of 25 Oct. 2012 on energy efficiency, amending Directives 2009/125/EC and 2010/30/EU and repealing Directives 2004/8/EC and 2006/32/EC, OJ L 315, 14 Nov. 2012, p. 1.
958. Section 7(4) Law No. 183(I)/2004, which corresponds to Art. 9(1)(b) Directive 2012/27/EU.

- ensure application of the competition rules in transmission, distribution and storage of natural gas;[959]
- protect the consumers' interests;[960]
- ensure the satisfaction of reasonable demand for natural gas;[961]
- ensure that the authorization holders are capable of financing the company for which the authorization is granted;[962]
- promote the development of a financially efficient and effective market of natural gas;[963]
- ensure the security, continuance of supply as well as quality and effectiveness of the natural gas supply;[964]
- care for the protection of the environment;[965]
- take into consideration the needs of vulnerable customers, disabled people and the elderly and care for sufficient guarantees for the protection thereof;[966]
- encourage research and development in relation to transmission, distribution, supply, storage and use of natural gas;[967]
- advise the Minister in matters within the scope of application of this law following its own initiative or after a referral of the Minister or the Council of Ministers;[968]
- ensure that the natural gas undertakings operate with the aim of achieving a competitive, safe and environmentally sustainable market of natural gas and do not discriminate between such undertakings with reference to rights or obligations;[969]
- ensure that the natural gas undertakings optimize the use of gas, for example, by providing energy management services, developing innovative pricing formulas or introducing intelligent metering systems or smart grids where appropriate;[970]
- promote and facilitate the cooperation of system operators at a regional level, including on cross-border issues with the aim of creating a competitive internal market, ensure the security of supply, foster the consistency of their legal, regulatory and technical framework and facilitate integration of the isolated systems forming gas islands that persist in the Union;[971]
- promote, in close cooperation with the Agency, regulatory authorities of other Member States and the European Commission, a competitive, secure and environmentally sustainable internal market in natural gas within the Union, and effective market opening for all customers and suppliers in the Union, and ensure

959. Section 6(1)(a) Law No. 183(I)/2004 and s. 31 Law No. 122(I)/2003.
960. Section 6(1)(b) Law No. 183(I)/2004.
961. Section 6(1)(c) *ibid.*
962. Section 6(1)(d) *ibid.*
963. Section 6(1)(e) *ibid.*
964. Section 6(1)(f) *ibid.*
965. Section 6(1)(g) *ibid.*
966. Section 6(1)(h) *ibid.*
967. Section 6(1)(i) *ibid.*
968. Section 6(1)(j) *ibid.*
969. Section 6(1)(k) *ibid.*
970. Section 6(1)(l) *ibid.*, which corresponds to Art. 3(8) Directive 2009/73/EC.
971. Section 6(1)(m) Law No. 183(I)/2004, which partially corresponds to Art. 7(1) Directive 2009/73/EC, as the directive refers solely to transmission system operators.

appropriate conditions for the effective and reliable operation of gas networks, taking into account long-term objectives;[972]

- develop competitive and properly functioning regional markets within the Union in view of the achievement of the aforementioned objectives of sustainable internal market, effective market opening and reliable operation of gas networks;[973]
- eliminate restrictions on trade in natural gas between the Member States, including developing appropriate cross-border transmission capacities to meet demand and enhance the integration of national markets which may facilitate natural gas flow across the Union;[974]
- help to achieve, in the most cost-effective way, the development of secure, reliable and efficient non-discriminatory systems that are consumer-oriented, and promote system adequacy and are in line with general energy policy objectives, energy efficiency as well as the integration of large and small-scale production of gas from renewable energy sources and distributed production in both transmission and distribution networks;[975]
- facilitate access to the network for new production capacity, in particular, to remove barriers that could prevent access for new market entrants and gas from renewable energy sources;[976]
- ensure that system operators and system users are granted appropriate incentives, in both, the short and the long term, to increase efficiencies in system performance and foster market integration;[977]
- ensure that customers benefit through the efficient functioning of their national market, promote effective competition and help to ensure consumer protection;[978] and
- help to achieve high standards of public service for natural gas, contribute to the protection of vulnerable customers and contribute to the compatibility of necessary data exchange processes for customer switching.[979]

226. During the fulfilment of those duties, the authority has regard for its public service duties and takes measures for its compliance with those. These measures are to be communicated to the European Commission.[980]

227. While exercising said powers and duties, Cyprus Energy Regulatory Authority may issue regulatory decisions setting out the manner in which the

972. Section 6(1)(n) Law No. 183(I)/2004, which corresponds to Art. 40(a) Directive 2009/73/EC.
973. Section 6(1)(o) Law No. 183(I)/2004, which corresponds to Art. 40(b) Directive 2009/73/EC.
974. Section 6(1)(p) Law No. 183(I)/2004, which corresponds to Art. 40(c) Directive 2009/73/EC.
975. Section 6(1)(q) Law No. 183(I)/2004, which corresponds to Art. 40(d) Directive 2009/73/EC.
976. Section 6(1)(r) Law No. 183(I)/2004, which corresponds to Art. 40(e) Directive 2009/73/EC.
977. Section 6(1)(s) Law No. 183(I)/2004, which corresponds to Art. 40(f) Directive 2009/73/EC.
978. Section 6(1)(u) Law No. 183(I)/2004, which corresponds to Art. 40(g) Directive 2009/73/EC.
979. Section 6(1)(t) Law No. 183(I)/2004, which corresponds to Art. 40(h) Directive 2009/73/EC.
980. Sections 6(2) and 41 Law No. 183(I)/2004.

natural gas market is regulated as well as specifying the natural gas undertakings that are bound by such a decision.[981]

228. Lastly, Cyprus Energy Regulatory Authority drafts and implements long-term planning in relation to security of supply, energy efficiency/demand side management and for the fulfilment of environmental goals and goals for energy from renewable sources, considering the possibility of third parties seeking access to the system.[982] Long-term planning is drafted on a ten-year rolling basis and has regard to any instructions of the Minister, which are published from time to time and have regard to governmental policy. It is also published on the website of the authority.[983]

II. The Minister of Energy, Commerce, Industry and Tourism

229. The Minister of Energy, Commerce, Industry and Tourism issues guidelines on governmental policy[984] and long-term planning,[985] regulations regarding dispute settlements relating to access to upstream networks[986] and is entrusted with ensuring that dispute mechanisms regarding decisions of Cyprus Energy Regulatory Authority, to which anyone can turn, are in place.[987] He also imposes public service obligations[988] and issues decrees for the determination of eligible customers.[989] Lastly, he decides on derogation due to serious economic and financial difficulties[990] and informs the European Commission on necessary safeguard measures taken in the event of sudden crisis[991] and about derogations or alternatively, he applies for such.[992]

III. The Agency for the Cooperation of Energy Regulators

230. The Agency plays an important role in this law in a manner similar to the aforementioned on Law No. 130(I)/2021. In particular, Cyprus Energy Regulatory Authority may request the opinion of the Agency on the compliance of a decision taken by the same with the Guidelines referred to in this legislation or Regulation

981. Section 7A(1)(a) *ibid.*
982. Section 39(6) *ibid.*, which corresponds to Art. 3(2) Directive 2009/73/EC.
983. Section 39(6) Law No. 183(I)/2004.
984. Section 10 *ibid.*
985. Section 39(6) *ibid.*
986. Section 36 *ibid.*
987. Section 7(2)(l) *ibid.*
988. Section 39 *ibid.*
989. Section 33(1) *ibid.*
990. Section 43(1) *ibid.*
991. Sections 40(12) and 44(1)(d) and (2)(c) *ibid.*
992. Section 44(3) *ibid.*

EC) No. 715/2009.[993,994] The authority is obliged to comply with its opinion within 'our months from the date of receipt of said opinion.[995]

993. Regulation (EC) No. 715/2009 of the European Parliament and of the Council of 13 Jul. 2009 on conditions for access to the natural gas transmission networks and repealing Regulation (EC) No. 1775/2005, OJ L 211, 14 Aug. 2009, p. 36.
994. Section 7E(1) Law No. 183(I)/2004, which corresponds to Art. 43(1) Directive 2009/73/EC.
995. Section 7E(2) Law No. 183(I)/2004, which corresponds to Art. 43(2) Directive 2009/73/EC. However, the directive foresees that the national authority must comply with the opinion of the Agency within three months.

Chapter 2. Production

§1. Natural Gas Undertakings Engaged in Supply

231. Every natural gas undertaking engaged in supply underlies the general dut of safe, sufficient and good standard supply of natural gas to their customers at rea sonable prices that are approved by Cyprus Energy Regulatory Authority.[996] Sav for provisions of section 40 Law No. 183(I)/2004, every such undertaking is in par ticular responsible for:

- contracting with clients under fair and in advance well-known terms. All infor mation must be provided by the undertaking to the customers prior to the con clusion or confirmation of the contract;[997]
- supplying natural gas of a specified quality, for the purchase of which he ma enter into contracts with more than one supplier, making use of existing infra structure;[998]
- providing the customers with good standards of service, including mainte nance;[999]
- not charging the customer for changing suppliers;[1000]
- offering customers a wide choice of payment methods;[1001]
- following the applicable trading and balancing rules;[1002]
- offering the customers transparent, fair and just methods of sale;[1003]
- providing the consumption data of customers to any other authorized natural ga undertaking engaged in supply, following their consent;[1004]
- providing a final closure account to customers following any change of natura gas supplier no later than six weeks after the change of supplier has take place;[1005] and
- publishing annually the Charter of Customer's Rights that includes the rights tha derive from section 40 of this law.[1006]

232. In addition to the above-mentioned, suppliers have special informatio obligations. They must inform the customers in writing and within a reasonable tim about any intention of changing the contract's terms as well as about the customers right to terminate the contract.[1007] They further communicate to customers an increase in charges at an appropriate time but no later than one normal billing perio

996. Section 23(1) Law No. 183(I)/2004.
997. Section 23(2)(a) *ibid.*
998. Section 23(2)(b) *ibid.*
999. Section 23(2)(c) *ibid.*
1000. Section 23(2)(d) *ibid.*
1001. Section 23(2)(e) *ibid.*
1002. Section 23(2)(f) *ibid.*
1003. Section 23(2)(g) *ibid.*
1004. Section 23(2)(h) *ibid.*
1005. Section 23(2)(i) *ibid.*
1006. Section 23(2)(j) *ibid.*
1007. Section 23(3)(a) *ibid.*

after the increase comes into effect in a transparent and comprehensible manner.[1008] Lastly, they are obliged to inform with transparency and in writing their customers on applicable prices and tariffs,[1009] on standard terms and conditions, in respect of access to and use of gas services,[1010] as well as on consumption data, the form of which is determined by Cyprus Energy Regulatory Authority.[1011]

§2. Authorization for Natural Gas Related Activities

233. Activities related to natural gas need to be authorized by Cyprus Energy Regulatory Authority.[1012] These activities involve building and/or operating natural gas facilities and/or storage facilities and/or pipeline network, pipelines and associated equipment,[1013] carrying out any of the duties of a natural gas facility owner and/or storage facility and/or pipeline network, pipelines and associated equipment,[1014] carrying out any of the responsibilities of system operation,[1015] supplying natural gas to wholesale customers, among others,[1016] supplying natural gas to non-eligible customers,[1017] carrying out any of the duties of the importation/storage/transmission/distribution system operator[1018] and carrying out any of the duties of the importation/storage/transmission/distribution system owner.[1019] Interestingly the term 'importation' is defined neither in the national legislation nor in the European directive, although the activity of importation is included in the functions of an LNG system operator.[1020] Hence, it is safe to assume that it has its ordinary meaning. It should be further noted that granting such authorization does not free the authorization holder from the obligation to obtain any other permit or authorization in accordance with national laws as well as the obligation to conform with the law.[1021]

234. Still, the Council of Ministers may decide not to apply the provisions on authorizations, those being sections 8–14 Law No. 183(I)/2004, with respect to distribution insofar as their application would obstruct, in law or in fact, the performance of the obligations imposed on natural gas undertakings in the general economic interest and insofar as the development of trade would not be affected to

1008. Section 23(3)(b) *ibid.*
1009. Section 23(4)(a) *ibid.*
1010. Section 23(4)(b) *ibid.*
1011. Section 23(4)(c) *ibid.*
1012. Section 8(1) *ibid.*
1013. Section 8(1)(a) *ibid.*
1014. Section 8(1)(b) *ibid.*
1015. Section 8(1)(c) *ibid.*
1016. Section 8(1)(d) *ibid.*
1017. Section 8(1)(e) *ibid.*
1018. Section 8(1)(f) *ibid.*
1019. Section 8(1)(g) *ibid.*
1020. Article 2(12) Directive 2009/73/EC, which was transposed in s. 2 Law No. 183(I)/2004.
1021. Section 8(2) *ibid.*

such an extent as would be contrary to the interests of the Union. Such interests include, *inter alia*, competition with regard to eligible customers in accordance with this legislation.[1022]

I. Application for Authorization

235. The particulars of the application for authorization are specified in secondary legislation.[1023] Briefly, the application needs to be filed in the specified form,[1024] along with specific documentation and data[1025] and the applicable fees.[1026] The documentation that needs to be submitted includes recent financial statements that reflect the financial status of the undertaking(s) operated by the applicant,[1027] a statement of the business plan for the next five years,[1028] a summary of the financial planning for the activities requested to be authorized for the next five years or the time period of the plan, should this be longer[1029] and a statement on the possible financial sources of the applicant and the plan.[1030] Especially when applying the authorization of natural gas extraction the following need to be submitted along with the above documentation: (i) a schedule of due dates for the construction and activation of the facilities, (ii) the details of the applicant or any business partner or any subcontractor, whose experience the applicant shall use, so that it will be proved that they possess the know-how to materialize the activities of the application, (iii) details on the level of efficiency expected to be accomplished by the proposed facilities, (iv) an environmental impact assessment, and (v) a risk-assessment study.[1031] Via obtaining, preparing and filing the above-mentioned documents, it is intended to allow the applicant to establish its prima facie technical and financial ability and resources to carry out the activities included in the application.[1032]

236. Within two months of receiving the application, Cyprus Energy Regulatory Authority may request in writing from the applicant any additional information regarding any submitted document within the time period specified therein.[1033] Should the applicant not provide the requested information, the authority may refuse the application. The applicant is informed accordingly in writing.[1034] Alternatively,

1022. Section 40(13) *ibid.*, which corresponds to Art. 3(10) Directive 2009/73/EC.
1023. Sections 9, 43(2)(a) Law No. 183(I)/2004.
1024. Regulation 3(1)(a) Regulations on Regulating the Natural Gas Market (Granting of Authorizations) ('περί Ρύθμισης της Αγοράς Φυσικού Αερίου (Έκδοση Αδειών) Κανονισμοί') No. 298 of 2006, OG III(I) No. 4122, 21 Jun. 2006, p. 2412 (hereinafter 'KDP 298/2006').
1025. Regulation 3(1)(b) *ibid.*
1026. Regulation 3(1)(c) *ibid.*
1027. Annex 1II(1) *ibid.*
1028. Annex 1II(2) *ibid.*
1029. Annex 1II(4) *ibid.*
1030. Annex 1II(5) *ibid.*
1031. Annex 1II(3) *ibid.*
1032. Regulation 3(2) *ibid.*
1033. Regulation 4(1) *ibid.*
1034. Regulation 4(3) *ibid.*

should the applicant provide the requested information, the authority may ask for more information within one month. In such a case and following the compliance of the applicant, the application is considered to be full.[1035] The same applies in the case that the authority does not require additional information in the specific time period(s).[1036]

II. Granting of Authorization

237. When the application is full, Cyprus Energy Regulatory Authority publishes without any delay the fact that such has been submitted in a daily newspaper in Cyprus for two days in sequence. In said publication, it is additionally stated that any person may submit any information related to the application to the authority within a specific time frame. Any information provided later than that is not taken into consideration.[1037] Such information, apart from being accessible to the public,[1038] is communicated to the applicant and a response to that can be submitted to the authority within a time limit specified by the latter.[1039] In addition, Cyprus Energy Regulatory Authority has the power to summon any person to submit in writing information to the same within a certain time period.[1040]

238. The lapse of the above said time periods initiates the beginning of the application's examination.[1041] Cyprus Energy Regulatory Authority examines the application and takes a decision based on data and information that lay before it.[1042] Further, factors that are taken into consideration are the safety of the facilities and the natural gas systems,[1043] environmental protection,[1044] location of processing plant or terminal or final coastal landing terminal of LNG,[1045] the potential of the applicant, including his technical and financial one,[1046] financial sufficient use of energy,[1047] applicable public service obligations[1048] and importance of the project for the natural gas market, where applicable.[1049] The decision is to be reached within three months.[1050] However, an extension for a maximum period of three additional months may be decided, whereas the applicant is informed accordingly

1035. Regulation 4(4) *ibid.*
1036. Regulation 4(2) *ibid.*
1037. Regulation 5(1) *ibid.*
1038. Regulation 5(2)(b) *ibid.*
1039. Regulation 5(2)(a) *ibid.*
1040. Regulation 5(3) *ibid.*
1041. Regulation 6(1) *ibid.*
1042. Regulation 6(2) *ibid.*
1043. Section 10(a) Law No. 183(I)/2004.
1044. Section 10(b) *ibid.*
1045. Section 10(c) *ibid.*
1046. Section 10(d) *ibid.*
1047. Section 10(e) *ibid.*
1048. Section 10(f) *ibid.*
1049. Section 10(g) *ibid.*
1050. Regulation 6(3) KDP 298/2006.

along with the relevant grounds.[1051] The final decision that the authority reaches must be reasoned, served to the applicant and published.[1052] It contains terms and conditions[1053] such as the standard ones set out in the law,[1054] as well as further such, as long as special grounds support them.[1055] The time period during which the relevant activities are authorized is equally defined in it.[1056] Within forty-five days of reaching the decision, the authorization is issued.[1057] In the same time period, the positive or negative decision on the request for authorization is published in the OG or in any other way the authority deems necessary.[1058] Regardless of granting the authorization, the applicant must in addition obtain any further authorizations, licences or permits required by law before performing any authorized activities.[1059]

III. Denial of Authorization

239. Non-fulfilment of the above-mentioned mandatory requirements for issuing the authorization results in denial thereof. Especially with regard to building and operating a distribution pipeline network in any particular area, the authority may decline to grant further authorization once such pipeline systems have been or are proposed to be built within a reasonable time in that area and if existing or proposed capacity is not saturated or is not expected to be saturated within a reasonable time.[1060] In the event that Cyprus Energy Regulatory Authority rejects the application for authorization, it must inform the applicant accordingly within thirty days via a duly reasoned notification. A copy thereof is to be forwarded to the European Commission.[1061]

240. Regardless of the lack of any special provisions in Law No. 183(I)/2004, the applicant upon rejection of the application may file an appeal with the Supreme Court according to the general provision of Article 148 of the Constitution.

IV. Alteration and Revocation of Authorization

241. Within its validity period, the authorization can be altered by the Cyprus Energy Regulatory Authority[1062] following the procedure set out hereinafter.[1063]

1051. Regulation 6(4) *ibid.*
1052. Regulation 7(1) *ibid.*
1053. Regulation 7(2)(a) *ibid.*
1054. Annex I(2), (3), (4), (5) and (6) *ibid.*
1055. Regulation 7(2)(b) and (c) *ibid.*
1056. Regulation 8(2)(a) *ibid.*
1057. Regulation 8(1) *ibid.*
1058. Regulation 7(3) *ibid.*
1059. Regulation 7(5) *ibid.*
1060. Section 14(1) Law No. 183(I)/2004.
1061. Section 14(2) *ibid.*
1062. Regulation 8(2)(b)(i) KDP 298/2006.
1063. Regulation 9 *ibid.*

This can be initiated by information from third parties or by the authority's own initiative.[1064] First, a notification is served to the authorization holder as well as published in the OG and in a daily newspaper.[1065] This notification contains the proposed amendment as well as its effect,[1066] the grounds[1067] and the time period, within which objections or representations can be raised. The time period cannot be shorter than thirty days from publication.[1068] Any such timely performed objection and representation is duly taken into consideration by the authority.[1069] The decision reached by the authority is served to the authorization holder[1070] and published in the OG and in a daily newspaper within forty-five days.[1071]

242. Apart from the above-described procedure, an alteration of the authorization can take place in agreement with the holder under the following conditions. The authority must be of the opinion that the amendments are necessary to face particular circumstances.[1072] The authorization holder should further not be without valid excuse in a less-favoured competitive position towards other authorization holders for the same activities.[1073] The same applies to the other holders.[1074] The publication of the intended alterations described above along with the possibility of the holder filing objections and representations also apply in this procedure.[1075] The decided amendment is published within forty-five days of the relevant decision.[1076]

243. The authorization can be terminated by Cyprus Energy Regulatory Authority giving a five years' notice when specific grounds lay. However, this cannot be done within the first fifteen years of its issuance.[1077] The grounds that justify a termination are set out below:

- submission of a relevant application by the authorization holder *in consensus* with the authority;[1078]
- the belief of the authority that the authorization was granted on the basis of false information or misrepresentations, which were essential for its granting;[1079]
- change in the ownership status of the holder that is not in accordance with the terms of the authorization;[1080]

1064. Regulation 10(1) *ibid.*
1065. Regulation 10(3) *ibid.*
1066. Regulation 10(2)(a)(i) *ibid.*
1067. Regulation 10(2)(a)(ii) *ibid.*
1068. Regulation 10(2)(a)(iii) *ibid.*
1069. Regulation 10(2)(b) *ibid.*
1070. Regulation 10(4)(a) *ibid.*
1071. Regulation 10(5) *ibid.*
1072. Regulation 11(1)(a) *ibid.*
1073. Regulation 11(1)(b)(i) *ibid.*
1074. Regulation 11(1)(b)(ii) *ibid.*
1075. Regulation 11(2) and (3) *ibid.*
1076. Regulation 11(4) *ibid.*
1077. Regulation 8(2)(b)(ii) *ibid.*
1078. Regulation 13(a) *ibid.*
1079. Regulation 13(b) *ibid.*
1080. Regulation 13(c) *ibid.*

- non-payment of the due fees;[1081]
- violation of the terms and conditions of the authorization and failure to rehabil tate the violation;[1082]
- violation of a decision of Cyprus Energy Regulatory Authority or of the Ministe regarding the authorized activities;[1083]
- reasonable belief of the authority that the holder shall permanently stop fulfillin the authorized activities;[1084] and
- filing a petition in bankruptcy on behalf of the holder.[1085]

244. The procedure followed in such a case is initiated by serving the authori zation holder with a notice informing him of the revocation of the authorizatio unless the specified violation is restored within a specified time frame.[1086] This tim frame must be proportional to the nature of the violation.[1087] Should the authoriza tion holder fail to restore it or in the event that the violation is beyond restoration Cyprus Energy Regulatory Authority specifies the due date of revocation in the rel evant decision and informs the holder in writing accordingly.[1088] This decision i additionally published in the OG and is also noted in the Register.[1089]

§3. Unbundling of Accounts

245. Apart from the obligation to comply with the contents of issued authoriza tions, natural gas undertakings must unbundle their accounts. This is ensured by th Cyprus Energy Regulatory Authority.[1090] In particular, natural gas undertakings whatever their system of ownership or legal form, draw up, submit to audit and pub lish their annual accounts in accordance with Companies' Law.[1091,1092] Undertak ings which are not legally obliged to publish their annual accounts keep a copy thereof at the disposal of the public at their head office.[1093] Said audit relates, in par ticular, to the obligation to avoid discrimination and cross-subsidization, a explained below.[1094] Further, they keep separate accounts, in their internal account ing, for each of their transmission, distribution, LNG and storage activities as they would be required to do if the activities in question were carried out by separate

1081. Regulation 13(d) *ibid.*
1082. Regulation 13(e) *ibid.*
1083. Regulation 13(f) *ibid.*
1084. Regulation 13(g) *ibid.*
1085. Regulation 13(h) *ibid.*
1086. Regulation 14(1) *ibid.*
1087. Regulation 14(2) *ibid.*
1088. Regulation 14(2)(a) and (b) *ibid.*
1089. Regulation 14(3) *ibid.*
1090. Section 29(1) and (9) Law No. 183(I)/2004, which correspond to Art. 31(1) Directive 2009/73/EC.
1091. A Law to Consolidate and Amend the Law Relating to Companies ('Cap. 113') No. 7 of 1951 CG No. 3544, 19 Feb. 1951, p. 69, as amended.
1092. Section 29(2) Law No. 183(I)/2004, which corresponds to Art. 31(2) Directive 2009/73/EC.
1093. Section 29(3) Law No. 183(I)/2004, which corresponds to Art. 31(2) Directive 2009/73/EC.
1094. Section 29(9) Law No. 183(I)/2004.

undertakings, with a view to avoiding discrimination, cross-subsidization and distortion of competition. They shall also keep accounts, which may be consolidated, for other gas activities not relating to transmission, distribution, LNG and storage. Revenue from ownership of the transmission or distribution network shall be specified in the accounts.[1095] These internal accounts include a balance sheet and a profit and loss account for each activity.[1096] Furthermore, undertakings specify in their internal accounting the rules for the allocation of assets and liabilities, expenditure and income as well as for depreciation, without prejudice to nationally applicable accounting rules, which they follow in drawing up the separate accounts previously referred.[1097] Those internal rules are controlled by Cyprus Energy Regulatory Authority and may be amended only in exceptional cases under the approval of the authority. Such amendments are stated and duly substantiated.[1098] Lastly, the annual accounts indicate in notes any transaction of a certain size conducted with related undertakings.[1099]

246. It is possible, and in the case of Cyprus most probable, that natural gas undertakings enjoy derogation due to emergent and isolated market (section 44 Law No. 183(I)/2004) from the obligation of unbundling accounts. Nonetheless, they must keep internal accounts, as explained above.[1100]

§4. Protection of Fair Competition

247. The promotion of effective competition is interrelated to ensuring the proper functioning of the natural gas market. Measures that Cyprus Energy Regulatory Authority may take pursuant to Law No. 183(I)/2004 in order to ensure a level playing field is compatible with the Treaty on European Union (TEU) and the Treaty on the Functioning of the European Union (TFEU) and with the legislation of the EU.[1101] Those measures are proportionate, non-discriminatory and transparent and may only be put into effect following the notification to and approval of the European Commission.[1102] Besides those general guidelines, no further provision specifying the above generally drafted measures for the protection of the competition is foreseen in this law.

1095. Section 29(4)(a) and (b) *ibid.*, which corresponds to Art. 31(3) Directive 2009/73/EC.
1096. Section 29(5) Law No. 183(I)/2004, which corresponds to Art. 31(3) Directive 2009/73/EC.
1097. Section 29(6) Law No. 183(I)/2004, which corresponds to Art. 31(5) Directive 2009/73/EC.
1098. Section 29(7) Law No. 183(I)/2004, which corresponds to Art. 31(5) Directive 2009/73/EC.
1099. Section 29(8) Law No. 183(I)/2004, which corresponds to Art. 31(6) Directive 2009/73/EC.
1100. Section 29A Law No. 183(I)/2004, which corresponds to Art. 31(1) Directive 2009/73/EC.
1101. Section 55(1) Law No. 183(I)/2004, which corresponds to Art. 47(1) Directive 2009/73/EC.
1102. Section 55(2) Law No. 183(I)/2004, which corresponds to Art. 47(1) Directive 2009/73/EC.

§5. Derogations, Exceptions and Safeguard Measures

I. Derogation due to Serious Economic and Financial Difficulties

248. Derogations from the above-mentioned statutory provisions can be justified on the following grounds, as long as certain conditions are met. The first ground to be examined is serious economic and financial difficulties. When a natural gas undertaking encounters or considers it would encounter such difficulties because of its take-or-pay commitments accepted in one or more gas purchase contracts, it may submit an application for a temporary derogation from the provisions on access to the transmission and distribution systems and LNG facilities (section 30 Law No. 183(I)/2004).[1103] This application is accompanied by all relevant information on the nature and extent of the problem and on the efforts undertaken by the natural gas undertaking to solve the problem, whereas the competent authority is the Minister.[1104] The Council of Ministers in consultation with Cyprus Energy Regulatory Authority may decide that such applications are presented either before or after the refusal of access to the system. The relevant limitation period is set following the recommendations of the authority.[1105] However, where a natural gas undertaking has refused access, the application is presented without delay.[1106]

249. The Minister examines the presented application with regard to the need to fulfil public service obligations and to ensure security of supply,[1107] the position of the natural gas undertaking in the gas market and the actual state of competition in that market,[1108] the seriousness of the economic and financial difficulties encountered by natural gas undertakings and transmission undertakings or eligible customers,[1109] the dates of signature and terms of the contract or contracts in question, including the extent to which they allow for market changes,[1110] the efforts made to find a solution to the problem,[1111] the extent to which, when accepting the take-or-pay commitments in question, the undertaking could reasonably have foreseen, having regard to the provisions of this law, that serious difficulties were likely to arise,[1112] the level of connection of the system with other systems and the degree of interoperability of those systems,[1113] the effects the granting of a derogation would have on the correct application of this law as regards the smooth functioning of the internal market in natural gas[1114] and the objective of achieving a competitive gas

1103. Section 43(1) Law No. 183(I)/2004, which corresponds to Art. 48(1) Directive 2009/73/EC.
1104. Section 43(3) Law No. 183(I)/2004, which corresponds to Art. 48(1) Directive 2009/73/EC.
1105. Section 43(2)(a) and (b) Law No. 183(I)/2004, which corresponds to Art. 48(1) Directive 2009/73/EC.
1106. Section 43(2)(c) Law No. 183(I)/2004, which corresponds to Art. 48(1) Directive 2009/73/EC.
1107. Section 43(6)(a) Law No. 183(I)/2004, which corresponds to Art. 48(3)(b) Directive 2009/73/EC.
1108. Section 43(6)(b) Law No. 183(I)/2004, which corresponds to Art. 48(3)(c) Directive 2009/73/EC.
1109. Section 43(6)(c) Law No. 183(I)/2004, which corresponds to Art. 48(3)(d) Directive 2009/73/EC.
1110. Section 43(6)(d) Law No. 183(I)/2004, which corresponds to Art. 48(3)(e) Directive 2009/73/EC.
1111. Section 43(6)(e) Law No. 183(I)/2004, which corresponds to Art. 48(3)(f) Directive 2009/73/EC.
1112. Section 43(6)(f) Law No. 183(I)/2004, which corresponds to Art. 48(3)(g) Directive 2009/73/EC.
1113. Section 43(6)(g) Law No. 183(I)/2004, which corresponds to Art. 48(3)(h) Directive 2009/73/EC.
1114. Section 43(6)(h) Law No. 183(I)/2004, which corresponds to Art. 48(3)(i) Directive 2009/73/EC.

market.[1115] Following consultations with the Cyprus Energy Regulatory Authority and in case no reasonably available alternative solutions exist, the Ministry reaches a decision on the submitted derogation.[1116] Any decision that grants derogation must be due grounded.[1117] Should no derogation have been granted to natural gas undertakings, these shall not refuse or shall no longer refuse access to the system because of take-or-pay commitments accepted in a gas purchase contract.[1118]

250. Subsequent to this, the Minister notifies the European Commission without delay of its decision to grant a derogation, together with all the relevant information with respect to the derogation, so that the European Commission having before its well-founded data can reach a final decision.[1119] Within eight weeks of receipt of that notification, the European Commission may request that the Member State or the designated competent authority concerned amend or withdraw the decision to grant a derogation. In the event that the Minister does not comply with that request within a period of four weeks, a final decision is taken expeditiously.[1120]

II. Derogation due to Qualification as an Isolated Market

251. Derogation may be further justified under the condition that Cyprus is qualified as an isolated market. The conditions that need to be satisfied are not being directly connected to the interconnected system of any other Member State and having only one main external supplier, that being supply undertaking having a market share of more than 75%. In such an occasion the Council of Ministers may decide

---

1115. Section 43(6)(i) Law No. 183(I)/2004, which corresponds to Art. 48(3)(a) Directive 2009/73/EC.
1116. Section 43(4) Law No. 183(I)/2004, which corresponds to Art. 48(1) Directive 2009/73/EC.
1117. Section 43(8) Law No. 183(I)/2004. This provision could be characterized as superfluous as according to general principles of Administrative Law administrative actions need to be fully and due reasoned. The relevant provision reads:

> administrative actions issued following discretionary power must be fully and due reasoned, especially when these actions (a) are unfavourable for the citizen, (b) have content contrary to previous opinion, suggestion, proposal or study of the competent authority or the data of the administrative file, (c) are contrary to established policy or tactic, (d) constitute an extraordinary measure and (e) are to be grounded by the law (s. 26(1) Law No. 158(I)/1999).

See relevant case law: *Georghiades Athos G and Others v. The Republic of Cyprus through the Public Service Commission* (1967) 3 CLR 653; *Michalakis Constantinides v. The Republic* (1967) 3 CLR 7; *The Republic v. Lefcos Georghiades* (1972) 3 CLR 594; *Christou Takis v. The Republic of Cyprus through the Public Service Commission* (1972) 3 CLR 32; *Hadjiconstantinou Costas and Others v. The Republic of Cyprus through the Public Service Commission* (1973) 3 CLR 65; *Pissas Ioannis N v. The Republic of Cyprus through the Public Service Commission* (1974) 3 CLR 476; *Republic of Cyprus (Educational Service Commission) v. Panayiotis Ioannou Myrtiotis* (1975) 3 CLR 484; *Nicolaou v. The Republic* (1997) 3 CLR 259; *The Republic v. Bellfoods* (2008) 3 CLR 517.

1118. Section 43(7) Law No. 183(I)/2004, which corresponds to Art. 48(4) Directive 2009/73/EC.
1119. Section 43(5) Law No. 183(I)/2004, which corresponds to Art. 48(2) Directive 2009/73/EC.
1120. Article 48(2) *ibid.*

derogation from sections 8–14, 18, 33, 34 and/or 35 Law No. 183(I)/2004.[1121] The Council then issues regulations on the function of the natural gas market that are in force so long as the deviation is.[1122] The latter expires when Cyprus ceases to be qualified as an isolated market.[1123] Any such derogation is communicated to the European Commission.[1124] However, until the natural gas market in Cyprus is qualified as isolated, Cyprus Energy Regulatory Authority may derogate from those sections, especially the ones relating to issuing authorizations, whenever it deems appropriate so that achieving the objective of this section is ensured.[1125] This provision is puzzling, as it enables the authority to act beyond Law No. 183(I)/2004 and to be bound solely by the general principles of Administrative Law. Reference to the objective of a section of the said legislation is equally confusing as none are referred to in the same, and it is ordinary for laws and not sections to have objectives. In addition, this could be estimated as legalizing acts and omissions of the administration in deviation from the principle of legality.

III. Derogation due to Qualification as an Emergent Market

252. The Cyprus natural gas market is an emergent market under the condition that the first commercial supply of natural gas within the first relevant long-term contract took place during the last ten years.[1126] Should Cyprus, in addition to being qualified as an emergent market, experience substantial problems due to provisions of this law that are not related to its contractual obligations of compulsory purchase regardless of receiving, it can proceed with a derogation. This is decided by the Council of Ministers and refers to sections 8–14 and 16(1) solely in relation to appointing a transmission system operator, as well as to sections 16(2), (3) and (4), 18, 21, 22(5) and (6), 24, 29, 30, 33 and/or 35 Law No. 183(I)/2004.[1127] In such a case, the Council issues regulations on the function of the natural gas market that are in force so long as the deviation is.[1128] Any such derogation is communicated to the European Commission.[1129] However, until the natural gas market in Cyprus is qualified as isolated, the Cyprus Energy Regulatory Authority may act in derogation from those sections, especially the ones relating to issuing authorizations, whenever it deems appropriate, so that achieving the objective of this section is ensured.[1130] With reference to this provision, the aforementioned concerns on the similar one on derogations due to qualification as an isolated market equally apply.

1121. Section 44(1)(a) and (b) Law No. 183(I)/2004, which corresponds to Art. 49(1) Directive 2009/73/EC.
1122. Section 44(5) Law No. 183(I)/2004.
1123. Section 44(1)(c) *ibid.*, which corresponds to Art. 49(1) Directive 2009/73/EC.
1124. Section 44(1)(d) Law No. 183(I)/2004, which corresponds to Art. 49(1) Directive 2009/73/EC.
1125. Section 44(1)(e) Law No. 183(I)/2004.
1126. Section 44(2)(d) *ibid.*
1127. Section 44(2)(a) *ibid.*, which partially corresponds to Art. 49(2) Directive 2009/73/EC, as the European provision refers only to substantial problems relating to emergent market and not to any contractual obligations.
1128. Section 44(5) Law No. 183(I)/2004.
1129. Section 44(2)(c) *ibid.*, which corresponds to Art. 49(2) Directive 2009/73/EC.
1130. Section 44(2)(f) Law No. 183(I)/2004.

253. Said derogation automatically expires from the moment that Cyprus does not qualify as an emergent market.[1131] On the date at which such derogation expires, the definition of eligible customers results in an opening of the market equal to at least 33% of the total annual gas consumption of the national gas market. Derogation from section 8(b) and (c) Law No. 183(I)/2004 is automatically upheld. Two years thereafter, eligible customers are all non-household customers, and three years thereafter, eligible customers are all customers. Until the date of defining as eligible customers, all non-household customers in Cyprus may decide not to apply section 30 Law No. 183(I)/2004 as far as ancillary services and temporary storage for the re-gasification process and its subsequent delivery to the transmission system are concerned.[1132]

IV. Procedure for Transmission Lines with a Third Country

254. Without prejudice to the allocation of competence between the EU and the Member States, as stated in Article 4 of the TFEU, where Cyprus intends to enter into negotiations with a third country in order to amend, extend, adapt, renew or conclude an agreement on the operation of a transmission line with a third country concerning matters falling, entirely or partly, within the scope of this law, it shall notify the Commission of its intention in writing.[1133] Such notification shall include the relevant documentation and an indication of the provisions to be addressed in the negotiations or to be renegotiated, the objectives of the negotiations and any other relevant information, and shall be transmitted to the Commission at least five months before the intended start of the negotiations.[1134]

255. Cyprus may initiate negotiations with the third country only after the Commission, following its evaluation, adopts a decision authorizing negotiations.[1135] Following the conclusion of negotiations and before signing an agreement with the third country, Cyprus shall notify the Commission of the outcome of negotiations and shall transmit the text of the negotiated agreement to the Commission[1136] for the latter to approve or disapprove it within ninety days of receipt of the notification. Where the Commission, adopts a decision, authorizing Cyprus to sign and conclude the agreement with a third country, Cyprus shall conclude the ratification procedure under Article 169 of the Constitution. It shall then notify the Commission of the conclusion and entry into force of the agreement, as well as of any subsequent changes to the status of that agreement.[1137]

1131. Section 44(2)(b) *ibid.*, which corresponds to Art. 49(2) Directive 2009/73/EC.
1132. Section 44(2)(e) Law No. 183(I)/2004, which corresponds to Art. 49(3) Directive 2009/73/EC.
1133. Section 44A(1) Law No. 183(I)/2004, which corresponds to Art. 49b(2) Directive 2009/73/EC.
1134. Section 44A(2) and (3) Law No. 183(I)/2004, which corresponds to Art. 49b(2) Directive 2009/73/EC.
1135. Section 44A(4) Law No. 183(I)/2004.
1136. Section 44A(5) *ibid.*, which corresponds to Art. 49b(11) Directive 2009/73/EC.
1137. Section 44A(6) Law No. 183(I)/2004, which corresponds to Art. 49b(14) Directive 2009/73/EC.

V. Exemption due to New Infrastructure

256. Major new gas infrastructure, i.e., interconnectors, LNG and storage facilities, may lead to exemption for a defined period of time from the provisions of sections 7(2)(a), (c), (e) and 16(1) Law No. 183(I)/2004 solely with reference to the Transmission System Operator, as well as of sections 18, 30, 31, 36 and 38 Law No. 183(I)/2004.[1138] Such an exemption may cover all or part of the capacity of the new infrastructure, or of the existing infrastructure with significantly increased capacity.[1139] The same applies to significant increases of capacity in existing infrastructure and to modifications of such infrastructure which enable the development of new sources of gas supply.[1140] Such an exemption may be granted, when the following conditions are fulfilled:

- the investment must enhance competition in gas supply and enhance the security of supply;[1141]
- the level of risk attached to the investment must be such that the investment would not take place unless an exemption was granted;[1142]
- the infrastructure must be owned by a natural or legal person which is separate at least in terms of its legal form from the system operators in whose systems that infrastructure will be built;[1143]
- charges must be levied on users of that infrastructure;[1144] and
- the exemption must not be detrimental to competition in the relevant markets which are likely to be affected by the investment, to the effective functioning of the internal market in natural gas, the efficient functioning of the regulated systems concerned, or to security of supply of natural gas in the Union.[1145]

257. In deciding to grant an exemption, consideration is given on a case-by-case basis to the need to impose conditions regarding the duration of the exemption and non-discriminatory access to the infrastructure. When deciding on those conditions account, in particular, is taken of the additional capacity to be built or the modification of existing capacity, the time horizon of the project and national circumstances.[1146] Before granting an exemption, the Cyprus Energy Regulatory Authority decides upon the rules and mechanisms for management and allocation of capacity. The rules require that all potential users of the infrastructure are invited to indicate their interest in contracting capacity before capacity allocation in the new infrastructure, including for own use, takes place. The authority requires congestion management rules to include the obligation to offer unused capacity on the market

1138. Section 45(1) Law No. 183(I)/2004, which corresponds to Art. 36(1) Directive 2009/73/EC.
1139. Section 45(6) Law No. 183(I)/2004, which corresponds to Art. 36(6) Directive 2009/73/EC.
1140. Section 45(2) Law No. 183(I)/2004, which corresponds to Art. 36(1) Directive 2009/73/EC.
1141. Section 45(1)(a) *ibid.*, which corresponds to Art. 36(1)(a) Directive 2009/73/EC.
1142. Section 45(1)(b) Law No. 183(I)/2004, which corresponds to Art. 36(1)(b) Directive 2009/73/EC
1143. Section 45(1)(c) Law No. 183(I)/2004, which corresponds to Art. 36(1)(c) Directive 2009/73/EC.
1144. Section 45(1)(d) Law No. 183(I)/2004, which corresponds to Art. 36(1)(d) Directive 2009/73/EC
1145. Section 45(1)(e) Law No. 183(I)/2004, which corresponds to Art. 36(1)(e) Directive 2009/73/EC.
1146. Section 45(7) Law No. 183(I)/2004, which corresponds to Art. 36(6) Directive 2009/73/EC.

and requires users of the infrastructure to be entitled to trade their contracted capacities on the secondary market. In its assessment of the criteria mentioned above, the authority takes into account the results of that capacity allocation procedure.[1147] Moreover, the Cyprus Energy Regulatory Authority before the adoption of the decision on the exemption shall consult the national regulatory authorities of the Member States the markets of which are likely to be affected by the new infrastructure and the relevant authorities of the third countries, where the infrastructure in question is connected with the Union network under the jurisdiction of a Member State, and originates from or ends in one or more third countries. Where the third-country authorities consulted do not respond to the consultation within a reasonable time frame or within a set deadline not exceeding three months, the Cyprus Energy Regulatory Authority has the power to adopt the necessary decision.[1148]

258. In the event that the infrastructure in question is transboundary, the Cyprus Energy Regulatory Authority may consult the Agency, upon which its decision may be based, within two months from the date on which the request for exemption was received by the Agency. Where all the regulatory authorities concerned agree on the request for exemption within six months of the date on which it was received by the last of the regulatory authorities, they shall inform the Agency of their decision. Where the infrastructure concerned is a transmission line between a Member State and a third country and where the first interconnection point is located in Cyprus, before the adoption of the decision on the exemption, Cyprus Energy Regulatory Authority may consult the relevant authority of that third country with a view to ensuring, as regards the infrastructure concerned, that Directive 2009/72 is applied consistently both in the territory and in the territorial sea of Cyprus. Where the third-country authority consulted does not respond to the consultation within a reasonable time or within a set deadline not exceeding three months, the Cyprus Energy Regulatory Authority may adopt the necessary decision.[1149] Further, they may jointly request that the period referred to above be extended by up to three months.[1150]

259. The exemption decision, including any conditions, is duly reasoned and published.[1151] In addition, the decision is notified, without delay, by the competent authority of the European Commission, together with all the relevant information with respect to the decision. This information may be submitted to the European

1147. Section 45(8) Law No. 183(I)/2004, which corresponds to Art. 36(6) Directive 2009/73/EC.
1148. Section 45(3)(a) and (b) Law No. 183(I)/2004, which corresponds to Art. 36(3)(a) and (b) Directive 2009/73/EC.
1149. Section 45(4) Law No. 183(I)/2004, which corresponds to Art. 36(4) Directive 2009/73/EC, as amended.
1150. Section 45(5) Law No. 183(I)/2004, which corresponds to Art. 36(4) Directive 2009/73/EC.
1151. Section 45(9) Law No. 183(I)/2004, which corresponds to Art. 36(6) Directive 2009/73/EC.

Commission in aggregate form, enabling the latter to reach a well-founded decision. In particular, such information contains:[1152]

- detailed reasons on the basis of which the Cyprus Energy Regulatory Authority granted or refused the exemption together with reference to the above-stated conditions including the relevant condition(s) on which such decision is based, including the financial information justifying the need for the exemption;[1153]
- analysis undertaken of the effect on competition and the effective functioning of the internal market in natural gas resulting from the grant of the exemption;[1154]
- reasons for the time period and the share of the total capacity of the gas infrastructure in question for which the exemption is granted;[1155]
- in case the exemption relates to an interconnector, the result of the consultation with the regulatory authorities concerned;[1156] and
- contribution of the infrastructure to the diversification of gas supply.[1157]

260. Within a period of two months from the day following the receipt of a notification, the European Commission may take a decision requiring Cyprus Energy Regulatory Authority to amend or withdraw the decision to grant an exemption. This period may be extended by an additional period of two months, where further information is sought by the European Commission. That additional period begins on the day following the receipt of the complete information. The initial two-month period may also be extended with the consent of both the European Commission and the regulatory authority.[1158] The Cyprus Energy Regulatory Authority complies with the decision of the European Commission to amend or withdraw the exemption decision within a period of one month and informs the latter accordingly.[1159] If the European Commission approves the exemption, this decision loses its effect two years from its adoption in the event that construction of the infrastructure has not yet started, and five years from its adoption in the event that the infrastructure has not become operational unless the European Commission decides that any delay is due to major obstacles beyond the control of the person to whom the exemption has been granted.[1160]

1152. Section 45(10) Law No. 183(I)/2004, which corresponds to Art. 36(8) Directive 2009/73/EC. In addition to this notification, the directive foresees the obligation of the national authorities to transmit to the Commission, without delay a copy of every request for exemption. Such a provision does not exist in the national law.
1153. Section 45(10)(a) Law No. 183(I)/2004, which corresponds to Art. 36(8)(a) Directive 2009/73/EC.
1154. Section 45(10)(b) Law No. 183(I)/2004, which corresponds to Art. 36(8)(b) Directive 2009/73/EC.
1155. Section 45(10)(c) Law No. 183(I)/2004, which corresponds to Art. 36(8)(c) Directive 2009/73/EC.
1156. Section 45(10)(d) Law No. 183(I)/2004, which corresponds to Art. 36(8)(d) Directive 2009/73/EC.
1157. Section 45(10)(e) Law No. 183(I)/2004, which corresponds to Art. 36(8)(e) Directive 2009/73/EC.
1158. Article 36(9) *ibid.*
1159. Section 45(11) Law No. 183(I)/2004, which corresponds to Art. 36(9) Directive 2009/73/EC.
1160. Section 45(12) Law No. 183(I)/2004, which corresponds to Art. 36(9) Directive 2009/73/EC.

VI. Safeguard Measures

261. In the event of a sudden crisis in the energy market or where the physical safety or security of persons, apparatus or installations or system integrity is threatened, the Minister may temporarily take the necessary safeguard measures taking into account measures to safeguard security of gas supply that Cyprus Energy Regulatory Authority determines and applies within Regulation (EU) No. 2017/1938.[1161,1162] Such measures cause the least possible disturbance to the functioning of the internal market and are not wider in scope than is strictly necessary to remedy the sudden difficulties which have arisen.[1163] These are notified without delay to the other Member States and the European Commission.[1164] The latter may decide that the Minister must amend or abolish such measures, insofar as they distort competition and adversely affect trade in a manner which is at variance with the common interest.[1165]

§6. Monitoring Compliance

262. For the purpose of monitoring the implementation of this law, the Cyprus Energy Regulatory Authority has the inspection and control powers stated in sections 13, 14 and 20 Law No. 130(I)/2021 as well as the inspection powers set out in regulations issued pursuant to section 47(2) of this law.[1166] In addition, the authority has the right of access to the accounts of natural gas undertakings, insofar as necessary to carry out its functions,[1167] while preserving the confidentiality of commercially sensitive information.[1168] Compliance with the specific contents of issued authorizations and statutory obligations is safeguarded via criminal and administrative penalties imposed upon breach. These are elaborated below.

263. Violation of the obligation to hold an authorization prior to performing any activities in relation to natural gas results in criminal prosecution. More specifically, any person, who in person or via its employee or representative, in violation of section 8 of this law builds and/or operates natural gas facilities and/or storage and/or pipelines networks, pipelines and associated equipment is guilty of a penal offence.[1169] Should he be convicted by the Court, imprisonment of up to five years

1161. Regulation (EU) 2017/1938 of the European Parliament and of the Council of 25 Oct. 2017 concerning measures to safeguard the security of gas supply and repealing Regulation (EU) No. 994/2010, OJ L 280, 28 Oct. 2017, p. 1.
1162. Section 42(1) Law No. 183(I)/2004, which corresponds to Art. 46(1) Directive 2009/73/EC.
1163. Section 42(2) Law No. 183(I)/2004, which corresponds to Art. 46(2) Directive 2009/73/EC.
1164. Section 42(3) Law No. 183(I)/2004, which corresponds to Art. 46(3) Directive 2009/73/EC.
1165. Article 46(3) *ibid.*
1166. Section 52 Law No. 183(I)/2004.
1167. Section 28(1) *ibid.*, which corresponds to Art. 30(1) Directive 2009/73/EC.
1168. Section 28(2) Law No. 183(I)/2004, which corresponds to Art. 30(2) Directive 2009/73/EC. National law did not opt for disclosure of such information, where necessary for the authority's duties to be performed.
1169. Section 49(a) Law No. 183(I)/2004.

and/or a monetary penalty of up to EUR 85,000 will be imposed on him.[1170] The same applies in the events of performing the activities of a system operator,[1171] or any of the activities of a natural gas facilities owner and/or storage facilities and/or pipeline networks, pipelines and associated equipment[1172] and supplying natural gas, to wholesale customers, among others.[1173] It should be noted that in the event of committing a criminal offence foreseen in this law by a legal person, as long as solid evidence exists that said crime has been committed with the consent or in collaboration of or is attributed to a person being director, secretary, other officer or other management organs of it, this natural person along with the legal person is liable to criminal prosecution.[1174] Should the acting natural person not hold any such office, but nevertheless perform the responsibilities and duties attributed to such an office, this natural person is deemed to be an officer for the purpose of the above-mentioned criminal offence.[1175]

264. Violation of the terms and conditions of authorization as well as other statutory obligations leads to the same criminal penalties. In particular, any person, who in person or via its employee or representative, violates or fails to comply with any term, condition and/or restriction of an authorization,[1176] discriminates between persons, categories of persons or system users,[1177] violates or fails to comply with the obligation to keep accounts (section 29 Law No. 183(I)/2004),[1178] violates or fails to comply with prohibitive or compelling provisions of any regulations or decrees issued in accordance with this law,[1179] is guilty of a criminal offence, and if found guilty by the Court, he shall be imprisoned for a maximum period of five years and/or shall receive a monetary penalty of up to EUR 85,000.[1180] The above-mentioned on legal persons equally apply here.

265. Parallel to such criminal offences, violation of terms and conditions of authorization gives rise to administrative sanctions. Should Cyprus Energy Regulatory Authority have reasonable grounds to believe that the authorization holder violates or possibly violates a term or a condition of the authorization, it may issue and serve a notice to the holder. This includes the term or condition deemed to be violated,[1181] the actions and omissions constituting a violation of the relevant term or condition in the opinion of the authority,[1182] and a time period of no less than thirty days, within which objections and representations may be submitted.[1183] The

1170. Section 49 *ibid.*
1171. Section 49(b) *ibid.*
1172. Section 49(c) *ibid.*
1173. Section 49(d) *ibid.*
1174. Section 51(1) *ibid.*
1175. Section 51(2) *ibid.*
1176. Section 50(1)(a) *ibid.*
1177. Section 50(1)(b) *ibid.*
1178. Section 50(1)(c) *ibid.*
1179. Section 50(1)(d) *ibid.*
1180. Section 50(1) *ibid.*
1181. Section 13(1)(a) *ibid.*
1182. Section 13(1)(b) *ibid.*
1183. Section 13(1)(c) *ibid.*

authority after evaluating any objections and representations may issue an administrative act obliging the authorization holder to take necessary measures for restoring the violation or for preventing future violations. The authorization holder is informed accordingly.[1184]

266. Should the authorization holder not comply with this, the Cyprus Energy Regulatory Authority may impose on him administrative fines[1185] and/or revoke his licence.[1186] These fines include an administrative penalty of up to 10% of the gross profit received during the year that the violation took place or the previous one, depending on which one is the largest. The importance and the duration of the violation are taken into consideration when specifying the exact amount, which may not be less than EUR 1,700.[1187] In addition, in the event that the violation continues to exist, an administrative fine of EUR 85–EUR 8,500, depending on the gravity of the violation, for every day that such a breach takes place may be imposed.[1188] Should the holder have taken unfair advantage of the violation, an administrative penalty of up to twice the amount of such an advantage may be issued.[1189] Lastly, if the violation of the terms, conditions or restrictions of the authorization or of the technical rules results in imminent danger for lives or property, the Cyprus Energy Regulatory Authority may issue immediately an order revoking the authorization for as long as it deems proper under the relevant circumstances. This order is served to the holder.[1190] Lastly, revocation of the authorization may be triggered by failing to pay the annual fees within three months of them being due.[1191] In such an event, in addition to any sanctions, the owed amount bears interest, as determined by the Central Bank, to which 3% is added.[1192]

267. The above-mentioned administrative acts imposing administrative penalties must be duly reasoned.[1193] Within thirty days of its service, the addressee may submit written representations to Cyprus Energy Regulatory Authority.[1194] The law sets out neither an obligation of the authority to consider this submission nor the extent of its powers. In view of the fact that this does not constitute any legal remedy, the effect of the same lies in the dark. However, the possibility of the addressee to file an appeal with the Supreme Court in accordance with Article 146 of the Constitution is beyond any dispute. This does not produce any suspensive effect, and the addressee is obliged to pay the fine to the authority immediately.[1195] In the event that no such payment is performed, the authority may seek judicial protection and

1184. Section 13(2) and (3) *ibid.*
1185. Section 13(4)(a) *ibid.*
1186. Section 13(4)(b) *ibid.*
1187. Section 13(4)(a)(i) *ibid.*
1188. Section 13(4)(a)(ii) *ibid.*
1189. Section 13(4)(a)(iii) *ibid.*
1190. Section 13(4) *ibid.*
1191. Section 48A(1) *ibid.*
1192. Section 48A(2) *ibid.*
1193. Section 54(1) *ibid.*
1194. Section 54(2) *ibid.*
1195. Section 54(3) *ibid.*

file actions requesting it to be received as a civil debt owed to the Republic. In suc a case the amount will be deposited with the Ministry of Finance.[1196]

1196. Section 54(4) *ibid.*

Chapter 3. Exploitation

268. The above-mentioned on prospection, research and exploitation of hydrocarbons[1197] equally apply to such activities for natural gas.

1197. Paragraphs 68 et seq. *supra.*

Chapter 4. Transmission

§1. Transmission, Storage and LNG System Operators

269. Before examining the duties of the Transmission, Storage and LNG System Operators, it is essential to set out their meaning. Transmission System Operator ('Διαχειριστής Συστήματος Μεταφοράς') means a natural or legal person who carries out the function of transmission and is responsible for operating, ensuring the maintenance of, and, if necessary, developing the transmission system in a given area and, where applicable, its interconnections with other systems, and for ensuring the long-term ability of the system to meet reasonable demands for the transport of gas.[1198] Storage System Operator ('Διαχειριστής Δικτύου Αποθήκευσης') is a natural or legal person who carries out the function of storage and is responsible for operating a storage facility.[1199] Lastly, the term 'LNG System Operator' ('Διαχειριστής Συστήματος ΥΦΑ') stands for a natural or legal person who carries out the function of liquefaction of natural gas, or the importation, offloading, and re-gasification of LNG and is responsible for operating an LNG facility.[1200]

270. The respective Transmission, Storage and LNG System Operators are determined by the undertakings which own such facilities or the Council of Ministers. More specifically, the Council of Ministers following discussions with Cyprus Energy Regulatory Authority designates or requires natural gas undertakings which own storage or LNG facilities to designate, for a period of time to be determined by the Council of Ministers, having regard to considerations of efficiency and economic balance, one or more Transmission, Storage and LNG System Operators. The latter is responsible for the operation, maintenance and development of transmission, storage and LNG facilities.[1201]

271. These system operators have common duties. They operate, maintain and develop under economic conditions secure, reliable and efficient transmission, storage and/or LNG facilities to secure an open market, with due regard to the environment, and ensure adequate means to meet service obligations.[1202] Further, they are to refrain from discriminating between system users or classes of system users,

1198. Section 2 Law No. 183(I)/2004, which corresponds to Art. 2(4) Directive 2009/73/EC. The French term is 'gestionnaire de réseau de transport', the German 'Fernleitungsnetzbetreiber' and the Dutch 'transmissiesysteembeheerder'.
1199. Section 2 Law No. 183(I)/2004, which corresponds to Art. 2(10) Directive 2009/73/EC. The French term is 'gestionnaire d'installation de stockage', the German 'Betreiber einer Speicheranlage' and the Dutch 'opslagsysteembeheerder'.
1200. Section 2 Law No. 183(I)/2004, which corresponds to Art. 2(12) Directive 2009/73/EC. The French term is 'gestionnaire d'installation de GNL', the German 'Betreiber einer LNG-Anlage' and the Dutch 'LNG-systeembeheerder'.
1201. Section 16(1) Law No. 183(I)/2004, which partially corresponds to Art. 13(1) Directive 2009/73/EC, as the directive refers only to storage and LNG system operators and not to transmission system operators.
1202. Section 16(2)(a) Law No. 183(I)/2004, which corresponds to Art. 13(1)(a) Directive 2009/73/EC.

particularly in favour of its related undertakings.[1203] They also have to provide any other transmission system operator, any other storage system operator, any other LNG system operator and/or any distribution system operator, sufficient information to ensure that transport and storage of natural gas may take place in a manner compatible with the secure and efficient operation of the interconnected system.[1204] Lastly, it is their obligation to provide system users with the information they need for efficient access to the system.[1205] Tariffs, terms and conditions for the provision of services by the system operators are established in a non-discriminatory way. Following their approval by the Cyprus Energy Regulatory Authority, they are published and hence come into force.[1206] Lastly, along with the Distribution System Operator, they meet the minimum investment standards for the maintenance and development of the transmission, distribution systems and the LNG and storage facilities, including interconnection capacity.[1207]

272. Transmission System Operators adopt rules for balancing the gas transmission system, including such for the charging of system users of their networks for energy imbalance. These rules are objective, transparent and non-discriminatory and are set in the following way.[1208] Non-discriminatory and cost-effective balancing mechanisms aim to ensure effective market access for all market players, including new entrants, and are set out or alternatively approved by Cyprus Energy Regulatory Authority.[1209] To this end, the authority is responsible for establishing transparent market-based mechanisms for the supply and purchase of natural gas needed in the framework of balancing requirements.[1210] It further ensures that balancing tariffs are equally non-discriminatory and cost-reflective[1211] and sets out the requirements and the terms as well as the measures for achieving appropriate incentives to balance the input and off-take of gas and not to endanger the reliability, security and effective function of the system.[1212] It also sets out the criteria and the methodology for ensuring, in any case, the balance of delivery and receipt of natural gas in the

1203. Section 16(2)(b) Law No. 183(I)/2004, which corresponds to Art. 13(1)(b) Directive 2009/73/EC.
1204. Section 16(2)(c) Law No. 183(I)/2004, which corresponds to Art. 13(1)(c) Directive 2009/73/EC.
1205. Section 16(2)(d) Law No. 183(I)/2004, which corresponds to Art. 13(1)(d) Directive 2009/73/EC.
1206. Section 16(4) Law No. 183(I)/2004, which corresponds to Art. 13(3) Directive 2009/73/EC. However, it is beyond doubt due to the systematic of the directive that these obligations, as set out therein, are to be met only by the transmission system operator, whereas no such conclusion can be drawn by the Cypriot provision.
1207. Section 17 Law No. 183(I)/2004, which corresponds to Art. 13(4) Directive 2009/73/EC. However, the duty set out in the directive refers to minimum standards for maintenance and development and makes no mention of investment ('επενδύσεις'), as the national legislation.
1208. Section 16(3) Law No. 183(I)/2004, which corresponds to Art. 13(3) Directive 2009/73/EC.
1209. Section 19(1) Law No. 183(I)/2004, which corresponds to recital No. 31 to Directive 2009/73/EC.
1210. Section 19(1)(a) Law No. 183(I)/2004, which corresponds to recital No. 31 to Directive 2009/73/EC.
1211. Section 19(1)(b) Law No. 183(I)/2004, which corresponds to recital No. 31 to Directive 2009/73/EC.
1212. Section 19(1)(c) Law No. 183(I)/2004, which corresponds to recital No. 31 to Directive 2009/73/EC.

transmission and distribution systems by their users.[1213] Transmission and Distribution System Operators ensure load balancing having regard to losses in the transmission and distribution systems as well as the stored amounts in the transmission system aiming for the reliable, secure and effective function of the system.[1214]

273. Transmission system operators are supplied with the energy used for fulfilling their duties according to transparent, non-discriminatory and market-based procedures that are controlled by the Cyprus Energy Regulatory Authority.[1215] They also build sufficient cross-border capacity to integrate European transmission infrastructure, accommodating all economically reasonable and technically feasible demands for capacity and taking into account the security of gas supply.[1216]

274. In the case that a Transmission System Operator belongs to a vertically integrated undertaking, it must be independent of other activities not relating to transmission, at least with regard to the organization and decision-making. No unbundling of the ownership status of the assets of the transmission system from the vertically integrated undertaking is needed, but the Council of Ministers may decide whether the Transmission System Operator is independent as to its legal form.[1217] In order to ensure the independence of the transmission system operator, the following minimum criteria are applied, whereas compliance with those is monitored by the Cyprus Energy Regulatory Authority. First, persons responsible for the management of the Transmission System Operator do not participate in company structures of the integrated natural gas undertaking responsible, directly or indirectly, for the day-to-day operation of the production, distribution, LNG, storage and supply of natural gas.[1218] Further, appropriate measures are taken in order to ensure that the professional interests of persons responsible for the management of the transmission system are taken into account in a manner that ensures that they are capable of acting independently.[1219] In addition, the Transmission System Operator has effective decision-making rights, independent from the integrated natural gas undertaking, with respect to assets necessary to operate, maintain or develop the transmission system. The existence of appropriate coordination mechanisms to ensure that the economic and management supervision rights of the vertically integrated company in respect of return on assets in a subsidiary is not hindered.[1220] The Transmission System Operator establishes a compliance programme, which sets out

1213. Section 19(1)(d) Law No. 183(I)/2004.
1214. Section 19(2) *ibid.*
1215. Section 19(3) *ibid.*
1216. Section 16(5) *ibid.*, which corresponds to Art. 13(2) Directive 2009/73/EC.
1217. Section 18(1) Law No. 183(I)/2004. Interestingly, the directive foresees the independence of the legal form for the transmission system owner as well as for the storage system operator according to Art. 15(1) Directive 2009/73/EC.
1218. Section 18(2)(a) Law No. 183(I)/2004. The wording of this provision is similar to Art. 15(2)(a) Directive 2009/73/EC. However, the latter refers to the independence of the transmission system owner and storage system operator.
1219. Section 18(2)(b) Law No. 183(I)/2004. Again, the wording of this provision is similar to Art. 15(2)(b) Directive 2009/73/EC. However, the latter refers to the independence of the transmission system owner and storage system operator.
1220. Section 18(2)(c) Law No. 183(I)/2004.

measures taken to ensure that discriminatory conduct is excluded, and ensures that observance of it is adequately monitored. The compliance programme sets out the specific obligations of employees to meet those objectives. An annual report, setting out the measures taken, is further submitted to the Cyprus Energy Regulatory Authority and is published.[1221]

§2. ACCESS TO THE SYSTEMS

275. Access to the systems requires criteria of technical safety as well as technical rules. The Cyprus Energy Regulatory Authority ensures that such criteria are defined and that technical rules establishing the minimum technical design and operational requirements for the connection to the system of LNG facilities, storage facilities, other transmission or distribution systems, and direct lines are developed and made public.[1222] Those technical rules are objective and non-discriminatory and ensure the interoperability of systems.[1223] They are further issued in any form the authority deems necessary, taking into consideration any recommendations of the Agency towards achieving compatibility of those rules. Lastly, they are communicated to the European Commission.[1224]

I. Access to the Transmission and Distribution System and LNG Facilities

276. The implementation of a system of third-party access to the transmission and distribution system and LNG facilities is established on the basis of published tariffs, applicable to all system users, which are applied objectively and without discrimination between system users.[1225] These tariffs need to be approved by the Cyprus Energy Regulatory Authority prior to their entry into force.[1226] The transmission system operator has access to the network of other transmission system operators on the basis of the same terms and principles as stated above, if necessary for the purpose of carrying out its functions including in relation to cross-border

1221. Section 18(2)(d) *ibid.* Once more the wording of this provision is similar to Art. 15(2)(d) Directive 2009/73/EC. However, the latter refers to the independence of the transmission system owner and storage system operator.
1222. Section 15(1) Law No. 183(I)/2004, which corresponds to Art. 8 Directive 2009/73/EC.
1223. Section 15(2) Law No. 183(I)/2004, which corresponds to Art. 8 Directive 2009/73/EC.
1224. Section 15(3) Law No. 183(I)/2004, which corresponds to Art. 8 Directive 2009/73/EC. For the particulars of the communication *see* Directive (EU) 2015/1535 of the European Parliament and of the Council of 9 Sep. 2015 laying down a procedure for the provision of information in the field of technical regulations and of rules on Information Society services, OJ L 241, 21 Sep. 2015, p. 1.
1225. Section 30(1) Law No. 183(I)/2004, which corresponds to Art. 32(1) Directive 2009/73/EC.
1226. Section 30(2) Law No. 183(I)/2004, which corresponds to Art. 32(1) Directive 2009/73/EC. However, the directive imposes in addition prior publication of the tariffs as a prerequisite of their entry into force, but no such provision is foreseen in the national law.

transmission.[1227] Lastly, it should be noted that the provisions of this legislation d not prevent the conclusion of long-term contracts insofar as they comply with th competition rules of the EU.[1228]

II. Access to Storage Facilities and Linepacks

277. Directive 2009/73/EC gives the Member States the option to choos between the procedure applicable in the case of negotiated access, the case of regu lated access or both of them, when implementing the provisions on organization c access to storage facilities and linepack when technically and/or economically nec essary for providing efficient access to the system for the supply of customers, a well as for the organization of access to ancillary services into national law.[122 Cyprus chose for regulated access. In particular, regulated access is applied on th basis of objective, transparent and non-discriminatory criteria defined in regula tions.[1230] These criteria relate, among others, to technical standards that must be ful filled by the natural gas undertakings, which are to be connected to the storag facilities and linepack,[1231] ensuring non-discrimination of the technical term imposed on natural gas undertakings,[1232] efficiency and economy in using an developing the storage facilities[1233] and publishing on behalf of the storage an transmission system operators the storage facilities or parts of them and th linepacks being offered.[1234] Further, natural gas undertakings and eligible custom ers either inside or outside the territory covered by the interconnected system ar given the right to access storage, linepack and other ancillary services, on the basi of published tariffs and/or other terms and obligations for the use of that storage an linepack, when technically and/or economically necessary for providing efficien access to the system, as well as for the organization of access to other ancillary ser vices.[1235] The Cyprus Energy Regulatory Authority consults system users whe developing those tariffs or the methodologies for those tariffs.[1236] The right o access for eligible customers may be given by enabling them to enter into suppl contracts with competing natural gas undertakings other than the owner and/o operator of the system or a related undertaking.[1237] These, however, are not applie as far as ancillary services and temporary storage for the re-gasification process an its subsequent delivery to the transmission system are concerned.[1238]

1227. Section 30(3) Law No. 183(I)/2004, which corresponds to Art. 32(2) Directive 2009/73/EC.
1228. Section 30(4) Law No. 183(I)/2004, which corresponds to Art. 32(3) Directive 2009/73/EC.
1229. Article 33(1) *ibid.*
1230. Section 31(2) Law No. 183(I)/2004, which corresponds to Art. 33(1) Directive 2009/73/EC.
1231. Section 31(2)(a) Law No. 183(I)/2004.
1232. Section 31(2)(b) *ibid.*
1233. Section 31(2)(c) *ibid.*
1234. Section 31(2)(d) *ibid.*, which corresponds to Art. 33(1) Directive 2009/73/EC.
1235. Section 31(3) Law No. 183(I)/2004, which corresponds to Art. 33(4) Directive 2009/73/EC.
1236. Section 31(4) Law No. 183(I)/2004, which corresponds to Art. 33(4) Directive 2009/73/EC.
1237. Section 31(5) Law No. 183(I)/2004, which corresponds to Art. 33(4) Directive 2009/73/EC.
1238. Section 31(6) Law No. 183(I)/2004, which corresponds to Art. 33(2) Directive 2009/73/EC.

III. Access to Upstream Pipeline Networks

278. The necessary measures are taken to ensure that natural gas undertakings and eligible customers, wherever they are located, are able to obtain access to upstream pipeline networks, including facilities supplying technical services incidental to such access. These measures are communicated to the European Commission. It should be noted that these measures are not applied to parts of such networks and facilities which are used for local production operations at the site of a field where the gas is produced.[1239] The legislation enabling and regulating this access ensures fair and open access, achieving a competitive market in natural gas and avoiding any abuse of a dominant position, taking into account security and regularity of supplies, a capacity which is or can reasonably be made available, and environmental protection.[1240] Additionally, the need to refuse access where there is an incompatibility of technical specifications which cannot reasonably be overcome is taken into consideration.[1241] Equally, the need to avoid difficulties which cannot reasonably be overcome and could prejudice the efficient, current and planned future production of hydrocarbons, including that from fields of marginal economic viability is evaluated.[1242] Parallel to the need to respect the duly substantiated reasonable needs of the owner or operator of the upstream pipeline network for the transport and processing of gas and the interests of all other users of the upstream pipeline network or relevant processing or handling facilities who may be affected is considered.[1243] Lastly, the need to apply the laws and administrative procedures for the grant of authorization for production or upstream development is regarded.[1244]

IV. Closed Distribution Systems

279. A closed distribution system is a system which distributes gas within a geographically confined industrial, commercial or shared services site and does not, without prejudice to an exception,[1245] supply household customers. The Cyprus Energy Regulatory Authority may classify as such a system, so long the following conditions are fulfilled.[1246] First, the operations or the production process of the users of that system are integrated for specific technical or safety reasons.[1247] Second, that system distributes gas primarily to the owner or operator of the system or

1239. Section 38(1) Law No. 183(I)/2004, which corresponds to Art. 34(1) Directive 2009/73/EC.
1240. Section 38(2) Law No. 183(I)/2004, which corresponds to Art. 34(2) Directive 2009/73/EC.
1241. Section 38(2)(a) Law No. 183(I)/2004, which corresponds to Art. 34(2)(a) Directive 2009/73/EC.
1242. Section 38(2)(b) Law No. 183(I)/2004, which corresponds to Art. 34(2)(b) Directive 2009/73/EC.
1243. Section 38(2)(c) Law No. 183(I)/2004, which corresponds to Art. 34(2)(c) Directive 2009/73/EC.
1244. Section 38(2)(d) Law No. 183(I)/2004, which corresponds to Art. 34(2)(d) Directive 2009/73/EC. However, the European provision mentions in addition conformity with EU law. This was not transposed in national law, possibly because it was considered as being superfluous.
1245. Incidental use by a small number of households with employment or similar associations with the owner of the distribution system and located within the area served by a closed distribution system do not preclude a system from being classified as closed distribution system. Section 26(4) Law No. 183(I)/2004, which corresponds to Art. 28(4) Directive 2009/73/EC.
1246. Section 26(1) Law No. 183(I)/2004, which corresponds to Art. 28(1) Directive 2009/73/EC.
1247. Section 26(1)(a) Law No. 183(I)/2004, which corresponds to Art. 28(1)(a) Directive 2009/73/EC.

to their related undertakings.[1248] The operator of such a system is exempted from the obligation to have their tariffs or methodologies being approved prior to their coming into force by the Cyprus Energy Regulatory Authority.[1249] However, these may still be reviewed and approved upon request by a user of the closed distribution system.[1250]

V. Refusal of Access

280. Access to the system can be refused on three specific grounds. These are lack of capacity, serious economic and financial difficulties with take-or-pay contracts and where access to the system would prevent them from carrying out the public service obligations assigned to them.[1251] Duly substantiated reasons are to be given for any such refusal.[1252] When the refusal ground is lack of capacity and lack of connection, Cyprus Energy Regulatory Authority has the power to take measures to ensure that the natural gas undertaking refusing connection makes the necessary enhancements as far as it is economically prudent to do so. The same applies when a potential customer is willing to pay for them.[1253] These measures are taken by the authority itself in case an application for authorization for building and operating a distribution pipeline network has been declined pursuant to section 14(1) of this law.[1254] Against such refusal, an appeal may be filed with the Supreme Court of Cyprus in accordance with Article 146 of the Constitution.

§3. Confidentiality

281. During the exercise of their duties, it is not uncommon for the authorities and the operators to come across commercially sensitive information. They are obliged to preserve the confidentiality of this information and to prevent information about their own activities which may be commercially advantageous from being disclosed in a discriminatory manner. More specifically, they may not disclose any commercially sensitive information to the remaining parts of the undertaking unless this is necessary for carrying out a business transaction. In order to ensure the full respect of the rules on information unbundling, the Cyprus Energy Regulatory Authority ensures that the Transmission System Owner including, in the case of a combined operator, the Distribution System Operator, and the remaining part of the undertaking do not use joint services, such as joint legal services, apart from purely administrative or IT functions.[1255] Especially in the context of sales or purchases of natural gas by related undertakings, Transmission, Storage and/or LNG

1248. Section 26(1)(b) Law No. 183(I)/2004, which corresponds to Art. 28(1)(b) Directive 2009/73/EC.
1249. Section 26(2) Law No. 183(I)/2004, which corresponds to Art. 28(2) Directive 2009/73/EC.
1250. Section 26(3) Law No. 183(I)/2004, which corresponds to Art. 28(3) Directive 2009/73/EC.
1251. Section 32(1) Law No. 183(I)/2004, which corresponds to Art. 35(1) Directive 2009/73/EC.
1252. Section 32(2) Law No. 183(I)/2004, which corresponds to Art. 35(1) Directive 2009/73/EC.
1253. Section 32(3) Law No. 183(I)/2004, which corresponds to Art. 35(2) Directive 2009/73/EC.
1254. Section 32(4) Law No. 183(I)/2004, which corresponds to Art. 35(2) Directive 2009/73/EC.
1255. Section 20(1) Law No. 183(I)/2004, which corresponds to Art. 16(1) Directive 2009/73/EC.

System Operators do not misuse commercially sensitive information obtained from third parties in the context of providing or negotiating access to the system.[1256] However, information necessary for effective competition and the efficient functioning of the market is made public. This obligation is without prejudice to protect commercially sensitive information.[1257]

282. Confidential information and intellectual property are equally protected under this law. Cyprus Energy Regulatory Authority, Distribution System Operators, Transmission System, Storage and LNG facilities Operators, Transmission and Distribution System Owners, Storage and LNG facilities Owner or any other person exercising any duty of this law or regulations thereof, may not announce or give to third parties in any way confidential data or information made known to it during the exercise of its duties. It also has the duty to protect any intellectual property rights relating to such data or information.[1258] Any person who contrary to this obligation reveals any confidential data or information is guilty of a penal crime. Should he be found guilty, he shall be imprisoned for a period of no more than two years and/or a criminal fine of up to EUR 51,000 will be imposed.[1259] Through this provision, the obligation to establish appropriate measures to be triggered by the disregard of confidentiality rules[1260] is fulfilled. It should be noted that this obligation of discretion does not apply when written consent is available[1261] or before a court,[1262] an Investigation Committee,[1263] an examining magistrate,[1264] the Unit for Combating Money Laundering[1265] and the Cyprus Energy Regulatory Authority.[1266]

1256. Section 20(2) Law No. 183(I)/2004, which corresponds to Art. 16(2) Directive 2009/73/EC.
1257. Section 20(3) Law No. 183(I)/2004, which corresponds to Art. 16(3) Directive 2009/73/EC.
1258. Section 48(1) Law No. 183(I)/2004.
1259. Section 48(2) *ibid.*
1260. Section 7(2)(i) *ibid.*, which corresponds to Art. 41(14) Directive 2009/73/EC.
1261. Section 48(1)(a) Law No. 183(I)/2004.
1262. Section 48(1)(b) *ibid.*
1263. Section 48(1)(c) *ibid.* and Cap. 44.
1264. Section 48(1)(d) Law No. 184(I)/2004 and s. 4 Cap. 155.
1265. Section 48(1)(e) Law No. 183(I)/2004. This section mentions Law on Concealment, Investigation and Confiscation of Income from certain Criminal Acts ('περί Συγκάλυψης, Έρευνας και Δήμευσης Εσόδων από Ορισμένες Εγκληματικές Πράξεις Νόμος') No. 61 of 1996, OG I(I) No. 3056, 3 May 1996, p. 223, which implemented Council Directive 91/308/EEC of 10 Jun. 1991 on prevention of the use of the financial system for the purpose of money laundering, OJ L 166, 28 Jun. 1991, p. 77. In the meanwhile, this has been replaced by Law on Prohibition and Combating of Money Laundering ('περί της Παρεμπόδισης και Καταπολέμησης της Νομιμοποίησης Εσόδων από Παράνομες Δραστηριότητες Νόμος') No. 188 of 2007, OG I(I) No. 4154, 31 Dec. 2007, p. 1715, which implements Directive 2005/60/EC of the European Parliament and of the Council of 26 Oct. 2005 on the prevention of the use of the financial system for the purpose of money laundering and terrorist financing, OJ L 309, 25 Nov. 2005, p. 15. In the meanwhile, this has been repealed and replaced by Directive (EU) 2015/849 of the European Parliament and of the Council of 20 May 2015 on the prevention of the use of the financial system for the purposes of money laundering or terrorist financing, OJ L 141, 5 Jun. 2015, p. 73.
1266. Section 48(1)(f) Law No. 183(I)/2004.

§4. REGIONAL COOPERATION

283. The Cyprus Energy Regulatory Authority consults and cooperates closely with other regulatory authorities and communicates to them and to the Agency any necessary information for the performance of their duties. In respect of the information exchanged, the receiving authority ensures the same level of confidentiality as that required of the originating authority.[1267] The issues of regional cooperation cover fostering the creation of operational arrangements in order to enable an optimal management of the network, promote joint gas exchanges and the allocation of cross-border capacity, and enable an adequate level of interconnection capacity, including through new interconnections, within the region and between regions to allow for development of effective competition and improvement of security of supply without discriminating between supply undertakings in different Member States.[1268] They further include coordination of the development of all network codes for the relevant transmission system operators and other market actors,[1269] as well as of the rules governing the management of congestion.[1270] These actions are carried out, as appropriate, in close consultation with other relevant national authorities and without prejudice to their specific competencies.[1271]

284. Cyprus Energy Regulatory Authority has the right to enter into co-operative agreements with other national regulatory authorities to foster regulatory cooperation.[1272] The European proviso refers to the right of national authorities to enter into co-operative agreements with each other.[1273] Hence the applicability of the national proviso is much wider, possibly due to the geographical location of Cyprus. However, this raises questions as to the capacity of the national body, under which the signing of such international treaties could be materialized. This is no deadlock, as it can be overcome under the assumption that the Cyprus Energy Regulatory Authority enters into these international treaties due to its proper authorization by the state.

285. Transmission system operators or other economic operators are free to maintain in force or to conclude technical agreements on issues concerning the operation of transmission lines between Cyprus and a third country. These agreements need to be compatible with Union law and the relevant decisions of the Cyprus Energy Regulatory Authority. They also need to be notified by said national authority.[1274] Similarly, Cyprus Energy Regulatory Authority may consult and cooperate with the relevant authorities of third countries in relation to the operation of

---

1267. Section 7D(1) *ibid.*, which corresponds to Art. 42(1) Directive 2009/73/EC.
1268. Section 7D(2)(a) Law No. 183(I)/2004, which corresponds to Art. 42(2)(a) Directive 2009/73/EC.
1269. Section 7D(2)(b) Law No. 183(I)/2004, which corresponds to Art. 42(2)(b) Directive 2009/73/EC.
1270. Section 7D(2)(c) Law No. 183(I)/2004, which corresponds to Art. 42(2)(c) Directive 2009/73/EC.
1271. Section 7D(4) Law No. 183(I)/2004, which corresponds to Art. 42(4) Directive 2009/73/EC.
1272. Section 7D(3) Law No. 183(I)/2004.
1273. Article 42(3) Directive 2009/73/EC.
1274. Section 20A Law No. 183(I)/2004, which corresponds to Art. 48a Directive 2009/73/EC.

gas infrastructure to and from third countries with a view to ensuring, as regards the infrastructure concerned, that this law is applied consistently in the territory and territorial sea of Cyprus.[1275]

5. Derogation due to Development of the Transmission and Major Distribution System

286. The need to develop the transmission and major distribution system can lead to derogation. In particular, where the implementation of this law would cause substantial problems in a geographically limited area of Cyprus, in particular, concerning the development of the transmission and major distribution infrastructure, and with a view to encouraging investments, the Council of Ministers may apply to the European Commission for a temporary derogation from sections 8–14, 16(1) solely with reference to appointing a transmission system operator, as well as from sections 16(2), (3) and (4), 18, 21, 22(5) and (6), 24, 29, 30, 33 and/or 35 of this law for developments within that area.[1276]

287. The Council of Ministers when deciding to submit such an application for derogation to the European Commission mainly takes into consideration the need for infrastructure investments, which would not be economical to operate in a competitive market environment, the level and pay-back prospects of investments required, the size and maturity of the gas system in the area concerned, the prospects for the gas market concerned, the geographical size and characteristics of the area or region concerned and socio-economic and demographic factors.[1277] With reference to the time period of such derogation, a differentiation needs to be made pursuant to the activities. For gas infrastructure other than distribution infrastructure, a derogation may be granted only if no gas infrastructure has been established in the area or if gas infrastructure has been established for less than ten years. This derogation does not exceed ten years from the time gas is first supplied in the area. For distribution infrastructure, a derogation may be granted for a period not exceeding twenty years from the time gas was first supplied through the said infrastructure in the area.[1278]

288. Should the derogation be granted, the Council of Ministers issues regulations on the function of the natural gas market, as in the above cases of derogation. These remain in force for so long as the same derogation does.[1279]

1275. Section 7D(5) Law No. 183(I)/2004, which corresponds to Art. 42(6) Directive 2009/73/EC.
1276. Section 44(3) Law No. 183(I)/2004, which corresponds to Art. 49(4) Directive 2009/73/EC.
1277. Section 44(4)(a)(i)–(vi) Law No. 183(I)/2004. These criteria are mentioned in the directive, however as criteria taken into account by the Commission when deciding on the derogation pursuant to Art. 49(5) Directive 2009/73/EC.
1278. Section 44(4)(b), (c) and (d) Law No. 183(I)/2004. Again this is referred in the European provision as a factor to be considered by the Commission when granting the requested derogation in accordance with Art. 49(5) Directive 2009/73/EC.
1279. Section 44(5) Law No. 183(I)/2004.

§6. Disputes

289. Cyprus Energy Regulatory Authority is the competent authority for resolving disputes on several occasions. Access to upstream pipeline networks is one of them. The authority is the competent authority for the national dispute settlement arrangement, as an authority independent from the parties with access to all relevant information. To this effect, such disputes are settled expeditiously, taking into account objectives of fair and open access, achieving a competitive market in natural gas, avoiding any abuse of a dominant position, security and regularity of supplies, capacity which is or can reasonably be made available and environmental protection (section 38(2) Law No. 183(I)/2009) as well as the number of the parties which may be involved in negotiating access to such networks.[1280] Relevant regulations are issued by the Minister.[1281] In the event of cross-border disputes, the dispute settlement arrangements for the Member State having jurisdiction over the upstream pipeline network which refuses access shall be applied.[1282] Where, in cross-border disputes, more than one Member State covers the network concerned, Cyprus shall consult each other with a view to ensuring that the provisions of this Directive are applied consistently.[1283] Where the upstream pipeline network originates from a third country and connects to at least Cyprus, the Member States concerned shall consult each other and when the first entry point to the Member States network is located in Cyprus, it shall consult the third country concerned where the upstream pipeline network originates, with a view to ensuring, as regards the network concerned, that Directive 2009/73/EC is applied consistently in the territory of the Member States.[1284] Further, Cyprus Energy Regulatory Authority is the competent authority for resolving cross-border disputes regarding the prohibition of using the network and access to the same.[1285] When more than one competent authority covers the network concerned, the authority consults those for the consistent application of this law.[1286]

290. Generally, parties are qualified to file an appeal ('προσφυγή') in relation to a decision on methodology reached pursuant to section 7(2) Law No. 183(I)/2004. Especially in cases where the Cyprus Energy Regulatory Authority is obliged to resolve disputes on the suggested tariffs or the proposed methods, any party may within two months following the publication of the decision or the decision, draft to file an appeal for re-examination. This appeal does not have any suspensive effect.[1287] Furthermore, any party having a complaint against a Transmission, Storage, LNG or Distribution System Operator in relation to that operator's obligations under this law may refer the complaint to the Cyprus Energy Regulatory Authority which, acting as a dispute settlement authority, issues a decision within a period of

1280. Section 36(1) *ibid.*, which corresponds to Art. 34(3) Directive 2009/73/EC.
1281. Section 36(1) Law No. 183(I)/2003.
1282. Section 36(2) *ibid.*, which corresponds to Art. 34(4) Directive 2009/73/EC.
1283. Section 36(3) Law No. 183(I)/2004, which corresponds to Art. 34(4) Directive 2009/73/EC.
1284. Section 36(4) Law No. 183(I)/2004, which corresponds to Art. 34(4) Directive 2009/73/EC.
1285. Section 37(1) Law No. 183(I)/2004.
1286. Section 37(2) *ibid.*
1287. Section 7(2)(f) *ibid.*, which corresponds to Art. 41(12) Directive 2009/73/EC.

two months after receipt of the complaint. That period may be extended by two months where additional information is sought by the authority. That extended period may be further extended with the agreement of the complainant. The authority's decision has binding effect unless and until overruled on appeal.[1288] These appeals do not hinder the exercise of the right of appeal pursuant to EU and national law,[1289] that being an administrative appeal under Article 145 of the Constitution.

1288. Section 7(2)(g) Law No. 183(I)/2004, which corresponds to Art. 41(11) Directive 2009/73/EC.
1289. Section 7(2)(j) Law No. 183(I)/2004, which corresponds to Art. 41(15) Directive 2009/73/EC.

Chapter 5. Distribution

§1. Distribution System Operator

291. A Distribution System Operator is a natural or legal person who carries out the function of distribution and is responsible for operating, ensuring the maintenance of, and, if necessary, developing the distribution system in a given area and, where applicable, its interconnections with other systems, and for ensuring the long-term ability of the system to meet reasonable demands for the distribution of gas.[1290] This operator is appointed for a certain time period either by the Council of Ministers or by the Distribution System Owners, following a relevant request of the said council. Consultation with the Cyprus Energy Regulatory Authority precedes this appointment.[1291]

292. Its duties, as explicitly set out in the law, include ensuring the long-term ability of the system to meet reasonable demands for the distribution of gas, and operating, maintaining and developing under economic conditions a secure, reliable and efficient system in its area, with due regard for the environment and energy efficiency,[1292] whereas during the exercise thereof, it should not discriminate between system users or classes of system users, particularly in favour of its related undertakings.[1293] In addition, it is obliged to provide any other Distribution, Transmission, LNG, and/or Storage System Operator with sufficient information to ensure that the transport and storage of natural gas take place in a manner compatible with the secure and efficient operation of the interconnected system.[1294] System users are equally provided with the information they need for sufficient access to the system, including its use.[1295] The Distribution System Operator is also responsible for balancing the distribution system. Rules adopted by it for that purpose are objective, transparent and non-discriminatory, including rules for the charging of system users for energy imbalance based on section 19 of this law.[1296] Tariffs, terms and conditions for providing services by the Distribution System Operator are drafted in a non-discriminatory way that reflects the cost and is approved by the Cyprus Energy Regulatory Authority before their publication and their coming into force.[1297]

293. Turning to unbundling issues, where the Distribution System Operator is part of a vertically integrated undertaking, it is independent at least in terms of its legal form, organization and decision-making from other activities not relating to

1290. Section 2 Law No. 183(I)/2004, which corresponds to Art. 2(6) Directive 2009/73/EC.
1291. Section 21 Law No. 183(I)/2004, which corresponds to Art. 24 Directive 2009/73/EC.
1292. Section 22(1) Law No. 183(I)/2004, which corresponds to Art. 25(1) Directive 2009/73/EC.
1293. Section 22(2) Law No. 183(I)/2004, which corresponds to Art. 25(2) Directive 2009/73/EC.
1294. Section 22(3) Law No. 183(I)/2004, which corresponds to Art. 25(3) Directive 2009/73/EC.
1295. Section 22(4) Law No. 183(I)/2004, which corresponds to Art. 25(4) Directive 2009/73/EC.
1296. Section 22(5) Law No. 183(I)/2004, which corresponds to Art. 25(5) Directive 2009/73/EC.
1297. Section 22(6) Law No. 183(I)/2004.

distribution. However, no obligation to separate the ownership of assets of the distribution system from the vertically integrated undertaking is created.[1298] For safeguarding the said independence of the operator, the following criteria are applied, under the monitoring of Cyprus Energy Regulatory Authority:[1299]

- those persons responsible for the management of the Distribution System Operator may not participate in company structures of the integrated natural gas undertaking responsible, directly or indirectly, for the day-to-day operation of the production, transmission and supply of natural gas;[1300]
- appropriate measures must be taken to ensure that the professional interests of persons responsible for the management of the Distribution System Operator are taken into account in a manner that ensures that they are capable of acting independently;[1301]
- the Distribution System Operator must have effective decision-making rights, independent from the integrated natural gas undertaking, with respect to assets necessary to operate, maintain or develop the network. In order to fulfil those tasks, the Distribution System Operator shall have at its disposal the necessary resources including human, technical, financial and physical resources. This should not prevent the existence of appropriate coordination mechanisms to ensure that the economic and management supervision rights of the vertically integrated undertaking in respect of return on assets are protected. In particular, this shall enable the vertically integrated undertaking to approve the annual financial plan, or any equivalent instrument, of the distribution system operator and to set global limits on the levels of indebtedness of the distribution system operator. It shall not permit the vertically integrated undertaking to give instructions regarding day-to-day operations, nor with respect to individual decisions concerning the construction or upgrading of distribution lines, that do not exceed the terms of the approved financial plan or any equivalent instrument;[1302]
- the Distribution System Operator must establish a compliance programme, which sets out measures taken to ensure that discriminatory conduct is excluded, and ensures that observance of it is adequately monitored. The compliance programme sets out the specific obligations of employees to meet that objective. An annual report, setting out the measures taken, is submitted by the person or body responsible for monitoring the compliance programme, the compliance officer of the Distribution System Operator, to Cyprus Energy Regulatory Authority and is published. The compliance officer of the Distribution System Operator is fully independent and has access to all the necessary information of the Distribution System Operator and any affiliated undertaking to fulfil his task.[1303]

294. Where the Distribution System Operator is part of a vertically integrated undertaking, Cyprus Energy Regulatory Authority or other competent authorities

1298. Section 24(1) *ibid.*, which corresponds to Art. 26(1) Directive 2009/73/EC.
1299. Section 24(2) Law No. 183(I)/2004, which corresponds to Art. 26(2) Directive 2009/73/EC.
1300. Section 24(2)(a) Law No. 183(I)/2004, which corresponds to Art. 26(2)(a) Directive 2009/73/EC.
1301. Section 24(2)(b) Law No. 183(I)/2004, which corresponds to Art. 26(2)(b) Directive 2009/73/EC.
1302. Section 24(2)(c) Law No. 183(I)/2004, which corresponds to Art. 26(2)(c) Directive 2009/73/EC.
1303. Section 24(2)(d) Law No. 183(I)/2004, which corresponds to Art. 26(2)(d) Directive 2009/73/EC.

ensure monitoring of the activities of the Distribution System Operator so that it cannot take advantage of its vertical integration to distort competition. In particular, vertically integrated distribution system operators may not, in their communication and branding, create confusion with respect to the separate identity of the supply branch of the vertically integrated undertaking.[1304]

295. However, the Council of Ministers may decide that the above-mentioned obligations, as set out in sections 24(1), (2) and (3) Law No. 183(I)/2004, do not apply to integrated natural gas undertakings serving less than 100,000 connected customers.[1305]

§2. Confidentiality

296. Apart from the aforementioned confidentiality duties that are equally binding on the Distribution System Operator, it is explicitly responsible for preserving the confidentiality of commercially sensitive information obtained in the course of carrying out its business and preventing information about its own activities which may be commercially advantageous from being disclosed in a discriminatory manner.[1306] In addition, in the context of sales or purchases of natural gas by related undertakings, it may not abuse commercially sensitive information obtained from third parties in the context of providing or negotiating access to the system.[1307]

§3. Combined Operator

297. The above-mentioned provisions on independence of the Distribution System Operator (section 24(1) Law No. 183(I)/2004) do not prevent the Council of Ministers from appointing one person as the combined operator of transmission, LNG, storage and distribution. This person, in terms of legal form, organization and decision-making, must be independent of other activities not related to transmission, LNG, storage and distribution. The relevant decision, which must be published in the OG,[1308] does not create an obligation to separate the ownership of assets of the combined system from the vertically integrated undertaking(s).[1309] The criteria applied for ensuring the independence of the combined system operator are the same as those applied for the independence of the Distribution System Operator and are equally monitored by the Cyprus Energy Regulatory Authority.[1310] The aforementioned measures are equally taken to safeguard the protection of competition.[1311]

1304. Section 24(3) Law No. 183(I)/2004, which corresponds to Art. 26(3) Directive 2009/73/EC.
1305. Section 24(4) Law No. 183(I)/2004, which corresponds to Art. 26(4) Directive 2009/73/EC.
1306. Section 25(1) Law No. 183(I)/2004, which corresponds to Art. 27(1) Directive 2009/73/EC.
1307. Section 25(2) Law No. 183(I)/2004, which corresponds to Art. 27(2) Directive 2009/73/EC.
1308. Section 27(1)(a) Law No. 183(I)/2004.
1309. Section 27(1)(b) *ibid.*
1310. Section 27(2) *ibid.*
1311. Section 27(3) *ibid.*

4. Prohibition of Abusive Practices Affecting Wholesale Energy Markets

298. Regulation (EU) No. 1227/2011 essentially prohibits abusive practices affecting wholesale energy markets throughout the EU.[1312] It prohibits insider trading, in the sense that persons possessing inside information in relation to a wholesale energy product are prohibited from using that information by acquiring or disposing of wholesale energy products to which that information relates for their own account or for the account of a third party.[1313] They are equally prohibited from disclosing that information to any other person unless such disclosure is made in the normal course of the exercise of their business.[1314] They are also prohibited from recommending or inducing another person, on the basis of inside information, to acquire or dispose of wholesale energy products to which that information relates.[1315] Regulation (EU) No. 1227/2011 further prohibits any engagement in, or attempt to engage in, market manipulation on wholesale energy markets.[1316]

299. Regulation (EU) No. 1227 specifies the terms that are the backbone of the said prohibitions, those being wholesale energy products, inside information and market manipulation. 'Wholesale energy products' ('ενεργειακά προϊόντα χονδρικής' in Greek, 'produits énergétiques de gros' in French, 'Energiegroßhandelsprodukte' in German, 'voor de groothandel bestemde energieproducten' in Dutch) means the following contracts and derivatives, irrespective of where and how they are traded: (a) contracts for the supply of electricity or natural gas where delivery is in the Union; (b) derivatives relating to electricity or natural gas produced, traded or delivered in the Union; (c) contracts relating to the transportation of electricity or natural gas in the Union; (d) derivatives relating to the transportation of electricity or natural gas in the Union. Contracts for the supply and distribution of electricity or natural gas for the use of final customers are not wholesale energy products. However, contracts for the supply and distribution of electricity or natural gas to final customers with a consumption capacity greater than 600 gigawatt-hours per year are treated as wholesale energy products.[1317]

300. 'Inside information' ('εμπιστευτικές πληροφορίες' in Greek, 'information privilégiée' in French, 'Insider-Information' in German, 'voorwetenschap' in Dutch) means information of a precise nature which has not been made public, which relates, directly or indirectly, to one or more wholesale energy products and which, if it was made public, would be likely to significantly affect the prices of those wholesale energy products. Further for the purposes of this definition, 'information' means: (a) information which is required to be made public in accordance with Regulations (EC) No. 714/2009 and (EC) No. 715/2009, including guidelines and network codes adopted pursuant to those Regulations; (b) information relating

1312. Article 1(1) Regulation (EU) 1227/2011.
1313. Article 3(1)(a) *ibid.*
1314. Article 3(1)(b) *ibid.*
1315. Article 3(1)(c) *ibid.*
1316. Article 5 *ibid.*
1317. Article 2(4) *ibid.*

to the capacity and use of facilities for production, storage, consumption or transmission of electricity or natural gas or related to the capacity and use of LNG facilities, including planned or unplanned unavailability of these facilities; (c) information which is required to be disclosed in accordance with legal or regulatory provisions at Union or national level, market rules, and contracts or customs on the relevant wholesale energy market, in so far as this information is likely to have a significant effect on the prices of wholesale energy products; and (d) other information that a reasonable market participant would be likely to use as part of the basis of its decision to enter into a transaction relating to, or to issue an order to trade in a wholesale energy product. Information shall be deemed to be of a precise nature if it indicates a set of circumstances which exists or may reasonably be expected to come into existence or an event which has occurred or may reasonably be expected to do so, and if it is specific enough to enable a conclusion to be drawn as to the possible effect of that set of circumstances or event on the prices of wholesale energy products.[1318]

301. 'Market manipulation' ('χειραγώγηση της αγοράς' in Greek, 'manipulations de marché' in French, 'Marktmanipulation' in German, 'marktmanipulatie' in Dutch) stands for: (a) entering into any transaction or issuing any order to trade in wholesale energy products which: (i) gives, or is likely to give, false or misleading signals as to the supply of, demand for, or price of wholesale energy products; (ii) secures or attempts to secure, by a person, or persons acting in collaboration, the price of one or several wholesale energy products at an artificial level unless the person who entered into the transaction or issued the order to trade establishes that his reasons for doing so are legitimate and that that transaction or order to trade conforms to accepted market practices on the wholesale energy market concerned; or (iii) employs or attempts to employ a fictitious device or any other form of deception or contrivance which gives, or is likely to give, false or misleading signals regarding the supply of, demand for, or price of wholesale energy products; or (b) disseminating information through the media, including the internet, or by any other means, which gives, or is likely to give, false or misleading signals as to the supply of, demand for, or price of wholesale energy products, including the dissemination of rumours and false or misleading news, where the disseminating person knew, or ought to have known, that the information was false or misleading. When information is disseminated for the purposes of journalism or artistic expression, such dissemination of information shall be assessed taking into account the rules governing the freedom of the press and freedom of expression in other media unless: (i) those persons derive, directly or indirectly, an advantage or profits from the dissemination of the information in question; or (ii) the disclosure or dissemination is made with the intention of misleading the market as to the supply of, demand for, or price of wholesale energy products.[1319]

302. Cyprus Energy Regulatory Authority is the competent authority for ensuring compliance with Regulation (EU) 1227/2011, also in the gas sector (in regard to

1318. Article 2(1) *ibid.*
1319. Article 2(2) *ibid.*

electricity *see* paragraph 26 above) and especially the prohibitions and obligations set out therein.[1320] It may further issue regulatory decisions clarifying the application of Regulation (EU) 1227/2011, in particular, for the prohibition of exploitation of insider information, the obligation to publish insider information, the duty to prepare and manage a catalogue of holders of insider information, the prohibition to manipulate the wholesale market of energy, the obligations of the market participants and the application of prohibition of abuse practices in the wholesale energy market.[1321] Equally, it may issue binding directives to the market participants for the regulation of any matter of Law 183(I)/2004 and/ or Regulation (EU) 1227/2011 or any matter that may be subject to regulation.[1322] It is thus evident that the Cyprus Energy Regulatory Authority enjoys broad regulatory powers that seem to rest on a *carte blanche*, as the vagueness of the statutory provision suggests.

303. Regulation (EU) 1227/2011 provides for disclosure and collection of information and data. In particular, it is provided that market participants are obliged to publish inside information.[1323] It further sets out the obligation of market participants and others to provide the ACER with a record of wholesale energy market transactions.[1324] Said other persons are third parties acting on behalf of the market participants, a trade reporting system, an organized market, a trade-matching system or another person professionally arranging transactions, a trade repository registered or recognized under applicable Union legislation on derivative transactions, central counterparties and trade repositories, or a competent authority which has received that information by investment firms executing transactions in financial instruments or European Securities and Markets Authority when it has received that information in accordance with applicable Union legislation on derivative transactions, central counterparties and trade repositories.[1325] Finally, the ACER shares the said information with national regulatory authorities, competent financial authorities of the Member States, national competition authorities, the European Securities and Markets Authority and other relevant authorities.[1326] In this regard, Law No. 183(I)/2004 provides that any person obliged to submit, make public or announce publicly any information, data, documents or print-outs, is obliged to ensure that they are true, full and precise.[1327] If this is not the case or alternatively, if essential information is withheld, such an action or omission may lead to an administrative fine, as explained below (*see* in this regard paragraphs 268 et seq. above), or to penal sanctions, those being imprisonment of up to five years and/ or a monetary

1320. Section 6(4A) Law No. 183(I)/2004.
1321. Section 7A(1)(b)(i), (ii), (iii), (iv), (v) and (vi) *ibid.*
1322. Section 7A(1)(c) *ibid.*
1323. Article 4 Regulation (EU) No. 1227/2011.
1324. Article 8 *ibid.*
1325. Article 8 *ibid.*, and Art. 26 Regulation (EU) No. 600/2014 of the European Parliament and of the Council of 15 May 2014 on markets in financial instruments and amending Regulation (EU) No. 648/2012, OJ L 173, 12 Jun. 2014, p. 84.
1326. Article 10(1) *ibid.*
1327. Section 54A(1) Law No. 183(I)/2004.

fine of up to EUR 700,000.[1328] Particularly, when a violator is a legal person, liability bears upon the legal person itself, along with any members of its administrative managerial supervising or auditing organs when he had consented or participated in the commission of the crime.[1329] The said members and the legal person are joint and severally liable for any damage caused to third persons due to their actions or omissions.

304. Cyprus Energy Regulatory Authority while exercising the powers, authority and duties as the competent authority for the implementation of Regulation (EU) 1227/2011 may perform all necessary investigations and take all necessary measures, either by itself, or in cooperation with other authorities, or upon petition to the competent courts.[1330] In particular, it may have access to any relevant document regardless of the form that has been stored and make a copy thereof.[1331] It may further ask for information from any person involved including those who interfere successively with the transmission of orders or the execution of relevant actions, as well as their principals, and, to the extent that it is necessary, to invite any of those persons or principals to a hearing.[1332] Moreover, it has the power to conduct *in situ* searches and investigations and enter into premises of natural and legal persons, with the exception of residences, in order to confiscate documents and data of any form, under the condition that it is reasonably suspected that the documents or data related to the scope of the investigation may be crucial to the purpose of establishing a case of manipulating confidential information or the market in violation to the provisions of this law.[1333] Cyprus Energy Regulatory Authority, in addition, has the power to demand existing data on telephone conversations and records of data transfer,[1334] as well as the termination of any practice taking place against the law[1335] and request court orders for freezing or confiscating assets.[1336] In particular, with reference to undertakings falling within the scope of Regulation on Market Abuse,[1337] the Law on Market Abuse[1338] and the Law on Markets in Financial Instruments,[1339] Cyprus Energy Regulatory Authority has the authority to request from the Cyprus Securities and Exchange Commission or the competent court a temporary abatement order.[1340]

1328. Section 54A(2) and (3) *ibid.*
1329. Section 54A(4) *ibid.*
1330. Section 7(5) and (6) *ibid.*
1331. Section 7(5)(a) *ibid.*
1332. Section 7(5)(b) *ibid.*
1333. Section 7(5)(c) and (d) *ibid.*
1334. Section 7(5)(e) *ibid.*
1335. Section 7(5)(f) *ibid.*
1336. Section 7(5)(g) *ibid.*
1337. Regulation (EU) No. 596/2014 of the European Parliament and of the Council of 16 Apr. 2014 on market abuse (market abuse regulation) and repealing Directive 2003/6/EC of the European Parliament and of the Council and Commission Directives 2003/124/EC, 2003/125/EC and 2004/72/EC, OJ L 173, 12 Jun. 2014, p. 1.
1338. Law on Market Abuse ('περί Κατάχρησης της Αγοράς Νόμος') No. 102 of 2016, OG I(I) 4577, 14 Oct. 2016, p. 1094.
1339. Law on Financial Services and Activities and Regulated Markets ('περί Επενδυτικών Υπηρεσιών και Δραστηριοτήτων και Ρυθμιζόμενων Αγορών Νόμος') No. 87 of 2017, OG I(I) 4610, 7 Jul. 2017, p. 738, implementing Directive 2014/65/EU of the European Parliament

305. Failure to comply with the prohibitions of Regulation (EU) 1227/2011 constitutes a penal offence under Law No. 183(I)/2004. More specifically, any person violating or omitting compliance with the prohibition of exploitation of insider information is guilty of a penal offence and may face imprisonment for up to five years and/ or a monetary fine of up to EUR 350,000.[1341] This act or omission may be performed in person, via an employee or a representative. A convicted person automatically loses the right to trade, directly or indirectly, wholesale energy products or to make transactions, including the order to negotiate in one or more wholesale energy markets for a period of five years since his conviction, save for the completion of prior lawful actions.[1342] Violation of these prohibitions constitutes a separate penal offence that may lead to imprisonment of up to one year and/ or a monetary fine of up to EUR 50,000.[1343] Such a conviction automatically leads to the convicted person losing the right to trade, directly or indirectly, wholesale energy products or to make transactions, including the order to negotiate in one or more wholesale energy markets for a further period of five years since its conviction for violating the prohibition of exploitation of insider information.[1344] Persons failing to comply with the prohibition to manipulate the wholesale energy market face the same penalties, prohibitions and exclusions from trading wholesale energy products.[1345] Should a legal person violate the prohibition of exploitation of insider information and manipulation of the wholesale energy market, further faces a monetary fine of up to EUR 500,000, whereas the court may in addition order its exclusion from state aid and benefit, interim or final prohibition of performing commercial activity, wind-up, or interim or final termination of operation of the premises used for committing the crime.[1346] Any persons bearing penal liability for offences carried out by a legal person are equally jointly and severally liable for any damage caused to third parties due to the action or omission constituting the penal offence.[1347]

306. Any person attempting to exploit insider information or manipulate the wholesale energy market may face imprisonment of up to three years and/or a monetary fine of up to EUR 150,000.[1348] It is specified that 'attempt to manipulate the market' ('απόπειρα χειραγώγησης της αγοράς' in Greek, 'tentative de manipulation du marché' in French, 'Versuch der Marktmanipulation' in German, 'poging tot marktmanipulatie' in Dutch) means: (a) entering into any transaction, issuing any order to trade or taking any other action relating to a wholesale energy product with the intention of: (i) giving false or misleading signals as to the supply of, demand

---

and of the Council of 15 May 2014 on markets in financial instruments and amending Directive 2002/92/EC and Directive 2011/61/EU, OJ L 173, 12 Jun. 2014, p. 349.

1340. Section 7(5)(h) Law No. 183(I)/2004.
1341. Sections 50(2)(a) and 7A(1)(b)(i) *ibid.*
1342. Section 50(2)(b) *ibid.*
1343. Section 50(2)(c) *ibid.*
1344. Section 50(2)(d) *ibid.*
1345. Sections 50(4)(a), (b), (c) and (d) and 7A(1)(b)(iv) *ibid.*
1346. Section 50(6)(i), (ii), (iii), (iv) *ibid.*
1347. Section 51(3) *ibid.*
1348. Section 50(5) *ibid.*

for, or price of wholesale energy products; (ii) securing the price of one or several wholesale energy products at an artificial level, unless the person who entered into the transaction or issued the order to trade establishes that his reasons for doing so are legitimate and that that transaction or order to trade conforms to accepted market practices on the wholesale energy market concerned; or (iii) employing a fictitious device or any other form of deception or contrivance which gives, or is likely to give, false or misleading signals regarding the supply of, demand for, or price of wholesale energy products; or (b) disseminating information through the media, including the internet, or by any other means with the intention of giving false or misleading signals as to the supply of, demand for, or price of wholesale energy products.[1349]

307. The courts of Cyprus are competent to hear a case on violation of the prohibition of exploitation of insider information and manipulation of the wholesale energy market, along with the opposite provisions of Cyprus Penal Law, when the alleged penal offences have been performed in whole or in part in Cyprus. Cyprus courts are equally competent when the alleged penal offences have been conducted to the benefit of a legal person having a seat in Cyprus.[1350]

308. Failure to comply with the obligation to publish insider information is a penal offence and may take place either in person, via an employee or a representative. If a person is found guilty, he may face imprisonment of up to five years and/or a monetary fine of up to EUR 85,000.[1351] Any persons bearing penal liability for offences carried out by a legal person are equally jointly and severally liable for any damage caused to third parties due to the action or omission constituting the penal offence.[1352]

309. Violation of the prohibition of exploitation of insider information and manipulation of the wholesale energy market, failure to publish insider information and prepare and manage a catalogue of holders of insider information, aforementioned penal offences aside, may cause the imposition of administrative measures by Cyprus Energy Regulatory Authority.[1353] In particular, the Cyprus Energy Regulatory Authority has the power to:

- Order the person responsible for the violation to terminate it and refrain from repeating it.[1354]
- Deprive the gains obtained or losses avoided due to the violation, if these are quantifiable.[1355]

1349. Article 2(3) Regulation (EU) No. 1227/2011.
1350. Section 50(7)(a) and (b) Law No. 183(I)/2004.
1351. Section 50(3) *ibid.*
1352. Section 51(3) *ibid.*
1353. Sections 54(5) and 7A(b)(i), (ii), (iii), (iv) *ibid.*
1354. Section 54(6)(a) *ibid.*
1355. Section 54(6)(b) *ibid.*

- Issue a public warning stating the person responsible and the nature of the violation.[1356]
- Revoke or suspend the operation licence.[1357]
- Prohibit the manager from exercising his duties in the particular undertaking either temporarily or – in case of repeated offences – permanently.[1358]
- Temporarily prohibit the manager from performing transactions for the same account.[1359]
- Order administrative fines of up to three times the amount of gains obtained or the losses avoided due to the violation if these are quantifiable.[1360]
- In case of natural persons, order administrative fines of up to EUR 5,000,000 for the exploitation of insider information or manipulation of the wholesale energy market, up to EUR 1,000,000 for failing to publish insider information, and up to EUR 500,000 for failing to compile and manage a catalogue of persons possessing insider information.[1361]
- In case of legal persons, order administrative fines of up to EUR 15,000,000, EUR 2,500,000 and EUR 1,000,000 respectively.[1362]

Should a person fail to comply with the aforementioned orders and prohibitions, Cyprus Energy Regulatory Authority may impose an administrative fine of up to EUR 350,000, and in case that non-compliance is repeated, a further fine of up to EUR 700,000.[1363] In the event that the violator gained profit from the found violation, the authority may further impose an administrative fine of up to twice the amount of obtained gain, as evidenced.[1364]

310. Should the aforementioned actions and omissions be performed by a legal person, the administrative fine may be imposed on the legal person and/or the board of directors, director, officer or any other person, when it is found that the violation was due to its fault, wilful omission or negligence, as Cyprus Energy Regulatory Authority may think fit.[1365]

311. In the event that the provisions of this law or of Regulation (EU) 1227(I)/2011 are violated, and no specific administrative fine is set out, Cyprus Energy Regulatory Authority has the authority to impose an administrative fine of up to EUR 350,000, and in case that the relevant action or omission is repeated a further fine of up to EUR 700,000.[1366] Should the violator has profited from such action or

1356. Section 54(6)(c) *ibid.*
1357. Section 54(6)(d) *ibid.*
1358. Section 54(6)(e) and (f) *ibid.*
1359. Section 54(6)(g) *ibid.*
1360. Section 54(6)(h) *ibid.*
1361. Section 54(6)(i) *ibid.*
1362. Section 54(6)(j) *ibid.*
1363. Section 54(8) *ibid.*
1364. Section 54(9) *ibid.*
1365. Section 54(7)(a) and (b) *ibid.*
1366. Section 54(8) *ibid.*

omission, it may further order an administrative fine of up to twice the amount c profit, as this is supported by evidence.[1367]

312. While specifying the manner of administrative penalty and its exa amount, the Cyprus Energy Regulatory Authority has to comply with the followin statutory provisions. It takes into account all relevant facts, including the followin as the case may be: (a) seriousness and duration of the violation; (b) the extent c the liability of the violator; (c) the financial prosperity of the violator, as evidence by the turnover of a legal person, or the annual income of a natural person; (d) th importance of the obtained profit or the loss avoided to the extent that may b proved; (e) violator's willingness to cooperate, save for taking the obtained profit c avoided damage; (f) any previous violations of the violator; and (g) the measure implemented by the violator for the purpose of preventing the violation from bein repeated.[1368]

313. Decisions of Cyprus Energy Regulatory Authority imposing administrativ fines or other sanctions for violating Regulation (EU) 1227/2011 are uploaded to it website[1369] following their service to the violator. The publication includes at leas information on the manner and nature of the violation and the identity of the vic lator.[1370] However, the law sets out two exceptions to this rule. The first one relate to decisions imposing investigatory measures which are exempt.[1371] The second on relates to the name of a legal person or personal data of a natural person, where thei publication would be disproportionate taking into account the risk of endangerin the stability of the wholesale energy market or an ongoing investigation. In suc cases, the Cyprus Energy Regulatory Authority has the power to suspend the pub lication of the decision until reasons supporting such a suspension lapse or to pub lish the decision while withholding the name of the legal person or the identity o the natural person, under the condition that such publication ensures sufficient pro tection of the relevant personal data. Finally, it equally has the power not to publis the decision.[1372] All published decisions are maintained on its website for a perio of five years.[1373] Should a legal remedy be launched against such a decision wit the Supreme Court of Cyprus, the authority equally makes public this information as well as any later information on the outcome of the court proceedings.[1374]

1367. Section 54(9) *ibid.*
1368. Section 54(10) *ibid.*
1369. These are available at: https://www.cera.org.cy/el-gr/apofasis (visited on 9 Nov. 2019).
1370. Section 54B(1)(a) Law No. 183(I)/2004.
1371. Section 54B(1)(b) *ibid.*
1372. Section 54B(1)(c) *ibid.*
1373. Section 54B(3) *ibid.*
1374. Section 54B(2) *ibid.*

Chapter 6. Consumption

§1. Customers

314. Different kinds of customers with different meanings enjoy different rights and bear different obligations in this law. Hence, their determination is necessary. Customer ('πελάτης') means a wholesale or final customer of natural gas or a natural gas undertaking which purchases natural gas.[1375] Eligible customer ('επιλέγων πελάτης') is a customer who is free to purchase gas from the supplier of his choice, within the meaning of section 33 Law No. 183(I)/2004.[1376] Final customer ('τελικός πελάτης') means a customer purchasing natural gas for his own use,[1377] whereas household customer ('οικιακός πελάτης') is a customer purchasing natural gas for his own household consumption.[1378] However, non-household customer ('μη οικιακός πελάτης') stands for a customer purchasing natural gas which is not for his own household use.[1379] Lastly, wholesale customer ('χονδρικός πελάτης') is a natural or legal person other than a Transmission System Operator or Distribution System Operator who purchases natural gas for the purpose of resale inside or outside the system where he is established.[1380]

§2. Public Service Obligations and Customer Protection

315. Public service obligations and customer protection play an important role in the regulation of the natural gas market. The Minister can give instructions to the Cyprus Energy Regulatory Authority to impose public service obligations to any natural gas undertaking through decisions or regulations. These may include obligations relating to security, including the security of supply,[1381] regularity, quality and price of supplies,[1382] and environmental protection, including energy efficiency,

1375. Section 2 *ibid.*, which corresponds to Art. 2(24) Directive 2009/73/EC. The French term is 'client', the German 'Kunde' and the Dutch 'afnemer'.
1376. Section 2 Law No. 183(I)/2004, which corresponds to Art. 2(28) Directive 2009/73/EC. The French term is 'client éligible', the German 'zugelassener Kunde' and the Dutch 'in aanmerking komende afnemer'. It should be noted however that in the Greek version of the European provision mention to *επιλέξιμος πελάτης* is made.
1377. Section 2 Law No. 183(I)/2004, which corresponds to Art. 2(27) Directive 2009/73/EC. The French term is 'client final', the German 'Endkunde' and the Dutch 'eindafnemer'.
1378. Section 2 Law No. 183(I)/2004, which corresponds to Art. 2(25) Directive 2009/73/EC. The French term is 'client résidentiel', the German 'Haushaltskunde' and the Dutch 'huishoudelijke afnemer'.
1379. Section 2 Law No. 183(I)/2004, which corresponds to Art. 2(26) Directive 2009/73/EC. The French term is 'client non résidentiel', the German 'Nichthaushaltskunde' and the Dutch 'niet-huishoudelijke afnemer'.
1380. Section 2 Law No. 183(I)/2004, which corresponds to Art. 2(29) Directive 2009/73/EC. The French term is 'client grossiste', the German 'Großhändler' and the Dutch 'grootafnemer'. It should be noted however that in the Greek version of the European provision mention to *πελάτης χονδρικής* is made.
1381. Section 39(1)(a) Law No. 183(I)/2004, which corresponds to Art. 3(2) Directive 2009/73/EC.
1382. Section 39(1)(b) Law No. 183(I)/2004, which corresponds to Art. 3(2) Directive 2009/73/EC.

energy from renewable sources and climate protection.[1383] Such obligations are clearly defined, transparent, non-discriminatory, verifiable and guarantee equality of access for natural gas undertakings of the Union to national consumers.[1384] The decision or regulations issued set out the time period within which the addressee has to comply with the same.[1385] It may further foresee that recovery of any additional expenses relates to a specified period of a year and that the amount paid at the end of this period to the natural gas undertakings is the amount of additional expenses incurred by the natural gas undertaking due to the public service obligations as certified by the Cyprus Energy Regulatory Authority.[1386] The above-mentioned decision of the authority can be amended or revoked by the Minister. In such a case, provisions for the recovery of the above-mentioned additional expenses until their full recovery must be included.[1387]

316. Turning to customers' rights, all customers connected to the gas network are entitled to have their gas provided by a supplier, subject to the supplier's agreement, regardless of the Member State in which the supplier is registered, as long as the supplier follows the applicable trading and balancing rules and subject to security of supply requirements. In this regard, the Cyprus Energy Regulatory Authority takes all measures necessary to ensure that administrative procedures do not constitute a barrier for supply undertakings already registered in another Member State.[1388]

317. Regulations issued in accordance with section 47(2)(e) Law No. 183(I)/2004 are equally related to the rights of customers as well as to suppliers' obligations. In short, they set out appropriate measures to protect final customers and to ensure high standards of customers protection, especially with reference to the transparency of contractual terms and conditions, general information and dispute resolve mechanisms,[1389] as well as appropriate measures that sufficiently guarantee the protection of vulnerable customers.[1390] In particular, these measures ensure that:

– final customers have a right to a contract with their gas service provider that specifies: (i) the identity and address of the supplier,[1391] (ii) the services provided,

1383. Section 39(1)(c) Law No. 183(I)/2004, which corresponds to Art. 3(2) Directive 2009/73/EC.
1384. Section 39(5) Law No. 183(I)/2004, which corresponds to Art. 3(2) Directive 2009/73/EC.
1385. Section 39(4) Law No. 183(I)/2004.
1386. Section 39(2) *ibid.*
1387. Section 39(3) *ibid.*
1388. Section 40(7) *ibid.*, which corresponds to Art. 3(5) Directive 2009/73/EC.
1389. Section 40(1)(a) Law No. 183(I)/2004, which partially corresponds to Art. 3(3) Directive 2009/73/EC.
1390. Section 40(1)(b) Law No. 183(I)/2004, which partially corresponds to Art. 3(4) Directive 2009/73/EC.
1391. Section 40(2)(a)(i) Law No. 183(I)/2004, which corresponds to Annex I(1)(a) Directive 2009/73/EC. However, the directive refers to rights of customers in general ('customers' in the English version, 'clients' in the French one, 'Kunden' in the German one and 'afnemers' in the Dutch one) and not solely of final customers as stated in the national law.

the service quality levels offered, as well as the time for the initial connection,[1392] (iii) the types of maintenance service offered,[1393] (iv) the means by which up-to-date information on all applicable tariffs and maintenance charges may be obtained,[1394] (v) the duration of the contract, the conditions for renewal and termination of services and of the contract, and whether withdrawal from the contract without charge is permitted,[1395] (vi) any compensation and the refund arrangements which apply if contracted service quality levels are not met including inaccurate and delayed billing,[1396] (vii) the method of initiating procedures for settlement of disputes,[1397] (viii) information relating to consumer rights, including on the complaint handling and all of the information referred to in this point, clearly communicated through billing or the natural gas undertaking's website,[1398] and (ix) where a customer, while respecting the contractual conditions, wishes to change supplier, the change is effected by the operator(s) concerned within three weeks, while customers are entitled to receive all relevant consumption data, which are granted to customers in a non-discriminatory manner as regards cost, effort or time;[1399]

- conditions are fair, clear and well-known in advance. In any event, the aforementioned information is provided prior to the conclusion or confirmation of the contract. Where contracts are concluded through intermediaries, the same information is also provided prior to the conclusion of the contract;[1400]
- final customers are given adequate notice of any intention to modify contractual conditions and are informed about their right of withdrawal when the notice is given. Service providers notify their subscribers directly of any increase in charges, at an appropriate time no later than one normal billing period after the increase comes into effect in a transparent and comprehensible manner. It is ensured that customers are free to withdraw from contracts if they do not accept the new conditions notified to them by their gas service provider;[1401]

1392. Section 40(2)(a)(ii) Law No. 183(I)/2004, which corresponds to Annex I(1)(a) Directive 2009/73/EC.
1393. Section 40(2)(a)(iii) Law No. 183(I)/2004, which corresponds to Annex I(1)(a) Directive 2009/73/EC.
1394. Section 40(2)(a)(iv) Law No. 183(I)/2004, which corresponds to Annex I(1)(a) Directive 2009/73/EC.
1395. Section 40(2)(a)(v) Law No. 183(I)/2004, which corresponds to Annex I(1)(a) Directive 2009/73/EC.
1396. Section 40(2)(a)(vi) Law No. 183(I)/2004, which corresponds to Annex I(1)(a) Directive 2009/73/EC.
1397. Section 40(2)(a)(vii) Law No. 183(I)/2004, which corresponds to Annex I(1)(a) Directive 2009/73/EC.
1398. Section 40(2)(a)(viii) Law No. 183(I)/2004, which corresponds to Annex I(1)(a) Directive 2009/73/EC.
1399. Section 40(2)(a)(ix) Law No. 183(I)/2004, which corresponds to Art. 3(6)(a) and (b) Directive 2009/73/EC.
1400. Section 40(2)(a)(x) Law No. 183(I)/2004, which corresponds to Annex I(1)(a) Directive 2009/73/EC.
1401. Section 40(2)(b) Law No. 183(I)/2004, which corresponds to Annex I(1)(b) Directive 2009/73/EC. Again, the directive refers to customers and not exclusively to final customers.

- transparent information on applicable prices and tariffs and on standard terms and conditions, in respect of access to and use of gas services, are provided to the public and especially to final customers;[1402]
- appropriate measures for the protection of vulnerable customers are applied;[1403]
- transparent, simple and inexpensive procedures for dealing with complaints of final customers are foreseen. In particular, all consumers have the right to a good standard of service and complaint handling by their gas service provider;[1404]
- customers are offered a wide choice of payment methods, which do not unduly discriminate between customers. Prepayment systems are fair and adequately reflect likely consumption. Any difference in terms and conditions reflects the costs to the supplier of the different payment systems. General terms and conditions are fair and transparent and are given in clear and comprehensible language, whereas they do not include non-contractual barriers to the exercise of customers' rights, for example, excessive contractual documentation. Customers are protected against unfair or misleading selling methods;[1405]
- customers are not charged for changing suppliers;[1406]
- customers connected to the gas system are informed about their rights to be supplied, under the national legislation applicable, with natural gas of specified quality at reasonable prices;[1407]
- customers have at their disposal their consumption data and are able to, by explicit agreement and free of charge, give any registered supply undertaking access to its metering data. The party responsible for data management shall be obliged to give those data to the undertaking. Customers are informed about the format for the data and the procedure for them and suppliers to have access to the same. No additional costs are charged to the consumer for that service;[1408]
- customers are properly informed of actual gas consumption and costs frequently enough to enable them to regulate their own gas consumption. That information is given by using a sufficient time frame, which takes account of the capability of the customer's metering equipment. A due account is taken of the cost-efficiency of such measures. No additional costs are charged to the consumer for that service.[1409] Moreover, the Cyprus Energy Regulatory Authority ensures that final

1402. Section 40(2)(c) Law No. 183(I)/2004, which corresponds to Annex I(1)(c) Directive 2009/73/EC.
1403. Section 40(2)(d) Law No. 183(I)/2004.
1404. Section 40(2)(e) *ibid.*, which corresponds to Annex I(1)(f) Directive 2009/73/EC. Once more the directive refers to customers and not exclusively to final customers.
1405. Section 40(2)(f) Law No. 183(I)/2004, which corresponds to Annex I(1)(d) Directive 2009/73/EC.
1406. Section 40(2)(g) Law No. 183(I)/2004, which corresponds to Annex I(1)(e) Directive 2009/73/EC.
1407. Section 40(2)(h) Law No. 183(I)/2004, which corresponds to Annex I(1)(g) Directive 2009/73/EC.
1408. Section 40(2)(i) Law No. 183(I)/2004, which corresponds to Annex I(1)(h) Directive 2009/73/EC.
1409. Section 40(2)(j) Law No. 183(I)/2004, which corresponds to Annex I(1)(i) Directive 2009/73/EC.

customers receive free of charge their accounts along with data on energy consumption. Their access to data on their consumption is also free of charge;[1410] and

- customers receive a final closure account following any change of natural gas supplier no later than six weeks after the change of supplier has taken place.[1411]

318. Nonetheless, and specifically within the exercise of the powers of competent authorities vested in Regulation (EU) No. 596/2014, the Cyprus Energy Regulatory Authority may take all necessary measures for the proper information of the public, including correction of false or misleading information that was made public, demanding from any person who did so, to make a correctional declaration public.[1412]

319. The regulations may also set out measures to be implemented for achieving the objectives of social and economic cohesion, environmental protection and security of supply, especially through maintenance and construction of the necessary network infrastructure, including interconnection capacity.[1413]

320. In view of bringing all these rights to an optimal materialization, Cyprus Energy Regulatory Authority ensures that consumers are provided with all necessary information concerning their rights, current legislation and the means of dispute settlement available to them in the event of a dispute. The content of this information is prepared by the authority and is available at least in electronic form at help desks for the citizens and at the district offices of the Ministry of Energy, Commerce, Industry and Tourism. These, along with the office of the authority, are contact points for consumers' information.[1414] The authority further ensures that gas suppliers or the transmission system operators in cooperation with the same take all necessary measures for providing to all consumers a copy of the energy consumer checklist of practical information relating to energy consumer rights. This is established by the European Commission in consultation with relevant stakeholders, including the Member States, the national regulatory authorities, consumer organizations and natural gas undertakings. It further ensures that this checklist is made publicly available.[1415]

321. Intelligent metering systems are introduced to assist the active participation of consumers in the gas supply market. Natural gas undertakings prepare a study that determines which form of intelligent metering is economically reasonable and cost-effective and which time frame is feasible for their distribution. Such a study must be submitted to the Cyprus Energy Regulatory Authority for

1410. Section 40(15) Law No. 183(I)/2004.
1411. Section 40(2)(k) *ibid.*, which corresponds to Annex I(1)(j) Directive 2009/73/EC.
1412. Section 7(5)(i) Law No. 183(I)/2004. *See* Annex I(1)(h) Directive 2009/72/EC on free of cost access to consumption data.
1413. Section 40(4) Law No. 183(I)/2004, which corresponds to Art. 3(7) Directive 2009/73/EC.
1414. Section 40(10) Law No. 183(I)/2004, which corresponds to Art. 3(9) Directive 2009/73/EC.
1415. Section 40(14) Law No. 183(I)/2004, which corresponds to Art. 3(12) Directive 2009/73/EC.

approval.[1416] The authority also ensures the interoperability of those metering sy tems to be implemented and has due regard to the use of appropriate standards an best practices and the importance of the development of the internal market in natu ral gas.[1417] When intelligent metering systems are implemented and smart mete for natural gas are rolled out, Cyprus Energy Regulatory Authority ensures that th metering systems provide final customers information on actual time of use and th the objectives of energy efficiency and benefits for final customers are fully take into account when establishing the minimum functionalities of the meters and th obligations imposed on market participants.[1418] It further ensures the security of th smart meters and data communication, and the privacy of final customers, in com pliance with the Law on the Protection of Natural Persons from Processing of Pe sonal Data and Free Movement of Those Data.[1419] Finally, it requires th appropriate advice and information be given to customers at the time of installatio of smart meters, in particular about their full potential with regard to meter readin management and the monitoring of energy consumption.[1420] Where smart meter are installed, they enable accurate billing information based on actual consumptior Cyprus Energy Regulatory Authority ensures that final customers have the possibil ity of easy access to complementary information on historical consumption, allow ing detailed self-checks. Complementary information on historical consumptio includes cumulative data for at least three previous years or the period since the star of the supply contract if this is shorter. The data correspond to the intervals fo which frequent billing information has been produced.[1421] It further include detailed data according to the time of use for any day, week, month and year. Thes data are made available to the final customer via the internet or the meter interfac for the period of at least the previous twenty-four months or the period since th start of the supply contract if this is shorter.[1422]

322. Special provisions are set out for vulnerable consumers ('*καταναλωτές*'),[142 the concept of which is defined with reference to energy poverty, among others, b the Minister following consultations with the Cyprus Energy Regulatory Authority First, the regulations mentioned above may foresee measures such as formulating

1416. Section 40(5)(a) Law No. 183(I)/2004, which corresponds to Annex I(2) Directive 2009/73/EC
1417. Section 40(5)(b) Law No. 183(I)/2004, which corresponds to Annex I(2) Directive 2009/73/EC
1418. Section 40(5)(c)(i) Law No. 183(I)/2004, which corresponds to Art. 9(2)(a) Directive 2012/27 EU.
1419. Section 40(5)(c)(ii) Law No. 183(I)/2004, which corresponds to Art. 9(2)(b) Directive 2012/27 EU.
1420. Section 40(5)(c)(iv) Law No. 183(I)/2004, which corresponds to Art. 9(2)(e) Directive 2012/27 EU.
1421. Section 40(5)(d)(i) Law No. 183(I)/2004, which corresponds to Art. 10(2)(a) Directive 2012/27 EU.
1422. Section 40(5)(d)(ii) Law No. 183(I)/2004, which corresponds to Art. 10(2)(b) Directive 2012/27 EU.
1423. National legislation as well as the Greek version of the Directive refer to vulnerable consumer ('ευάλωτους καταναλωτές'), whereas the English version mentions 'vulnerable customers', th French one 'consommateurs vulnérables', the German one 'schutzbedürftige Kunden' and th Dutch one 'kwetsbare afnemers'. Hence, it cannot be assumed with certainty whether the term 'customer' or 'consumer' should be best used. In any case, this problematic is of low value, as th term is to be defined by the national authorities.

national energy action plans, providing social security benefits to ensure the necessary gas supply to them, or providing for support for energy efficiency improvements to address energy poverty where identified, including in the broader context of poverty. Such measures do not impede the effective opening of the market set out in section 33 Law No. 183(I)/2004 and market functioning and are notified to the European Commission, where relevant. Still, this notification does not include measures taken within the general social security system.[1424] Additionally, the supplier may not disconnect natural gas to such persons in critical times.[1425]

323. Lastly, upon coming into force of this legislation, the Minister informs the European Commission of all measures adopted to fulfil public service obligations, including consumer and environmental protection, and their possible effect on national and international competition. He is further obliged to notify the European Commission subsequently every two years of any changes to such measures.[1426] In addition, the Cyprus Energy Regulatory Authority informs the European Commission of all measures adopted for fulfilling the public service obligations every two years. Such measures may, however, require derogation from this legislation.[1427] Said notification relates to measures for the protection of the environment, security of supply, customers' protection, including final customers, social and regional solidarity as well as preserving standards of services and the possible effect on national and international competition.[1428]

§3. Disputes

324. Cyprus Energy Regulatory Authority acts as an independent mechanism (energy ombudsman or consumer body) for the efficient treatment of complaints of consumers and out-of-court dispute settlements.[1429] Regulations may further establish a procedure for fair and speedy dispute resolution, with the provision, where warranted, for a system of reimbursement and/or compensation.[1430]

1424. Section 40(9) Law No. 183(I)/2004, which corresponds to Art. 3(4) Directive 2009/73/EC.
1425. Section 40(8) Law No. 183(I)/2004, which corresponds to Art. 3(3) Directive 2009/73/EC.
1426. Section 40(12) Law No. 183(I)/2004, which corresponds to Art. 3(11) Directive 2009/73/EC.
1427. Section 41(1) Law No. 183(I)/2004. It is self-evident that any measures not in compliance with Law No. 183(I)/2004, breach the principle of legality ('αρχή της νομιμότητας') established in s. 8(1) Law No. 158(I)/1999.
1428. Section 41(2) Law No. 183(I)/2004.
1429. Section 40(11) *ibid.*, which corresponds to Art. 3(9) Directive 2009/73/EC. Appointing the Cyprus Energy Regulatory Authority as an independent mechanism does seem odd. In Germany, the Federal Ministry for Economic Affairs and Energy ('Bundesministerium für Wirtschaft und Technologie') and the Federal Ministry of Food and Agriculture ('Bundesministerium für Ernährung, Landwirtschaft und Verbraucherschutz') have appointed *Schlichtungsstelle Energie e.V.*, a legal person governed by private law that further complies with the requirements foreseen in 98/257/EC: Commission Recommendation of 30 Mar. 1998 on the principles applicable to the bodies responsible for out-of-court settlement of consumer disputes, OJ L 115, 17 Apr. 1998, p. 31, pursuant to §111 b Abs. 3, 4 EnWG.
1430. Section 40(3) Law No. 183(I)/2004, which corresponds to Annex I(1)(f) Directive 2009/73/EC.

Part III. Regulatory Framework Concerning Petrol

Chapter 1. Introduction

325. Storage, transport and sale of petrol are regulated by the Petroleum Law[1431] (hereinafter 'Cap. 272'), whereas laying and using of pipelines is regulated by the Petroleum (Pipelines) Law[1432] (hereinafter 'Cap. 273'). These laws, which were issued at the time of British Rule, foresee the necessity of licences for the performance of such actions.

1431. A Law to consolidate and amend the law relating to the storage, transport and sale of petroleum, CG No. 2795, 22 Nov. 1939, p. 69, as amended.
1432. Relating to the laying of pipes for the purpose of conveying oil, CG No. 1376, 2 May 1919, p. 198, as amended.

Chapter 2. Licence to Store and Keep Petroleum

326. Within Cap. 272 Petroleum means any inflammable substance, which is derived from petroleum comprised in the following three classes. The first one is 'Petroleum Class A', which includes the products usually known as gasoline ('υγραέρια'), aviation spirit ('βενζίνη αεροπλάνων'), benzene ('βενζίνη για κινητήρες'), crude petrol ('αργό πετρέλαιο') and other petroleum having a flashpoint below 37.5° Celsius. 'Petroleum Class B' includes the products usually known as kerosene-type jet fuel ('καύσιμο αεριωθουμένων τύπου κηροζίνης'), illuminating oil ('φωτιστικό πετρέλαιο'), gas oil/diesel ('πετρέλαιο εσωτερικής καύσης / ντίζελ') and other petroleum having a flashpoint, not below 37.8° Celsius but below 60° Celsius. 'Petroleum Class C' includes the products usually known as fuel oil ('πετρέλαιο θέρμανσης'), light fuel oil ('ελαφρύ μαζούτ'), heavy fuel oil ('βαρύ μαζούτ') and other petroleum having a flashpoint, not below 60° Celsius.[1433] This petroleum underlies the provisions of this law. However, certain petroleum is excluded from the application of the same. This is petroleum kept or stored in any premises in separate glass, earthenware or metal vessels safely hermetically sealed, provided that the aggregate amount of petroleum contained therein does not exceed four gallons of petroleum class A in vessels of no more than one litre each,[1434] 100 gallons of petroleum class B[1435] and 250 gallons of petroleum class C,[1436] so long as this petroleum is not kept or stored for sale. Equally excluded from the application of this law is petroleum contained in the storage vessel of any motor vehicle or other vehicles, whose propelling power is derived from petroleum,[1437] as well as petroleum contained in the storage vessel of any aircraft or motor floating craft.[1438] Lastly, from the applicability of this law, petroleum carried on any motor vehicle or other vehicles as a reserve supply the propelling power of which is obtained from petroleum, provided that such reserve supply does not exceed eight gallons.[1439] Similarly, gasoline kept or stored in vessels, the aggregate amount of which is less than 450 litres, is excluded from the application of this law.[1440]

327. The Licensing Authority may in its discretion grant to any person a licence in the prescribed form to store and keep petroleum of a class specified therein. Such a licence is granted following an application of the applicant, which is accompanied by a certification from the labour inspectorate certifying that the relevant area or building is suitable and safe for such a purpose.[1441] It is valid for a two-year period[1442] unless annulled in the meantime. This may take place when a report of

1433. Section 2 Cap. 272.
1434. Section 4(5)(a)(i) *ibid.*
1435. Section 4(5)(a)(ii) *ibid.*
1436. Section 4(5)(a)(iii) *ibid.*
1437. Section 4(5)(b)(i) *ibid.*
1438. Section 4(5)(b)(ii) *ibid.*
1439. Section 4(5)(c) *ibid.*
1440. Section 4(6) *ibid.*
1441. Section 4(1) *ibid.*
1442. Section 4(2) *ibid.*

the director of labour inspectorate establishing that the relevant area or building is improper for storing petroleum is tabled before the Licensing Authority.[1443]

328. Any person aggrieved by the refusal to grant a licence or the cancellation of the licence by the Licensing Authority or the terms and conditions imposed by the Licensing Authority in any such licence may within ten days from such refusal or cancellation or from the date of grant of licence against which the appeal is made, appeal to the Council of Ministers. Its decision is final and conclusive.[1444]

329. Monitoring compliance is entrusted to the director of labour inspectorate and any police officer of any rank not lower than that of a sergeant. They may at any time without a warrant enter any premises or place wherein or whereon he has reasonable ground to suspect that petroleum is being stored, kept, sold or exposed for sale in contravention of Cap. 272. They may further seize and remove any such petroleum together with the vessel containing the same.[1445]

330. Lastly, criminal provisions are foreseen in this law. Any person storing or keeping petroleum without the aforementioned licence is guilty of an offence. He is liable to imprisonment for a term not exceeding one year and/or to a fine not exceeding EUR 1,710.[1446] Similarly, any person resisting search or obstructing the director of labour inspectorate or any police officer monitoring compliance with this law, as described above, is guilty of an offence. He is liable to imprisonment for a term not exceeding three months and/or to a fine not exceeding EUR 256.[1447]

1443. Section 4(3) *ibid.*
1444. Section 7 *ibid.*
1445. Section 8(1) *ibid.*
1446. Section 4(4) *ibid.*
1447. Section 8(2) *ibid.*

Chapter 3. Licence to Lay or Use Pipelines

331. Any person to whom an authorization under Law No. 4(I)/2007 to mine an win oil has been granted may apply to the Council of Ministers for a licence to la and use a pipeline on any land in Cyprus, whether such land is or is not the propert of such a person.[1448] Within this law, pipeline means any pipe for the purpose of c capable of being used for conveying oil, which includes gas.[1449] The application i accompanied by a plan of the land showing, as nearly may be, the names of th owners and occupiers thereof, and also the course and direction of the pipeline an the position of any pumping stations, tanks or other works in connection with suc pipeline.[1450]

332. The Council of Ministers may grant to such applicant, upon such terms an conditions as it may think fit, a licence to lay and use a pipeline over such land a may be the property of the applicant or over which he may have obtained way leave and as to such land, if any, as is not his property or over which he has not obtaine way leave, to proceed under the procedure stated below.[1451] A licensee desirous o laying a pipeline on the land of another person gives notice in writing to the owne of such land of his desire to lay down such pipeline. Such notice also includes hi intention after the expiration of fourteen days from the date of such notice on specified day to enter upon such land for the purpose of fixing the location of suc pipeline. Within fourteen days of such entry, he shall serve the owner with a state ment in writing containing full particulars of the description and proposed locatio of such pipeline.[1452]

333. Any such owner after receipt of such notice and statement of particular may by writing under his hand assent to the laying down of such pipeline upon pay ment of such compensation as may be agreed upon. Any assent so given is bindin on all parties having any estate or interest in the land. Any occupier or person othe than the owner interested in that land is entitled to compensation for any injury h may sustain by the laying of such pipeline so that the claim therefore be mad within twelve months after the laying of such pipeline. The amount of such com pensation is determined in the case of dispute in the manner in which disputed com pensation for injury of land is required to be determined by Cap. 273.[1453]

334. If an owner fails to express his assent to the proposal to lay a pipeline o his land within one month after the service of the aforementioned notice, he i deemed to have dissented from the relevant proposal. In the event of such dissent the question of whether the proposed pipeline will cause any injury to such owner or to the occupier or another person interested in the land, is decided by the Cour

1448. Section 4(1) Cap. 273.
1449. Section 2 *ibid.*
1450. Section 4(2) *ibid.*
1451. Section 4(3) *ibid.*
1452. Section 5 *ibid.*
1453. Section 6 *ibid.*

following an application of the licensee.[1454] The same applies to the question, whether any injury that may be caused is or is not of a nature to admit of being fully compensated for by money.[1455] The Court may summon the parties to appear before it at a time and place to be named in the summons. Upon the appearance of the parties, or in the absence of any of them upon proof of the due service of the summons, the Court may hear and determine the question as well as the amount of compensation, if applicable. To that purpose, it examines such parties and their witnesses upon oath. The costs of every such inquiry and by whom they are to be paid are at the discretion of the Court.[1456] Should the Court decide that no injury will be caused to the owner, occupier or another party interested in the land, the licensee may proceed forthwith to lay the pipeline.[1457] However, if it decides that injury will be caused to the same persons, but such injury is of a nature to admit of being fully compensated by money, the Court proceeds to assess such compensation and to apportion the same amongst the parties in its judgment entitled thereto. On payment of the sum so assessed, the licensee might proceed to lay the pipeline.[1458] Should the Court, however, find that such injury is not of a nature to admit of being fully compensated by money, the licensee is not entitled to lay the pipeline.[1459]

335. After the pipeline has been laid, following a relevant judgment of the Court, where such is necessary, it is lawful for the licensee or person in charge of such pipeline or any person authorized in writing by either of them, from time to time as it becomes necessary, to enter upon the land through which such pipeline has been laid for the purpose of inspecting and with such assistance as may be necessary repairing the same. In case the pipeline is no longer required, the purpose of entering may be that of removing the same. In such a case, the surface of the land is forthwith restored to its former condition. In default thereof, such restoration may be carried out by the owner of the land, whereas the costs thereof are recoverable from the person liable for this through a court order.[1460] Any person hindering, obstructing or interfering with the exercise of the above-mentioned entry rights is liable to a fine not exceeding EUR 171.[1461]

336. It should also be noted that the provisions of Cap. 273 do not relieve any licensee of the liability to make compensation to the owner or occupier of the land or the agents, workmen or servants of such owner or occupier for any damage or injury done or caused by the exercise or use of any power or authority hereby conferred or by any irregularity, trespass or other wrongful proceedings in the execution of this law or by the breaking or bursting of any pipe, or by reason of any defect

1454. Section 7(1)(a) *ibid.*
1455. Section 7(1)(b) *ibid.*
1456. Section 8 *ibid.*
1457. Section 7(2)(a) *ibid.*
1458. Section 7(2)(b) *ibid.*
1459. Section 7(2)(c) *ibid.*
1460. Section 12 *ibid.*
1461. Section 13 *ibid.*

in any pipe. Provided that if before action brought in respect thereof such licensee makes tender of sufficient amends to the party injured, such last-mentioned party shall not recover in any action.[1462]

337. Laying or using a pipeline without the relevant licence, or committing a breach of the terms and conditions of such licence or any provisions of this law results in liability to a fine not exceeding EUR 427.[1463]

1462. Section 14 *ibid.*
1463. Section 15 *ibid.*

Part IV. Regulatory Framework Concerning Coal

338. Coal is neither produced nor used in Cyprus. Most probably due to those facts, no regulatory framework concerning coal is to be found in the national legislation.

Part V. Regulatory Framework Concerning Renewables

Chapter 1. Introduction

§1. Objective

339. The objective of Law No. 107(I)/2022 is to promote and encourage the use of electricity from renewable sources,[1464] that being energy from renewable non-fossil sources, namely wind, solar (solar thermal and solar photovoltaic) and geothermal energy, ambient energy, tide, wave and other ocean energy, hydropower, biomass, landfill gas, sewage treatment plant gas and biogas.[1465] *Ambient energy* ('ενέργεια του περιβάλλοντος') means naturally occurring thermal energy and energy accumulated in the environment with constrained boundaries, which can be stored in the ambient air, excluding in exhaust air, or in surface or sewage water,[1466] whereas *geothermal energy* ('γεωθερμική ενέργεια') is energy stored in the form of heat beneath the surface of solid earth.[1467] *Biomass* ('βιομάζα') means the biodegradable fraction of products, waste and residues from biological origin from agriculture, including vegetal and animal substances, from forestry and related industries, including fisheries and aquaculture, as well as the biodegradable fraction of waste, including industrial and municipal waste of biological origin.[1468] EU law further specifies that agricultural biomass ('γεωργική βιομάζα') is biomass produced from agriculture,[1469] forest biomass ('δασική βιομάζα') biomass produced

1464. Section 3 Law No. 107(I)/2022.
1465. Section 2 *ibid.*, which corresponds to Art. 2(1) Directive (EU) 2018/2001. The French term is 'énergie produite à partir de sources renouvelables', the German 'Energie aus erneuerbaren Quellen' and the Dutch 'energie uit hernieuwbare bronnen'.
1466. In French 'énergie ambiante', in German 'Umgebungsenergie', in Dutch 'omgevingsenergie'. Section 2(1) Law No. 107(I)/2022, which corresponds to Art. 2(2) Directive (EU) 2018/2001.
1467. Section 2(1) Law No. 107(I)/2022, which corresponds to Art. 2(3) Directive (EU) 2018/2001. The French term is 'énergie géothermique', the German 'geothermische Energie' and the Dutch 'geothermische energie'.
1468. Section 2 Law No. 107(I)/2022, which corresponds to Art. 2(24) Directive (EU) 2018/2001. The French term is 'biomasse', the German 'Biomasse' and the Dutch 'biomassa'.
1469. In French 'biomasse agricole', in German 'landwirtschaftliche Biomasse', in Dutch 'agrarische biomassa'. Article 2(25) Directive (EU) 2018/2001.

from forestry[1470] and biogas ('βιοαέρια') gaseous fuels produced from biomass.[1471] Wind, solar, tide, wave and other ocean energy, as well as landfill gas, an sewage treatment plant gas, are not defined in the law. Hence, they must be interpreted in their ordinary sense. Nonetheless, this law provides that terms not define in the same have the meaning specified in the following legislations: (a) Law No 130(I)/2021; (b) Law on Reduction of Emission Fuels;[1472] (c) Law on Energy Efficiency of Buildings;[1473] (d) Law on Energy Efficiency in Heating and Cooling;[1474] (e) Law on Energy Efficiency;[1475] (f) Law on Ecodesign;[1476] (g) Law on Labelling of Energy Efficiency;[1477] (h) Law on Renewables' Fund;[1478] (i) Law on Installation of Alternative Fuels;[1479] and (j) Law No. 13(I)/2022.[1480]

340. Such an objective is intended to be achieved via the establishment of common framework for the promotion of energy from renewable sources. It sets binding Union target for the overall share of energy from renewable sources in th

---

1470. In French 'biomasse forestière', in German 'fortwirtschaftliche Biomasse', in Dutch 'bosbiomassa'. Article 2(26) Directive (EU) 2018/2001.
1471. In French 'biogaz', in German 'Biogas', in Dutch 'biogas'. Article 2(28) Directive (EU) 2018/2001.
1472. Law on Standards, Sustainability Criteria and Reducing Emmissions of Fuels ('ο περί Προδιαγραφών, Κριτηρίων Αειφορίας και Μείωσης των Εκπομπών των Καυσίμων Νόμος') No 106 of 2022, OG I(I) No. 4902 of 15 Jul. 2022, p. 986.
1473. Law on Regulating Energy Performance of Buildings ('περί Ρύθμισης της Ενεργειακής Απόδοσης των Κτιρίων Νόμος') No. 142 of 2006 (OG I(I) No. 4095, 3 Nov. 2006, p. 1517), as amended, which implements Directive 2010/31/EU of the European Parliament and of the Council of 19 May 2010 on the energy performance of buildings, OJ L 153, 18 Jun. 2010, p. 13.
1474. Law on Promoting Energy Efficiency in Heating and Cooling and Co-Production of Electricity and Heating ('ο περί Προώθησης της Ενεργειακής Απόδοσης στη Θέρμανση και Ψύξη και της Συμπαραγωγής Ηλεκτρισμού και Θερμότητας Νόμος') No. 174 of 2006, OG I(I) No 4105 of 29 Dec. 2006, p. 1905.
1475. Law on Energy Efficiency ('ο περί της Ενεργειακής Απόδοσης Νόμος') No. 31 of 2009, OGI(I) No. 4200 of 3 Apr. 2009, p. 170.
1476. Law on Setting of Ecodesign Requirements for Energy-Related Products ('ο περί του Καθορισμού των Απαιτήσεων Οικολογικού Σχεδιασμού των Συνδεόμενων με την Ενέργεια Προϊόντων Νόμος') No. 17 of 2011, OG I(I) No. 4271 of 25 Feb. 2011, p. 80, which implement Directive 2009/125/EC of the European Parliament and of the Council of 21 Oct. 2009 establishing a framework for the setting of ecodesign requirements for energy-related products, OJ L 285 31 Oct. 2009, p. 10, as amended.
1477. Law on Labelling of Energy Efficiency, Consumption of Energy and Other Sources by Products Associated with Energy During Their Use ('ο περί της Σήμανσης της Ενεργειακής Απόδοσης, της Κατανάλωσης Ενέργειας και Λοιπών Πόρων από τα Συνδεόμενα με την Ενέργεια Προϊόντα κατά τη Χρήση τους Νόμος') No. 44 of 2021, OG I(I) No. 4826 of 7 Apr 2021, p. 241, which facilitates the effective application of Regulation (EU) 2017/1369 of the European Parliament and of the Council of 4 Jul. 2017 setting a framework for energy labelling and repealing Directive 2010/30/EU, OJ L 198, 28 Jul. 2017, p. 1, as amended.
1478. Law on the Operation of the Fund for Renewable Sources of Energy and Saving Energy ('ο περί της Λειτουργίας Ταμείου Ανανεώσιμων Πηγών Ενέργειας και Εξοικονόμησης Ενέργειας Νόμος') No. 108 of 2022, OG I(I) No. 4902 of 15 Jul. 2022, p. 1081.
1479. Law on Promoting and Developing Installations for Alternative Fuels ('ο περί Προώθησης και Ανάπτυξης των Υποδομών Εναλλακτικών Καυσίμων Νόμος') No. 59 of 2017, OG I(I) No 4604 of 16 Jun. 2017, p. 503.
1480. Section 2(2) Law No. 107(I)/2022.

Union's gross final consumption of energy in 2030.[1481] It also lays down rules on financial support for electricity from renewable sources, on self-consumption of such electricity, on the use of energy from renewable sources in the heating and cooling sector and in the transport sector, on regional cooperation between Member States, and between Member States and third countries, on guarantees of origin, on administrative procedures and on information and training.[1482]

341. Mandatory national overall targets for Cyprus are specified as follows. Cyprus together with other Member States collectively ensure that the share of energy from renewable sources in the Union's gross final consumption of energy in 2030 is at least 32% or any other target set by the Union. The national contribution of Cyprus to meet the binding overall Union target is set within the frame of the Integrated National Energy and Climate Plan.[1483] Especially, the share of energy from renewable sources in gross final consumption of energy in Cyprus by 1 January 2021 and thereafter must be at least 13%.[1484] The Commission supports the just transition of carbon-intensive regions towards increased shares of renewables through enhanced use of Union funds in particular for the purposes of reducing the cost of capital for renewable energy projects, developing projects for integrating renewable sources into the energy system, developing transmission and distribution grid infrastructure, intelligent networks, storage facilities and interconnections, and enhancing regional cooperation both between Member States and Member States and third countries.[1485]

§2. Regulatory Mechanism

342. The players in this legislation are the Minister of Energy, Commerce and Industry ('the Minister'), the Council of Ministers, Cyprus Energy Regulatory Authority, the Director of the Department of Energy of the Ministry of Energy, Commerce and Industry ('the Director') and they have the following duties and responsibilities.

343. The Minister prepares drafts to be submitted to the Council of Ministers in the matters of national contribution to the binding overall target for 2030, on support schemes, joint support schemes and pilot support schemes, statistical transfers of certain amount of electricity by renewables sources between Cyprus and other Member States, joint projects of any type and simplified authorization procedures.[1486] He also reports to the House of Representatives on the progress of

1481. Section 4(a) Law No. 107(I)/2022, which corresponds to Art. 1 Directive (EU) 2018/2001.
1482. Section 4(b) Law No. 107(I)/2022, which corresponds to Art. 1 Directive (EU) 2018/2001.
1483. Section 5(1) & (2) Law No. 107(I)/2022, which corresponds to Art. 3(1) & (2) Directive (EU) 2018/2001.
1484. Section 5(3)(1) Law No. 107(I)/2022, which corresponds to Art. 3(4) and Annex I Part A Directive (EU) 2018/2001.
1485. Article 3(5)(a) to (d) *ibid.*
1486. Sections 5(3)(b), 6(1) & (2) & 15(1), 7(7), 10(1), 11(1) & 13(1) and 18(12) Law No. 130(I)/2022 respectively.

national contribution to said binding overall target for 2030.[1487] At the same time the Minister contributes to shaping the principles, under which producers located in other Member States may participate in the support schemes.[1488] Most importantly the Minister has the power to issue Decrees ('διάταγμα') on certain issues,[1489] including the share of energy from renewable sources to gross final consumption of electricity from renewable sources,[1490] special procedure for certain authorizations,[1491] issuing guarantees of origin for electricity from renewable sources for heating or cooling,[1492] Finally, the Minister issues Notifications ('Γνωστοποιήσεις') with regard to a series of issues[1493] and acts as a dispute resolution body.[1494]

344. The Council of Ministers makes decisions following drafts prepared by the Minister on the aforementioned range of matters.[1495] It is also entrusted with legislative powers, as it has the power to issue Regulations ('Κανονισμοί') on any issue that may be regulated under this law. Regulations are published in the official gazette.[1496] Finally, the Council of Ministers is involved in organizing the authorization process.[1497]

345. Cyprus Energy Regulatory Authority is the competent authority for guarantees of origin.[1498] It may also issue regulatory decisions and decisions in this regard.[1499] Still, it mainly consults the Minister on issues such as support schemes, joint projects, and simplified authorizations.[1500] At the same time, it advises the Director of the Department of Energy of the Ministry,[1501] while issuing regulatory decisions with regard to renewable energy communities and jointly acting renewables self-consumers.[1502] Finally, it may impose administrative fines to persons violating this law, as long as the breached obligation or duty falls within its competence.[1503]

346. The Director drafts and publishes long-term schedules anticipating the expected allocation of support for projects of renewable sources[1504] and promotes

1487. Section 5(4)(a) & (b)*ibid.* respectively.
1488. Section 7(5) *ibid.*
1489. Section 46 *ibid.*
1490. Section 9 *ibid. See also* Art. 7 Directive (EU) 2018/2001.
1491. Section 18(12)(e) Law No. 107(I)/2022.
1492. Sections 23(4) and 26(12)(c) *ibid.*
1493. Section 40(3) *ibid.*
1494. Section 41(5) & (7), 42 *ibid.*
1495. Sections 5(3)(b), 6(1) & 7(5) & (7), 10(1), 11(1), 13(1) and 15(1) *ibid.*
1496. Section 46(1) & (2) *ibid.*
1497. Section 18(1) *ibid.*
1498. Section 23(3), (4) & (5) *ibid.*
1499. Section 33(2) *ibid.*
1500. Section 6(2), 11(1) & 13(1), 18(9), *ibid.*
1501. Section 8(7) *ibid.*
1502. Sections 37(2) & 38(2) *ibid.*
1503. Section 41(8) *ibid.*
1504. Sections 8(2) *ibid. See also* ss 37(7) and 40(1) *ibid.*

increase in the share of energy from renewable sources in heating and cooling.[1505] At the same time, it performs assessments on the effectiveness of national support schemes, and the regulatory and administrative obstacles to long-term renewable power purchase agreements,[1506] It further conveys to the Commission with regard to the electricity or energy for heating and/ or cooling from renewable sources produced by any joint project in Cyprus or other Member States.[1507] Importantly, it is the competent authority for providing information on support schemes to the public, on optimal combination of energy from renewable sources, high efficiency, as well as district heating and cooling to interested parties, such as engineers and architects, and on actualizing information programmes for the citizens to be informed on how to exercise their rights as active customers.[1508] At the same time, it keeps the record of small-scale installations.[1509] The Director also determines the standards for equipment and energy systems for renewable sources.[1510] Finally, it is the competent authority for guarantees of origin solely with regard to energy from renewable sources for heating or cooling[1511] and has the power to perform inspections in order to ensure compliance with this law.[1512]

1505. Section 34(1) to (6).
1506. Section 8(5) & (7).
1507. Sections 11(2), 12(1), 13(4), 14(2), 15(3).
1508. Section 19(1) *ibid*. *See also* ss 22(1), (5) to (7) and 35(1) *ibid*.
1509. Section 36(1) *ibid*.
1510. Section 20(1) *ibid*.
1511. Sections 23(2), 24(1), 26(10), (12) & (13) *ibid*.
1512. Sections 39(1) and 41(1) to (8) *ibid*.

Chapter 2. Production

§1. Permissions

347. At the outset, it is underlined that all rules concerning the authorization, certification and licensing procedures are proportionate and necessary, while contributing to the implementation of the energy efficiency first principle. Such procedures are applied to plants and associated transmission and distribution networks: (a) for the production of electricity; (b) for heating or cooling from renewable sources; (c) to the process of transformation of biomass into biofuels, bioliquids, biomass fuels or other energy products, to renewable liquid and gaseous transport fuels of non-biological origin; and (d) to energy storage. All competent authorities of Cyprus are under the statutory duty to ensure this.[1513] In fact, said authorities take the necessary steps to confirm that: (a) administrative procedures are streamlined and expedited at the appropriate administrative level and predictable timeframes are established for aforementioned procedures; (b) rules concerning authorization, certification and licensing are objective, transparent and proportionate, do not discriminate between applicants and take fully into account the particularities of individual renewable energy technologies; (c) administrative charges paid by consumers, planners, architects, builders and equipment and system installers and suppliers are transparent and cost-related; and (d) simplified and less burdensome authorization procedures, including a simple-notification procedure, are established for decentralized devices, and for producing and storing energy from renewable sources.[1514]

348. Cyprus has created a contact point named *Single Service Point* ('Υπηρεσία Ενιαίας Εξυπηρέτησης') upon request by the applicant, guide through and facilitate the entire administrative permit application and granting process. This is the only point of communication for the entire process. The authorization process for units of energy production via renewable sources covers all relevant administrative authorizations to build, repower and operate plants for the production of energy from renewable sources. It further covers the administrative process for authorizations for the construction of necessary infrastructure for connecting units to transmission or distribution networks, as well as for any other necessary procedures.[1515] The Single Service Point guides the applicant through the administrative permit application process in a transparent manner up to the delivery of one or several decisions by the responsible authorities at the end of the process. At the same time, it provides the applicant with all necessary information and involves other administrative authorities that are possibly involved with the application.[1516] Specifically for developers of renewable energy production projects, the

1513. Section 17(1)(a) to (d) Law No. 107(I)/2022, which partially corresponds to Art. 15(1) Directive (EU) 2018/2001.
1514. Section 17(2)(a) to (d) Law No. 107(I)/2022, which partially corresponds to Art. 15(1) Directive (EU) 2018/2001.
1515. Section 18(1) & (2) Law No. 107(I)/2022, which partially corresponds to Art. 16(1) Directive (EU) 2018/2001.
1516. Section 18(3)(a) to (c) Law No. 107(I)/2022, which corresponds to Art. 16(2) Directive (EU) 2018/2001.

Single Service Point prepares, in cooperation with competent authorities, a manual of procedures and conditions that addresses distinctly also small-scale projects and renewable self-consumer projects. Said manual is made available online. The online information indicates the contact point relevant to the applicant's application.[1517]

349. The applicant has the option to submit all relevant documentation in digital form; the competent authorities have simultaneous access to the system, where said documents have been submitted.[1518]

350. The above-mentioned provisions simply transfer the European ones imposing obligations on national authorities into national law without actually materializing those, as the national planning law[1519] makes no reference to renewables, contrary to relevant laws of other Member States.[1520] This has taken place through secondary legislation issued by the Minister of Interior,[1521] which adds further requirements to the application for planning permission ('πολεοδομική άδεια'), as regulated in the national planning law. The additional requirements depend on the type of renewable energy intended to be generated. Wind farms ('αιολικά πάρκα') cannot be built in certain areas,[1522] whereas they are to be localized at a certain distance from specific areas and buildings. This is a distance longer than 850 metres from established development limits and 350 metres from existing housing located outside the urban development zone,[1523] longer than 300 metres from established natural protection area,[1524] longer than 150% and 100% of the maximum height of the windmill from any road or other public work,[1525] longer than 350 metres from any aerial corridor or any other distance set by the Department of Civil

1517. Section 18(5)(a) to (c) Law No. 107(I)/2022, which corresponds to Art. 16(3) Directive (EU) 2018/2001.
1518. Section 18(4) Law No. 107(I)/2022, which partially corresponds to Art. 16(2) Directve 2018/2001.
1519. Law on Urban and Land Planning ('περί Πολεοδομίας και Χωροταξίας Νόμος') No. 90 of 1972, OG I(I) No. 977, 8 Dec. 1972, p. 929, as last amended by Law on Urban and Land Planning ('περί Πολεοδομίας και Χωροταξίας (Τροποποιητικός) Νόμος') No. 16 of 2019, OG I(I) No. 4689, 8 Mar. 2019, p. 55.
1520. *See* for example, the German legislation, where explicit mention on energy from renewable sources ('Strom, Wärme oder Kälte aus erneuerbaren Energien oder Kraft-Wärme-Kopplung') is made in §5 Abs. 2 Nr. 1 (b) BauGB relating to land-use plan ('Flächennutzungsplan'), §9 Abs. 1 Nr. 12 and 23(b) BauGB elaborating area development plan ('Bebauungsplan'), §11 Abs. 1 Nr. 4 BauGB referring to urban area development contract ('städtebaulicher Vertrag') and §148 Abs. 1 Nr. 5 BauGB explaining building measures ('Baumaßnahmen').
1521. Order No. 2 of 2006 on the basis of s. 6 of Law on Urban and Land Planning regarding localization of renewable energy plants, http://www.moi.gov.cy/ (hereinafter 'Order 2/2006').
1522. No windfarms can be established within an urban development zone ('όριο ανάπτυξης'), within roads, in archaeological areas or ancient monuments, in state forest, in nature reserves, such as protected landscape and special area of conservation Natura 2000, in special protection areas of wild birds and habitats, in airports, in airways and military facilities, works or areas (para. 4.1.2(a)–(g) Order 2/2006).
1523. Paragraph 4.2.1(a) *ibid.*
1524. Paragraph 4.2.1(b) *ibid.*
1525. Paragraph 4.2.1(c) *ibid.*

Aviation or the Ministry of Defence,[1526] longer than 150% and 100% of the max mum height of the windmill from overhead power lines,[1527] longer than 500 metre from an archaeological area under consideration of the views of the department c archaeology and the department of environment,[1528] longer than 200 metres fro the outskirts of a forest,[1529] longer than 500 metres from transit areas used b migrating birds and from special protection areas, while the views of the huntin authority will be taken into consideration,[1530] longer than 100 metres from area where radio signals are transmitted and 600 metres from areas where radio wave are transmitted.[1531] Further, special provisions on the location of each windmi within each wind farm, the level of noise pollution and the fluttering of shadows ar foreseen.[1532]

351. The localization of isolated windmills ('ανεμόμυλος') depending on the capacity, height and purpose are also regulated. Isolated windmills of capacity up t 30 kilowatts and a maximum height of up to 36 metres used additionally for th needs of agricultural, livestock or industrial development may be permitted onl within the urban development zone in property of the proper size and shape accord ing to the estimation of the planning authority, as long as the windmill is situated a least 150% of its maximum height from the boundaries of the property.[1533] Isolate windmills of capacity of up to 10 kilowatts and a maximum height of up to 1 metres or a windmill combined with other renewable energy generation system used primarily to contribute to the electricity consumed for needs other than agri cultural, livestock or industrial development needs may be permitted outside th urban development zone. The relevant property should also have the appropriat size and shape according to the estimation of the planning authority. Again, th windmill must be situated at least 150% of its maximum height from the bound aries of the property.[1534] In cases of many windmills of overall capacity from 1 megawatts to 300 megawatts or a couple of windmills of 300 kilowatts to 1 mega watt, the planning authority may impose the necessary terms and conditions depend ing on the facts of each case.[1535]

352. With reference to wind farms and isolated windmills in general, the plan ning authority is instructed to choose fewer windmills with greater capacity per uni over more windmills with lesser capacity per unit.[1536] The exact localization o windmills within a wind farm needs to be well planned, whereas the exact locatio

1526. Paragraph 4.2.1(d) *ibid.*
1527. Paragraph 4.2.1(e) *ibid.*
1528. Paragraph 4.2.1(f) *ibid.*
1529. Paragraph 4.2.1(g) *ibid.*
1530. Paragraph 4.2.1(h) *ibid.*
1531. Paragraph 4.2.1(i) *ibid.*
1532. Paragraph 4.2.2 *ibid.*
1533. Paragraph 4.3.1 *ibid.*
1534. Paragraph 4.3.2 *ibid.*
1535. Paragraph 4.3.3 *ibid.*
1536. Paragraph 4.4(a) *ibid.*

of each depends on the specific features of the given area.[1537] This is equally applicable to isolated windmills.[1538] Harmony and optical balance need to be ensured,[1539] whereas in the case of two wind farms having in total fifteen windmills need to be at least 2 kilometres apart.[1540] In addition, to the above-described, the planning authority has the regard of the cumulative effect from renewable energy plans in a given area.[1541] Lastly while evaluating the application for planning permission, the competent authority consults the Ministry of Energy, Commerce, Industry and Tourism, the Ministry of Agriculture, Rural Development and Environment, the Departments of Forest, Agriculture, Geological Survey, Water Development, Fishery and Marine Research, the Meteorological Service, the Environmental and Mines Service, the Ministry of Interior, the Department of Land Registry and Hunting Authority, the Ministry of Transportation and Works, the Departments of Electronical Communication, Electromechanical Services, Public Works, Road Transport, Civil Aviation and the Archaeological Department, the Ministry of Defence, the Ministry of Health, Cyprus Energy Regulatory Authority, the local authorities, the Commander of the British bases, where applicable, and Cyprus Electricity Authority.[1542]

353. Planning permission granted for a wind farm or an isolated windmill includes terms on mitigating the effects on birds,[1543] embodying the necessary electromechanical equipment in pylons of the windmills,[1544] safety signs on every windmill for the sake of air security,[1545] restricting the display of the wind farm or the isolated windmills from public places of interest through proper localization of each unit[1546] and construction of electricity transmit system along existing roads.[1547] The duration of such planning permissions is of a limited period in correspondence with the duration of the relevant authorization of electricity generation issued by Cyprus Energy Regulatory Authority.[1548] Lastly, each planning permission related to renewables includes a term imposing the obligation to dismantle and remove all equipment of the wind farm or isolated windmill in the event of interruption of electricity generation. This, along with the recovery of landscape, is performed under the guidance of the planning authority within the specified time limits.[1549]

354. Photovoltaic systems for the generation and supply of electricity may be allowed in a proper area, as this is estimated by the planning authority, whereas they cannot be built in the same areas as the wind farms, with the exception of airports,

1537. Paragraph 4.4(b) *ibid.*
1538. Paragraph 4.4(e) *ibid.*
1539. Paragraph 4.4(c) *ibid.*
1540. Paragraph 4.4(d) *ibid.*
1541. Paragraph 4.4(f) *ibid.*
1542. Paragraph 7.5(a)–(j) *ibid.*
1543. Paragraph 4.5(i) *ibid.*
1544. Paragraph 4.5(ii) *ibid.*
1545. Paragraph 4.5(iii) *ibid.*
1546. Paragraph 4.5(iv) *ibid.*
1547. Paragraph 4.5(v) *ibid.*
1548. Paragraph 4.6.2 *ibid.*
1549. Paragraph 4.6.3 *ibid.*

airways and transit areas of migrating birds.[1550] They must further cause no negative effects on the microclimate of their surroundings and the enjoyment of the neighbouring uses of land and development.[1551] Smaller photovoltaic systems installed on buildings to meet the energy needs of persons staying there need additional planning permission, only if they are not regarded as auxiliary works in the approved building. Should an application need to be filed for additional planning permission, this is to be granted as long as they are incorporated into the building in a harmonic way and no negative effect on their surroundings and the enjoyment of neighbouring uses of land and developments is caused.[1552]

355. Other generation facilities of energy from renewable sources may be permitted in any area considered appropriate by the planning authority that neighbours the area where the raw material is produced as long as it is possible to be connected with the transmission system. Certain provisions on wind farms and photovoltaic systems are also applied.[1553]

§2. Integration of Energy from Renewable Sources

356. Integration of renewables into planning is explicitly foreseen in the law and it has been given the form of taking it into account while planning, while building and while forming renewable energy communities. At the outset, it is provided that, all competent authorities, including governmental departments and services, independent authorities and organizations, as well as local authorities, while planning, have the duty to regulate the integration and development of renewable energy, including renewables self-consumption and renewable energy communities, and the use of unavoidable waste heat and cold. Said planning allows for early spatial planning, designing, building and renovating urban infrastructure, industrial, commercial or residential areas and energy infrastructure, including electricity, district heating and cooling, natural gas and alternative fuel networks.[1554] Same authorities encourage local and regional administrative bodies to include heating and cooling from renewable sources in the planning of city infrastructure where appropriate and to consult the network operators to reflect the impact of energy efficiency and demand response programs as well as specific provisions on renewables self-consumption and renewable energy communities, on the infrastructure development plans of the operators.[1555]

357. In the building sector, the following are foreseen. For the cases when new buildings are constructed or when existing buildings undergo major renovations or

1550. Paragraphs 5.3, 4.2.1 *ibid.*
1551. Paragraph 5.3 *ibid.*
1552. Paragraph 5.1 *ibid.*
1553. Paragraphs 6, 4.1.2, 4.6.4, 4.6.5 *ibid.*
1554. Section 21(1)(a) & (b) Law No. 107(I)/2022, which partially corresponds to Art. 15(3) Directive (EU) 2018/2001.
1555. Section 21(2) Law No. 107(I)/2022, which partially corresponds to Art. 15(3) Directive (EU) 2018/2001.

other equivalent results, the Director introduces appropriate measures to achieve promotion of renewables by adding to the minimum requirements for energy efficiency of buildings further requirements for use of energy from renewable sources.[1556] While drafting such measures, the Director may take into consideration national measures on increasing self-consumption of energy from renewable sources, local storage of energy and energy efficiency with regard to co-production and buildings of high energy efficiency or nearly zero-energy buildings. Same measures may be applied to security forces only to the extent that their application does not collide with the nature and the main purpose of their activities, but for material used exclusively for military purposes.[1557] In cases where such buildings are public, they are expected to play an exemplary role in complying with the explained obligation. Such exemplary role can be their construction or renovation as nearly zero-energy buildings or use of their roofs for the installation of energy production from renewable sources.[1558]

358. With respect to buildings in general, the Director promotes the use of heating and cooling systems using renewable sources of energy and achieving significant decrease in energy consumption. To this end, energy signs, eco signs, other certificates or standards are used.[1559] Similarly, with the aim of promoting the replacement of old heating and cooling systems, the Director informs and advises on alternative options of renewable energy of high efficiency, as well as on the available financial motives.[1560]

359. Finally, the Director makes an estimation of the stock in the sector of energy from renewable sources and the use of residual heat and waste cooling for heating and cooling. It includes territorial analysis of areas exemplary for the development of low ecological risk and the stock for small-scale projects at the level of households. Said estimation is included in the assessment that is foreseen under the Law on Regulation of Energy Efficiency of Buildings (*see* in this regard paragraph 225 above).[1561]

360. Furthermore, it is ensured that final customers, in particular, household customers, have the right to participate in a renewable energy community[1562] ('κοινότητα ανανεώσιμης ενέργειας'). This has been specified as a legal entity (a) which is based on open and voluntary participation, is autonomous, and is effectively controlled by shareholders or members that are located in the proximity of the renewable energy projects that are owned and developed by that legal entity; (b) the shareholders or members of which are natural persons, SMEs or local authorities, including municipalities; and (c) the primary purpose of which is to provide

1556. Section 22(1) Law No. 107(I)/2022.
1557. Section 22(2) & (3) *ibid.*
1558. Section 22(4) *ibid.*
1559. Section 22(5) *ibid.*
1560. Section 22(6) *ibid.*
1561. Section 22(7) *ibid.*
1562. Section 37(1) *ibid.*, which corresponds to Art. 22(1) Directive (EU) 2018/2001.

environmental, economic or social community benefits for its shareholders or members or for the local areas where it operates, rather than financial profits.[1563] While doing so, they maintain their rights and obligations as final customers and they are not being subject to unjustified or discriminatory conditions or procedures that would prevent their participation in such a community. Nonetheless for private undertakings, such participation must not constitute their primary commercial or professional activity.[1564]

361. To the end of facilitating this right, as well as in order to provide a favourable frame for promoting and enabling the development of renewable energy communities, Cyprus Energy Regulatory Authority, via regulatory decisions, ensures the following, among others:

- the right of renewable energy communities to: (a) produce, consume, store and sell renewable energy, including through renewables power purchase agreements; (b) share, within the renewable energy community, renewable energy that is produced by the production units owned by that renewable energy community, subject to the other requirements as described in this paragraph and to maintaining the rights and obligations of the renewable energy community members as customers; (c) access all suitable energy markets both directly or through aggregation in a non-discriminatory manner;
- the removal of unjustified regulatory and administrative barriers to renewable energy communities;
- that renewable energy communities that supply energy or provide aggregation or other commercial energy services are subject to the provisions relevant for such activities;
- the cooperation of the Distribution System Operator with them in order to facilitate energy transfers within such communities;
- that renewable energy communities are subject to fair, proportionate and transparent procedures, including registration and licensing procedures, and cost-reflective network charges, as well as relevant charges, levies and taxes, ensuring that they contribute, in an adequate, fair and balanced way, of the overall cost sharing of the system in line with a transparent cost-benefit analysis of distributed energy sources developed by Cyprus Energy Regulatory Authority under Law No. 130(I)/2021;
- that renewable energy communities are not subject to discriminatory treatment with regard to their activities, rights and obligations as final customers, producers, suppliers, distribution system operators, or as other market participants;
- the participation in the renewable energy communities is accessible to all consumers, including those in low-income or vulnerable households;
- making available tools to facilitate access to finance and information;

1563. In French 'communauté d'énergie renouvelable', in German 'Erneuerbare-Energie-Gemeinschaft', in Dutch 'hernieuwbare-energiegemeenschap'. Section 2(1) Law No. 112(I)/2022, which corresponds to Art. 2(16) Directive (EU) 2018/2001.

1564. Section 37(1) Law No. 107(I)/2022, which corresponds to Art. 22(1) Directive (EU) 2018/2001.

- providing regulatory and capacity-building support to public authorities in enabling and setting up renewable energy communities, and in helping authorities to participate directly;
- having in place rules to secure the equal and non-discriminatory treatment of consumers that participate in such communities.[1565]

362. At the same time, Cyprus Energy Regulatory Authority assesses the obstacles and options for the development of renewable energy communities in Cyprus.[1566]

363. For all the aforementioned purposes, support schemes may be put into place. While designing these support schemes, the Director takes into account specificities of renewable energy communities, in order to allow them to compete for support on an equal footing with other market participants.[1567]

§3. JOINT PROJECTS

364. Joint projects relating to the production of electricity, heating or cooling from renewable energy sources can be agreed upon and conducted between Cyprus and the other Member States, as well as Cyprus and third countries. The related provisions on estimating compliance with the requirements concerning national overall targets and notification obligations are explained below.

I. Joint Projects Between Cyprus and the Other Member States

365. Joint projects for the production of electricity from renewable sources between Cyprus and other Member States, the duration of which may extend beyond 2030[1568] are implemented in the process described below. The Minister drafts proposals for such projects and has consultations with Cyprus Energy Regulatory Authority, while having the option to ask the opinions of the Transmission System Operator, the Distribution System Operator or other competent authorities. In the event that the Minister and Cyprus Energy Regulatory Authority reach no agreement, the authority's views are attached to the proposal of the Minister. This proposal is submitted to the Council of Ministers that has the power to decide on concluding bilateral or multilateral agreements with the other Member States about joint projects of any type relating to the production of electricity, heating or cooling from renewable energy sources. Private operators may participate in such agreements and propose to the competent authority the technology that is going to develop within the frame of joint project, as well as the installed capacity and the

1565. Section 37(2)(a) to (j) Law No. 107(I)/2022, which corresponds to Art. 22(2)(a) to (c) and (4)(a) to (i) Directive 2018/2001.
1566. Section 37(4) Law No. 107(I)/2022.
1567. Section 37(6) & (7) *ibid.*, which partially corresponds to Art. 22(7) Directive (EU) 2018/2001.
1568. Section 11(4) Law No. 107(I)/2022, which corresponds to Art. 9(6) Directive (EU) 2018/2001.

place, where the project shall be made. Local authorities may also do so. The Coun-cil of Ministers and the other Member States that approve the agreements have th power to attach conditions thereto.[1569]

366. The Director notifies the Commission of the proportion or amount of elec-tricity, heating or cooling from renewable energy sources produced by any joir project in Cyprus that became operational after 25 June 2009, or by the increase capacity of an installation that was refurbished after that date, which is to b regarded as counting towards the renewable energy share of another Member Stat for the purposes of this law.[1570] This notification includes at least the followin items:

- description of the proposed installation or identification of the refurbished instal-lation;[1571]
- specification of the proportion or amount of electricity or heating or cooling pro-duced from the installation which is to be regarded as counting towards th national overall target of another Member State;[1572]
- identification of the Member State in whose favour the notification is bein made;[1573] and
- specification of the period, in whole calendar years, during which the electricit or heating or cooling produced by the installation from renewable energy source is to be regarded as counting towards the national overall target of the othe Member State.[1574]

367. Any such notification may not be varied or withdrawn without the join agreement of all Member States involved in the same.[1575]

368. The establishment of such projects may be facilitated by the Commission following a request by Cyprus and the other interested Member States, in particular via dedicated technical assistance and project development assistance.[1576]

369. The effects of such joint projects are notified to the Commission and are taken into consideration in calculating the renewable energy share. Within three months from the end of the above-mentioned period (*see* paragraph 368 above), the Director forwards to the Commission and the Member State, on behalf of which this

1569. Section 11(1)(a), (b) & (c) Law No. 107(I)/2022, which partially corresponds to Art. 9(1) Direc-tive (EU) 2018/2001.
1570. Section 11(2) Law No. 107(I)/2022, which corresponds to Art. 9(2) Directive (EU) 2018/2001.
1571. Section 11(4)(a) Law No. 107(I)/2022, which corresponds to Art. 9(3)(a) Directive (EU) 2018/2001.
1572. Section 11(4)(b) Law No. 107(I)/2022, which corresponds to Art. 9(3)(b) Directive (EU) 2018/2001.
1573. Section 11(4)(c) Law No. 107(I)/2022, which corresponds to Art. 9(3)(c) Directive (EU) 2018/2001.
1574. Section 11(4)(d) Law No. 107(I)/2022, which corresponds to Art. 9(3)(d) Directive (EU) 2018/2001.
1575. Section 11(5) Law No. 107(I)/2022, which corresponds to Art. 9(5) Directive (EU) 2018/2001.
1576. Section 11(6) Law No. 107(I)/2022, which corresponds to Art. 9(6) Directive (EU) 2018/2001.

is performed, a letter of notification[1577] stating the total amount of electricity, heating or cooling produced during that year from renewable energy sources by the installation which was the subject of the above notification[1578] and the amount of electricity, heating or cooling produced during the year from renewable energy sources by that installation which is to count towards the national overall target of the other Member State in accordance with the terms of the notification.[1579] For the purposes of this law measuring target compliance with the requirements of the present legislation concerning national overall targets, the amount of electricity, heating or cooling produced from renewable energy sources notified as described above is deduced from the amount of energy from renewable sources that is taken into account, in calculating the renewable energy share of Cyprus, that has issued the letter of notification.[1580] The same is added to the amount of energy from renewable sources that are taken into account in calculating the renewable energy share of the Member State receiving the letter of notification from Cyprus.[1581]

II. Joint Projects Between Cyprus and Third Countries

370. In a similar manner, joint projects regarding the production of electricity from renewable energy sources with third countries may be decided, notified and implemented. The Council of Ministers, following a proposal of the Minister, has the power to decide on concluding bilateral or multilateral treaties with one or more third countries as well as with one or more Member States on all types of such projects.[1582] This cooperation of Cyprus and third countries established via international treaties may involve private operators and takes place in full respect of international law.[1583] The duration of such projects may extend beyond 2030.[1584] Private operators and local authorities, as stated in the preceding paragraphs, may propose to the competent authority the technology to be developed within such joint projects, as well as the installed capacity and the location of the project under the conditions set out in the agreements approved by the Council of Ministers.[1585]

1577. Section 12(1) Law No. 107(I)/2022, which corresponds to Art. 10(2) Directive (EU) 2018/2001.
1578. Section 12(1)(a) Law No. 107(I)/2022, which corresponds to Art. 10(1)(a) Directive (EU) 2018/2001.
1579. Section 12(1)(b) Law No. 107(I)/2022, which corresponds to Art. 10(1)(b) Directive (EU) 2018/2001.
1580. Section 12(2)(a) Law No. 107(I)/2022, which corresponds to Art. 10(3)(a) Directive (EU) 2018/2001.
1581. Section 12(2)(b) Law No. 107(I)/2022, which corresponds to Art. 10(3)(b) Directive (EU) 2018/2001.
1582. Section 13(1)(a) Law No. 107(I)/2022, which corresponds to Art. 11(1) Directive (EU) 2018/2001.
1583. Section 13(1)(b) Law No. 107(I)/2022, which corresponds to Art. 11(2) Directive (EU) 2018/2001.
1584. Section 13(6) Law No. 107(I)/2022, which corresponds to Art. 11(6) Directive (EU) 2018/2001.
1585. Section 13(1)(c) Law No. 107(I)/2022.

371. Electricity from renewable energy sources produced in a third country is taken into account only for the purposes of measuring compliance with the statutory requirements concerning national overall targets if the following conditions are met. First, the electricity must be consumed in the EU. This is deemed to be met when: (i) an equivalent amount of electricity to the electricity accounted for has been firmly nominated to the allocated interconnection capacity by all responsible transmission system operators in the country of origin, the country of destination and, if relevant, each third country of transit; (ii) an equivalent amount of electricity to the electricity accounted for has been firmly registered in the schedule of balance by the responsible transmission system operator on the Union side of an interconnector; and (iii) the nominated capacity and the production of electricity from renewable energy sources by the installation mentioned below refer to the same period of time.[1586] In addition to that, the electricity must be produced by a newly constructed installation that became operational after 25 June 2009 or by the increased capacity of an installation that was refurbished after that date under a joint project and the amount of electricity produced and exported should not have received support from a support scheme of a third country other than investment aid granted to the installation.[1587] Finally, the electricity must have been produced in accordance with international law in a third country that is a signatory to the Council of Europe Convention for the Protection of Human Rights and Fundamental Freedoms, or other international conventions or treaties on human rights.[1588]

372. The proportion or amount of electricity produced by any installation in the territory of a third country is to be regarded as counting towards the renewable energy share of Cyprus for the purposes of this law. The Director notifies the Commission of said proportion or amount along with the distribution of proportion or amount between Member States. In the latter case, the proportion or amount does not exceed the one actually exported to, and consumed in, the Union. At the same time, it corresponds to the amount explained in points (i) and (ii) stated in the preceding paragraph and meets all the conditions explained in the same paragraph. The Director makes the notification, when the proportion or amount of electricity counts to the overall national target of Cyprus.[1589] To this end, the Director may apply to the Commission to consider electricity from renewable sources produced and consumed in a third country, in the context of the construction of an interconnector with a very long lead-time between Cyprus and a third country under certain conditions. These include the beginning of construction by 31 December 2026, becoming operational sometime between four and six years later and, upon operating, use of the interconnector for the export to the Union of electricity from renewable sources.

1586. Section 13(2)(a) *ibid.*, which corresponds to Art. 11(2)(a) Directive (EU) 2018/2001.
1587. Section 13(2)(b) & (c) Law No. 107(I)/2022, which corresponds to Art. 11(2)(b) & (c) Directive (EU) 2018/2001.
1588. Section 13(2)(d) Law No. 107(I)/2022, which corresponds to Art. 11(2)(d) Directive (EU) 2018/2001.
1589. Section 13(4)(a) to (c) Law No. 107(I)/2022, which corresponds to Art. 11(4) Directive (EU) 2018/2001.

Lastly, the application must relate to certain joint projects[1590] and to a quantity of electricity that is no greater than the quantity that will be exported to the Union.[1591]

373. The notification of the Director to the Commission has the following content: (a) description of the proposed installation or identification of the refurbished installation; (b) specification of the proportion or amount of electricity produced from the installation which is to be regarded as counting towards the renewable energy share of Cyprus as well as, subject to confidentiality requirements, the corresponding financial arrangements; (c) specification of the period, in whole calendar years, during which the electricity is to be regarded as counting towards the renewable energy share of Cyprus; and (d) a written acknowledgement of aforementioned points (b) and (c) by the third country in whose territory the installation is to become operational and an indication of the proportion or amount of electricity produced by the installation which will be used domestically by that third country.[1592]

374. Any notification mentioned in this subsection may not be varied or withdrawn without the joint agreement of the Member State making the notification, that being Cyprus, and the third country that has acknowledged the joint project.[1593]

375. Cyprus, along with Member States and the Union encourages the relevant bodies of the Energy Community to take, in conformity with the Energy Community Treaty, the measures necessary to allow the Contracting Parties to apply the provisions on cooperation between Member States laid down in this law.[1594]

376. In regard to the effects of such joint projects, within twelve months of the end of each year within a certain period,[1595] the Director makes a notification stating the following: (a) the total amount of electricity produced from renewable sources during that year by the installation which was the subject of the aforementioned notification (*see* in this respect paragraph 374 above); (b) the amount of electricity produced from renewable sources during that year by that installation which is to count towards its renewable energy share in accordance with the terms of the same aforementioned notification (*see* in this respect paragraph 375 above); and (c) evidence of compliance with certain conditions (*see* in this respect paragraph 373 above).[1596] This notification is made to the Commission and to the third country,

1590. *See* in this regard s. 13(2)(b) & (c) Law No. 107(I)/2022, which corresponds to Art. 11(2)(b) & (c) Directive (EU) 2018/2001.
1591. Section 13(3)(a) to (e) Law No. 107(I)/2022, which corresponds to Art. 11(3)(a) to (e) Directive (EU) 2018/2001.
1592. Section 13(5)(a) to (d) Law No. 107(I)/2022, which corresponds to Art. 11(5)(a) to (d) Directive (EU) 2018/2001.
1593. Section 13(7) Law No. 107(I)/2022, which corresponds to Art. 11(7) Directive (EU) 2018/2001.
1594. Section 13(8) Law No. 107(I)/2022, which corresponds to Art. 11(8) Directive (EU) 2018/2001.
1595. This is the period, in whole calendar years, during which the electricity is to be regarded as counting towards the renewable energy share of Cyprus. Section 13(5)(c) Law No. 107(I)/2022, which corresponds to Art. 11(5)(c) Directive (EU) 2018/2001.
1596. Section 14(1)(a) to (c) Law No. 107(I)/2022, which corresponds to Art. 12(1)(a) to (c) Directive (EU) 2018/2001.

which has acknowledged the project.[1597] For the purposes of calculating the renewable energy shares under this law, the amount of electricity from renewable sources notified in the process stated above is added to the amount of energy from renewable sources that is taken into account in calculating the renewable energy shares of Cyprus.[1598]

§4. Monitoring Compliance

377. Inspectors-in-chief ('εντεταλμένοι επιθεωρητές'), who are appointed by the Director, bear the duty to inspect and monitor compliance with all provisions of this law and Regulations and Decrees issued under the same;[1599] thus, they have been given the following statutory powers. They may enter at any reasonable time freely and without any prior notice to any building or area, where facilities and/or equipment of renewable sources of energy are situated. In addition, they may control and inspect constructions, machines and equipment that lay in said premises in order to ensure adherence to said provisions as well as Decrees issued under this law. However, entering a place of residence requires a court order when the owner does not agree.[1600] Inspectors-in-chief may carry with them any equipment and material considered necessary as well as perform any necessary measurements, take photos and make registrations for the purpose of fulfilling their duties.[1601] They have further the right to ask for presentations, data and updates, and inspection of any entries, registers, books, digital data or other documentation, which are considered to contain useful information.[1602] They may also demand from the owner of the premises or from his representatives or employees in location to facilitate safe access to any part of the facilities[1603] or to provide reasonable means for the intended inspection[1604] and to give any useful information that they possess or to which they have access.[1605] Lastly, they have the power to confiscate any relevant documentation, equipment or samples, in case it is reasonably assumed that a penal offence has been committed and these are expected to be used as evidence.[1606]

378. Should inspectors-in-chief establish that an installer or supplier of renewable energy equipment and systems generating electricity, heating and cooling does not comply with the provisions of the law, they inform the competent authority accordingly. The latter may issue a notification ('ειδοποίηση') to the relevant installer or supplier. This notification mentions the violation and invites the addressee to comply within a reasonable time, which depends on the nature of the

1597. Section 14(2) Law No. 107(I)/2022, which corresponds to Art. 12(2) Directive (EU) 2018/2001.
1598. Section 14(3) Law No. 107(I)/2022, which corresponds to Art. 12(3) Directive (EU) 2018/2001.
1599. Sections 39(1) Law No. 107(I)/2022.
1600. Section 39(2)(a) *ibid.*
1601. Section 39(2)(b) *ibid.*
1602. Section 39(2)(c) *ibid.*
1603. Section 39(2)(d)(i) *ibid.*
1604. Section 39(2)(d)(ii) *ibid.*
1605. Section 39(2)(d)(iii) *ibid.*
1606. Section 39(2)(e) *ibid.*

violation.[1607] It also includes the measures to be taken by the addressee for the purpose of complying with the law.[1608] Nothing further regarding the enforcement of said notification is set out in the law.

379. The Director, taking into consideration the seriousness and the duration of each violation, has the power to impose monetary administrative sanctions in the following cases. When suppliers of equipment or systems of renewable energy fail to comply with their statutory information duties, they may impose a fine of up to EUR 20,000 on them.[1609] Apart from that, any equipment supplier of energy from renewable sources or importer of same not complying with or violating its information duty towards the competent authority may face an administrative fine of no more than EUR 50,000 by the same authority. The same applies if those persons fail to provide any reasonably asked information or in the event that the provided information is false, misleading or inaccurate.[1610] A supplier of electricity, the Transmission System Operator, the Distribution System Operator or an electricity undertaking failing to comply with the same information duty towards the competent authority, may face a fine of up to EUR 100,000.[1611] Lastly, any other person violating any other provision of this law may be liable to a monetary fine of up to EUR 100,000.[1612]

380. Still, the Director before imposing the administrative fine, notifies the affected natural or legal person of his intention to do so, while informing it about the reasons, for which he has such an intention. At the same time, the Director gives that person the right to submit representations within thirty days.[1613] Thereafter, the relevant duly reasoned decision is served to the person responsible for the violation via action or omission, as the case may be.[1614] The imposed fine becomes due upon its service; filling neither an administrative complaint nor an appeal may hinder its enforceability.[1615] Should the addressee fail to pay the imposed monetary fine, the Director is given the authority to claim it as a civil debt towards the Republic.[1616]

381. Parallel to the powers of the Director explained above, Cyprus Energy Regulatory Authority may impose fines with regard to violation of provisions of this law that fall within its competence. In doing so, it acts upon the relevant statutory provisions of the legislation on electricity, Law No. 130(I)/2021.[1617]

1607. Section 39(3)(a) *ibid.*
1608. Section 39(3)(b) *ibid.*
1609. Sections 41(1)(a) and 19(2) *ibid.*
1610. Sections 41(1)(b) and 40(1) & (2) *ibid.*
1611. Sections 41(1)(c) and 40(1) & (2) *ibid.*
1612. Section 41(1)(d) *ibid.*
1613. Secton 41(3) *ibid.*
1614. Section 41(4) *ibid.* Specifically on service *see* s. 43 *ibid.*
1615. Section 41(5) & (7) *ibid.*
1616. Section 41(6) *ibid.*
1617. Section 41(8) *ibid.*

382. Besides the administrative fines already portrayed, violating statutory pro visions may initiate criminal prosecution. In particular, any person performin duties of an installer after the revocation or the termination of his registration in th register kept by the competent authority commits a criminal offence, and in case c conviction, he shall be imprisoned for a period of no longer than one year and/or monetary fine not exceeding EUR 100,000.[1618] The same penalties face a perso violating terms and regulations specified in regulations issued in accordance wit this law[1619] or a person obstructing inspectors-in-chief to perform their statutor duties.[1620] Any accessory or any person consenting to the above-stated pen offences also faces the same penalties.[1621] Lastly, a person obstructing actions an inspections with regard to guarantees of origin also commits a crime and may b imprisoned for up to one year and/ or a monetary fine of up to EUR 100,000.[162

1618. Sections 44(1)(a) and 36 & 46(2) *ibid.*
1619. Section 44(1)(b) and 46(2) *ibid.*
1620. Section 44(1)(c) and 39(2) *ibid.*
1621. Section 44(3) *ibid.*
1622. Section 44(2)(a) & (b) *ibid.*

Chapter 3. Consumption

§1. Support Schemes

383. Support schemes can be national and joint ones, those being support schemes decided and implemented by more than one Member State of the EU. At the outset, it is clarified that support schemes ('καθεστώτα στήριξης') have been defined as any instrument, scheme or mechanism applied by Cyprus, or by Cyprus in cooperation with other Member States, that promotes the use of energy from renewable sources by reducing the cost of that energy, increasing the price at which it can be sold, or increasing, by means of a renewable energy obligation or otherwise, the volume of such energy purchased, including but not restricted to, investment aid, tax exemptions or reductions, tax refunds, renewable energy obligation support schemes including those using green certificates, and direct price support schemes including feed-in tariffs and sliding or fixed premium payments.[1623]

I. National Support Schemes

384. Support schemes underpin the binding overall Union target that the share of energy from renewables in the Union's gross final energy consumption reaches at least 32% by 2030. To this end, the Council of Ministers, following a proposal of the Minister in consultation with Cyprus Energy Regulatory Authority and, as the case may be, the Transmission System Operator, the Distribution System Operator or other competent body,[1624] have the authority to issue support schemes aiming to promote the use of renewables. These schemes are designed with due regard to the waste hierarchy as set out in the national legislation[1625] in order to avoid undue distortive effects on the raw material markets. They grant no support for renewable energy produced from the incineration of waste if the separate collection obligations laid down in the same legislation have not been complied with.[1626] Furthermore, they grant no support for energy from biofuels, bioliquids and biomass fuels that do not fulfil the sustainability criteria and the criteria of minimizing greenhouse gas emissions, as set out in the national legislation.[1627] The support schemes may include detailed provisions on any technical specifications which are to be met by renewable energy equipment and systems in order to benefit from such schemes.[1628] Moreover, they may include the terms and conditions that the applicants must satisfy, as well as the manner, the time and the procedure of granting such support.[1629]

1623. In French 'régime d'aide', in German 'Förderregelung', in Dutch 'steunregeling'. Section 2(1) Law No. 107(I)/2022, which corresponds to Art. 2(5) Directive (EU) 2018/2001.
1624. Section 6(2) Law No. 107(I)/2022.
1625. On the national law of waste *see* para. 109 above. Waste hierarchy is set in s. 9 Law No. 185(I)/2011, which corresponds to Art. 4 Directive 2008/98/EC.
1626. Section 6(1)(a) & (b) Law No. 107(I)/2022, which corresponds to Art. 3(3) Directive (EU) 2018/2001.
1627. Section 6(1) last sentence Law No. 107(I)/2022.
1628. Section 6(3)(a) *ibid.*, which corresponds to Art. 15(2) Directive (EU) 2018/2001.
1629. Section 6(3)(b) & (c) Law No. 107(I)/2022.

Save for the support provisions of Law No. 130(I)/2021, same support schemes provide incentives for the integration of electricity from renewable sources in the electricity market in a market-based and market-responsive way, while avoiding unnecessary distortions of electricity markets as well as taking into account possible system integration costs and grid stability.[1630] Further, they are designed so as to maximize the integration of electricity from renewable sources in the electricity market and to ensure that renewable energy producers are responding to market price signals and maximizing their market revenues. To that end, with regard to direct price support schemes, support shall be granted in the form of a market premium, which could be, *inter alia*, sliding or fixed.[1631] Also, they support electricity from renewable sources in an open, transparent, competitive, non-discriminatory and cost-effective manner. Moreover, they may also provide for establishing mechanisms to ensure regional diversification in the deployment of renewable electricity, in particular, to ensure cost-efficient system integration.[1632] Specifically, where such support is granted by means of a tendering procedure, the criteria set to qualify for the tendering procedure are non-discriminatory and transparent, and they set clear dates and rules for delivery of the project. At the same time, information about previous tendering procedures, including project realization rates is published. All these are set with the aim of ensuring a high project realization rate.[1633] Tendering procedures may be limited to specific technologies, where opening support schemes to all producers of electricity from renewable sources would lead to a suboptimal result, in view of: (a) the long-term potential of a particular technology; (b) the need to achieve diversification; (c) grid integration costs; (d) network constraints and grid stability; and (e) for biomass, the need to avoid distortions of raw materials markets.[1634]

385. Producers of electricity from renewable sources located in other Member States may participate in the support schemes under conditions determined by Cyprus Energy Regulatory Authority and, as the case may be, the Transmission System Operator, the Distribution System Operator or other competent bodies.[1635] Support may be provided for an indicative share of the newly-supported capacity, or of the budget allocated thereto, in each year open to producers located in other Member States. Such indicative shares may, in each year, amount to at least 5% from 2023 to 2026 and at least 10% from 2027 to 2030, or, where lower, to the level of interconnectivity of the Member State concerned in any given year.[1636] Such support schemes may require proof of physical import of electricity from renewable

1630. Section 6(4)(a) *ibid.*, which corresponds to Art. 4(2) Directive (EU) 2018/2001.
1631. Section 6(4)(b) Law No. 107(I)/2022, which corresponds to Art. 4(3) Directive (EU) 2018/2001.
1632. Section 6(4)(c) & (d) Law No. 107(I)/2022, which corresponds to Art. 4(4) Directive (EU) 2018/2001.
1633. Section 6(5)(a) & (b) Law No. 107(I)/2022, which corresponds to Art. 4(6)(a) & (b) Directive (EU) 2018/2001.
1634. Section 6(6)(a) to (e) Law No. 107(I)/2022, which corresponds to Art. 4(5)(a) to (e) Directive (EU) 2018/2001.
1635. Sections 7(1) & 6(2) Law No. 107(I)/2022, which partially correspond to Art. 5(1) Directive (EU) 2018/2001.
1636. Section 7(2) & (3) Law No. 107(I)/2022, which in part corresponds to Art. 5(1) Directive (EU) 2018/2001.

sources. To that end, participation may be limited to producers located in Member States with which there is a direct connection via interconnectors. Still, cross-zonal schedules and capacity allocation shall neither change nor be otherwise affected due to producers participating in cross-border support schemes. Cross-border electricity transfers shall be determined only by the outcome of capacity allocation pursuant to Union law on the internal market in electricity.[1637] The principles of such participation are agreed upon by the Minister of Energy, Commerce and Industry and other Member States covering at least the principles of allocation of renewable electricity that is the subject of cross-border support.[1638] While preparing these agreements, Cyprus and other Member States may ask the Commission to assist them throughout the negotiation process with the setting up of cooperation arrangements by providing information and analysis, including quantitative and qualitative data on the direct and indirect costs and benefits of cooperation, as well as with guidance and technical expertise.[1639]

386. The support granted to renewable energy projects is stable, in the sense that the level of, and the conditions attached to, the support granted to renewable energy projects are not revised in a way that negatively affects the rights conferred thereunder and undermines the economic viability of projects that already benefit from support. Nonetheless, the level of support may be adjusted in accordance with objective criteria, provided that such criteria are established in the original design of the support scheme.[1640] The Director of the Department of Energy of the Ministry of Energy, Commerce and Industry, that is the competent authority in this case, makes and publishes a long-term schedule anticipating the expected allocation of support covering at least three years. This includes the indicative timing, the frequency of tendering procedures where appropriate, the expected capacity and budget or maximum unitary support expected to be allocated, and the expected eligible technologies, if applicable. That schedule is updated on an annual basis or, where necessary, to reflect recent market developments or expected allocation of support.[1641] Same authority assesses, publishes and communicates to the House of Representatives, at least every three years, the effectiveness of the national support schemes for electricity from renewable sources and their major distributive effects on different consumer groups, and on investments taking into account the effect of possible changes to the support schemes. The results of this assessment are considered for updating the long-term planning of support and preparing the support schemes while being included in the relevant progress reports of the Integrated National Energy and Climate Plan.[1642]

1637. Section 7(4) Law No. 107(I)/2022, which corresponds to Art. 5(2) Directive (EU) 2018/2001.
1638. Section 7(5) Law No. 107(I)/2022, which corresponds to Art. 5(3) Directive (EU) 2018/2001.
1639. Section 7(6) Law No. 107(I)/2022, which corresponds to Art. 5(4) Directive (EU) 2018/2001.
1640. Section 8(1)(a) & (b) Law No. 107(I)/2022, which corresponds to Art. 6(1) & (2) Directive (EU) 2018/2001.
1641. Section 8(2) to (4) Law No. 107(I)/2022, which corresponds to Art. 6(3) Directive (EU) 2018/2001.
1642. Section 8(5) & (6) Law No. 107(I)/2022, which corresponds to Art. 6(4) Directive (EU) 2018/2001.

II. Joint Support Schemes

387. Without prejudice to the obligations of Cyprus with regard to national mandatory overall targets set out in section 7 of this law (*see* in this regard paragraph 342 above), support schemes may be joined or become partly coordinated. The Council of Ministers has the authority to decide this, following a relevant proposal of the Minister and thereafter to sign relevant bilateral or multilateral agreements with one or more Member States.[1643] In such cases, a certain amount of energy from renewable sources produced in the territory of one participating Member State may count towards the national overall target of Cyprus or vice versa under specific conditions.[1644] These include performing a statistical transfer of specified amounts of energy from renewable sources from one Member State to another in accordance with section 10 of this law[1645] and setting up a distribution rule agreed by participating Member States that allocates amounts of energy from renewable sources between the participating Member States. Such a rule is notified to the Commission no later than three months after the end of the first year in which it takes effect.[1646] The competent authority performing such notification must issue a letter of notification stating the total amount of electricity or heating or cooling from renewable energy sources produced during the year which is to be the subject of the distribution rule within three months of the end of each year.[1647] For the purposes of calculating the renewable energy shares under this Directive, the amount of electricity or heating or cooling from renewable sources notified in accordance with paragraph 2 shall be reallocated between the Member States concerned in accordance with the notified distribution rule.[1648] Cyprus, together with the interested Member State, may request the Commission to facilitate the establishment of joint support schemes through dissemination of guidelines and best practices.[1649]

§2. Renewable Energy Communities

388. Final customers, in particular, household customers, have the right to participate in a renewable energy community.[1650] Renewable energy community ('κοινότητα ανανεώσιμης ενέργειας') is a legal entity: (a) which, in accordance with the applicable national law, is based on open and voluntary participation, is autonomous, and is effectively controlled by shareholders or members that are located in the proximity of the renewable energy projects that are owned and developed by that legal entity; (b) the shareholders or members of which are natural persons, SMEs or

1643. Section 15(1) Law No. 107(I)/2022, which corresponds to Art. 13(1) Directive (EU) 2018/2001.
1644. Section 15(1) Law No. 107(I)/2022, which corresponds to Art. 11(1) Directive (EU) 2018/2001.
1645. Section 15(2)(a) Law No. 107(I)/2022, which corresponds to Art. 13(1)(a) Directive (EU) 2018/2001.
1646. Section 15(2)(b) Law No. 107(I)/2022, which corresponds to Art. 13(1)(b) Directive (EU) 2018/2001.
1647. Section 15(3) Law No. 107(I)/2022, which corresponds to Art. 13(2) Directive (EU) 2018/2001.
1648. Section 15(4) Law No. 107(I)/2022, which corresponds to Art. 13(3) Directive (EU) 2018/2001.
1649. Section 15(5) Law No. 107(I)/2022, which corresponds to Art. 13(4) Directive (EU) 2018/2001.
1650. Section 27(1) Law No. 107(I)/2022, which corresponds to Art. 22(1) Directive (EU) 2018/2001.

local authorities, including municipalities; and (c) the primary purpose of which is to provide environmental, economic or social community benefits for its shareholders or members or for the local areas where it operates, rather than financial profits.[1651] While doing so, they maintain their rights or obligations as final customers, without being subject to unjustified or discriminatory conditions or procedures that would prevent their participation in a renewable energy community, provided that for private undertakings, their participation does not constitute their primary commercial or professional activity.[1652]

389. To this purpose, as well as to provide a favourable frame for promoting and facilitating the development of such communities, Cyprus Energy Regulatory Authority creates an enabling framework. It ensures, among others that: (a) renewable energy communities have the right to produce, consume, store and sell renewable energy, including through renewables power purchase agreements, to share, within the renewable energy community, renewable energy that is produced by the production units owned by that renewable energy community, subject to the other requirements laid down in this law and to maintaining the rights and obligations of the renewable energy community members as customers, to access all suitable energy markets both directly or through aggregation in a non-discriminatory manner; (b) unjustified regulatory and administrative barriers to renewable energy communities are removed; (c) renewable energy communities that supply energy or provide aggregation or other commercial energy services are subject to the provisions relevant for such activities; (d) the relevant distribution system operator cooperates with renewable energy communities to facilitate energy transfers within renewable energy communities; (e) renewable energy communities are subject to fair, proportionate and transparent procedures, including registration and licensing procedures, and cost-reflective network charges, as well as relevant charges, levies and taxes, ensuring that they contribute, in an adequate, fair and balanced way, to the overall cost sharing of the system in line with a transparent cost-benefit analysis of distributed energy sources developed by Cyprus Energy Regulatory Authority; (f) renewable energy communities are not subject to discriminatory treatment with regard to their activities, rights and obligations as final customers, producers, suppliers, distribution system operators, or as other market participants; (g) the participation in the renewable energy communities is accessible to all consumers, including those in low-income or vulnerable households; (h) tools to facilitate access to finance and information are available; (i) regulatory and capacity-building support is provided to public authorities in enabling and setting up renewable energy communities, and in helping authorities to participate directly; and (j) rules to secure the equal and non-discriminatory treatment of consumers that participate in the renewable energy community are in place.[1653]

1651. In French 'communauté d'énergie renouvelable', in German 'Erneuerbare-Energie-Gemeinschaft', in Dutch 'hernieuwbare-energiegemeenschap'. Section 2(1) Law No. 107(I)/2022, which corresponds to Art. 2(16) Directive (EU) 2018/2001.
1652. Section 37(1) Law No. 107(I)/2022, which corresponds to Art. 22(1) Directive (EU) 2018/2001.
1653. Section 37(2) Law No. 107(I)/2022, which corresponds to Art. 22(2) & (4) Directive (EU) 2018/2001.

390. The main elements of the enabling framework are part of the Integrate National Energy and Climate Plan and the progress reports under Regulation (EU 2018/1999.[1654]

391. With regard to support schemes, the Director takes into account specific ties of renewable energy communities when designing them, with the aim of allow ing them to compete for support on an equal footing with other mark participants.[1655]

§3. Renewables Self-Consumers

392. Consumers have the right to act as *renewables self-consumer* ('αυτοκαταναλωτές ενέργειας από ανανεώσιμες πηγές') both individually an through aggregators without being subject to discriminatory or disproportionate pro cedures.[1656] Renewables self-consumers has been defined as a final customer oper ating within its premises located within confined boundaries or, where permitted b a Member State, within other premises, who generates renewable electricity for it own consumption, and who may store or sell self-generated renewable electricity provided that, for a non-household renewables self-consumer, those activities do no constitute its primary commercial or professional activity.[1657] It is clarified that th renewables self-consumer's installation may be owned by a third party, as long a that third party remains subject to the renewables self-consumer's instructions. Such an installation may also be managed by a third party under the same condition.[1658]

393. In view of this, Cyprus Energy Regulatory Authority creates a facilitating framework, where the following rights are ensured. Renewables self-consumers are given the option to generate renewable energy, including for their own consump tion, store and sell their excess production of renewable electricity, including through renewables power purchase agreements, electricity suppliers and peer-to peer trading arrangements. These have to be possible without being subject to dis criminatory or disproportionate procedures and charges and network charges tha are not cost-reflective, with regard to consumed electricity, whereas regarding self generated electricity remaining within their premises, to same procedures and to any charges or fees, save for certain cases.[1659] Self-consumers further have the right to

---

1654. Section 37(3) Law No. 107(I)/2022, which corresponds to Art. 22(5) Directive (EU) 2018/2001
1655. Section 37(7) Law No. 107(I)/2022, which corresponds to Art. 22(7) Directive (EU) 2018/2001
1656. Section 38(1) Law No. 107(I)/2022, which partially corresponds to Art. 21(1) Directive (EU 2018/2001.
1657. In French 'autoconsommateur d'énergies renouvelables', in German 'Eigenversorger im Bereich erneuerbare Elektrizität', in Dutch 'zelfverbruiker van hernieuwbare energie'. Section 2(1) Law No. 107(I)/2022, which corresponds to Art. 2(14) Directive (EU) 2018/2001.
1658. Section 38(2)(c) Law No. 107(I)/2022, which corresponds to Art. 21(5) Directive (EU) 2018 2001.
1659. Section 38(2)(a)(i) to (iii) Law No. 107(I)/2022, which corresponds to Art. 21(2)(a) Directive (EU) 2018/2001. On these cases *see* s. 22(12) Law No. 130(I)/2021, which corresponds to Art 21(3) Directive (EU) 2018/2001.

instal and operate electricity storage systems combined with installations generating renewable electricity for self-consumption without liability for any double charge including network charges for stored electricity remaining within their premises.[1660] They are also entitled to receive remuneration, including, where applicable, through support schemes, for the self-generated renewable electricity that they feed into the grid, which reflects the market value of that electricity and which may take into account its long-term value to the grid, the environment and society.[1661] Parallel to all aforementioned rights, they preserve both their rights and their duties as final customers and consumers.[1662] Moreover, Cyprus Energy Regulatory Authority issues regulatory decisions: (a) addressing accessibility of renewables self-consumption to all final customers, including those in low-income or vulnerable households; (b) addressing unjustified barriers to the financing of projects in the market and measures to facilitate access to finance; (c) addressing other unjustified regulatory barriers to renewables self-consumption, including for tenants; (d) addressing incentives to building owners to create opportunities for renewables self-consumption, including for tenants; (e) granting renewables self-consumers, for self-generated renewable electricity that they feed into the grid, non-discriminatory access to relevant existing support schemes as well as to all electricity market segments; (f) ensuring that renewables self-consumers contribute in an adequate and balanced way to the overall cost sharing of the system when electricity is fed into the grid; (g) including provisions on safeguarding the origin of renewable sources of the electricity produced by self-consumers; (h) ensuring that tenants have the right to self-consumption of energy from renewable sources without discrimination.[1663] A summary of the policies and measures under the enabling framework and an assessment of their implementation is included in the National Plan for Climate and Energy.[1664]

394. Specifically, renewables self-consumers located in the same building, including multi-apartment blocks, have the right to engage jointly in the aforementioned activities. They are also permitted to arrange sharing of renewable energy that is produced on their site between themselves, without prejudice to the network charges and other relevant charges, fees, levies and taxes applicable to each renewables self-consumer. Any differentiation between individual renewables self-consumers and jointly acting renewables self-consumers has to be both proportionate and duly justified.[1665]

1660. Section 38(2)(a)(iv) Law No. 107(I)/2022, which corresponds to Art. 21(2)(b) Directive (EU) 2018/2001.
1661. Section 38(2)(a)(vi) Law No. 107(I)/2022, which corresponds to Art. 21(2)(d) Directive (EU) 2018/2001.
1662. Section 38(2)(a)(v) Law No. 107(I)/2022, which corresponds to Art. 21(2)(c) Directive (EU) 2018/2001.
1663. Section 38(4)(a) to (h) Law No. 107(I)/2022, which partially corresponds to Art. 21(6)(a) to (f) Directive (EU) 2018/2001.
1664. Section 38(5) Law No. 107(I)/2022, which partially corresponds to Art. 21(6) Directive (EU) 2018/2001.
1665. Section 38(2)(b) Law No. 107(I)/2022, which corresponds to Art. 21(4) Directive (EU) 2018/2001.

§4. Statistical Transfers Between Member States

395. The initial proposal for a directive on the promotion of the use of energy from renewable sources did not entail the notion of statistical transfers.[1666] This was first suggested by the European Parliament in the first reading[1667] with different content than the one now in force.[1668]

This was discussed within the climate-energy legislative package by the Council of the EU, and it was welcomed as a cooperation mechanism between the Member States.[1669] The content was subsequently changed following various proposals.[1670] The European Parliament approved the Commission proposal as amended,[1671] and the act was unanimously adopted by the Council of the EU.[1672]

396. Statistical transfer of a specified amount of energy from renewable sources from Cyprus to the other Member States or vice versa is decided by the Council of

1666. Commission, *Proposal for a Directive of the European Parliament and of the Council on the promotion of the use of energy from renewable sources*, 2008/0016 (COD) COM(2008) 19 final, dd. 23 Jan. 2008, http://www.europarl.europa.eu/oeil/home/home.do.
1667. Committee on Industry, Research and Energy, *on the proposal for a directive of the European Parliament and of the Council on the promotion of the use of energy from renewable sources* (COM(2008)0019 – C6-0046/2008 – 2008/0016(COD)), A6-0369/2008, dd. 26 Sep. 2008, proposed Art. 9 a (new), http://www.europarl.europa.eu/oeil/home/home.do.
1668. The proposal read:

    Statistical transfers between Member States
    1. Two or more Member States may agree to transfer energy from renewable sources statistically between themselves with the effect of counting towards their national targets.
    2. The volume which a Member State may transfer to other Member States under this Article is restricted to the total volume of energy from renewable sources which has benefited from a support scheme operated by the Member State in question in the respective year.
    3. A Member State may transfer energy from renewable sources statistically to another Member State only if, at the moment of transfer, its share of energy from renewable sources has exceeded the trajectory as set out in Part B of Annex I.
    4. Transfers under this Article must remain valid until at least 2020 and be effective for a minimum of one year. They shall become effective only after all Member States involved in the transfer have notified the transfer to the Commission.

1669. The climate-energy legislative package involved apart the promotion of the use of renewable, proposals on greenhouse gas emission allowance trading system, reduction of the same and geological storage of CO_2. Council of the EU, *Note from Presidency to the Council 14395/08*, dd. 14 Oct. 2008, pp. 1, 17, http://register.consilium.europa.eu/.
1670. Council of the EU, *Note from Presidency to COREPER 1473/08*, dd. 24 Oct. 2008, p. 21; Council of the EU, *Note from General Secretariat of the Council to Delegations, 15281/08*, dd. 6 Nov. 2008, p. 12; Council of the EU, *Note from General Secretariat of the Council to Delegations*, 17086/08, dd. 11 Dec. 2008, p. 37 f., http://register.consilium.europa.eu/.
1671. European Parliament, *Legislative resolution on the proposal for a directive of the European Parliament and of the Council on the promotion of the use of energy from renewable sources* (COM(2008)0019 – C6-0046/2008 – 2008/0016(COD)), A6-0369/2008, dd. 17 Dec. 2008, http://www.europarl.europa.eu/oeil/home/home.do.
1672. Council of the EU, *Note on voting result, 8533/09*, dd. 6 Apr. 2009, p. 2, http://register.consilium.europa.eu/.

Ministers following the relevant proposal of the Minister.[1673] The transferred quantity is deducted from the amount of energy from renewable sources that is taken into account in measuring compliance with accomplishing its national target by the Member State making the transfer[1674] and added to the amount of energy from renewable sources that is taken into account in calculating the renewable energy share of the Member State accepting the transfer.[1675] The arrangements for such transfer may have a duration of one or more years and are to be notified to the Commission no later than twelve months after the end of each year in which they have an effect. Alternatively, they must be finalized on the Union Renewable Development Platform, that is established by the Commission, within the same period.[1676] The European Commission is informed of the quantity and price of the energy involved, whereas for transfers finalized on the Union Renewable Development Platform, the parties involved as well as the information on the particular transfer shall be disclosed to the public.[1677] Transfers are effective only after all Member States involved in it comply with the above-described notification obligation to the Commission or after all clearing conditions are met on the Union Renewable Development Platform, as applicable.[1678]

§5. Guarantees of Origin

397. Guarantee of origin ('εγγύηση προέλευσης') is a notion not defined in this law, unlike in the repealed legislation.[1679] It is a regime first created by Directive 2001/77/EC in order to facilitate domestic or international trade in renewable electricity, such as proof of the green nature of the electricity, and to increase transparency in consumers' choice between renewable and non-renewable electricity.[1680] Despite the lack of definition, the law provides its content. Accordingly, a guarantee of origin must describe at least the following, although installations of less than 50 kW may require simplified information: (a) the energy source from which the energy was produced and the start and end dates of production; (b) whether it relates to electricity, gas, including hydrogen, or heating or cooling; (c) the identity, location, type and capacity of the installation where the energy was produced; (d)

1673. Section 10(1) Law No. 107(I)/2022, which corresponds to Art. 8(1) Directive (EU) 2018/2001.
1674. Section 10(2)(a) Law No. 107(I)/2022, which corresponds to Art. 8(1)(a) Directive (EU) 2018/2001.
1675. Section 10(2)(b) Law No. 107(I)/2022, which corresponds to Art. 8(1)(b) Directive (EU) 2018/2001.
1676. Section 10(3) Law No. 107(I)/2022, which corresponds to Art. 8(4) Directive (EU) 2018/2001.
1677. Section 10(4) & (5) Law No. 107(I)/2022, which corresponds to Art. 8(4) Directive (EU) 2018/2001.
1678. Section 10(6) Law No. 107(I)/2022, which corresponds to Art. 8(5) Directive (EU) 2018/2001.
1679. *See* s. 2 Law No. 112(I)/2013, which corresponded to Art. 2(j) Directive 2009/28/EC and read: 'an electronic document which has the sole function of providing proof to a final customer that a given share or quantity of energy was produced from renewable sources as required by Art. 3(6) of Directive 2003/54/EC'.
1680. Council of the EU, *Cover Note from Secretary-General of the European Commission signed by Mr Jordi Ayet Puigarnau, Director, to Mr. Javer Solana, Secretary-General/ High Representative, 5421/08*, dd. 30 Jan. 2008, p. 12, http://register.consilium.europa.eu/.

whether the installation has benefited from investment support and whether the unit of energy has benefited in any other way from a national support scheme, and the type of support scheme; (e) the date on which the installation became operational; and (f) the date and country of issue and a unique identification number.[1681] They are valid for twelve months after the production of the relevant energy unit and in fact expire at least eighteen months after the production of the energy unit, if they have not been cancelled by the authorized issuers. Such expired guarantees of origin are included in the calculation of the residual energy mix of Cyprus.[1682]

398. The *authorized issuer* ('εξουσιοδοτημένος εκδότης') is pivotal to the function of guarantees of origin. This is the authority that issues guarantees of origin. Depending on whether the requested guarantees of origin relate to energy from renewable sources for heating or cooling or to electricity from renewable sources and gas, including hydrogen from renewable sources, this authority is determined by the Minister or by Cyprus Energy Regulatory Authority. In the first case, the Minister has the power to appoint the Director as authorized issuer. In any event, it is pertinent that the authorized issuer is independent of production, commerce and supply of energy.[1683]

399. The authorized issuer is a person other and different from the *competent authority for guarantees of origin* ('αρμόδιος φορέας εγγυήσεων προέλευσης'). This term dictates the authority that supervises the issuance, transfer, revocation, amendment and cancellation of guarantees of origin for energy from renewable sources for heating or cooling and or guarantees of origin for electricity from renewable sources and gas, including hydrogen, from renewable sources. In the first case, the competent authority is the Director, and in the latter Cyprus Energy Regulatory Authority.[1684] These authorities are further under the statutory duty to put in place appropriate mechanisms to ensure that guarantees of origin are issued, transferred and cancelled electronically and are accurate, reliable and fraud-resistant. At the same time, they have to ensure that the requirements they impose comply with the standard CEN – EN 16325.[1685]

400. The authorized issuer issues guarantees of origin in response to a request from a producer of energy from renewable sources.[1686] Such a request may refer only to energy from renewable sources produced in Cyprus by the following installations: facilities of renewable sources of energy connected to the transmission and distribution systems; facilities of cogeneration; facilities of self-consumers from renewable sources of energy that are not connected to the transmission or distribution systems; facilities of gas production from renewable sources of energy; hydrogen production facilities; and facilities of heating or cooling using energy from

1681. Section 25(1) Law No. 107(I)/2022, which corresponds to Art. 19(7) Directive (EU) 2018/2001.
1682. Section 25(2) & (3) Law No. 107(I)/2022, which corresponds to Art. 19(3) & (4) Directive (EU) 2018/2001.
1683. Section 2(1) Law No. 107(I)/2022. *See also* s. 23(4) & (5) *ibid.*
1684. Section 23(2) & (3) *ibid.*
1685. Section 23(6) *ibid*,, which corresponds to Art. 19(6) Directive (EU) 2018/2001.
1686. Section 26(1) Law No. 107(I)/2022.

renewables.[1687] Each kilowatt generated from said sources correlates to one guarantee of origin.[1688] The relevant application can be submitted within sixty working days from the expiration date of accounting for the energy, which will be set out in the guarantee of origin. No guarantees of origin are issued for a time period beyond this one.[1689] The application is further accompanied by all necessary information required by the authorized issuer and the relevant registration and/or certification fee with the electronic registry, which is set by the competent authorized issuer.[1690]

401. The origin of electricity produced from renewable energy sources is guaranteed as such in accordance with objective, transparent and non-discriminatory criteria.[1691] The authorized issuer examines the application only if all necessary information is submitted.[1692] In order to evaluate the information provided, the authorized issuer may enter the facilities of the supplier, but not his residence unless a relevant court order has been obtained, and perform the necessary controls, examinations, testings, calculations, estimations and measurements for the purpose of identification and verification of the said information.[1693] He may equally use any equipment, measuring instruments, devices and material for the purpose of performing the above-mentioned duties.[1694] In addition, the authorized issuer may delegate to an independent body the performance of certain tasks and works related to granting the guarantees of origin, under the condition that the competent authority for guarantees of origin or the Minister are in agreement. These tasks and works include *in situ* inspection of the supply facilities, measurements and collection of data. The independent body must be specialized in technical inspections according to good professional practice rules and of recognized competence.[1695] The authorized issuer may refuse to issue a guarantee of origin, in the event that one or more of the following circumstances apply: (a) when the applicant refused access to the authorized issuer to the premises of his facility without valid excuse, (b) when the supplier refuses to provide information and documentation, which is considered to be useful to verify the accuracy and reliability of the information related to the specific guarantee of origin, and (c) when the authorized issuer establishes that the submitted information is not complete or is inaccurate, false or misleading.[1696]

1687. Section 26(7)(a) to (g) *ibid.*
1688. Section 26(4) *ibid.*
1689. Section 26(8) *ibid.*
1690. Section 26(9) *ibid.*
1691. Section 23(1) *ibid.*, which corresponds to Art. 19(1) Directive (EU) 2018/2001.
1692. Section 26(2) Law No. 107(I)/2022.
1693. Section 26(3)(a) *ibid.*
1694. Section 26(3)(b) *ibid.*
1695. Section 26(10) *ibid.*
1696. Section 26(11)(a)–(c) *ibid.*

402. The authorized issuer ensures that guarantee of origin is accurate, reliab and fraud-resistant.[1697] Following the issuance of such a guarantee and under th condition that it has not been revoked, no further guarantees of origin for the sam amount of energy may be issued.[1698]

403. Each guarantee of origin is communicated to the competent authority fc guarantees of origin.[1699] Specifically, a negative decision of an authorized issuer i communicated immediately to the competent authorities for guarantees of origin c to the Minister, as the case may be. It is also communicated to the supplier that ha submitted the request, informing him about its right to submit a complaint befor the competent authority for guarantees of origin or the Minister, as the case may b within seven days. The authority hearing the complaint examines it within a reasonable time and issues a final decision.[1700]

404. Guarantees of origin issued by other Member States may be recognized i Cyprus by the competent authorities for guarantees of origin, exclusively as evidence of certain elements following the submission of an electronic application. Th competent authorities for guarantees of origin have the power to refuse to recogniz a guarantee of origin only where it has well-founded doubts about its accuracy, reliability or veracity. This, including its reasoning, is notified to the Commission.[170 Should the Commission opine that the refusal was unfounded and issue a corresponding decision, the competent authority for guarantees of origin is obliged t comply with this approach and recognize it.[1702] Nonetheless, same authority doe not recognize guarantees of origin issued by a third country. Exceptionally, it ma do so, when three conditions are met. Firstly, an agreement must have been concluded between the Union and the third country and in that same country, compatible guarantees of origin systems must be in place. Lastly, the guarantee of origi must concern only direct import or export of energy.[1703]

405. The authorized issuer ensures that the guarantee of origin may be electronically transferred, as well as revoked, amended and cancelled.[1704] Transfer o such a guarantee requires an application of the holder to the authorized issuer an relevant notification of the competent authorities for guarantees of origin or th Minister, as the case may be.[1705] This amount of energy from renewable sources corresponding to guarantees of origin transferred by an electricity supplier to a thir

1697. Section 23(1) *ibid.*, which corresponds to Art. 19(1) Directive (EU) 2018/2001.
1698. Section 27(5) Law No. 107(I)/2022.
1699. Section 26(1) *ibid.*, which corresponds to Art. 19(5) Directive (EU) 2018/2001.
1700. Section 26(12)(a)(i) & (13) Law No. 107(I)/2022.
1701. Section 31(1) & (2) *ibid.*, which corresponds to Art. 19(9) Directive (EU) 2018/2001.
1702. Section 31(3) Law No. 107(I)/2022, which corresponds to Art. 19(10) Directive (EU) 2018/2001
1703. Section 31(4) Law No. 107(I)/2022, which corresponds to Art. 19(11) Directive (EU) 2018/2001
1704. Section 26(6) Law No. 107(I)/2022, which partially corresponds to Art. 15(5) Directive (EU 2018/2022.
1705. Section 28(1) Law No. 107(I)/2022.

party is deducted from the share of energy from renewable sources in its energy mix for the purposes of proving to its final customers the amount of electricity included in its energy mix.[1706]

406. Amendment or revocation of guarantee of origin may take place solely in the following cases. The holder has submitted a relevant written request to the authorized issuer, and the latter agrees with it.[1707] Another case is when the authorized issuer has established that the information, on the basis of which the guarantee of origin was issued, is not complete, misleading, false, inaccurate or based on false representations.[1708] Lastly, amendment or revocation may take place when the holder violates any terms, conditions or provisions of these laws, Law No. 174(I)/2006, Law No. 130(I)/2021, Law No. 183(I)/2004 or of the Transmission and Distribution Rules or relevant decisions of Cyprus Energy Regulatory Authority.[1709] The relevant decision on amendment or revocation of the authorized issuer must be due reasoned,[1710] and the holder must be informed without any delay on this along with his right to file a complaint either with the competent authority for guarantees of origin, or with the Minister, as the case may be.[1711]

407. Finally, the guarantees of origin are cancelled by the authorized issuer, when they are used for the purpose of proving to final consumers the share or amount of energy from renewable sources. They are also cancelled when their validity period expires. No new guarantees of origin may be issued for the purposes of replacing cancelled ones.[1712]

408. The competent authorities for guarantees of origin regulate, monitor, control and supervise the functions of the guarantee of origin system and establish the necessary measures for the purpose of objectivity, transparency and impartiality of the above-mentioned processes of issuance, amendment, revocation, transfer and cancellation.[1713] Hence, these authorities may control and verify the accuracy and reliability of all information, data and issues contained in the application of the supplier.[1714] They may further ensure that the authorized issuer performs the necessary controls, calculations, measurements and verifications of information, data and issues in suppliers' applications.[1715] They also have the authority to order the authorized issuer to revoke or amend a guarantee of origin when it establishes that issues, measurements, calculations, data and information are not complete or are inaccurate, false or misleading. Should he fail to comply within one month, the authority

1706. Section 28(2) *ibid.*
1707. Section 27(1)(a) *ibid.*
1708. Section 27(1)(b) *ibid.*
1709. Section 27(1)(c) *ibid.*
1710. Section 27(1) *ibid.*
1711. Section 27(2) *ibid.*
1712. Section 29(1) *ibid.*
1713. Section 32(1) *ibid.* The obligation to supervise the issuance, transfer and cancellation of guarantees of origin is foreseen in Art. 19(5) Directive (EU) 2018/2001.
1714. Section 32(2)(a) Law No. 112(I)/2013.
1715. Section 32(2)(b) *ibid.*

imposes revocation or amendment of the guarantee of origin.[1716] They are equally entitled to instruct the authorized issuer to terminate the issuance procedure of a specific guarantee of origin if they establish that the information provided with the relevant application does not comply with the provisions of this law, that is sections 26 and 27 Law No. 107(I)/2022. In the event that the authorized issuer does not comply within one month, the authority imposes termination of the relevant issuance procedure.[1717] For the effective application of these powers, every supplier allows competent public servants of the competent authorities for guarantees of origin or the Minister to access the supply facilities. He also provides them with any possible information, data and help that they might require.[1718] In addition, the authorized issuer supplies said authorities with any information, data, certified measurements and calculations upon their request.[1719]

§6. Information and Registers

409. The public enjoys the right to be informed about certain matters of energy from renewable sources. The obligation to provide those is entrusted to the Director in cooperation with other governmental bodies, local authorities, foundations and organizations.[1720] This right materializes in providing, in particular, information on support schemes to all interested parties, such as consumers, including low-income, vulnerable consumers, renewables self-consumers, renewable energy communities, builders, constructors, installers, architects, engineers, suppliers of equipment, heating and cooling systems, as well as energy from renewable sources and vehicles compatible with the use of such energy and of intelligent transport systems.[1721] It is further ensured that guidance is provided to all relevant actors, notably planners and architects so that they are properly able to consider the optimal combination of renewable energy sources, high-efficiency technologies and district heating and cooling when planning, designing, building and renovating industrial, commercial or residential areas.[1722] Suitable information, awareness-raising, guidance or training programmes are developed in order to inform citizens of how to exercise their rights as active customers, and of the benefits and practicalities, including technical and financial aspects of developing and using energy from renewable sources, including by renewables self-consumption or in the framework of renewable energy communities.[1723] Suppliers of equipment and systems of energy from renewable sources have further the obligation to provide the public with information on the net

1716. Section 32(2)(c) *ibid.*
1717. Section 32(2)(d) *ibid.*
1718. Section 32(3)(a) *ibid.*
1719. Section 32(3)(b) *ibid.*
1720. Section 19(1) *ibid.*
1721. Section 19(1)(a) *ibid.*, which corresponds to Art. 18(1) Directive (EU) 2018/2001.
1722. Section 19(1)(b) Law No. 107(I)/2022, which corresponds to Art. 18(5) Directive (EU) 2018/2001.
1723. Section 19(1)(c) Law No. 107(I)/2022, which corresponds to Art. 18(6) Directive (EU) 2018/2001.

benefits, cost and energy efficiency of equipment and systems for the use of heating, cooling and electricity from renewable energy sources, sustainable use and eco-characteristics of products. The information and the manner of registration are provided in Law No. 17(I)/2011 and Law No. 44(I)/2021.[1724]

410. Apart from the above-mentioned public information, the establishment of a number of registers is additionally foreseen in this law. First, the Director keeps a registry of installers of small-scale biomass boilers and stoves, solar photovoltaic and solar thermal systems, shallow geothermal systems and heat pumps. Information on the procedure for registering in said register, which at all times shall be voluntary, is made public, as is the registry itself and its content.[1725]

411. Further, the authorized issuer of guarantees of origin has the statutory duty to keep two registers. The first is an electronic register in which all facilities having guarantees of origin are recorded. In addition, in special accounts, all issued, revoked, amended, transferred and cancelled guarantees of origin are kept, along with the holders of authorization for supply of electricity to final customers.[1726] The authorized issuer of guarantees further keeps a separate electronic registry for every: (a) guarantee of origin for electricity from renewable sources; (b) guarantee of origin for gas including hydrogen from renewable sources; and (c) guarantee of origin for energy from renewable sources for heating or cooling.[1727]

412. Finally, electricity suppliers, transmission and distribution system operators and retail companies of energy have the statutory duty to communicate statistical data to the Director, when he requests so. These data can be of any kind, such as aggregated data on energy consumption, the use of renewables and the new facilities of renewable sources of energy of last year.[1728] Suppliers of renewable energy equipment must also provide the same authority with the same information.[1729] The same obligation lies with the suppliers of energy from renewable sources, who are not connected with the transmission or distribution system,[1730] the same suppliers, who are connected with such systems and channel the energy into the system,[1731] and suppliers, who are connected with said systems and receive energy in order to meet their own needs.[1732] Finally, public authorities, departments, services, offices, local and district authorities, authorities, institutions and organizations have the duty to provide the Director with any statistical data relating to their activities, including

1724. Section 19(2)(a) & (b) Law No. 107(I)/2022, which corresponds to Art. 18(2) Directive (EU) 2018/2001.
1725. Section 36(1) to (3) Law No. 107(I)/2022, which corresponds to Art. 18(3) Directive (EU) 2018/2001.
1726. Section 30(1)(a), (b) & (c) Law No. 107(I)/2022.
1727. Section 30(2) *ibid.*
1728. Section 40(1)(a) *ibid.*
1729. Section 40(1)(ii) *ibid.*
1730. Section 40(2)(i) *ibid.*
1731. Section 40(2)(ii) *ibid.*
1732. Section 40(2)(iii) *ibid.*

aggregated data on energy consumption, the use of renewables and the new facilities of renewable sources of energy, when they are asked to do so. It is irrelevant whether these suppliers were the beneficiaries of support schemes.[1733] The specific statistical data that the suppliers must submit are portrayed in a decision of the Minister, which is duly published in the OG.[1734] Should this information contain commercially sensitive information, this is considered confidential in the meaning of Law on Statistics.[1735] Hence, this is published in a manner that direct or indirect revealing of the identity of the person providing this or the persons to whom it refers will not be effected.[1736]

1733. Section 40(2) *ibid.*
1734. Section 40(3) *ibid.*
1735. Section 40(4) *ibid.*
1736. Section 13 Law No. 15(I)/2000.

Part VI. Interaction Between Energy Law and Environmental Law

413. The energy industry underlies certain obligations arising from environmental legislation that relate mainly to the issuance of certain permits as well as compliance with the terms and conditions set out therein.

Chapter 1. Environmental Impact Assessment

414. It has already been noted above[1737] that the application for authorization o exploitation of hydrocarbons must be accompanied by an Environmental Impa Assessment Report according to Law No. 127(I)/2018. In addition, such a repo must be accompanied by the application for a building permit when a refining pla a power station with a thermal output of more than 50 megawatts and a nucle power plant are intended to be built.[1738] Due to the fact that this law implemen Directive 2014/92/EU and Directive 2011/92/EU, as well as its predecessor th being Directive 85/337/EC, the relevant case law of the Court of Justice of the E is much helpful in interpreting the national legislation.[1739]

1737. *See* in this respect *supra* para. 84.

1738. Sections 17, 18, 19 and 20 and Annex I Law No. 127(I)/2018.

1739. This case law includes among others: Case C-396/92, *Bund Naturschutz in Bayern e.V. and Rich-ard Stahnsdorf and others v. Freistaat Bayern, Stadt Vilsbiburg and Landkreis Landshut* [1994] ECR I-03717; Case C-72/95, *Aannemersbedrijf P.K. Kraaijeveld BV e.a. v. Gedeputeerde State van Zuid-Holland* [1996] I-05403; Case C-81/96, *Burgemeester en wethouders van Haarlemmer liede en Spaarnwoude and Others v. Gedeputeerde Staten van Noord-Holland*, [1998] EC I-03923; Case C-435/97, *World Wildlife Fund (WWF) and Others v. Autonome Provinz Bozen an Others* [1999] ECR I-05613; Case C-287/98, *Grand Duchy of Luxemburg v. Berthe Linster, Aloys Linster and Yvonne Linster* [2000] ECR I-06917; Case C-201/02, *The Queen, on the applicatio of Delena Wells v. Secretary of State for Transport, Local Government and the Regions* [2004] ECR I-00723; Case C-290/03, *The Queen, on the application of: Diane Barker v. London Bor ough of Bromley* [2006] ECR I-03949; Case C-2/07, *Paul Abraham and Others v. Région wal lonne and Others* [2008] ECR I-01197; Case C-142/07, *Ecologistas en Acción-CODA v Ayuntamiento de Madrid* [2008] ECR I-06097; Case C-156/07, *Salvatore Aiello and Others v Regione Lombardia and Others* [2008] ECR I-05215; Case C-75/08, *The Queen on the applica tion of Christopher Mellor v. Secretary of State for Communities and Local Government* [2009] ECR I-03799; Case C-205/08, *Umweltanwalt von Kärnten v. Kärntner Landesregierung*, [2009] ECR I-11525; Case C-263/08, *Djurgården-Lilla Värtans Miljöskyddsförening v. Stockholms kom mun genom dess marknämnd* [2009] ECR I-09967; Joined cases C-128/09 to C-131/09, C-134/09 and C-135/09, *Antoine Boxus and Willy Roua* (C-128/09), *Guido Durlet and Others* (C-129/09), *Paul Fastrez and Henriette Fastrez* (C-130/09), *Philippe Daras* (C-131/09), *Association des riv erains et habitants des communes proches de l'aéroport BSCA (Brussels South Charlero Airport)(*ARACh)(C-134/09 and C-135/09), *Bernard Page* (C-134/09) *and Léon L'Hoir an Nadine Dartois* (C-135/09) *v. Région wallonne* [2011] ECR I-09711.

Chapter 2. Waste Dumping Permit

415. Pursuant to the Law on Control of Water and Soil Pollution,[1740] the operation of any facility that causes or may cause pollution of waters and soil is prohibited unless the operator holds a licence for waste dumping.[1741] In view of the fact that this law implements a number of directives of the EU,[1742] relevant case law is valuable for its interpretation.[1743]

1740. Law on Regulating the Pollution of Waters and Soil ('περί Ελέγχου της Ρύπανσης των Νερών και του Εδάφους Νόμος') No. 106 of 2002, OG I(I) No. 3621, 12 Jun. 2002, p. 2123.
1741. Section 8 Law No. 106(I)/2002.
1742. In particular these directives are the following: Directive 2000/60/EC of the European Parliament and of the Council of 23 Oct. 2000 establishing a framework for Community action in the field of water policy, OJ L 327, 22 Dec. 2000, p. 1, as amended; Directive 2006/7/EC of the European Parliament and of the Council of 15 Feb. 2006 concerning the management of bathing water quality and repealing Directive 76/160/EEC, OJ L 64, 4 Mar. 2006, p. 37, as amended; Directive 2006/11/EC of the European Parliament and of the Council of 15 Feb. 2006 on pollution caused by certain dangerous substances discharged into the aquatic environment of the Community, OJ L 64, 4 Mar. 2006, p. 52; Directive 2006/44/EC of the European Parliament and of the Council of 6 Sep. 2006 on the quality of fresh waters needing protection or improvement in order to support fish life, OJ L 264, 25 Sep. 2006, p. 20, as amended; Directive 2006/113/EC of the European Parliament and of the Council of 12 Dec. 2006 on the quality required of shellfish waters, OJ L 376, 27 Dec. 2006, p. 14, as amended; Directive 2006/118/EC of the European Parliament and of the Council of 12 Dec. 2006 on the protection of groundwater against pollution and deterioration, OJ L 372, 27 Dec. 2006, p. 19, as amended and replaced by Commission Directive 2014/80/EU of 20 Jun. 2014 amending Annex II to Directive 2006/118/EC of the European Parliament and of the Council on the protection of groundwater against pollution and deterioration, OJ L 182, 21 Jun. 2014, p. 52; Directive 2008/105/EC of the European Parliament and of the Council of 16 Dec. 2008 on environmental quality standards in the field of water policy, amending and subsequently repealing Council Directives 82/176/EEC, 83/513/EEC, 84/156/EEC, 84/491/EEC, 86/280/EEC and amending Directive 2000/60/EC of the European Parliament and of the Council, OJ L 348, 24 Dec. 2008, p. 84, as amended; and Directive 2008/1/EC of the European Parliament and of the Council of 15 Jan. 2008 concerning integrated pollution prevention and control, OJ L 24, 29 Jan. 2008, p. 8.
1743. *See* in this regard: Case C-24/09, *Djurgården-Lilla Värtans Miljöskyddsförening v. AB Fortum Värme samägt med Stockholms stad* [2010] ECR I-00035; Joined cases C-165/09 to C-167/09, *Stichting Natuur en Milieu and Others v. College van Gedeputeerde Staten van Groningen* (C-165/09) *and College van Gedeputeerde Staten van Zuid-Holland* (C-166/09 and C-167/09), [2011] ECR I-04599; Case C-381/07, *Association nationale pour la protection des eaux et rivières – TOS v. Ministère de l'Écologie, du Développement et de l'Aménagement durables* [2008] ECR I-08281; Case C-43/10, *Nomarchiaki Aftodioikisi Aitoloakarnanias and Others v. Ypourgos Perivallontos, Chorotaxias kai Dimosion ergon and Others*, digital ECR; Case C-461/13, *Bund für Umwelt und Naturschutz Deutschland e.V. v. Bundesrepublik Deutschland,* digital ECR; Case C-207/14, *Hotel Sava Rogaška, gostinstvo, turizem in storitve, d.o.o. v. The Republic of Slovenia*, digital ECR.

Chapter 3. Permit for Industrial Waste Gas

416. In accordance with the Law on Control of Pollution of Air,[1744] undertakings producing lubricants from crude oil, facilities producing, processing and storing oil, natural and synthetic gas, facilities producing coal and combustion plants using light and/or heavy fuel oil containing sulphur of more than 1% must obtain a licence for industrial waste gas prior to their operation.[1745] Once more, this national law has been enacted for the purpose of implementing EU legislation,[1746] and therefore, relevant case law is helpful to resolve any interpretation questions.[1747]

1744. Law on Regulating the Pollution of Air ('περί Ελέγχου της Ρύπανσης της Ατμόσφαιρας Νόμος') No. 187 of 2002, OG I(I) No. 3649, 1 Nov. 2002, p. 2893, as amended.
1745. Section 8, Annex II Law No. 187(I)/2002.
1746. In particular the following instruments are implemented into national law: Council Directive of 19 Mar. 1987 on the prevention and reduction of environmental pollution by asbestos (87/217/EEC), OJ L 085, 28 Mar. 1987, p. 40, as amended; Directive 2001/80/EC of the European Parliament and of the Council of 23 Oct. 2001 on the limitation of emissions of certain pollutants into the air from large combustion plants, OJ L 309, 27 Nov. 2001, p. 1, as amended; Directive 2008/1/EC of the European Parliament and of the Council of 15 Jan. 2008 concerning integrated pollution prevention and control, OJ L 24, 29 Jan. 2008, p. 8; Directive 2008/98/EC of the European Parliament and of the Council of 19 Nov. 2008 on waste and repealing certain Directives, OJ L 312, 22 Nov. 2008, p. 3; and Directive 2010/75/EU of the European Parliament and of the Council of 24 Nov. 2010 on industrial emissions (integrated pollution prevention and control), OJ L 334, 17 Dec. 2010, p. 17.
1747. This case law includes among others: Case 172/82, *Syndicat national des fabricants raffineurs d'huile de graissage and Others v. Groupement d'intérêt économique 'Inter-Huiles' and Others* [1983] ECR 00555; Case 295/82, *Groupement d'Intérêt Economique 'Rhône-Alpes Huiles' and Others v. Syndicat National des Fabricants Raffineurs d'Huile de Graissage and Others* [1984] ECR 00575; Case 240/83, *Procureur de la République v. Association de défense des brûleurs d'huiles usagées (ADBHU)* [1985] ECR 00531; Case C-37/92, *Criminal proceedings against José Vanacker and André Lesage and SA Baudoux combustibles* [1993] ECR I-04947; Joined cases C-307/00 to C-311/00, *Oliehandel Koeweit BV and Others v. Minister van Volkshuisvesting, Ruimtelijke Ordening en Milieubeheer* [2003] ECR I-01821; Case C-24/09, *Djurgården-Lilla Värtans Miljöskyddsförening v. AB Fortum Värme samägt med Stockholms stad* [2010] ECR I-00035; Joined cases C-165/09 to C-167/09, *Stichting Natuur en Milieu and Others v. College van Gedeputeerde Staten van Groningen* (C-165/09) *and College van Gedeputeerde Staten van Zuid-Holland* (C-166/09 and C-167/09), [2011] ECR I-04599; Case C-24/09, *Djurgården-Lilla Värtans Miljöskyddsförening v. AB Fortum Värme samägt med Stockholms stad* [2010] ECR I-00035; Case C-358/11, *Lapin elinkeino-, liikenne- ja ympäristökeskuksen liikenne ja infrastruktuuri -vastuualue v. Lapin luonnonsuojelupiiri ry*, digital ECR; Case C-292/12, *Ragn-Sells AS v. Sillamäe Linnavalitsus*, digital ECR; Case C-251/07, *Gävle Kraftvärme AB v. Länsstyrelsen i Gävleborgs län* [2008] ECR I-07047; Case C-317/07, *Lahti Energia Oy* [2008] ECR I-09051; Case C-209/09, *Lahti Energia Oy* [2010] ECR I-01429.

Chapter 4. Waste Management Permit

417. Pursuant to Law on Waste (Law No. 185(I)/2011), undertakings engaged in energy activities, to the extent that they are waste producers, are obliged to forward waste to dealers or persons performing disposal operations. In case, however, they decide to treat their waste themselves, they must hold a waste management permit.[1748] This law implements EU directives.[1749] Hence, the case law of the Court of Justice of the EU is helpful in interpreting national legislation.[1750]

1748. Sections 15 and 24 Law No. 185(I)/2011.

1749. These are: Council Directive 96/59/EC of 16 Sep. 1996 on the disposal of polychlorinated biphenyls and polychlorinated terphenyls (PCB/PCT), OJ L 243, 24 Sep. 1996, p. 31, as amended; Council Directive 1999/31/EC of 26 Apr. 1999 on the landfill of waste, OJ L 182, 16 Jul. 1999, p. 1; Directive 2002/96/EC of the European Parliament and of the Council of 27 Jan. 2003 on waste electrical and electronic equipment (WEEE), OJ L 037, 13 Feb. 2003, p. 24, as amended; Directive 2006/66/EC of the European Parliament and of the Council of 6 Sep. 2006 on batteries and accumulators and waste batteries and accumulators, OJ L 266, 26 Sep. 2006, p. 1, as amended; Directive 2008/98/EC of the European Parliament and of the Council of 19 Nov. 2008 on waste, OJ L 312, 22 Nov. 2008, p. 3; and Directive 2011/65/EU of the European Parliament and of the Council of 8 Jun. 2011 on the restriction of the use of certain hazardous substances in electrical and electronic equipment, OJ L 174, 1 Jul. 2011, p. 88, as amended.

1750. Case C-6/03, *Deponiezweckverband Eiterköpfe v. Land Rheinland-Pfalz* [2005] ECR I-02753; Case C-172/08, *Pontina Ambiente Srl v. Regione Lazio* [2010] ECR I-01175; Case C-97/11, *Amia SpA v. Provincia Regionale di Palermo*, digital ECR; Case C-121/11, *Pro-Braine ASBL and Others v. Commune de Braine-le-Château*, digital ECR; Case C-225/13, *Ville d'Ottignies-Louvain-la-Neuve and Others v. Région wallonne*, digital ECR; Case C-292/12, *Ragn-Sells AS v. Sillamäe Linnavalitsus*, digital ECR; Case C-358/11, *Lapin elinkeino-, liikenne- ja ympäristökeskuksen liikenne ja infrastruktuuri -vastuualue v. Lapin luonnonsuojelupiiri ry*, digital ECR.

Chapter 5. Greenhouse Gas Emission Permit

418. Pursuant to Law Establishing a Scheme for Greenhouse Gas Emission Allowance Trading,[1751] activities involving combustion installations with a rated thermal input exceeding 20 megawatts (except hazardous or municipal waste installations), mineral oil refineries and coke ovens that emit CO_2 must hold a greenhouse gas emission permit.[1752] This law has been enacted for the purpose of implementing directives of the EU.[1753] Thus, any interpretation matters may be resolved by reference to the relevant case law of the Court of Justice of the EU.[1754]

1751. Law Establishing a Scheme for Greenhouse Gas Emission Allowance Trading ('Ο περί της Θέσπισης Συστήματος Εμπορίας Δικαιωμάτων Εκπομπής Αερίων του Θερμοκηπίου Νόμος') No. 110 of 2011, OG I(I) 4290 of 29 Jul. 2011, p. 1040, which implements Directive 2003/87/EC of the European Parliament and of the Council of 13 Oct. 2003 establishing a scheme for greenhouse gas emission allowance trading within the Community and amending Council Directive 96/61/EC, OJ L 275, 25 Oct. 2003, p. 32, Directive 2004/101/EC of the European Parliament and of the Council of 27 Oct. 2004 amending Directive 2003/87/EC establishing a scheme for greenhouse gas emission allowance trading within the Community, in respect of the Kyoto Protocol's project mechanisms, OJ L 338, 13 Nov. 2004, p. 18, Directive 2008/101/EC of the European Parliament and of the Council of 19 Nov. 2008 amending Directive 2003/87/EC so as to include aviation activities in the scheme for greenhouse gas emission allowance trading within the Community, OJ L 8, 13 Jan. 2009, p. 3, Directive 2009/29/EC of the European Parliament and of the Council of 23 Apr. 2009 amending Directive 2003/87/EC so as to improve and extend the greenhouse gas emission allowance trading scheme of the Community, OJ L 140, 5 Jun. 2009, p. 63.
1752. Section 13 and Annex II Law No. 110(I)/2011.
1753. These are: Directive 2003/87/EC of the European Parliament and of the Council of 13 Oct. 2003 establishing a scheme for greenhouse gas emission allowance trading within the Community, OJ L 275, 25 Oct. 2003, p. 32; Directive 2004/101/EC of the European Parliament and of the Council of 27 Oct. 2004 amending Directive 2003/87/EC establishing a scheme for greenhouse gas emission allowance trading within the Community, in respect of the Kyoto Protocol's project mechanisms, OJ L 338, 13 Nov. 2004, p. 18; Directive 2008/101/EC of the European Parliament and of the Council of 19 Nov. 2008 amending Directive 2003/87/EC so as to include aviation activities in the scheme for greenhouse gas emission allowance trading within the Community, OJ L 8, 13 Jan. 2009, p. 3; Directive 2009/29/EC of the European Parliament and of the Council of 23 Apr. 2009 amending Directive 2003/87/EC so as to improve and extend the greenhouse gas emission allowance trading scheme of the Community, OJ L 140, 05 Jun. 2009, p. 63.
1754. This includes, among others: Case C-366/10, *Air Transport Association of America and Others v. Secretary of State for Energy and Climate Change*, digital ECR; Case T-16/04, *Arcelor v. Parliament and Council* [2010] ECR II-00211; Case C-127/07, *Société Arcelor Atlantique et Lorraine and Others v. Premier ministre and Others* [2008] ECR I-09895; Case C-524/09, *Ville de Lyon v. Caisse des dépôts et consignations* [2010] ECR I-14115; Joined cases C-566/11, C-567/11, C-580/11, C-591/11, C-620/11 and C-640/11, *Iberdrola SA and Others*, digital ECR; Case C-203/12, *Billerud Karlsborg AB and Billerud Skärblacka AB v. Naturvårdsverket*, digital ECR; Case C-43/14, *KO-ENERGO, s.r.o. v. Odvolací finanční ředitelství*, digital ECR; Case C-148/14, *Bundesrepublik Deutschland v. Nordzucker AG*, digital ECR; Joined Cases C-191/14, C-192/14, C-295/14, C-389/14 and C-391/14 to C-393/14, *Borealis Polyolefine GmbH and Others v. Bundesminister für Land-, Forst-, Umwelt und Wasserwirtschaft and Others*, digital ECR.

Chapter 6. Environmental Liability

419. Undertakings engaged in energy activities are further obliged to take the necessary preventive measures in case of an imminent threat of environmental damage.[1755] In the event of actual occurrence of environmental damage, they inform the competent authority and take all practicable steps to immediately control, contain, remove or otherwise manage the relevant contaminants and/or any other damage factors in order to limit or to prevent further environmental damage and adverse effects on human health or further impairment of services as well as the necessary remedial measures.[1756] The cost of these measures is borne by the said undertakings unless they prove that such damage was caused by a third party and occurred despite the fact that appropriate safety measures were in place or resulted from compliance with a compulsory order or instruction emanating from a public authority other than an order or instruction consequent upon an emission or incident caused by the operator's own activities.[1757] This law has been issued for the purpose of implementing EU legislation,[1758] and therefore, the relevant case law is very valuable for its optimal perception.[1759]

1755. Section 7(1) Law on Environmental Liability with Regard to the Prevention and Remedying of Environmental Damage ('περί της Περιβαλλοντικής Ευθύνης όσον αφορά την Πρόληψη και την Αποκατάσταση Περιβαλλοντικής Ζημιάς Νόμος') No. 189 of 2007, OG I(I) No. 4154, 31 Dec. 2007, p. 1849.
1756. Section 9(1) *ibid.*
1757. Sections 8(1) and 11(1) *ibid.*
1758. Directive 2004/35/CE of the European Parliament and of the Council of 21 Apr. 2004 on environmental liability with regard to the prevention and remedying of environmental damage, OJ L 143, 30 Apr. 2004, p. 56, as amended.
1759. Case C-378/08, *Raffinerie Mediterranee (ERG) SpA, Polimeri Europa SpA, Syndial SpA v. Ministero dello Sviluppo economico and Others* [2010] ECR I-01919; Joined Cases C-379/08 and C-380/08, *Raffinerie Mediterranee (ERG) SpA, Polimeri Europa SpA and Syndial SpA v. Ministero dello Sviluppo economico and Others* (C-379/08) *and ENI SpA v. Ministero Ambiente e Tutela del Territorio e del Mare and Others* (C-380/08) [2010] ECR I-02007; Joined Cases C-478/08 and C-479/08, *Buzzi Unicem SpA and Others v. Ministero dello Sviluppo economico and Others* (C-478/08) *and Dow Italia Divisione Commerciale Srl v. Ministero Ambiente e Tutela del Territorio e del Mare and Others* (C-479/08) [2010] ECR I-00031; Case C-534/13, *Ministero dell'Ambiente e della Tutela del Territorio e del Mare and Others v. Fipa Group and Others*, digital ECR; Case C-592/13, *Ministero dell'Ambiente e della Tutela del Territorio e del Mare, Ministero della Salute, Ministero dello Sviluppo Economico v. Ediltecnica SpA*, digital ECR; Case C-156/14, *Tamoil Italia v. Ministero dell'Ambiente e della Tutela del Territorio e del Mare*, digital ECR.

Part VII. Interaction Between Energy Law and Tax Laws

Chapter 1. Introduction

420. Taxation on energy products is regulated by Law No. 91(I)/2004,[1760] which implements Directive 2003/96/EC.[1761] Energy products are specified on the base of goods nomenclature (hereinafter 'combined nomenclature or CN').[1762] This was introduced in the Member States of the EU for the purpose of collection and exchange of data on the statistics trade.[1763] Having these in mind, energy products are those falling within CN codes 1507–1518, if these are intended for use as heating fuel or motor fuel,[1764] within CN codes 2701, 2702 and 2704–2715,[1765] within CN codes 2901 and 2902,[1766] within CN code 2905 11 00, which are not of synthetic origin, if these are intended for use as heating fuel or motor fuel,[1767] within CN code 3403,[1768] within CN code 3811,[1769] within CN code 3817[1770] and within CN codes 3824 91 00, 3824 99 86, 3824 84 00, 3824 85 00, 3824 86 00, 3824 87 00, 3824 88 00, 3824 99 92, 3826 00 10 and 3826 00 90, if these are intended for

1760. Law on Consumption Taxes ('ο Περί Φόρων Κατανάλωσης Νόμος') No. 91 of 2004, OG I(I) No. 3846A of 29 Apr. 2004.
1761. Council Directive 2003/96/EC of 27 Oct. 2003 restructuring the Community framework for the taxation of energy products and electricity, OJ L 283, 31 Oct. 2003, p. 51. On the scope of the directive *see*: Joined Cases C-145/06 and C-146/06, *Fendt Italiana Srl v. Agenzia Dogane – Ufficio Dogane di Trento* [2007] ECT I-05869.
1762. Article 1 Council Regulation (EEC) No. 2658/87 of 23 Jul. 1987 on the tariff and statistical nomenclature and on the Common Customs Tariff, OJ L 256, 7 Sep. 1987, p. 1, as amended.
1763. Preamble to Regulation No. 2658/87.
1764. Section 33(1)(a) Law No. 91(I)/2004, which implements Art. 2(1)(a) Directive 2003/96/EC. CN codes are explained in Commission Implementing Regulation (EU) No. 1001/2013 of 4 Oct. 2013 amending Annex I to Council Regulation (EEC) No. 2658/87 on the tariff and statistical nomenclature and on the Common Customs Tariff, OJ L 290, 31 Oct. 2013, p. 1.
1765. Section 33(1)(b) Law No. 91(I)/2004, which corresponds to Art. 2(1)(b) Directive 2003/96/EC.
1766. Section 33(1)(c) Law No. 91(I)/2004, which corresponds to Art. 2(1)(c) Directive 2003/96/EC.
1767. Section 33(1)(d) Law No. 91(I)/2004, which corresponds to Art. 2(1)(d) Directive 2003/96/EC.
1768. Section 33(1)(e) Law No. 91(I)/2004, which corresponds to Art. 2(1)(e) Directive 2003/96/EC.
1769. Section 33(1)(f) Law No. 91(I)/2004, which corresponds to Art. 2(1)(f) Directive 2003/96/EC.
1770. Section 33(1)(g) Law No. 91(I)/2004, which corresponds to Art. 2(1)(g) Directive 2003/96/EC.

use as heating fuel or motor fuel.[1771] Lastly, for the purposes of the present legislation, electricity is the one falling within CN code 2716.[1772]

§1. OBJECTIVE

421. The objective is to impose and collect an excise tax on energy products electricity,[1773] any other product used as motor fuel or as an additive or extender in motor fuels[1774] and any other hydrocarbon, except for peat, intended for use, offered for sale or used for heating purposes.[1775]

422. Production of these products, with the exception of electricity, is performed by an authorized producer at facilities approved as tax warehouses. The Director of Customs and Excise may, however, allow production at other facilities under the terms and conditions that he deems proper.[1776] The term 'production' includes acquiring energy products, substitutes of energy products, electricity from any material of solid, fluid or gaseous composition, natural source or energy,[1777] as well as acquiring energy products or substitutes of those from other energy products or substitutes of the same.[1778] Production further constitutes any introduction of an energy product or substitutes of the same to the production process for rectification or mixing[1779] and extraction.[1780] However, the term 'production' does not fall heat and pressure of energy products that result in invariance of the energy product when this is replenished,[1781] as well as energy product water separation and filtering.[1782] Equally, production is not to be understood for electricity produced by small producers for their own consumption, as long as the energy products used for such production derive from taxed stocks and stocks exempted from excise tax pursuant to this law.[1783]

1771. Section 33(1)(h) Law No. 91(I)/2004, which corresponds to Art. 2(1)(h) Directive 2003/96/EC.
1772. Section 33(2) Law No. 91(I)/2004, which corresponds to Art. 2(2) Directive 2003/96/EC. *See* relevant case law Case C-517/07, *Afton Chemical Limited v. Commissioners for Her Majesty's Revenue and Customs* [2008] ECR I-10427; Joined cases C-43/13 and C-44/13, *Hauptzollamt Köln v. Kronos Titan GmbH* (C-43/13) and *Hauptzollamt Krefeld v. Rhein-Ruhr Beschichtungs-Service GmbH* (C-44/13), digital ECR.
1773. Section 36(a) and (b) Law No. 91(I)/2004, which corresponds to Art. 2(3) Directive 2003/96/EC.
1774. Section 36(c) Law No. 91(I)/2004, which corresponds to Art. 2(3) Directive 2003/96/EC.
1775. Section 36(d) Law No. 91(I)/2004, which corresponds to Art. 2(3) Directive 2003/96/EC.
1776. Section 40(1) Law No. 91(I)/2004.
1777. Section 40(2)(a) *ibid.*
1778. Section 40(2)(b) *ibid.*
1779. Section 40(2)(c) *ibid.*
1780. Section 40(2)(d) *ibid.*
1781. Section 40(2)(a) *ibid.*
1782. Section 40(2)(b) *ibid.*
1783. Section 40(2)(c) *ibid.*

Chapter 2. Excise Tax

§1. Determination of Excise Tax

423. For the purpose of determining excise tax on energy products, the rates are set out in Annex I Law No. 91(I)/2004 along with the product's temperature of 15° Celsius.[1784] These rates vary from EUR 0 to EUR 479 per 1,000 litres or gigajoules and are set out in Table 1.

Table 1 Excise Tax Rates on Energy Products

Product	*Excise Tax Rate*
Products that bear CN codes 2707 10 00, 2707 30 00, 2707 30 90 and solvent naphtha bearing CN code 2707 50 00.	EUR 429/1,000 litres
Oils partially treated including partially distilled ones that bear CN code 2710 19 99 and 2710 20 90 with the exception of other lubricant oils or other oils that are not for sale or are used as motor fuels or as additive motor fuels.	EUR 429/1,000 litres
Pentanes, hexanes, heptanes and octanes that bear CN code 2901 10 00, benzene that bears CN code 2902 20 00 and mixed xylol isomers that bear CN code 2902 44 00	EUR 429/1,000 litres
Unleaded petrol bearing CN code 2710 12 41, 2710 12 45 and 2710 12 49	EUR 429/1,000 litres
Petrol bearing CN codes 2710 12 31, 2710 12 51, 2710 12 59 και 2710 12 70	EUR 421/1,000 litres
Gas oil used as engine fuel that bears CN codes 2710 19 43, 2710 19 46, 2710 19 47, 2710 19 48, 2710 20 11, 2710 20 15, 2710 20 17 and 2710 20 19	EUR 400/1,000 litres
Gas oil used as heating fuel bearing CN codes 2710 19 43, 2710 19 46, 2710 19 47, 2710 19 48, 2710 20 11, 2710 20 15, 2710 20 17 and 2710 20 19	EUR 74.73/1,000 litres
Gas oil used as fuel for agricultural purposes bearing CN codes 2710 19 43, 2710 19 46, 2710 19 47, 2710 19 48, 2710 20 11, 2710 20 15, 2710 20 17 and 2710 20 19	EUR 21/1,000 litres

1784. Section 37 and Annex I *ibid.*, which corresponds to Arts 8, 9, 10 and Annex I Tables A, B, C Directive 2003/96/EC. *See* relevant case law: Case C-426/12, *X v. Voorzitter van het managementteam van het onderdeel Belastingdienst/Z van de rijksbelastingdienst*, digital ECR (*See* Falkenberg, Matthias, *Dual use von Energieerzeugnissen, Eine Erwiderung auf Liebheit/Schiebold*, 91 ZfZ 230 (2015)).

Product	*Excise Tax Rate*
Gas oil used for other purposes that bears CN codes 2710 19 43, 2710 19 46, 2710 19 47, 2710 19 48, 2710 20 11, 2710 20 15, 2710 20 17 and 2710 20 19	EUR 74.73/1,000 litres
Kerosene used as engine fuel that bears CN codes 2710 19 21 and 2710 19 25	EUR 400/1,000 litres
Kerosene used as heating fuel that bears CN codes 2710 19 21 and 2710 19 25	EUR 74.73/1,000 litres
Kerosene used as fuel for agricultural purposes that bears CN codes 2710 19 21 and 2710 19 25	EUR 21/1,000 litres
Kerosene used for other purposes bearing CN codes 2710 19 21 and 2710 19 25	EUR 74.73/1,000 litres
Heavy oil used as heating fuel that bears CN codes 2710 19 62, 2710 19 64, 2710 19 68, 2710 20 31, 2710 20 35 and 2710 20 39	EUR 15/1,000 kilograms
Propane used as engine fuel that bears CN codes 2711 12 11–2711 19 00	EUR 125/1,000 kilograms
Propane used as heating fuel that bears CN codes 2711 12 11–2711 19 00	EUR 0.00/1,000 kilograms
Propane used for other purposes that bears CN codes 2711 12 11–2711 19 00	EUR 0.00/1,000 kilograms
Natural gas used as engine fuel that bears CN codes 2711 11 00 and 2711 21 00	EUR 2.60/ gigajoules mixed heat value
Natural gas used as heating fuel that bears CN codes 2711 11 00 and 2711 21 00	EUR 2.60/ gigajoules mixed heat value
Natural gas used for other purposes that bears CN codes 2711 11 00 and 2711 21 00	EUR 2.60/ gigajoules mixed heat value
Anthracite and coke used as heating fuel that bear CN codes 2701, 2702 and 2704	EUR 0.31/ gigajoules
Anthracite and coke used for other purposes that bear CN codes 2701, 2702 and 2704	EUR 0.00/ gigajoules
Electrical energy bearing CN code 2716	EUR 0.00/ megawatt hours

424. Should one or more rates of the excise tax change, the Council of Ministers may issue a decree ordering increased or decreased rate of the excise tax change on reserves of energy products that have been disposed of for home use in the

rate.[1785] The Council of Ministers may further specify different rates of excise tax on energy products and electrical energy, when the differentiated rates are directly linked to product quality, when the differentiated rates depend on quantitative consumption levels for electricity and energy products used for heating purposes, for uses of local public passenger transport (including taxis), waste collection, armed forces and public administration, disabled people and ambulances. In such a case, it may impose any terms and conditions deemed necessary, as long as the minimum rates set out in the said directive are taken into consideration.[1786] Different excise tax rates may also be imposed on gas oil used as a propellant, depending on its commercial and non-commercial use, under the terms and conditions that the Council of Ministers deems proper, provided that the minimum levels of the EU are observed.[1787]

§2. Chargeable Events

425. In general, excise duty becomes chargeable at the time of release for consumption. This means any departure, including irregular departure, from a suspension arrangement of products that underlie excise tax,[1788] any manufacture, including irregular manufacture, of those products outside a suspension arrangement,[1789] any importation of those products, including irregular importation, where those products have not been placed under a suspension arrangement[1790] and holding such products outside a suspension agreement, for which no excise tax has been imposed according to this law.[1791] With reference to other products, excise tax is chargeable upon departure from customs' suspension agreement, free zone or free warehouse,[1792] any importation of those products, including irregular importation, where those products have not been placed under a customs' suspension arrangement, free zone or free warehouse,[1793] transaction of said products from the warehouse or place of manufacture into Cyprus' territory, including irregular one, with

1785. Section 39 Law No. 91(I)/2004.
1786. Section 45(1) *ibid.*, Art. 5 Directive 2003/96/EC.
1787. Section 45(2) Law No. 91(I)/2004, Art. 7 Directive 2003/96/EC.
1788. Section 5(1)(a) Law No. 91(I)/2004, which corresponds to Art. 6(1)(a) Directive 92/12/EEC, as amended. *See* relevant case law: Case C-325/99, *G. van de Water v. Staatssecretaris van Financiën* [2001] ECR I-02729; Case C-230/08, *Dansk Transport og Logistik v. Skatteministeriet*, [2010] ECR I-03799; Case C-333/11, *Koninklijke Federatie van Belgische Transporteurs en Logistiek Dienstverleners (Febetra) v. Belgische Staat*, digital ECR.
1789. Section 5(1)(b) Law No. 91(I)/2004, which corresponds to Art. 6(1)(b) Directive 92/12/EEC, as amended.
1790. Section 5(1)(c)(i) Law No. 91(I)/2004, which corresponds to Art. 6(1)(c) Directive 92/12/EEC, as amended.
1791. Section 5(1)(c)(ii) Law No. 91(I)/2004, which corresponds to Art. 7(1) Directive 92/12/EEC, as amended. *See* relevant case law: Case C-5/05, *Staatssecretaris van Financiën v. B. F. Joustra* [2006] ECR I-11075; Case C-663/11, *SC Scandic Distilleries SA v. Direcţia Generală de Administrare a Marilor Contribuabili*, digital ECR; Case C-315/12, *Metro Cash & Carry Danmark ApS v. Skatteministeriet*, digital ECR; Case C-175/14, *Ralph Prankl*, digital ECR.
1792. Section 5(1)(d) Law No. 91(I)/2004.
1793. Section 5(1)(f) *ibid.*

the exception of their placement in customs' suspension agreement[1794] and ent into Cyprus' territory of such products, including irregular one, when forwarde from the other Member States.[1795]

426. In particular about energy products and electrical energy, the amount taxation on energy products becomes due on the occurrence of one of the charg able events, those being the intention of use, offer for sale or use as motor fuel heating fuel or as an additive or extender in motor fuels.[1796] Taxation on energ products and electricity also becomes due when it is established that a final use co dition laid down for the purpose of a reduced level of taxation or exemption is no or is no longer, fulfilled.[1797] The consumption of energy products within the curt lage of an establishment producing energy products is not considered a chargeab event giving rise to taxation if the consumption consists of energy products pr duced within the curtilage of the establishment. Still, if the consumption is for pu poses not related to the production of energy products and in particular, for th propulsion of vehicles, this is considered a chargeable event, giving rise to tax tion.[1798] Electricity and natural gas become chargeable at the time of supply by th distributor or redistributor,[1799] whereas coal, coke and lignite become chargeable the time of delivery by companies, which have to be registered for that purpose b the Director of Customs and Excise. He may allow the producer, trader, importer c fiscal representative to substitute the registered company for the fiscal obligation imposed upon it according to this law.[1800]

§3. Mixing of Energy Products

427. Mixing of energy products and their substitutes or any other relevant actio within production facilities of energy products or tax warehouses must be approve by the Director of Customs and Excise.[1801] Any person performing such mixing out side production facilities of energy products or tax warehouses in violation of thi law is committing a criminal offence. If found guilty, a penal fine of up to EU 2,550 may be imposed on him and/or three times the amount of excise tax appli cable on the products involved in the crime. He may further be imprisoned for period not longer than one year. Products, vessels and other objects used are con fiscated.[1802]

1794. Section 5(1)(e) *ibid.*
1795. Section 5(1)(g) *ibid.*
1796. Section 38(1)(a) *ibid.*, which corresponds to Art. 21(1) Directive 2003/96/EC.
1797. Section 38(1)(b) Law No. 91(I)/2004, which corresponds to Art. 21(4) Directive 2003/96/EC.
1798. Section 38(2) Law No. 91(I)/2004, which corresponds to Art. 21(3) Directive 2003/96/EC.
1799. Section 38(3) Law No. 91(I)/2004, which corresponds to Art. 21(5) Directive 2003/96/EC. *Dis tributor* ('διανομέας') is an entity producing electricity for its own use (s. 38(3) Law No. 91(I) 2004, which corresponds to Art. 21(5) Directive 2003/96/EC).
1800. Section 38(4) Law No. 91(I)/2004, which corresponds to Art. 21(5) Directive 2003/96/EC.
1801. Section 42(1) Law No. 91(I)/2004.
1802. Section 42(2) *ibid.*

§4. Refunds, Exemptions and Reductions of Excise Tax

428. Excise tax may be refunded if the Director of Customs and Excise is convinced that taxed energy products have been randomly contaminated or mixed, and due to this event, they may not be used for their intended purpose. Said tax is refunded under the condition that these products are returned to tax warehouse for recycling.[1803]

429. Certain energy products are exempted from excise tax under the terms and conditions set by the Director of Customs and Excise. These products are jet fuel (CN code 2710 19 21) delivered with the purpose of refuelling aircraft performing international and intra-Union flights, with the exception of private pleasure flights, those being the use of an aircraft by its owner or the natural or legal person who enjoys its use either through hire or through any other means, for other than commercial purposes and, in particular, other than for the carriage of passengers or goods or for the supply of services for consideration or for the purposes of public authorities.[1804] Exemption is further granted for energy products supplied for use as fuel for the purposes of navigation within Union waters (including fishing), other than private pleasure craft, and electricity produced on board a craft. Private pleasure craft is any craft used by its owner or the natural or legal person who enjoys its use either through hire or through any other means, for other than commercial purposes and, in particular, other than for the carriage of passengers or goods or for the supply of services for consideration or for the purposes of public authorities.[1805] Equally, energy products and electricity used to produce electricity and electricity used to maintain the ability to produce electricity are exempted from excise tax. However, the Council of Ministers may, for reasons of environmental policy, subject these products to taxation without having to respect the minimum levels of taxation laid down in this law.[1806] Lastly, energy products used in the production of cement are exempted from the said tax.[1807]

430. The Council of Ministers may further issue decrees regarding application of reduced rates on gas oil, kerosene, gas and natural gas in agricultural, horticultural or piscicultural works, and in forestry, stationary motors, plant and machinery used in construction, civil engineering and public works, vehicles intended for use off the public roadway or which have not been granted authorization for use mainly on the public roadway, as long as the minimum rates set out in this law are respected.[1808] The same may be ordered in cases of business use, that being the use

1803. Section 43(1) *ibid.*
1804. Section 44(1)(a) *ibid.*, which corresponds to Art. 14(1)(b) Directive 2003/96/EC. *See*: Case C-79/10, *Systeme Helmholz GmbH v. Hauptzollamt Nürnberg*, digital ECR; Case C-250/10, *Haltergemeinschaft LBL GbR v. Hauptzollamt Düsseldorf*, digital ECR.
1805. Section 44(1)(b) Law No. 91(I)/2004, which corresponds to Art. 14(1)(c) Directive 2003/96/EC.
1806. Section 44(1)(c) Law No. 91(I)/2004, which corresponds to Art. 14(1)(a) Directive 2003/96/EC. *See*: Case C-226/07, *Flughafen Köln/Bonn GmbH v. Hauptzollamt Köln* [2008] ECR I-05999; Case C-355/14, *Polihim-SS EOOD v. Nachalnik na Mitnitsa – Svishtov*, digital ECR.
1807. Section 44(1)(d) Law No. 91(I)/2004.
1808. Section 44(2) *ibid.*, Art. 8(2) Directive 2003/96/EC.

by a business entity,[1809] which independently carries out, in any place, the supply of goods and services, whatever the purpose or results of such economic activities whereas economic activities comprise all activities of producers, traders and persons supplying services including mining and agricultural activities and activities of the professions.[1810] Further decrees imposing reduced excise tax rates or even full or partial exceptions to the following products may be issued:

- taxable products used under fiscal control in the field of pilot projects for the technological development of more environmentally friendly products or in relation to fuels from renewable resources;
- electricity of solar, wind, wave, tidal or geothermal origin;
- electricity of hydraulic origin produced in hydroelectric installations;
- electricity generated from biomass or from products produced from biomass;
- electricity generated from methane emitted by abandoned coal mines;
- electricity generated from fuel cells;
- energy products and electricity used for combined heat and power generation;
- electricity produced from combined heat and power generation provided that the combined generators are environmentally friendly. Member States apply national definitions of 'environmentally friendly' (or high-efficiency) cogeneration production until the Council, on the basis of a report and a proposal from the European Commission, unanimously adopts a common definition;
- energy products and electricity used for the carriage of goods and passengers by rail, metro, tram and trolley bus;
- energy products supplied for use as fuel for navigation on inland waterways (including fishing) other than in private pleasure craft, and electricity produced onboard a craft;
- natural gas in Cyprus in which the share of natural gas in final energy consumption was less than 15% in 2000;
- electricity, natural gas, coal and solid fuels used by households and/or by organizations recognized as charitable by Cyprus. In the case of such charitable organizations, Cyprus may confine the exemption or reduction to use for the purpose of non-business activities. Where mixed-use takes place, taxation applies in proportion to each type of use. If use is insignificant, it may be treated as nil;
- natural gas and liquid petroleum gas (LPG) used as propellants;
- motor fuels used in the field of the manufacture, development, testing and maintenance of aircraft and ships;
- motor fuels used for dredging operations in navigable waterways and in ports;
- products falling within CN code 2705 used for heating purposes;
- energy products and electricity used for agricultural, horticultural or piscicultural works and in forestry may be tax-free;
- products falling within CN codes 1507–1518;

1809. Business entity cannot be considered as smaller than a part of an enterprise or a legal body that from an organizational point of view constitutes an independent business, that is to say an entity capable of functioning by its own means (Art. 11(2) Directive 2003/96/EC).

1810. Section 44(3) Law No. 91(I)/2004, Art. 11 Directive 2003/96/EC.

- products falling within CN codes 3824 90 55 and 3824 90 80–3824 90 99 for their components produced from biomass;[1811]
- products falling within CN codes 2207 20 00 and 2905 11 00 which are not of synthetic origin;
- products produced from biomass, including products falling within CN codes 4401 and 4402;
- energy products where such products contain water (CN codes 2201 and 2851 00 10);
- in favour of energy-intensive business;[1812] and
- where agreements are concluded with undertakings or associations of undertakings, or where tradable permit schemes or equivalent arrangements are implemented, as far as they lead to the achievement of environmental protection objectives or to improvements in energy efficiency.[1813]

431. The above-mentioned provisions on refunds or deduced rates are equally applied to subsidies of energy products, as long as they are intended to be used likewise.[1814]

432. Lastly, energy products released for consumption in a Member State, contained in the standard tanks of commercial motor vehicles and intended to be used as fuel by those same vehicles, as well as in special containers, and intended to be used for the operation, during the course of transport, of the systems equipping those same containers are not subject to taxation in Cyprus.[1815] Standard tanks are the tanks permanently fixed by the manufacturer to all motor vehicles of the same type as the vehicle in question and whose permanent fitting enables fuel to be used directly, both for the purpose of propulsion and, where appropriate, for the operation, during transport, of refrigeration systems and other systems. Gas tanks fitted to motor vehicles designed for the direct use of gas as a fuel and tanks fitted to the other systems with which the vehicle may be equipped are also considered to be standard tanks. Standard tanks are equally tanks permanently fixed by a manufacturer to all containers of the same type as the container in question and whose permanent fitting enables fuel to be used directly for the operation, during transport, of

---

1811. *Biomass* means the biodegradable fraction of products, waste and residues from agriculture (including vegetal and animal substances), forestry and related industries, as well as the biodegradable fraction of industrial and municipal waste (Art. 16(1) *ibid.*).
1812. *Energy-intensive business* means a business entity, where either the purchases of energy products and electricity amount to at least 3% of the production value or the national energy tax payable amounts to at least 0.5% of the added value, whereas *purchases of energy products and electricity* is the actual cost of energy purchased or generated within the business. Only electricity, heat and energy products that are used for heating purposes or for the purposes of stationary motors and plant and machinery used in construction, civil engineering and public works are included. All taxes are included, except deductible Value Added Tax (VAT). Lastly, *production value* means turnover, including subsidies directly linked to the price of the product, plus or minus the changes in stocks of finished products, work in progress and goods and services purchased for resale, minus the purchases of goods and services for resale (Art. 17(1)(a) *ibid.*).
1813. Section 44(4) and (5) Law No. 91(I)/2004, Arts 15, 16 and 17 Directive 2003/96/EC.
1814. Section 46 Law No. 91(I)/2004.
1815. Section 48(1) *ibid.*, which corresponds to Art. 24(1) Directive 2003/96/EC.

the refrigeration systems and other systems with which special containers are equipped. Special containers mean any container fitted with specially designed apparatus for refrigeration systems, oxygenation systems, thermal insulation systems or other systems.[1816]

1816. Section 48(2) Law No. 91(I)/2004, which corresponds to Art. 24(2) Directive 2003/96/EC. *See*: Case C-152/13, *Holger Forstmann Transporte GmbH & Co. KG v. Hauptzollamt Münster*, digital ECR.

Chapter 3. Monitoring Compliance

433. Any person who uses, possesses, transports or offers energy products or their subsidies or electrical energy for purposes other than the ones stated in provisions relating to tax exemptions or reductions, or in violation of the provisions of any regulations, Orders or Notifications issued under this law, commits an offence. If found guilty, he may be imprisoned for a maximum period of up to two years or a penalty of up to three times of applicable excise tax or of EUR 2,550, whichever is higher, may be imposed on him. Energy products, vessels, vehicles or other transport means used are confiscated. Same penalties are imposed in case of failure or refusal to comply with terms and conditions imposed for tax exemption or reduction,[1817] as well as when a person produces energy products in facilities not authorized as tax warehouses in violation of section 40(1) Law No. 91(I)/2004.[1818]

1817. Section 47(1) Law No. 91(I)/2004.
1818. Section 40(3) *ibid*.

Part VIII. Interaction Between Energy Law and Competition Laws

Chapter 1. Introduction

434. Competition is being regulated in Cyprus by Law No. 13(I)/2022.[1819] Pursuant to its preamble, this law has been enacted for the purpose of regulation and protection of free competition in Cyprus as well as for the application of Council Regulation (EC) No. 1/2003[1820] and the implementation of Directive 2019/1.[1821] Especially with reference to a concentration between undertakings, Law No. 83(I)/2014 is applicable.

1819. *See* in this respect *supra* n. 143.

1820. Council Regulation (EC) No. 1/2003 of 16 Dec. 2002 on the implementation of the rules on competition laid down in Arts 81 and 82 of the Treaty, OJ L 1, 4 Jan. 2003, p. 1, as last amended by Council Regulation (EC) No. 487/2009 of 25 May 2009 on the application of Art. 81(3) of the Treaty to certain categories of agreements and concerted practices in the air transport sector (Codified version), OJ L 148, 11 Jun. 2009, p. 1.

1821. Directive (EU) 2019/1 of the European Parliament and of the Council of 11 Dec. 2018 to empower the competition authorities of the Member States to be more effective enforcers and to ensure the proper functioning of the internal market, OJ L 11, 14 Jan. 2019, p. 3.

Chapter 2. Limitation or Distortion of Competition

435. All agreements between undertakings as well as all decisions of associations of undertakings and every harmonized practice that have as an object or as a result obstruction, limitation or distortion of competition within Cyprus are forbidden.[1822] Under such prohibition especially fall the ones that directly or indirectly fix purchase or sell prices or other terms of transactions,[1823] that limit or control production, disposal, technological development or investments,[1824] that geographically or otherwise allocate goods or sources of supply,[1825] that foresee the application of unequal terms for equivalent transactions towards undertakings transacting commercially, resulting into some undertakings to be left behind[1826] and that depend on the entering into agreements from acceptance of obligations, which according to their nature or the prevailing trade practice are not related to the object of such agreements.[1827] Such forbidden cartels are void *ex initio*.[1828]

436. However, every such agreement, decision and harmonized practice that is forbidden in accordance with the above may be valid, as long as the following conditions are met. These are a contribution to the improvement of production or distribution of goods or to the promotion of technical or financial progress, whereas consumers reasonably participate in resulting benefits.[1829] In addition, restrictions imposed on undertakings must not exceed those strictly necessary for achieving the above-mentioned scope,[1830] while undertakings concerned with the cartel do not enjoy the possibility of abolishing an important part of the market of the relevant product.[1831] No relevant decision of the Commission for the Protection of Competition is necessary.

437. In addition to that, the Council of Ministers may issue decrees ordering the non-applicability of the above-mentioned prohibition on certain categories of cartels following a reasoned opinion of the Commission for the Protection of Competition.[1832] The burden of proof that a cartel falls under such a decree lies with the undertaking purporting this.[1833] However, the Commission for the Protection of Competition may decide that a cartel does not fall within the application area of a decree. In such a case, the relevant cartel is prohibited.[1834]

1822. Section 3(1) Law No. 13(I)/2022.
1823. Section 3(1)(a) *ibid.*
1824. Section 3(1)(b) *ibid.*
1825. Section 3(1)(c) *ibid.*
1826. Section 3(1)(d) *ibid.*
1827. Section 3(1)(e) *ibid.*
1828. Section 3(2) *ibid.*
1829. Section 4(1)(a) *ibid.*
1830. Section 4(1)(b) *ibid.*
1831. Section 4(1)(c) *ibid.*
1832. Section 5(1) *ibid.*
1833. Section 5(3)(a) *ibid.*
1834. Section 5(4)(a) *ibid.*

438. For any violation of the above-stated restrictions and/or Articles 101 and 102 TFEU, the Commission for the Protection of Competition may impose administrative fines of up to 10% of the turnover of the undertaking or of the sum of turnover of the undertakings involved that was achieved in the previous financial year, depending on the seriousness and duration of the violation. An undertaking may be released of the imposed fine, if it cooperates, and provides assistance or evidence that helps the commission with proving the violation.[1835] The commission may also oblige the involved undertakings or associations of undertakings within a specific time period to terminate the established violation and to avoid the same in the future.[1836] It may also impose terms and measures depending on the violation that is necessary to stop said violation.[1837] In the event that the relevant undertaking or association of undertakings does not comply with a decision of the commission, it may impose an administrative fine of up to 5% of the average annual turnover of the previous year for every day of this violation.[1838]

1835. Section 24(a) *ibid.*
1836. Section 24(b) *ibid.*
1837. Section 24(c) *ibid.*
1838. Section 24(d) *ibid.*

Chapter 3. Abuse of Dominant Position

439. Abuse of dominant position ('καταχρηστική εκμετάλλευση δεσπόζουσας θέσης') of an undertaking in the market of a product is prohibited. As such is understood especially any action of one or more undertakings that have a dominant position in the whole or part of the internal market of a product, when this imposes directly or indirectly unfair sale or purchase prices or other unfair trading conditions,[1839] restricts the production or supply or technological development to the expense of consumers,[1840] applies dissimilar terms for equal transactions resulting into some undertakings being exposed to unfair competition,[1841] or when the conclusion of a contract depends from the acceptance of obligations, which do not connect to the object of such contracts in accordance with their nature or the dominant trading practice.[1842] Equally, abuse of financial dependence ('καταχρηστική εκμετάλλευση σχέσης οικονομικής εξάρτησης') by one or more undertakings that is a customer, supplier, representative, distributor or commercial partner even only of a special kind of products or services provided that no equal alternative is available, is prohibited. Such abuse may consist especially of imposing arbitrary trading conditions, discrimination, interruption of commercial relations in a way that vitally affects competition or sudden and unreasoned interruption of long-term commercial relations.[1843]

440. The above-mentioned provisions on administrative fines in case of violation of the provisions on limitation or distortion of competition equally apply here.

1839. Section 6(1)(a) *ibid.*
1840. Section 6(1)(b) *ibid.*
1841. Section 6(1)(c) *ibid.*
1842. Section 6(1)(d) *ibid.*
1843. Section 6(2) *ibid.* The Commission for Protection of Competition has confirmed abuse of dominant position in the following cases: *Alpha Electric House Ltd v. Fissler GmbH* (File No.: 11.17.010.16, Decision No. 42/2012); *P & M Air-Sea-Land Services Ltd v. Salamis Shipping Services Ltd* (File No.: 11.17.007.33, Decision No. 01/2013); *Andros Kiosk Ltd v. Fereos Ltd* (File No. 11.17.06/2006, Decision No. 09/2013). All decisions are available at: http://www.competition.gov.cy/.

Chapter 4. Concentration Between Undertakings

441. No concentration may be materialized prior to receiving a notification of approval by the Service of the Commission for the Protection of Competition ('Υπηρεσία της Επιτροπής') or the lapse of the relevant time limits without receiving a response by the same.[1844]

442. A concentration ('συγκέντρωση') is deemed to arise under Law No. 83(I)/2014, where a change of control on a lasting basis results from the merger of two or more previously independent undertakings or parts of undertakings.[1845] This equally happens through acquisition, by one or more persons already controlling at least one undertaking, or by one or more undertakings, whether by the purchase of securities or assets, by contract or by any other means, of direct or indirect control of the whole or parts of one or more other undertakings.[1846] Similarly, the creation of a common undertaking that fulfils all functions of an autonomous financial entity forms a concentration.[1847] Control is constituted by rights, contracts or any other means which, either separately or in combination and having regard to the considerations of fact or law involved, confer the possibility of exercising decisive influence on an undertaking, in particular, by ownership or the right to use all or part of the assets of an undertaking,[1848] and/or rights or contracts which confer decisive influence on the composition, voting or decisions of the organs of an undertaking.[1849] Control is acquired by persons or undertakings that are holders of the rights or entitled to rights under the contracts concerned[1850] or while not being holders of such rights or entitled to rights under such contracts have the power to exercise the rights deriving therefrom.[1851]

443. Concentrations of major importance are notified to the service prior to their implementation and following the conclusion of the agreement, the announcement of the public bid or the acquisition of a controlling interest.[1852] Notification may also be made where the undertakings concerned demonstrate to the service good faith to conclude an agreement or, in the case of a public bid, where they have publicly announced an intention to make such a bid, provided that the intended agreement or bid would result in a concentration of major importance.[1853] A concentration which consists of a merger[1854] or the acquisition of joint control[1855] is notified jointly by the parties to the merger or by those acquiring joint control, as the case

1844. Section 11(1) Law No. 83(I)/2014.
1845. Section 6(1)(a)(i) *ibid.*
1846. Section 6(1)(a)(ii) *ibid.*
1847. Section 6(1)(b) *ibid.*
1848. Section 6(2)(a) *ibid.*
1849. Section 6(2)(b) *ibid.*
1850. Section 6(3)(a) *ibid.*
1851. Section 6(3)(b) *ibid.*
1852. Section 10(1) *ibid.*
1853. Section 10(2) *ibid.*
1854. *Merger* ('συγχώνευση') has here the same meaning as in s. 6(1)(a)(i) *ibid.*
1855. *Acquisition of joint control* ('απόκτηση από κοινού του ελέγχου') has here the same meaning as in s. 6(1)(a)(ii) *ibid.*

may be. In all other cases, the notification is effected by the person or undertakir to acquire control of the whole or parts of one or more undertakings.[1856] Followir such notification, the service publishes in the OG the fact of the notification, at tl same time, indicating the names of the undertakings concerned, the nature of tl concentration and the economic sectors involved,[1857] while taking account of tl legitimate interest of undertakings in the protection of their business secrets.[1858]

444. Concentrations are then appraised with a view to establishing whether not they are compatible with this law. In making this appraisal, the Committee (' Επιτροπή') takes into account the need to maintain and develop effective compe tition within the common market in view of, among other things, the structure of a the markets concerned and the actual or potential competition from undertaking located either within or out with Cyprus.[1859] It also takes into consideration the ma ket position of the undertakings concerned and their economic and financial powe the alternatives available to suppliers and users, their access to supplies or market any legal or other barriers to entry, supply and demand trends for the relevant good and services, the interests of the intermediate and ultimate consumers, and th development of technical and economic progress, provided that it is to consumers advantage and does not form an obstacle to competition.[1860] A concentration whic would significantly impede effective competition, in Cyprus or in a substantial pa of it, in particular, as a result of the creation or strengthening of a dominant posi tion, is declared incompatible with the function of competition in the market.[1861] A the same time, a concentration which would not significantly impede effective com petition in Cyprus or in a substantial part of it, in particular, as a result of the cre ation or strengthening of a dominant position, is declared compatible with th function of competition in the market.[1862]

1856. Section 10(3) *ibid.*
1857. Section 10(4)(a) *ibid.*
1858. Section 10(4)(b) *ibid.*
1859. Section 19(1)(a) *ibid.*
1860. Section 19(1)(b) *ibid.*
1861. Section 20 *ibid.*
1862. Section 21 *ibid.*

Selected Bibliography

Renato Alessi. *Diritto Amministrativo Italiano* (1960).

Elena Andreou. *Cyprus Economy in the Last Three Decades (1960–1994)*, in *The Development of the Cypriot Economy* 232 et seq. (V. Karageorghis & D. Michaelides eds, University of Cyprus and Bank of Cyprus 1996).

Simoni Angelides. *The Cyprus Economy under British Rule (1878–1960)*, in *The Development of the Cypriot Economy* 209 et seq. (V. Karageorghis & D. Michaelides eds, University of Cyprus and Bank of Cyprus 1996).

Anastasios Antoniou LLC. *Oil Regulation & Natural Gas*, in *Cyprus Law Digest* (1st ed., Nomiki Bibliothiki 2012).

Vassos Argyrou. Under a Spell: The Strategic Use of Magic in Greek Cypriot Society, 20 *AAA/AE* 256 (1993).

Sebastian Becker. Kurzbesprechung der Schlussanträge des Generalanwalts Jan Mazak vom 12.12.2007 in der Rechtssache C-439/06 (citiworks AG/Sächsiches Staatsministerium für Wirtschaft und Arbeit), 11 *EuZW* 101 (2008).

Gianluca Bellomo. Riso 'salato' per le Antille olandesi: la Corte difende nuovamente il mercato comunitario dall'invasione di prodotti agro-alimentari dagli ACP via PTOM, 12 *Dir. pubbl. comp. eur.* 432 (2002).

Robert Biddulph. *Cyprus* (For. & Cmmw. Off. Collection 1889).

Samuel Kwaw Nyameke Blay. Self-Determination in Cyprus: The New Dimensions of an Old Conflict, 10 *Austrl. Y.B. Intl. L.* 67 (1987).

Christian Bolze. Règles de concurrence. Décision – Notification – Délai de recours – Point de départ, 48 *RTD com.* 687 (1995).

Joël Boudant. L'activité Anti-dumping Communautaire (1996), 7 *R.M.C.U.E.* 470 (1997).

Spyros Calogeropoulos-Stratis. Le Problème de Chypre, 31 *Pol ètr* 344 (1966).

Central Intelligence Agency. *The World Factbook, Europe: Cyprus*, 26 September 2018, https://www.cia.gov/library/publications/the-world-factbook/.

Nicos Charalambous. *Handbook of Cyprus Administrative Law* (in Greek) (3rd ed., 2016).

C. Gilbert Cullis. A Sketch of the Geology and Mineral Resources of Cyprus, 72 (3741) *J. Royal Socy. Arts* 624 (1924).

Ioannides Demetriou LLC. *Electricity in Cyprus*, in *Cyprus Law Digest* (1st ed., Nomiki Bibliothiki 2012).

Meinrad Dreher & Kerstin Neumann. Keine Nichtigkeit der EGRL 19/94, 13 *EWiR* 159 (1997).

Selected Bibliography

Michael Doherty. The Status of the Principles of EC Environmental Law, 11 *J. Envtl. L.* 378 (1999).

Editors. Höhere Gewalt bei Versäumung gemeinschaftsrechtlicher Antragsfrist, 1(*DVBl.* 1249 (2004).

Camile Enlart. *Gothic Art and the Renaissance in Cyprus,* 378 et seq. (David Hun ed., 1st ed., Trigraph 1987).

European Commission, *Post-Programme Surveillance Report, Cyprus Spring 2018 Institutional Paper 083* (Luxembourg, July 2018), https://ec.europa.eu/info. publications/economic-and-financial-affairs-publications_en.

Ulrich Everling. Einlagensicherung der Banken im Europäischen Binnenmarkt, 162 *ZHR* 403 (1998).

Marios Evriviades. The Legal Dimensions of the Cyprus Conflict, 10 *Tex. Intl. L.J.* 227 (1975).

Matthias Falkenberg, Dual use von Energieerzeugnissen, Eine Erwiderung auf Liebheit/Schiebold, 91 *ZfZ* 230 (2015).

Maurice Flory. La Partition de Chypre, 30 *Ann. fr. dr. intern.* 177 (1985).

Yves Gautier. Chronique de jurisprudence du Tribunal et de la Cour de justice des Communautés européennes, 129 *J* 524 (2002).

Wouter Geldhof & Stefan Tormans. Case C-439/06 – ECJ Leaves Limited Scope for Exemptions from Third Party Access Obligations for So-Called Operational Networks, 17 *Eur. Energy & Envtl. L. Rev.* 256 (2008).

Michael Given. Mining Landscapes and Colonial Rule in Early-Twentieth-Century Cyprus, 39 *Hist. Archaeology* 49 (2005).

Adabella Gratani. Misure a protezione dello strato di ozono e lotta ai gas nocivi, 7 *Ambiente Cons.* 78 (1999).

Katia Hadjidemetriou. *History of Cyprus* (in Greek) 380 (Nicosia 2010).

John L. Hargrove. Cyprus: International Law and the Prospects for Settlement, 78 *Am. Socy. Intl. L. Procs.* 107 (1984).

Thomas Incalza. De meldingsplicht wegens witwassen ten aanzien van de ontvangstlidstaat in het licht van de vrijheid van dienstverrichting: een Spaanse armada tussen droom en daad?, 78 *RW* 1362 (2014).

Andreas J. Jacovides. Cyprus: The International Law Dimension, 10 *Am. J. Intl. L. & Policy* 1221 (1995).

Walter Jellinek. *Gesetz und Verordnung* (1887).

Arnaud Lecocq. Arrêt 'Jyske Bank Gibraltar': le contrôle exercé sur la libre prestation de services financiers au titre de la lutte contre le terrorisme et le blanchiment de capitaux, 14 *J.D.E.* 231 (2013).

Ronald SJ. McDonald. International Law and the Conflict in Cyprus, 19 *Can. Y.B. Intl. L.* 3 (1981).

Costantino Mortati. *Diritto Pubblico* (1962).

Matthias Möschel. Race Discrimination and Access to the European Court of Justice: Belov, 50 *Com. Mkt. L. Rev.* 1433 (2013).

Andreas Neocleous & Co LLC. *Handbook of Cypriot Laws* (in Greek), (2nd ed., Nomiki Bibliothiki 2013).

Andreas Neocleous. *Neocleous's Introduction to Cyprus Law* (C. Melides et al. (eds), 3rd ed., Andreas Neocleous & Co LLC 2011).

J.T. Nowak. Zaak C-136/11 Westbahn Management, zaak C-363/11 Epitropos tou Elegktikou Synedriou sto Ypourgeio Politismou kai Tourismou en zaak C-394/11 Valeri Hariev Belov, 54 *SEW* 559 (2013).

Raymond Odent. *Contentieux Administratif* (1961).

Chiara Petruzzo. Accesso dei terzi alla rete elettrica: un diritto 'biunivoco' e direttamente applicabile, 18 *Riv. it. dir. pubbl. com.* 1558 (2008).

Renate Pirstner-Ebner. Kein Recht zum Anschluss an das Übertragungsnetz, 12 *EuZW* 15 (2009).

S. Pront-van Bommel. Particuliere elektriciteitsnetten onder communautair vuur?, 50 *SEW* 244 (2009).

Prountzos & Prountzos LLC. *Production of Electricity from the Private Sector in Cyprus: Renewable and Conventional – Towards a Competitive and Diversified Market?*, in *Cyprus Law Digest* (1st ed., Nomiki Bibliothiki 2012).

Hifsiye Pulhan & Numan Ibrahim. The Traditional Urban House in Cyprus as Material Expression of Cultural Transformation, 19 *J. Design History* 105 (2006).

Panayiota Pyla & Petros Phokaides. Architecture and Modernity in Cyprus, 2 *EAHN Newsltr.* 36 (2009).

Lea Querzola. Spunti sui limiti oggettivi del giudicato comunitario, 52 *Riv. trim. dir. proc. civ.* 331 (1998).

Euphrosyne Rizopoulou-Egoumenidou. *The House of the Dragoman of Cyprus Hadjigeorgakis Kornessions* (Bank Cyprus Cultural Foundation 1991).

John Rosser. Crusader Castles of Cyprus, 39 *Archaeology* 40 (1986).

John Rosser. Excavations at Saranda Kolones, Paphos, Cyprus 1981–1983, 39 *Dumbarton Oaks Papers* 81 (1985).

Boris Scholtka & Sebastian Helmes. Das Objektnetz ist tot. Es lebe das Industrienetz, 21 *NVwZ* 1310 (2008).

H.G. Sevenster. Milieubeginselen uit EG-Verdrag toetssteen voor CFK-verordening, 3 *NTER* 226 (1998).

Malcom N. Shaw. *International Law* (4th ed., Cambridge University Press 1997).

George Sinclair. Cyprus since Independence, 110 *J. Royal Socy. Arts* 511 (1962).

Kai-Uwe Steck. Rechtsunsicherheit in Kollisionsfällen kann Rückzug von Banken aus bestimmten Zielstaaten zur Folge haben, 68 *BB* 1684 (2013).

E. Steyger. Subsidiariteit en de motiveringsplicht van de wetgever, 2 *NTER* 183 (1997).

Stefan Talmon. The EU-Turkey Controversy over Cyprus or a Tale of Two Declarations, 5 *Chinese J. Intl. L.* 579 (2006).

Piet Van Nuffel. Gebruiksaanwijzing voor subsidiariteit. Een bijsluiter bij de eerste toepassing door het Hof van justitie, 61 *RW* 273 (1997).

Michael Volmer. Das EuGH-Urteil zur Einlagensicherungsrichtlinie vom 13.5.1997, 9 *EWS* 54 (1998).

Stephan Wernicke. Subsidiaritätsprinzip im Zúsammenhang mit der Einlagensicherung durch Kreditinstitute, 8 *EuZW* 442 (1997).

Glanville Williams. The Defence of Necessity, 6 *Current Leg. Problems* 216 (1953).

David Wippman. International Law and Ethnic Conflict on Cyprus, 31 *Tex. Intl. L.J.* 141 (1996).

Selected Bibliography

Jan Wouters. The Community Legislature's Role Regarding the Freedom of Establishment and the Freedom to Provide Services: Theory and Practice, 9 *Euredia* 241 (1999).

Altug Yilmaz. Conflit Chypriote, 27 *Annales de la Faculté de Droit d'Istanbul* 375 (1980).

Table of Cases

Case Law of the Court of Justice of the European Union (In Chronological Order)

Table of Cases

Case Law of Cyprus (In Alphabetical Order)

Index

The numbers here refer to paragraph numbers.

Index

Index

www.ingramcontent.com/pod-product-compliance
Lightning Source LLC
Chambersburg PA
CBHW071431230926
51846CB00001B/193

* 9 7 8 9 4 0 3 5 3 9 1 7 1 *